Limiting Secularism

Limiting Secularism

The Ethics of Coexistence in Indian Literature and Film

Priya Kumar

University of Minnesota Press
Minneapolis • London

Sections of chapters 3 and 5 were published as "Testimonies of Loss and Memory: Partition and the Haunting of a Nation," *Interventions: An International Journal of Postcolonial Studies* 1, no. 2 (1999): 201–16. A portion of chapter 5 was published in "Islamic 'Terrorism,' Secularism, and Visions of Justice in Khalid Mohamed's *Fiza*," in *Cinema, Law, and the State in Asia,* ed. Corey K. Creekmur and Mark Sidel (New York: Palgrave Macmillan Press, 2007).

Published by the University of Minnesota Press
111 Third Avenue South, Suite 290
Minneapolis, MN 55401-2520
http://www.upress.umn.edu

Library of Congress Cataloging-in-Publication Data

Kumar, Priya.
   Limiting secularism : the ethics of coexistence in Indian literature and film / Priya Kumar.
      p.   cm.
   Includes bibliographical references and index.
   ISBN: 978-0-8166-5072-9 (hc : alk. paper)
   ISBN-10: 0-8166-5072-1 (hc : alk. paper)
   ISBN: 978-0-8166-5073-6 (pbk. : alk. paper)
   ISBN-10: 0-8166-5073-X (pbk. : alk. paper)
   1. South Asian literature—20th century—History and criticism.   2. South Asian literature—Moral and ethical aspects.   3. Motion pictures—Moral and ethical aspects—India.   4. Secularism in literature.   5. Secularism in motion pictures.   I. Title.
   PK5407.K86 2008
   809'.8954—dc22

                                                                    2007032357

Printed in the United States of America on acid-free paper

The University of Minnesota is an equal-opportunity educator and employer.

15 14 13 12 11 10 09 08   10 9 8 7 6 5 4 3 2 1

To my parents
Madhu and Tapishwar Kumar
for the unconditional gift
of their love

Contents

Acknowledgments

This book has been the culmination of a long journey—both intellectually and literally. It is a pleasure to thank the many people who have helped me see this project to its completion.

I am deeply grateful to Rajeswari Sunder Rajan, who has been a teacher and mentor since my days at Jawaharlal Nehru University, India. Professor Sunder Rajan's faith in my project, her generosity of intellect and time—often across continents—and her responses to my work have been crucial to the path this project has traversed. I also owe an invaluable debt to Meenakshi Mukherjee, G. J. V. Prasad, and Harish Narang, my teachers at J.N.U. who first introduced me to the possibility of reading and studying literatures outside Anglo America.

At McGill University, Canada, the example and support of my adviser, Karin Cope, gave me the courage to embark on this project. I will always be grateful to Karin not only for her constant encouragement and enthusiasm about my work but also for her kindness to a somewhat confused and lonely international student. I owe special thanks to a number of peers and professors at McGill and Concordia from whose intellect and knowledge I have benefited greatly: Marianne Conroy, Marike Finlay de Monchy, Janine Marchessault, Mette Hjort, Gabrielle McIntire, Sherry Simon, Paul St. Pierre, and Proma Tagore.

During the year I spent teaching and doing research at the University of Virginia, I received invaluable help from Robert Hueckstedt, Nazen Merjian, Ajay Skaria, Shiney Verghese, Christi Merrill, and Joyce Allan. I am indebted to them for their kindness and hospitality.

At the University of Iowa, I have had the pleasure of learning from many wonderful colleagues. Mary Lou Emery, Claire Fox, and Corey Creekmur have provided me with much guidance and advice over the years. I am extremely indebted to them for their meticulous readings of my manuscript. I am also deeply grateful to Barbara Eckstein, Laura Rigal, and Judith Pascoe for their generous and insightful responses to my work; I have learned much from each of them about intellectual rigor and precision. I owe special thanks to Kathy Lavezzo, Teresa Mangum, and Doris Witt for responding to different parts of the manuscript and for providing much-needed direction in the early stages. Philip Lutgendorf offered valuable guidance with the *Ramayana* subtext of chapter 4. I am also indebted to Kathleen Newman for providing me with a basic course on film studies in two inspiring and informative sessions. Finally, my sincerest gratitude belongs to Linda Bolton for thoughtful and fun conversations on ethics and hospitality.

I am grateful to Iowa graduate students Ania Spyra, Lisa Angelella, Bidisha Banerjee, Sucheta Mallick, Dorothy Giannakouros, and Amit Baishya for vital research assistance. I am especially grateful to Amit for many fascinating and thought-provoking discussions on a number of wide-ranging topics. I owe thanks to the wonderful students who took my seminar on secularism and religious violence in the fall of 2002 for their stimulating comments and questions. Eddie Mallot and Ellen Sweeney have shared many important insights with me—my thanks to them. Swarnavel Pillai has taught me a lot about cinema in the course of several enjoyable discussions and movie-watching sessions. Finally, to the "Brown Light" group of Iowa City: Murli Natrajan, Vidya Kalaramadam, and Prasenjit Gupta, I miss our many loud and passionate debates. Thank you for your friendship.

Along the way, I have had the privilege of receiving feedback from several wonderful and inspiring scholars who read parts of this project in its incipient form. In particular, I thank Professor Veena Das, Ritu Menon, and Roberta Culbertson. I also express my gratitude to Ajay Skaria and Simona Sawhney for inviting me to give a talk at the University of Minnesota's South Asian Studies program; I thank them and other members of the audience for valuable comments on the first chapter. Khalid Mohamed has been very generous in responding to my many questions about his films and his writing; I am deeply indebted to him.

I am especially grateful to the two external readers for the University of Minnesota Press, Anuradha Needham and Sangeeta Ray, for their thorough and incisive readings of the manuscript. Both of them provided many important and useful suggestions that helped me to clarify and hone my arguments. Finally, many thanks to my editor at Minnesota, Douglas Armato, for his support and enthusiasm for this project; Mike Stoffel and Andrea Patch for their help with putting the manuscript together; and Carol Lallier, my manuscript editor, for her meticulous reading. I am also indebted to Celeste Newbrough for her painstaking work on the index.

This project received generous financial support from several institutions. I am grateful to the Virginia Foundation for the Humanities and the Institute on Violence, Culture, and Survival for awarding me a Rockefeller Fellowship in the spring of 2000. McGill University provided support in the form of a J. W. McConnell McGill Major Fellowship and a Margaret Gillett Graduate Research Award. The University of Iowa generously supported this project through several grants, including two Arts and Humanities Initiative Fellowships, an Obermann Summer Research Fellowship, an International Programs Summer Research Fellowship, and an Old Gold Fellowship. I would also like to thank the Office of the Vice President for Research for a book subvention that helped me to bring this project to completion.

When you work and live so far away from "home," family comes to be everything. To my family away from home: Kama Bua, Gopal Uncle, Juhi, and Sami, I know I can never repay the gift of your love, so I can only express my gratitude. I am also very grateful to my aunt and (late) uncle, Asha and Jagdish Minocha, who have always been there to guide and support me. My aunts Sushma Mehta and Veena Mallal provided crucial help and encouragement in the early stages. Amma, Achan, Malu, and Rajesh have given me much love and support over the years—I am especially grateful to Amma for her help as I finished the last part of the manuscript. My brother and sister-in-law, Munishwar and Pooja, continue to be a mainstay of strength and love for me; I hope their children, Manahar and Noor, will read their Bua's "sweet fat book" someday. I also owe special thanks to my wonderful friends: Preeti Walia, Shapoor Marolia, Mayjee Philips, Nipun Prem, and Edward Roberts for their help and support at different stages.

My parents, Madhu and Tapishwar Kumar, have brought me to this place. My father's breadth of knowledge, his wisdom, and his compassion for others continue to amaze and inspire me. His feedback on the manuscript and our many conversations on these questions shaped my work in formative ways. My mother has been my wellspring of love, strength, and support in ways that she does not even begin to realize. This book is therefore dedicated to them for everything they will always mean to me.

Finally, to Vinu Warrier, my husband and my best friend, who traveled across the world to make it possible for us to be together, I could never have done this without you. Your wide-ranging knowledge and your passion for reading are an example to me. Your writing continues to set the bar higher.

Introduction: At Home with the Stranger

This book considers the fraught question of religious coexistence in post-Partition India and its entanglement with the concept of secularism. At least since independence, secularism has been called upon to represent several intractable agendas and interests, primary among which is the hope of a united and peaceful Indian nation. Closely aligned with the term *nationalism,* secularism has come to connote an ideal of tolerance and multireligious coexistence among elite groups brought up on the Nehruvian vision of India as a plural and diverse nation made up of many religions and cultures, nonetheless one that is marked by a "unity in diversity." Yet recent decades have witnessed a crisis in the idea of Nehruvian secularism, marked by a rising Hindu fundamentalist movement that has targeted the minority Muslim community as the enemy within the nation. The accelerated ascendance of the Hindu Right since the 1980s presents one of the central conundrums of contemporary Indian history and politics. Hindu nationalism's designs for a majoritarian, authoritarian, militaristic, and exclusionary India are fairly evident, yet it continues to make dangerous advances in vast segments of Indian society. A number of commentators have noted that the Hindu Right gains a great deal of its staying power and effectiveness by speaking simultaneously in several languages.[1] Hindu nationalists speak at once in the language of democracy and authoritarianism, secularism and religious intolerance, as well as modernity and a "genuine" cultural nationalism. Banu Subramaniam's potent phrase, "archaic modernity," effectively captures the paradoxical politics and the powerful appeal of this movement, which simultaneously upholds capitalism, technology, and western science as

xiv INTRODUCTION

elements of a modern *Hindu* nation along with epic visions of a glorious and hoary Hindu past.[2]

The vision of a homogenous Hindu *rashtra* (nation) that is congruous with upper-caste Hindu beliefs and practices is central to the Hindu Right's agenda. The notion of *Hindutva*—literally "Hinduness," more specifically, Hindu rule or Hindu nation—encapsulates the coercive and majoritarian manifesto of the *Sangh Parivar*, the "family" of right-wing political, cultural, and religious organizations that comprise the Hindu Right. Although the Hindutva league has targeted all minorities in its goal of making India a Hindu nation, Indian Muslims have merited a special place in its virulence. In fact, "the Muslim" in the discourses of the Hindu Right becomes the arch outsider, the enemy of the great Hindu nation. As the authors of *Khaki Shorts and Saffron Flags* note: "At the heart of Hindutva lies the myth of a continuous thousand-year-old struggle of Hindus against Muslims as the structuring principle of Indian history. Both communities are assumed to have been homogeneous blocs—of Hindu patriots, heroically resisting invariably tyrannical, 'foreign' Muslim rulers."[3] Despite the surprise defeat of the Hindu nationalist–led coalition in the last elections, we cannot afford to dismiss or trivialize its hegemony, because the anti-Muslim rhetoric of Hindu nationalists has come to consolidate a kind of popular common sense among many Indians. This othering of Muslims includes fearful notions about their prolific sexuality that will soon allow them to overtake the approximately 800 million Hindus of India; their inherent conservativeness; the violent temperament of Muslim men and the corresponding victimization of all Muslim women; and the familiar charge that all Indian Muslims are, at heart, Pakistanis. India's more than one hundred million Muslims are thus constructed as the nemesis of the benign and tolerant Hindu nation. If the milder face of the Hindu Right endorses a cultural nationalism that advocates assimilation, more virulent voices proclaim a program that stops just short of ethnic cleansing, as amply demonstrated in the horrific anti-Muslim pogrom that took place in Gujarat in 2002.

While the expanding role of religion in Indian political culture has led to a rallying of the forces of liberal secularism against this onslaught of religious "fundamentalism," it has also resulted in a fiercely divisive, yet productive, debate on the normative and progressive claims of the project of modern secularism itself. Above all, the destruction of the Babri

Masjid (mosque) in 1992 by self-styled Hindu nationalists, and the more recent state-orchestrated genocide of Muslims in Gujarat, have dramatically brought to the fore the question of whether and how secularism as state policy and as an ideal of liberal tolerance should be sustained.[4] The terrifying events of Gujarat, in particular, are a frightening reminder of how Muslims have been marked as the adversary within the nation. The many appalling stories of violence, rape, and torture—of wombs being ripped out and fetuses being burned in order to entirely obliterate the other—compel us to rethink and reinvigorate our theories of tolerance and living with the other.

This book takes up the task of *revising* the related and entangled notions of tolerance and secularism. My study traces the emergence of what I call an "ethics of coexistence" in postindependence South Asian literature and film, an ethics that has arisen as a deeply felt imaginative response to particular historical moments marked by rising religious violence in the Indian subcontinent. Beginning with the contention that secularism as a concept is not expansive enough to accommodate the vision of multireligious coexistence it has been asked to take on in India, I argue that literary and cultural productions can make a significant contribution to contemporary intellectual and political efforts to envision the peaceful coexistence of diverse religious groups in the Indian subcontinent. The fictions I examine include the works of contemporary English-language writers such as Salman Rushdie, Amitav Ghosh, Mukul Kesavan, and Shauna Singh Baldwin; subcontinental-language fictions by Saadat Hasan Manto, Khwaja Ahmad Abbas, Rajinder Singh Bedi, Jamila Hashmi, Jyotirmoyee Devi, and Lalithambika Antherjanam; and Hindi films by Khalid Mohamed, Mahesh Bhatt, and Shyam Benegal. In different ways, these works urge a shift in our ethical and political imaginations by offering ways of living together that exceed the political and juridical contract ensured by law, the constitution, or any kind of state apparatus. By envisioning possibilities of multireligious coexistence that go beyond liberal formulations of tolerance and an abstract secular citizenship, these literary and film narratives allow us to animate the theory and practice of tolerance and coexistence.

Any project that contemplates peaceful coexistence in the subcontinent must begin by addressing the ambivalent and liminal position occupied by Muslims in post-Partition India. The figure of the Indian Muslim has come to be constituted as the "intimate enemy" or the "stranger" in our midst, who is not quite a friend or an external enemy. "In general," as Jacques Derrida tells us, "it is the birthplace which will always have underpinned the definition of the stranger (the stranger as nonautochthonous, nonindigenous)."[5] A stranger *(étranger)* is one who is born elsewhere, one who is not considered a "natural" part of "home." In the Indian landscape, Muslims, along with Christians, have often been viewed as nonautochthonous not because they are born elsewhere but because they follow faiths that originated elsewhere.[6] But the "strangeness" of the Muslim is further exacerbated by Partition and the creation of Pakistan as a separate nation for the subcontinent's Muslims. In 1947, on the basis of a separatist movement led by Mohammed Ali Jinnah, India was divided into its Muslim-majority and Hindu-majority provinces. Jinnah's political party, the Muslim League, which had no popular support until the early 1940s, spearheaded a separatist movement that led to the division of India in less than a decade. His two-nation theory presented Partition as the logical and inevitable outcome of the irreconcilable differences between Hindus and Muslims. However, as Partition historian Mushirul Hasan points out, "Even at its most euphoric stage, the campaign for a 'Muslim' nation was hardly embedded in the historical logic of the two-nation theory. In fact the theory on its own hardly reflected the consciousness of a community, for it was conceived by a small group, in a specific context, as an ideological counterweight to secular nationalism."[7] Yet Partition came to pass, and the new nation of Pakistan was born on August 14, 1947. The effects and consequences of Partition were cataclysmic: the division of the country was accompanied by a communal holocaust of terrifying proportions, setting off one of the largest mass migrations of people in history, the death and devastation of millions of people, the rape and abduction of thousands of women by men of other communities, and innumerable other losses of property, ways of life, and community.

Taking Partition to be a foundational trauma of the Indian nation-state, this book returns to the proximate past of Partition in order to call into question the construction of the Indian Muslim as the stranger within the nation. My effort in this study is not only to bring the events of Partition to the forefront of national memory, as has been the focus of much recent scholarship, but to deconstruct the very concept of the Indian nation—the centered subject of much nationalist historiography—by returning to its moment of origin.[8] As Derrida explains, all institutions of origin conceal the splitting off of something other than the origin in order for the origin to be instituted.[9] Accordingly, my deconstructive approach returns to the moment of origin of the Indian nation-state in order to reveal "that which must be differed-deferred" precisely so that the Indian nation-state can posit itself as a unified and coherent entity.[10] I argue that an alternative understanding of the demand for the Muslim state of Pakistan must be at the forefront of any revisionary project of multireligious cohabitation in the subcontinent. The dominant narratives of secular nationhood tend to construct Partition as the logical culmination of the Muslim separatist impulse. However, recent revisionist historical scholarship on the Partition suggests that Jinnah did not really want Pakistan—the separate nation—but held up the specter of Pakistan as a cleverly disguised tactical maneuver, a bargaining chip with which to extract specific concessions for Muslims from Nehru and Gandhi's Congress party.[11] Behind the cry for Pakistan lay a host of complex, diverse, and often conflicting interests and causes, including the long history of provincial politics, the unyielding stance of the Congress on several issues, and the fear of elite Muslims that they would be marginalized once the British left; it was hardly the (sole) culmination of a monolithic Islamic movement. While Partition emerged contingently, it was also not an accidental event in the history of Indian nationalism. It becomes the only solution to the Muslim "problem" with which the secular state can live. In a radical reexamination of Muslim separatism, Aamir Mufti argues that since the problematic of Muslim identity "exceeded the categories within which nationalism sought to contain it," this *excess* had to be excised.[12] Thus, Partition must be read as a development necessary to the discourse of Indian nationhood, "a turning of two thirds of the Muslims of India [the largest Muslim polity in the world at the time] into non-Indians" (Pakistanis) so the re- maining one-third could successfully be *contained* in the role of national minority.[13] The Muslim separatist impulse in India, enunciated most explicitly by the Muslim League and Jinnah, must be understood primarily as a refusal to accept this ambivalently coded anomalous citizenship, a refusal to be cast in the excluded and cast-out position of minority. Such a fundamental rethinking of the very origins of the Indian nation-state is crucial for thinking coexistence in the present. It enables us to reconsider the demonized narrative of Muslim separatism as well as the persistent construction of the Indian Muslim as an undecidable figure, the stranger, whose loyalty is always suspect and must be ritually reaffirmed to quell nationalist anxieties.

Indian secular nationalism of the Nehruvian kind has typically relied on liberal idioms of "tolerance" and "protection of minorities" to ensure Muslims a relatively secure place in the polity. This is as true of secularism defined as a political doctrine guiding state policy as it is of the notion of secularism as an ideal of multicultural cohabitation among elites brought up on the Nehruvian consensus. In this book, I ask if a liberalist understanding of tolerance is adequate to describe the ideal of peaceful coexistence among different religious or cultural groups in a polity. The notion of tolerance as the telos and vision of multicultural cohabitation has been subjected to rigorous scrutiny in the recent work of Wendy Brown.[14] Eliciting attention to the connotations of tolerance as enduring, allowing, licensing, or indulging, Brown argues that tolerance expresses the extent to which one group, the "tolerant" (usually conceived as superior), may *withstand* the practices, behavior, or even the existence of another group, the "tolerated" (usually constituted as inferior and marginal). She writes, "In every lexicon [plant physiology, medicine, engineering], tolerance signifies the *limits* on what foreign, erroneous, objectionable, or dangerous element can be allowed to cohabit with the host without destroying the host" (Brown, "Reflections," 103). As tolerance has come to be incorporated into the discourse of identity politics and multiculturalism, it is seen to provide a tool for the management of what are viewed as permanent and essential antagonisms achieved through the conversion of overt hatred to forbearance.

The question of *who* tolerates *whom* is also at stake in state and societal practices of tolerance. Tolerance, in other words, is mainly granted by those in power who conform to the normative order to those who deviate from it. Thus the heterosexual tolerates the homosexual, the dominant racial or ethnic group tolerates minority cultures or races, the Hindu tolerates the Muslim, Christian, or the Sikh—though the extent to which tolerance is proffered or withheld differs largely. In each instance, however, the "nonreciprocity" of tolerance discourse is effectively masked, since the hegemonic group is typically constructed as universal and secular, while minority groups are viewed as saturated by their religious and cultural identities. A liberalist understanding of tolerance thus designates condescension or the overcoming of an attitude of disdain, contempt, or enmity toward the "other" ("Reflections," 102). The goal of this discourse, then, is not so much to arrive at equality or solidarity with others but rather *"how to put up with others* by weakening one's own connections to community and claims of identity."[15] The problem with this discourse of forbearance is that it does not take cognizance of its own profoundly paternalistic underpinnings. It continually re-creates minorities as "minors" who require the benevolent protection of the majority community, the genuine "adult" citizens, in order to be accepted as citizens of the nation.

To be sure, while a liberal discourse of tolerance can imply condescension, nonreciprocity, and inequality, the word *tolerance,* in a more idiomatic sense, can also connote mutual or reciprocal tolerance among diverse religious and ethnic groups. *Limiting Secularism: The Ethics of Coexistence in Indian Literature and Film* proposes different, more ethical ways of relating to others that go beyond not only a liberalist understanding of tolerance but also any relationship of exchange or reciprocity. My book argues for the critical relevance of Derrida's ethical philosophy for addressing the dilemmas of how to live with religious and cultural others in the context of the Indian subcontinent. "Living together," as Derrida points out, encompasses many heterogeneous connotations, ranging from the worst to the best, from notions of the last resort to the idea of living together in peace and in accord.[16] On the one hand, in its French idiom, the phrase *il faut bien vivre ensemble* (one must *well* live together) reminds us of what remains an unavoidable necessity—one must live together in any fashion, even if it is badly, in hatred or in conflict, for how can one live otherwise? For example, Israelis and Palestinians, Indians and Pakistanis, simply must coexist and cohabitate in the same space and time. On the other hand, this injunction, "must well" *(il faut bien),* can also be otherwise modulated—"one must live together *well*"—gesturing toward a mode of coexistence that is of trust, concord, and "good faith." In fact, "the best of the 'living together' is often associated with peace . . . a perpetual peace or a messianic peace, whose promise belongs to the very concept of peace and suffices to distinguish it from armistice, from ceasefire or even from any 'peace process'" (11). This peace or "ethics of living together" is not limited to the contract guaranteed by the law or any sort of state apparatus (17).

To "live together" *well*, we must be able to interrogate all statutory conventions, all totality, and the cohesiveness of any organism (natural or biological) or any social body (family, ethnic group, nation) that has been given to us by blood, birth, or belonging. Living together is neither reducible to "organic symbiosis" (life according to nature, birth, or soil) nor to the juridico-political contract ("life according to convention, contract or institution") (18). Indeed, the adverb form of the word *ensemble*, as in the phrase "vivre ensemble" (living together), must always contest and dislocate the authority of *ensemble* as a noun with its connotations of a *whole* or a coherent system. Living together must not be contained, limited, or governed by the authority of a natural (genetic or biological) or juridico-institutional whole. Thus, Derrida avers, one only lives together *well* with and as a stranger at home—there where one claims to be "at home with oneself"—in all the implications of "home," including the self, the family, the neighborhood, the religious or ethnic community, and the nation-state. A living together of peace and accord that exceeds the compulsory tolerance of the juridical contract can occur only when one opens one's self and one's home to the other—the stranger who is not considered a natural part of home—without subsuming the other into the self.[17] Derrida's vision of coexistence thus rests upon the possibility of an ethical relationship with the other—it asks us to welcome the other not only beyond any relation of exchange, calculation, or reciprocity, but also without negating the alterity of the other.[18] Elsewhere, Derrida speaks of the prospect of what he calls "another tolerance," one that would respect the distance of infinite alterity as singularity.[19] This "ethics of living together" ("another tolerance") implies justice and equity in multireligious polities, and as such, it is radically different from the arrogant tolerance of condescension.

Although this living together of justice and equity is "beyond and across the normality of a legal, political, and state-controlled bind," it does not require a rupture with the juridical contract or have to be in contradiction with it (Derrida, "Avowing," 17). In fact, the ethics of living well together can command the sense of the *must* well live together—the compulsory tolerance of the political contract—by guiding our vision of democracy, law, and the secular state. At the same time, we must recognize that the very historicity of these laws inevitably threatens or perverts the *well* of the living well together. This irreducible division—or what

Gaytari Spivak terms the "founding gap"—between the ethical and the historical-political has to do with an understanding of ethics as the "experience of the impossible."[20] If we grasp ethics as the "call of the wholly other, which must necessarily be answered . . . by a responsibility bound by accountable reason," we must also acknowledge that no self can reach the *wholly other* because radical alterity is "that which must be differed-deferred so that we can posit ourselves, as it were."[21] Hence, ethics as the experience of radical alterity can be understood as the experience of the impossible.[22] Consequently, any act or talk that we take as closest to the ethical—the historical and the political—is bound to be conditional and limited. However, we should not take this experience of the impossible to be an impasse; rather, we must always work toward narrowing or supplementing this founding gap between the ethical and the historical-political.

In light of this "division and sharing" of ethics and politics, chapter 1, "Rethinking Secularism," takes up the important task of considering how we might be able to reanimate and transform the political in light of the Derridean ethic of living well together.[23] Since secularism is the rubric under which most discussions of religious violence and tolerance take place in India, this chapter considers whether secularism can encapsulate the vision of peaceful coexistence it has been asked to fulfill in postindependence India. My intervention in the vigorously contested political and intellectual terrain of secularism begins with the premise that there remains considerable semantic and conceptual confusion about this key political idea and that we need a more specific understanding of this concept before we can begin to address its usefulness and limits for the historical instance of India. Drawing on the double sense of the word *limiting* in my title, I argue that secularism is a limited concept that must be restricted (limited) in its scope if it is to play a role in contesting religious majoritarianism. The chapter traces the history of secularism from its origins in the European Enlightenment, through its globalization by way of colonialism, and to its institutionalization in modern forms of governance. I argue that the liberal secularist dictum about the privatization of religion—which is premised on the idea of separate religious and secular spheres—cannot suffice for ensuring peace and amity among disparate religious groups (though I continue to uphold the notion of a reason-based secularism for dissenting against religious dogmas and orthodoxies). Traditional secularist claims notwithstanding, I assert that religion is inseparable from its social and political nexus, particularly the contested realms of nationalism, citizenship, and the state. In opposition to the view that religion has declined in modernity, I argue that majority religions (most notably a reformed Protestantism in western countries) are diffused under the signature of knowledge, culture, ethics, and morals in modern "secular" nation-states (and hence rendered transparent), while minority religions are often consigned to the margins of national culture and constructed as strange and excessive to the nation.

If (majority) religious structures continue to buttress and support national secular culture in fundamental, if indirect, ways, how can we begin to address the marginalization of religious minorities in a liberal state and society? In response to this question, my project turns to contemporary India as an important example of what is at stake in reconceptualizing secularism (without rejecting it entirely). In particular, I address the question of the secular state in India. While acknowledging the recent failures, apathy, and complicity of the Indian state in the suffering of Indian Muslims, I continue nevertheless to hold on to the necessity of the state and its rights discourses for ensuring *reasonable* coexistence of diverse religious groups by means of the juridico-political contract. I further underline the importance of the state and constitutionalism in bringing about a more substantial notion of equality in society. Recognizing that religion (along with gender, class, caste, etc.) is an important axis of oppression in a liberal secular state, I argue that identitarian religiocultural claims must be brought into the democratic political process. But we must move past the multiculturalist paradigms of "recognition" and a "politics of difference" to think rather in terms of power sharing and equality within the form of the nation-state. Informed by recent work on pluralism and minority rights, I make the case for reinventing structures of citizenship such that minority religious groups may participate as groups in democratic politics in order to ensure social justice.

However, the remaining four chapters take these questions outside the domain of the state. Clearly, unless we wish to blind ourselves to the limitations of the liberal political contract, we must think beyond the state and the law. State secularism must be supplemented by efforts in the social and cultural spheres, including civil society initiatives by various peace organizations, grassroots efforts at restoring accord, and the long-term ethical effort that moves past identity politics to imagine the other as a self. In the spirit of Spivak's recent work, I affirm the importance of literature for a training in ethics. The ethical is a means of interrupting the epistemological—the domain of the law—which attempts to constitute the other as an object of knowledge. Ethical practices seek to "listen to the other as if it were a self."[24] Spivak affirms the humanities in the university as an important ethical site for "cultural instruction in the exercise of the imagination," which enables us to "figure the other as imaginative actant" (94). Concurrently, she also underscores the necessity of othering the self—rendering our familiar self and home uncanny—by means of the imagination in order to respond to the call of the other.[25] Although literature must not be viewed as a "blueprint to be followed in unmediated social action," by figuring the impossible, it shows us how we might be able to access the other in the imagination, even if incompletely and imperfectly.[26] I share Spivak's faith in the significance of fiction and film as important sites for imaginative making that must be drawn on to imagine radical possibilities of living well together. In different ways, the literary and cultural productions that I explore in this book show us how we might be able to inaugurate a living together of peace and accord between Hindus and Muslims, Indians and Pakistanis. Calling attention to the insidious agenda of majoritarian nationalisms, these works assert the importance of minoritarian claims on national culture and women's particular and corporeal investments in the peaceful cohabitation of groups. Enabling us to move past identity politics and to go toward the other, these fictional narratives offer important resources for narrowing the gap between the political and the ethical.

Chapter 2, "For God's Sake, Open the Universe a Little More: Cosmopolitan Fictions," examines Salman Rushdie's *The Moor's Last Sigh* and Amitav Ghosh's *In an Antique Land* in light of contemporary theoretical reflections on cosmopolitanism and hospitality. Derrida's injunctions about thinking beyond the ensemble and welcoming the stranger as crucial conditions for the living together of peace and accord provide a touchstone for my readings of Rushdie's and Ghosh's narratives. I argue that these literary works in their evocative accounts of a cosmopolitan world—where everyone lives as a stranger among strangers and where no one claims ownership or mastery of the home—offer compelling representations of Derrida's vision of hospitality and living well together. Both writers seek to imagine a more inclusive and hospitable world, but where Rushdie's novel affirms the idea of a cosmopolitan *nation* that is welcoming to all others, particularly those groups who have been rendered as strangers within the nation, Ghosh's text locates a more *transnational* cosmopolitanism in the medieval past of Indian Ocean trading cultures to call into question the post-Partition binaries of "Indian" and "Pakistani." In their visions of an interconnected, accommodative, and hospitable world—where all are welcome and where no one group has antecedent claim—these literary works allow us to think about possibilities of multireligious coexistence that exceed living together according to blood, birth, or statutory conventions. However, when I turn to Rushdie's version of cosmopolitanism, I draw attention to its tendency to dissolve differences altogether in its desire for a world without borders, and paradoxically, to its inability to move past the modernist category of the nation-state. In contrast, Ghosh offers a more complex account of the intermeshing of religions and cultures, one that is not limited by, and indeed exceeds the bounds of, the nation-state. Finally, while affirming the immense appeal of these works, I also interrogate Rushdie for his failure to conceive of religion in lexicons other than regressive or fundamentalist and Ghosh for his inability to call into question his narrator's secular universalist positioning in his ethnographic account. This examination allows me to underscore the necessity of rethinking the binaries between the religious and the secular for any agenda of coexistence and living well together.

The question of national memory—in particular, the memory of Partition—is also central to the living together of different religious groups and nations in the subcontinent. It continues to be a major and conflictual stake in any discussion of multireligious coexistence. Accordingly, in chapters 3 and 4, I direct my attention to the moment of Partition in order to provide a radically different—defamiliarized—understanding of Partition and its continuing ramifications. Chapter 3, "Acts of Return: Literature and Post-Partition Memory," examines the attempts made by Amitav Ghosh's *The Shadow Lines,* Mukul Kesavan's *Looking through Glass,* and Shauna Singh Baldwin's evocative short story, "Family Ties," to return to Partition as the founding trauma of Indian nationalism. This chapter takes up complex questions about the dialectic between remembering and forgetting Partition in conversation with Holocaust models of memorialization and acts of witnessing by the second generation. In light of Derrida's proposal that avowing the impossible (often a violent and shameful past) and forgiving the impossible are both crucial for thinking coexistence, I argue that these fictions through their return to a painful past open up possibilities of living together in the present. What is especially interesting about these literary narratives as compared to other recent literary works on the Partition, such as Bapsi Sidhwa's *Cracking India* (1988) and Baldwin's later novel *What the Body Remembers* (1999), is that they enact the process of return within their narratives. In each text, a post-Partition narrator who belongs to a subsequent generation returns to the shameful past of Partition through different literary devices ranging from time travel to the uncovering of familial and national secrets in order to grapple with its lingering legacies. Characterized by belatedness and distance, these fictions show us the way to what I call an "uncanny practice of remembrance" that decenters the normative nationalist subject—the representative Indian nationalist self—that was inaugurated by Partition. I contend that the uncanny mode of remembrance posited by these narratives is crucial for moving past the law of identity and going toward the other. The discussion of retrospective acts of cultural memory in this chapter directly leads to an investigation of trauma as a form of bodily memory in the next chapter.

What role can inhuman stories of violence and trauma play in inaugurating a living together of peace and concord? As the editors of a recent issue of *Postcolonial Studies* ask, "Can any good come of the desire to recall (enumerate, understand, lament, . . .) the disorderly singularities of violence?"[27] What might be the risks of such an enterprise? Why and how should we remember violence? Chapter 4, "Fictions of Violence: Witnessing and Survival in Partition Literature," takes up these urgent questions by offering a sustained reading of Urdu, Bengali, and Malayalam fictions, written in the immediate aftermath of Partition, works that center around women's experience of sexual violation during communal riots. I explore the short fictions of Saadat Hasan Manto, Khwaja Ahmad Abbas, Rajinder Singh Bedi, Jamila Hashmi, Jyotirmoyee Devi, and Lalithambika Antherjanam in order to address the issue of sexual violence in mass conflict and the ways in which violence gets inscribed onto the bodies of survivors. Taking as my premise the fact that secular academic discourse has rarely, if at all, concerned itself with the issue of violence in its terrifying impact on people's lives and everyday worlds, I argue for the immense significance of these early imaginative works in their efforts to write and tell a gendered story of loss, trauma, and survival in the aftermath of such tremendous violence. These literary fictions of inhuman sexual violence do not merely serve as exposés or testimonies—though they perform an important testimonial function—but they have a crucial role to play in imagining and inaugurating a world without hatred and violence. By means of their moving portrayals of a radical crisis of masculinity in male witnesses and perpetrators, and by imaginatively taking us to the enduring trauma of life after rape for the female survivor, these fictions make eloquent and compelling pleas for a perpetual peace rather than the living together of pragmatism, necessity, or expediency. In underscoring the ways in which women's bodies become the sites and the stakes in the war between communities, these fictions of sexual violence also allow me to underscore the centrality of a feminist agenda not only for debates about personal law and the secular state but also for revising our notions of tolerance and coexistence.

While chapters 3 and 4 focus on Partition as a founding trauma in the history of the subcontinent, chapter 5, "It's My Home, Too: Minoritarian Claims on the Nation," engages the particular legacies of a divided nation for the minority Muslim community of post-Partition India. This chapter works over a somewhat different domain—Hindi film—to examine the significance of minoritarian claims on the Indian nation. Popular Hindi cinema is a form of entertainment that until recently was too easily dismissed in film and postcolonial studies, but as one of the most prominent and popular forms of public culture in contemporary India, it provides a fascinating site for addressing issues such as nationalism, state violence, religious conflict, and minoritarian identities. I argue that Hindi cinema's potential as an affective and imaginative medium must be drawn upon to envision the living together of peace and justice. The films I examine, Mahesh Bhatt's *Zakhm,* Khalid Mohamed's *Fiza,* and Shyam Benegal's *Mammo,* are part of an emergent genre in Hindi cinema that I call the "Muslim minoritarian film." These films take us to the predicaments of living as a Muslim in India at the turn of the twenty-first century. If the cosmopolitan fictions I explore in chapter 2 affirm a vision of a hospitable community that is welcoming to all others, especially the stranger and the enemy, these films *lay claim* to the nation from the perspective of those who have been dislocated by the politics of the nation-state. They allow me to affirm the centrality of minoritarian claims on national culture. Crucially, the last film I consider, Benegal's *Mammo*, stakes a claim to the nation from the liminal position of a refugee displaced at Partition, a woman who is not quite "Indian," nor "Pakistani." In doing so, it exemplifies Derrida's notion of a justice that exceeds the (unjust) laws of both the Indian and Pakistani nation-states. It allows us to envision the radical possibility of a living together with the (self-consolidating) "other" of Indian nationalism, not just the intimate stranger—the Indian Muslim—but the Pakistani enemy.

While my arguments emerge largely from the specificities of questions and dilemmas emanating from the South Asian context, these arguments are relevant as well on a global stage, to a world increasingly ruptured by the claims of distinct religious identities. I am hopeful that attention to these narratives of a beleaguered minoritarian Muslim identity in contemporary India can help to interrogate the current proliferation of discourses about a monolithic transnational fundamentalist Islam.

1

Rethinking Secularism

What does it mean that a project dedicated to stemming religious hatred and fostering coexistence has come together under the sign of "secularism"? Secularism has been expanded from its traditional concern with emancipation from religion or the privatization of religion to a far more wide-ranging and heterogeneous agenda in postcolonial India. It has been called upon to resolve a number of thorny social and political issues, including primarily (but not only) the possibility of multireligious and multicultural coexistence within the nation and the complex question of the place of religious minorities in a liberal democratic state. Indeed, secularism has become associated with a generalized language of anticommunalism among elites in India. This book asks if secularism, both as a cultural project and as a political doctrine, is useful for enabling the peaceful coexistence of diverse religious groups. If living together *well* necessarily implies justice and equity between disparate religious groups in a polity, is secularism sufficient for envisioning a more radical politics of equality among and within different religious groups? If not, what other models of democratic citizenship must be reinvigorated in order to counter the politics of religious majoritarianism? Moreover, what other kinds of contemporaneous projects of justice must be imagined and implemented if the desired goal is not just the mitigation of suffering caused by communal violence but also a living together of peace and harmony? Through an exploration of secularism's limits and possibilities, this chapter argues that the concept must be minimized and restricted in its purview if it is to be effective at all in checking communal violence and religious majoritarianism. A *reformulated* secularism—both as a cultural project and as a doctrine underwriting the liberal state—does have an important role to play in ensuring the living together of diverse religious groups, but I contend that secularism as a political and cultural term is not capacious enough to house the vision of multireligious coexistence that it has been asked to achieve in postindependence India.

Indian debates about secularism and religious strife have largely limited themselves to defending or rethinking the role of the secular state. Theorists of secularism have not devoted enough attention to the exploration of secularism as a broader and more ambitious disciplinary project for regulating public life. While the liberal secular state and the secularization of society are not unrelated notions, they must be disentangled in order to ask what aspects of each are useful for addressing religious conflict in contemporary India and what elements need to be reformulated or rejected. Accordingly, the first section of this chapter sets out to unravel the complicated meanings of secularism as a cultural and ideological project constitutive of modernity. Providing a brief account of the concept of the secular and the doctrine of secularism that took shape during the European Enlightenment, I examine how secularism has come to be constituted as a normative model for the rest of the world's peoples in their path toward progress and modernity. I argue that the liberal dictum about the privatization of religion—which is premised on the idea of separate religious and secular spheres—is no longer tenable (and never was) as a strategy for peace and coexistence. However, unlike those who reject secularism in its entirety because of its origins in the Enlightenment and in Reformation Christianity, I maintain that a reformulated reason-based secularism must be put to the service of challenging religious orthodoxies, particularly those that legitimize caste hierarchies and patriarchies.

In the next section, I focus on the trajectory of secularism in India, particularly on the implications of secularism as a political doctrine underwriting the liberal state and whether it provides the means through which multireligious coexistence may be sought or achieved. I affirm the importance of the secular state in multireligious societies—if the secular state is understood as the separation of state from any *one* religion rather than the exclusion of religion from politics as such—for ensuring the reasonable coexistence of groups in society. However, I argue that a secular state by itself is not enough to ensure equality among different religious groups in a bounded nation-state. Thus, I emphasize the crucial role of the state in effecting substantive equality in society through the *participation* of minority religious groups (as groups) in democratic institutions and structures of representation rather than through the relegation of these groups to a realm outside the state. In my view, the discourse of constitutionalism and the state continues to remain an important site of intervention both for preventing religious violence and for redressing institutionalized inequalities in society, though I also believe that the state cannot be the final horizon of action. In the concluding section, I discuss briefly the limits of secularism as an ethical ideal, one most often understood as a liberalist version of tolerance or protection of minorities in the Indian context. I argue that we need to devise more resonant terms and concepts for thinking about the encounter with otherness. With that goal in mind, I turn to postindependence literary and cinematic productions in order to demonstrate how these works can serve to revise our notions of tolerance and living with the other.

Secularism and Religion

Secularism is understood to be at the core of modernity. The narrative of secularization is typically recounted as a story of progress and gradual emancipation from religion through the exercise of reason and in the wake of the destructive and terrible sectarian wars that overtook Europe in the sixteenth and seventeenth centuries.[1] According to this account, the emergence of rationalistic and evidentiary modes of thought enabled the undoing of religion and led to the development of an autonomous public realm constituted by "mature," self-sufficient human beings. In this traditional and still canonical description, secularism and religion function as binaries along the axes of rational–irrational, progressive–regressive, and modern–traditional. However, secularism has come to be the subject of increasing scrutiny and interrogation in much recent scholarship.[2] Taking my cue from this revisionist work, I view secularism as the product of a particular moment in post-Reformation Christian history, the European Enlightenment. It becomes institutionalized as a doctrine with the historical separation of church and state in nineteenth-century liberal society and eventually becomes globalized through colonialism and the dispersal of modern forms of governance and of corporate, market, and professional values.

Enlightenment rationalism stands as the forerunner of liberal secularism as a doctrine, though secularization itself was a more complex process that had already been taking place within the Reformation (and particularly within Puritanism and Dissent).[3] Kant's essay "What Is Enlightenment?" articulates the characteristic Enlightenment idea that religious beliefs cannot be compelled and that these beliefs arise from interior forces such as reason and conscience:

> A prince who does not find it beneath him to say that he takes as his duty to prescribe nothing, but rather to allow men complete freedom in religious matters—*who thereby renounces the arrogant title of tolerance*—is himself enlightened and deserves to be praised by a grateful present and by posterity as the first, at least where the government is concerned, to release the human race from immaturity and *to leave everyone free to use his own reason in all matters of conscience.* (my emphasis)[4]

Much Enlightenment thinking sought to disassociate religious affiliations from loyalty to the monarchial state at a time when the legitimacy of monarchs derived in part from their allegiance to a particular religious sect. Secularist political and social movements of disassociation and reform were underpinned by the idea of the rational and individualistic believer, one who had to make his own choices about salvation and eternal life.

In locating secularism or secular thought in the Enlightenment, however, we have to be careful not to conflate different and heterogeneous perspectives on religion and reason.[5] The common account of the Enlightenment is that it saw religion as a threat to freedom, progress, and modernity. While hostility toward religion may be a feature of a particular tradition of the Enlightenment, that of the French *Lumières*, which exercised a "critical and antireligious vigilance" articulated most volubly in Voltaire's battle cry, *"Ecrasez l'infâme"* (and which influenced thinkers such as Marx, Nietzsche, and Feuerbach), it does not encapsulate the complexity and variety of Enlightenment thought on religion.[6] For example, Derrida notes that the German Enlightenment (Aufklärung) is profoundly rooted in Reformation thought.[7] In fact, recent historical work has taught us to move away from a singular conception of what has come to be called *the* Enlightenment with its focus on a canon of great thinkers to more multiple and varied accounts of Enlightenment. Enlightenment produced a wide variety of responses to religion, ranging from Voltaire's (secular) hostility to Kant's attempts to come up with a rational or "reflecting religion," as well as powerful religious movements like Methodism and Pietism.[8]

While secularism took shape during the Enlightenment and culminated in the great secularization movements of the nineteenth century that brought about the historic separation of church and state, the concept of the secular was constituted in the preceding centuries, particularly in early modernity. As Talal Asad points out, the genealogy of secularism has to be traced by means of the concept of the secular—"in part to the Renaissance doctrine of humanism, in part to the Enlightenment concept of nature, and in part to Hegel's philosophy of history."[9] The Oxford English Dictionary provides the following meanings for the word *secular:* (1) concerned with the affairs of this world: not spiritual or sacred, (2) not concerned with religion or religious belief, (3) a. not ecclesiastical or monastic b. not bound by a religious rule, (4) occurring once in an age or century. The opposition between *this* world as comprised of autonomous human agents responsible for their own actions (the makers of History) and a distinct supernatural world that is the domain of the Christian God, Asad tells us, is a particular (early) modern construction that *demarcates* the human and divine spheres; the gods of the Greeks, by contrast, were not viewed as transcendent but directly involved in natural and social processes (27). In this construction, "nature" is viewed as a manipulable realm subject to man's domination, while anything beyond that realm is "supernatural," inhabited by irrational events and imagined beings. The projection of a transcendent God at one remove from the world enabled the construction of *this* world as the sphere of rational and empirical exploration—therefore secular; however, this kind of separation of spheres may not be as likely in religiocultural contexts in which the notion of divinity is not as clearly locatable in a separate, supernatural realm.

Underpinned by this notion of the secular as "of this world" (a world of autonomous human beings), secularism is typically understood to be the doctrine that is indifferent to or excludes religion or religious considerations, which are henceforth constituted as otherworldly. Based on the idea of distinct religious and worldly spheres, secularism constitutes these spheres along the lines of the private and public distinction that has been so central to modernity, with religion being consigned to the "private" sphere. Proponents of liberal secularism hoped that the functional differentiation of spheres would lead to eventual emancipation from, and therefore the decline of, religion. Typically, the secularist notion of well-defined sacred and profane spheres has also been deployed to make the case for tolerance among disparate religious sects in liberal societies. Locke's "Letter concerning Toleration" is one of the earliest articulations of a liberalist mode of tolerance that draws its rationale from secularism.[10] Written in part as a response to the hegemony of the Anglican Church, Locke's work attempts to clearly demarcate religion from what he calls "civil life." He argues that while the powers of civil government must be confined to "the care of the things of this world," the church itself is "absolutely separate and distinct from the commonwealth" (120/126). The claim is that since religious beliefs are intensely private and subjective, an individual must not and cannot be coerced—by the state or by any ecclesiastical authority—to believe in any particular religion. The argument for religious tolerance is thus buttressed by the ideology of secularism: "He jumbles heaven and earth together, the things most remote and opposite, who mixes these two societies, which are in their original, end, business, and in everything perfectly distinct and infinitely different from each other" (126). This clear distinction between religious and civil life allows Locke to render religion solely as a matter of "private" belief. Tolerance of different religions is thus made contingent on the privatization of belief. Yet, what are the implications and consequences of this modern differentiation of religious and secular spheres along private and public lines?

In an important argument, José Casanova notes that the private/public distinction has been crucial to all conceptions of the modern social order; religion, in particular, has been intrinsically connected to the modern historical differentiation of private and public spheres.[11] The notion that "religion is a private affair" is constitutive of western modernity in a dual sense—it points to the liberal and bourgeois belief in religious freedom as the first freedom as well as the precondition of all modern freedoms. In this view, freedom of conscience is intrinsically related to the "right to privacy," that is, to the modern institutionalization of a private sphere removed from governmental as well as ecclesiastical control. But the obverse of this formulation is perhaps even more crucial to the emergence of the modern social order: religion was progressively evacuated from the modern secular state, the capitalist economy, and science in an attempt to contain and limit it within the newly constituted private sphere. Much like the concept of private property, the privatization of religion therefore serves as the very foundation of modern liberalism and modern individualism.

From the secularist viewpoint, religion becomes legitimate and acceptable so long as it does not intrude upon the jurisdiction of what has been constituted as the "public" realm. The self-validating narrative of modernity marks the privatization of religion as crucial in our eventual path toward emancipation from religion, and paradoxically, also as significant to the freedom of religion itself from worldly politics. Yet how exactly the boundaries between private and public are to be demarcated is a question that continues to trouble secularists and indeed is central to the confusions that surround much secular discourse. At issue of course is what constitutes the private and public in such distinctions—often this seems to depend on which end of the two polar oppositions we define clearly. On the one hand, if we understand the private sphere to be the realm of the domestic, the family, interpersonal relations, and intimacy, then "the public" is often constituted by opposition as everything that cannot be subsumed under the "private," including both state and civil society. On the other hand, if we limit our conceptions of the public to the domain of the state and its institutions, then everything else is collapsed into an undifferentiated residual category of the "private."[12] The place of what has come to be constituted as "civil society," the "public sphere," or society at large remains nebulous and vague in all such attempts at defining clear boundaries between private and public. This inability to clearly define private and public spheres is reflected in contemporary discussions of religion and secularism—there is no consensus about what the privatization of religion entails.

It is not surprising then that many recent scholarly conversations on secularism and religious strife have tended to limit themselves to clarifying the role of the secular state (particularly in Indian debates on secularism). Secularism is often understood solely as the political doctrine that underpins the liberal secular *state*. However, I argue that secularism, in its hegemonic versions, must be understood as a broader disciplinary project of regulating "public" life that seeks to confine religion within the *domestic sphere*. Modernity assigns religion—along with women—to the sphere of the "home." As Casanova notes, "Home is the sphere of love, intimacy, subjectivity, sentimentality, emotions, irrationality, morality, spirituality, and religion"; it is also the "female sphere par excellence" (33). This process of privatization has led to the feminization and sentimental- ization of religion such that religion is rendered irrelevant to all worldly (public) concerns; concomitantly, women are often invested with the onus of upholding a (privatized) religion. Clearly, the doctrine of secular- ism was never limited to the question of the state, but it was central to the modernization and liberalization of society itself. William Connolly goes so far as to propose that the question of rights, tolerance, and the role of the state are more properly the concerns of liberalism, while the matter of the "role of religion and nonreligion in public life" belongs to the concep- tual domain of secularism.[13] In my view, while the notion of separation of religion from state is a central *aspect* of the liberal thesis of secular- ism, the "public" in formulations of secularism is certainly not restricted to the sphere of the state. A broader emancipation of the "social," the "public sphere," or "civil society" from religion is the desired outcome of secularism in its normative versions. Those who seek to make the case for secularism today as a political doctrine guiding the secular state in multi- religious polities first must come to grips with secularism as a cultural and sociological project that is at the core of modernity.

The question that confronts us as we consider today's escalating religious violence and what is called fundamentalism is whether the secularist privatization of religion and the separation of spheres are possible—or even desirable—as an adequate response. Feminist in- sights about the impossibility of isolating and separating clearly demar- cated private and public spheres are instructive in this context. Gayatri Spivak writes, "[I]f the fabric of the so-called public sector is woven of the so-called private, the definition of the private is marked by a public potential since it is the weave, or texture of public activity."[14] Private and public are thus seen as porous and unstable conceptual distinc- tions that take on different meanings in different contexts such that each sphere may be said to infuse and spill into the other. (Indeed, feminism has much at stake in destabilizing the private/public distinction that is so central to the liberal trajectory of secularism. Religious practices, *when seen as privatized,* can become a source of immense violence for women given the positioning of the female body in the private sphere. Women are made to carry the burden of the "home"—both in the sense of the household and the privatized religious community.)[15] If it is indeed impossible to mark out private from public, what are the specific consequences of this understanding for thinking about religion and secularism? To what extent has religion been "evacuated" from the domain of the state, economy, and science?

What is important and far-reaching about secularization is not that religion has waned in western modernity (a highly debatable proposition) but that there is a radical and paradigmatic shift in the way in which religion itself is socially and institutionally constituted. The modern differentiation of religious and social spheres has resulted in a fundamental shift in the configuration and (public) role of religion rather than its disappearance or decline. With secularization, Christianity, specifically post-Reformation Christianity, invents religion as a separate institution that is now held to be purely about inner, privatized belief, shorn of everyday embodied practices (as opposed to organized worship).[16] This intellectualized abstract system of internalized beliefs is assumed to constitute some sort of transcultural "essence of religion," making it the object of systematic discourse and study across cultures. Once all religions are made to fit into a normative model along the lines of a reformed Protestantism, different religions can be compared and constructed as essentially the same. And yet, any of those "other" religions can never quite be the original itself; at best, they can be poor imitations.[17] Religions that do not conform to this post-Reformation Christian model of privatization are rendered outside the pale of modernity and construed as inherently fundamentalist.

I argue that a truly secular public sphere freed of all religious understandings, figures of thought, or practices does not exist even in western liberal societies that define themselves as "secular." Rather, religious discourses get diffused and redistributed as ethics, morals, and culture in modernity. Derrida suggests that the religious stratum resurfaces in the most unexpected ways, not necessarily as explicit religiosity or submission to some scriptural authority but as the repressed or as a figure of haunting.[18] He reminds us that our fundamental juridico-political concepts, such as the sovereign state, the citizen-subject, and private and public space, are religious or "theologico-political."[19] Religious structures (specifically the appeal to faith) suppose and underpin all social interaction, all intersubjectivity, "every act of language and every address to the other" (56). Moreover, and this is Derrida's more radical claim, reason itself can only suppose trustworthiness or faith, what he terms (here and elsewhere) the "mystical foundation of authority" (57). The very emergence of justice and law, the inauguration and founding moment of law, implies a *"call to faith."*[20] He points out that without this elementary act of faith, this supposition of trustworthiness, "there would neither be 'social bond' nor address of the other . . . neither convention nor institution, nor constitution, nor sovereign state, nor law" ("Faith and Knowledge," 80). This elementary faith is at least "in its essence or calling religious (the elementary condition, the milieu of the religious if not religion itself)" (81). In suggesting that modern "secular" culture continues to be underwritten in fundamental, if indirect, ways by religious discourse, Derrida's view renders deeply problematic and complex the historical claims of secularization by western modernity.

Significantly, therefore, Derrida eschews the language of secularization and chooses to use the resonant term *mondialatinisation* instead (translated as "globalatinization" by Samuel Webcr). He uses this neologism to designate what he sees as the phenomenon of "Latinity" and its globalization via Anglo-America. Latinity is the Christianization of the world but a particular form of "secularized" Christianity that we have inherited from the Enlightenment (what we have come to term "secularism" retrospectively). For Derrida, Kant's notion of a true or "reflecting faith" is central to the globalatinization of the world. Kant affirms that in order to conduct oneself in a moral manner, man must not ask what God has done for his salvation but know what he must do to become worthy of this help; *therefore, he must act as though God had abandoned us.* Christianity is thus announced as the "death of God" by Kant to the Enlightenment:

> In enabling us to think (but also to suspend in theory) the existence of God, [and] the freedom or the immortality of the soul, . . . the concept of 'postulate' of pure practical reason guarantees this radical dissociation and assumes ultimately rational and philosophical responsibility, the consequence here in this world, in experience of this abandonment. (51)

It is this emphasis on the world as peopled by autonomous rational human beings that we have come to term *secularism*, though Derrida rarely uses the term. His deployment of the term *globalatinization* rather than secularization to describe the process sparked by Enlightenment thought underscores that this is a particularly Christian notion emerging from a Christian tradition but that it has become hegemonic through the dispersal of modern forms of governance and through Europe's colonial encounters, which played a key role in the diffusion of Enlightenment culture.[21] Secularism is thus understood to be the invention of a particular religion—Reformed Christianity.[22]

One of the central contributions of recent work on secularism, religion, and modernity, then, has been a demystification of the progress narrative anchoring the project of European secularism. I have dwelt at some length on the normative (western) version of secularism because it finds little purchase in Indian discussions about secularism and coexistence other than as the routine gesture of proclaiming the difference of the Indian variant of secularism. I see this critique of western secularism as a crucial and necessary point of departure for those of us who, struggling to contend with rising religious majoritarian movements in postcolonial contexts, seek to reconsider modernity's passionate investment in the notion of secularism.

But does this mean that secularism—as a cultural project and as a political doctrine—must be abandoned entirely? Or should it be reconfigured? Is there no place for Enlightenment (reason-based) secularism in the project of promoting peaceful coexistence among disparate religious groups? I argue that while we need to move away from the goal of emancipating society from *all* religion (the ambition of a particular trajectory of Enlightenment), we must also hold on to the notion of secularism as a form of rational critique, especially in order to be able to dissent from established religious orthodoxies and dogmas (even as we must continue to be wary of the kind of strident antireligious thinking that fetishizes reason). Spivak provides some direction for this project by finding ground within Enlightenment thought itself for a revised notion of secularism that continues to ally itself with reason but that is also able to make room for "the transcendental" (which she asserts should not be given the "blanket name 'religion' too quickly").[23] Like Derrida, she returns to Kant for some answers to contemporary dilemmas about religion and "fundamentalism" even as she asserts that the universal secular intellectual—so beloved of Kant and Said—will no longer suffice for what the university must produce today. In Spivak's view, a revisioned secularism cannot exist without some notion of the transcendental (and the transcendental has different cultural names); yet the transcendental must also be subject to rational critique. Secularism must learn to be more accommodative of forms of transcendentalism like religion; thus, she is extremely critical of those "sanitized secularists who are hysterical at the mention of religion." At the same time, she also underscores the need for "persistently de-transcendentalizing the radically other ['God' in many languages] into a space of effect" or what she terms as a "metalepsis" (111).[24] Such a de-transcendentalized radical alterity can coexist "however discontinuously, with faith itself" (103). The humanities have a special role to play in bringing about such a world where religion can shrink to a level of "mundane normality" rather than provide the basis for mobilization in identity politics (105).[25] This radical secularism is quite different from the most common version of secularism—"laundered Judeo-Christianity"— and has tremendous relevance not only for contesting contemporary global manifestations of the abstraction "terror" (the immediate context for this essay) but also for resisting Hindu majoritarianism and Muslim militancy in India. It is also of immense use for feminist and anticasteist politics that oppose patriarchal and casteist religious practices. The place of reason thus remains implacable in this revisioned version of *"what we may as well call secularism,"* even as we acknowledge that the liberal secularist dictum about the privatization of religion will no longer suffice for achieving the peaceful cohabitation of diverse religious groups (107). Enlightenment thinking on religion and reason, therefore, must not be dismissed summarily. It must be put to use in a careful and qualified manner to undermine the accelerated global phenomenon of an unprecedented and dangerous identity politics around religion.

Of course, western Christian juridico-political concepts (like secularism) and their conceptual apparatuses, however hegemonic and normative, have not been dispersed intact in their diaspora across the world. Rather, the differential diasporas of these "ideoscapes" demand a careful qualification of concepts in order to acknowledge different historical and cultural experiences of modernity.[26] The next section takes contemporary India, overtaken by the Hindu Right, as a compelling example of what is at stake in reformulating secularism both as a doctrine guiding the state in a multireligious polity and as a cultural/ethical project of tolerance.

India's political-social landscape speaks to some of the most crucial tensions at work in arguments about secularism, particularly the place—and claims—of religious minorities in liberal democracies. I begin by exploring the varied and slippery connotations of this fraught term in India by way of ground clearing before I address the particular uses and limits of secularism for ensuring the living together of diverse communities.

Secularism in India: Qualifying the Term

An argument that often emerges in Indian debates on secularism addresses how the concept has come to mark out an independent conceptual domain of its own in postindependence India, giving it rather different inflections from the standard English meaning. For example, Brenda Cossman and Ratna Kapur, in a book appropriately titled *Secularism's Last Sigh,* an allusion to Salman Rushdie's *The Moor's Last Sigh,* give voice to a feeling prevalent in left and liberal circles in India that Indian secularism is in a state of crisis:

> On 6 December, 1992, . . . the RSS, BJP, and VHP combined,
> impaled the cause of secularism on the *trishul* (Shiva's spear)
> of Hindutva ideology. With their 'bare hands and teeth' they an-
> nihilated the five hundred years of bricks and mortar that held
> together a simple mosque—the Babri Masjid. Within minutes, the
> mobs of the Hindu Right had left the ancient structure in ruins,
> the remaining rubble occasionally belching clouds of smoke and
> dust, *as if gasping for the last breath of secularism.* The mosque
> lay belly up, harpooned with saffron flags and swarmed by the
> apostles of the God Squad ebullient in their victory over *toler-
> ance, faith and the secular ideal.* (my emphasis)[27]

In this somewhat dramatic and literary rendering of the events at Ayodhya, the scene of the destruction of the mosque becomes the stage for the figurative death of secularism itself. It is evident that what is meant and conveyed by the term *secularism* here is in *excess* of the western notion of separation of religious and political spheres, or state from religion. The sense of defeat that emerges from the passage does not simply have to do with the failure of the secular state in its inability to prevent the expansion of the Hindu Right, or the project of secularization as such. It has to do with the fundamental issue of whether Hindus and Muslims can continue to live together, peacefully, in a contiguous nation-space given the widespread successes Hindu nationalism has achieved in establishing its unabashedly majoritarian and anti-Muslim agenda.

Secularism in India has been asked to resolve a number of difficult issues. As Anuradha Needham and Rajeswari Sunder Rajan note, secularism in the postcolonial world is a "more comprehensive and diffuse package of ideas, ideals, politics, and strategies than its representation solely as religion's Other would lead us to expect."[28] It has been a foundational political concept since the time of the nationalist struggle against colonial rule. In order to mobilize people from various parts of British India, the anticolonial nationalist movement, led by the Indian National Congress, sought to characterize itself as an inclusive and secular organization, which could accommodate people of different languages, religions, castes, and classes. Congress-led nationalism needed the concept of the secular in order to legitimize its representative claims and to establish hegemony over the different religious groups that comprised British India. It could not afford to be seen as privileging one religious group over the other, even as it was underpinned by an upper-caste Hindu idiom. And, since independence was attended by the partition of the country along religious lines, secularism came to be viewed as crucial for ensuring a reasonable degree of civility in a fragmented and polarized sociopolitical context and for unifying a populace still reeling from the impact of the horrific communal violence that accompanied Partition. For the recently truncated India recovering from the trauma of losing part of its territory to a Muslim Pakistan, secularism therefore came to be a highly charged notion invested with a great degree of nationalist sentiment. Indeed, the notion of secularism came to be crucial to India's self-fashioning as a nation (especially as defined by Jawaharlal Nehru), and served to mark off its "difference" from a separatist Islamic Pakistan, though this self-professed stance is constantly contested even in the early years after independence with other leaders clamoring to establish India as a Hindu state.[29]

Given the complex circumstances and motivations underlying the inception and institutionalization of the concept in India, it is not surprising that the term *secularism* has taken on a meaning in excess of the separation of spheres. As Amartya Sen insightfully points out, "[secularism] is in fact, a part of a more comprehensive idea—that of India as an integrally pluralist country, made up of different religious beliefs, distinct language groups, divergent social practices."[30] It has come to underwrite the idea of India as a multireligious and multiethnic polity. Thus, secularism in India principally connotes a valorized structure of feeling that is cast as the antithesis of *communalism*—the term that Gyanendra Pandey succinctly defines as the "condition of suspicion, fear and hostility between members of different religious communities."[31] Closely allied with the term nationalism, secularism has expanded to describe an ethical ideal of tolerance and coexistence that allows different religious groups to live together amicably.[32]

Indeed, I argue that the idea of "tolerance" has come to serve as the hallmark of secularism in India both in its constitutional form as well as in its ideal of multireligious cohabitation. After Partition, state secularism became the nationalist leaders' way of assuring minorities, mainly Muslims, of their commitment to notions of "neutrality" and equal citizenship. State secularism was interpreted as tolerance or freedom of all religions rather than as the exclusion of religion from state. Paradoxically, secularism, when understood as the tolerance of all religions, has also been made to serve the agenda of minority rights—to provide special treatment to marginalized religious groups. More often than not, however, the notion of tolerance, in its hegemonic versions, is articulated in the liberal and paternalistic idiom of the "protection of minorities"—both as a basis for state policy and as an ideal of peaceful coexistence in society.

Secularism, then, has been called upon to serve different and often contradictory functions in the Indian nation-state. If it has been asked to grapple with the thorny question of multireligious and multiethnic coexistence and to serve as a means of unifying the nation, then it has also been deployed to provide state protection to minority religious communities. Thus, it has been asked to negotiate between uniform rights and liberal citizenship, on the one hand, and special rights for minority religious groups, on the other. And, in keeping with its Enlightenment provenance, secularism has also been mobilized to reform—mainly upper-caste Hindu—religious practices as part of the Nehruvian state's program of modernization, although this program never took off with much force.

To claim, then, that there is a well-defined and distinct referent for the word secularism in the Indian context would be very problematic. Partha

Chatterjee points out that "the loud and often acrimonious Indian debate on secularism is never entirely innocent of its Western genealogies."[33] He observes that the Indian meanings of secularism did not emerge in ignorance of the European or American meanings of the word. I would go further and propose that even the idea of tolerance is not so removed from its western genealogy, since tolerance was the ostensible rationale for the secular state in nineteenth-century liberal society. As a result, contemporary secularism discourse in India is often marked by confusion and by a conceptual slippage between the range of meanings that become encompassed by the terms *secular* and *secularism,* a slippage that occurs not just between the so-called Indian and western meanings of the term but also between political or state secularism and the notion of secularism as an ideal of tolerance and forbearance.

In the next section, I focus on secularism as political doctrine underpinning the liberal state in order to consider its usefulness for the peaceful cohabitation of diverse religious groups in India.

The Indian Secular State

Donald Smith, one of the earliest commentators on Constitutional secularism in India, provides a useful and fairly comprehensive account of secularism as a political doctrine. He argues that in the liberal democratic tradition secularism is not limited to the principle of separation of religion and state but has to be understood in terms of three interrelated components: (1) freedom of religion, which has to do with an individual's relationship to religion so long as it does not impinge upon other basic rights; (2) citizenship, which has to do with the relationship between an individual and the state, whereby the state deals with the *individual as citizen* rather than as member of this or that religious persuasion; (3) neutrality, which bears upon the relationship between the state and religion and demands that the state not uphold the religious over the secular.[34] While the actual word *secularism* does not enter the Indian Constitution until 1976, the Preamble and the chapter on fundamental rights lay out a comprehensive statement on secularism in terms of these three interconnected concepts. I deploy Smith's tripartite structure as a framework for my examination of the discourse of constitutional secularism in India. My effort is to inquire into each of these constituent elements to ask whether secularism needs to be rejected, reconceptualized, clarified, or accompanied by some other project(s) in order to address the vexed issue of religious coexistence.

Freedom of Religion

The guarantee of religious freedom is found in Article 25 (1) of the Constitution, which states that "subject to public order, morality and health and to the other provisions of this Part, all persons are equally entitled to freedom of conscience and the right freely to profess, practice and propagate religion." The limits to this right are provided by the qualifier "public order, morality and health" as well as by other provisions that enable the state to enact laws for social reform and welfare. For example, the practice of untouchability cannot be protected under this right; moreover, the state can ban patriarchal social practices like *sati* or *devdasi* dedication. Freedom of religion is further limited by the proviso that the state can regulate any "economic, financial, political or other *secular* activity which may be associated with religious practice." However, the question of the distinction between the "religious" and the "secular" remains troubled in formulations of religious freedom. The difficulties of demarcating the essential aspects of the religious from the secular were especially evident during the Constitutional debates that went into the framing of the right to religious freedom.

Shefali Jha's work on Constituent Assembly debates from 1946 to 1950 has uncovered a provocative and fascinating discussion on what comprises "religion." She usefully identifies three positions in the Constituent Assembly's discussions on the question of religious freedom: (1) a "no-concern" position of separation of state and religion that comes very close to the hegemonic western understanding of the privatization of religion; (2) the flip side of the first position, which demands separation but does so out of a concern with protecting religion rather than with emancipating the state; (3) the "equal-respect" theory, which affirms that the state should respect all religions equally rather than staying away from them altogether.[35] This last position claimed that in a largely religious society like India ("spiritual," unlike the "materialistic" west), the state cannot afford to trivialize religion. K. M. Munshi, one of the upholders of this view, declared that the nonestablishment clause of the U.S. constitution would not work in Indian conditions. Others went so far as to demand that the state participate in imparting spiritual training to citizens. By and large, however, those who affirmed the notion of equal respect believed that the Indian state could not afford to be founded on a secularism that was disparaging of religion.[36]

The no-concern and equal respect positions came to loggerheads in a seemingly trivial argument, but one that has interesting ramifications for our thinking about "religion." While proponents of the first position wanted the right to freedom of religion to be defined narrowly as the right to freedom of conscience and worship, the upholders of equal respect wanted freedom of religion to be instituted more broadly as the "right freely to *profess, practice and propagate* religion." The crucial disagreement centered around the terms "practice" and "worship"—those who wanted to use the term practice argued that defining religion as worship would be to limit it to a set of performative rituals such as those performed in a church, whereas they claimed that religion in India (specifically Hinduism) was a "way of life." By contrast, others such as B. R. Ambedkar, Amrit Kaur, and P. K. Salve—who opposed use of the term "practice"—were wary of the many patriarchal and casteist customs that could be given validity by the Constitutional institutionalization of such a broad understanding of religion. Ambedkar expressed his concerns in a famous statement to the Constituent Assembly on December 2, 1948:

> There is nothing extraordinary in saying that we ought to strive hereafter to *limit the definition of religion* in such a manner that we shall not extend it beyond beliefs and such rituals as may be connected with ceremonials which are *essentially religious*. . . . I do not see why religion should be given this vast, expansive jurisdiction as to cover the whole of life and to prevent the legislature from encroaching upon that field. (my emphasis)[37]

In Ambedkar's well-meaning efforts to circumscribe the purview of "religion" by marking of the "essentially religious" from other aspects of culture, we encounter a classic expression of the secularist impulse to demarcate religion as a separate institution. However, as Derrida reminds us, if *religion* today implies an institution that is separate and identifiable (tied to the Roman *ius*), there has not always been, nor will there always be everywhere, "a thing that is *one and identifiable*, identical with itself, which whether religious or irreligious, all agree to call 'religion'" ("Faith and Knowledge," 69, 72–73). Since the very term *religion* is a Latin noun, we need to be more specific about this concept and its genealogy—that is, all kinds of experiences of the divine or the sacred are not (and weren't always) identifiable with a distinct institution called "religion."[38] To be sure, the Latin word *religion* has contracted a particular kind of bond with the Abrahamic revelations (the three great monotheisms); however, these are different from other experiences of faith, of the holy, the un-scathed, the divine, or the sacred, but we may be tempted "by a dubious analogy" to call such experiences "religion" (48). Thus, all sacredness and holiness are not necessarily "religious"; however, with the dispersal of Enlightenment culture across the globe, the word *religion* is "calmly and violently applied to things which have always been and remain foreign to what this word names and arrests in its history" (67). Derrida goes on to suggest that the history of the word *religion* should not, *in principle*, be applied to non-Christian religions, especially where such a "separate institution" is not recognized (72).

It may be more interesting, however, to consider how the term *religion* itself is being expanded and reimagined through its dispersal. In the Indian attempts to resist the narrow definition of religion as (organized) worship (the equal respect position), we see how the Latin noun *religion* is being opened up and transformed to accommodate different experiences of sacredness and holiness that cannot be disentangled from cultural practices. In fact, after much debate, the equal respect position won out, but subject to the various limits of public order, social reform, and welfare. Despite aspects of overlap with western secularisms, the right to freedom of religion as it comes to be articulated in the Indian Constitution, then, has important implications for contesting one aspect of globalatinization—the effort to apply a post-Reformation Christian discourse of *religion* on to all experiences of the sacred and the holy. Jha's historical work is a useful reminder to those who dismiss secularism as an elitist and western ideology that Indian secularism, as institutionalized in the Constitution, is far from contemptuous of religion. On the contrary, Constitutional secularism allows a broad freedom of religion, which is not understood as a separate institution that can then be quarantined but as a set of practices that are closely imbricated with culture.

To be sure, the anxieties of Ambedkar and others about religion-legitimized patriarchies and about casteist and majoritarian practices are more relevant today than ever before, but I continue to assert that state-sponsored privatization and delimitation of religion is not a viable solution to these thorny social issues. Rather, the understanding of secularism as a long-term social and cultural project that works to shrink religion to a level of "mundane normality" is more useful in helping to contest religious dogmas and orthodoxies (Spivak, "Terror," 105).

Neutrality

The notion of neutrality is central to the liberal secular state, yet in much secular discourse it remains unclear if by neutrality we mean state "indifference" toward religion based on the notion of separate religious and political spheres or a state policy of *impartiality* toward all religions. Is an ultimate neutrality of the state or public sphere even possible in either understanding of the concept of neutrality? That is, is a complete dissociation of the secular state from religion—religion per se or the majority religion in particular—possible? If not, what is the value (if any) of this procedural notion of neutrality? How can it be used to make the secular state accountable for protecting at the very least the most elementary rights of all its citizens irrespective of their religious allegiance?

Smith's understanding of the principle of neutrality is the strict secularist one that reiterates Locke's arguments about distinct religious and civil spheres. He takes neutrality to mean the exclusion of religion from the state, "each operating within its own sphere of activity," with the state in charge of worldly human activity.[39] He views the U.S. "wall of separation"—a doctrine that provides that the state shall not make any law with respect to religion, nor shall it involve itself with religious affairs—as the closest approximation of this ideal, though he also acknowledges that such a complete separation of state and religion has not been perfectly achieved in any country. (Indeed, the very notion of a wall of separation in the United States has been interpreted differently at different times and is more complex than it is often made out to be.)[40] Nevertheless, in Smith's version of neutrality, "separation means separation, not something less" (226).

Clearly, the Indian state entails a minimum form of separation of state and religion, since it is not a theocratic state, but it can also be viewed as having many anomalies or "problems"—the most obvious of which is the continued existence of separate personal laws for different religions—when evaluated in light of Smith's strict formulation.[41] I have already suggested the impossibility of a truly secular ("neutral," in Smith's sense) public sphere that has been freed of all religious figures of thought, citations, or practices. However, a reformulated notion of the principle of neutrality could be useful for ensuring the reasonable coexistence of disparate religious groups. I suggest that we return to Nehru's notion of the secular state and consider its continued significance for present-day India despite its current disrepute with a number of scholars in the wake of Ashis Nandy and T. N. Madan's provocative critiques of Nehruvian secularism.[42]

It is useful to begin by reexamining the Nehru–Gandhi split on the issue of religion and secularism and rethinking the commonplace view that too easily polarizes and opposes their thinking. I propose that the Nehruvian understanding of state secularism as impartiality to religion is not that distinct from the Gandhian notion of *sarva dharma sambhava* (often understood as equal respect for all religions) in the ways that the Gandhian notion has come to be mobilized and appropriated for the secular state. To understand this overlap between what are often set up as two distinct bases for the secular state, it is important to come to a clearer sense of the principle of neutrality in the Nehruvian position. Although both Nehru and Gandhi were on the same side of the nationalist divide, and upheld the idea of a secular state, their perspectives on the place of religion were to all appearances quite different. While Nehru was a confirmed agnostic, Gandhi's life was permeated with his commitment to religion. In a famous early statement, Gandhi wrote: "[T]hose who say that religion has nothing to do with politics do not know what religion means."[43] Elsewhere, he affirms, "[P]olitics divorced of religion has absolutely no meaning."[44] Accordingly, he advocated the notion of *sarva dharma sambhava* rather than endorsing the exclusion of religion from public life. In fact, as Ajay Skaria explains, Gandhi defined his religious "politics" *in opposition* to a state-centered politics and to modern practices of governmentality.[45] Gandhi's notion of politics, then, is more akin to ethics in its preoccupation with self–other relationships without the necessity of a middle term such as the state to moderate, mediate, or manage such relationships. Since Gandhi's politics was set up in opposition to the state, it is difficult to gauge the precise implications of his notion of *sarva dharma sambhava* for a statist politics, but ironically, it is often used to provide justification for a particularly Indian understanding of the secular state as one that respects all religions equally. In this view, the secular state is viewed as the benevolent representative and protector of all religions rather than one that excludes religion altogether.

In contrast, Nehru was firmly committed to a vision of public life that was derived from the principles of Enlightenment rationality and saw the secular state as the primary agent of societal secularization. In *The Discovery of India* he states:

> We have to get rid of that narrowing religious outlook, that obsession with the supernatural and metaphysical speculations, that loosening of the mind's discipline in religious, ceremonial and mystical emotionalism, which come in the way of our understanding ourselves and the world. We have to come to grips with the present, *this life, this world, this nature* which surrounds us in its infinite variety. (my emphasis)[46]

Clearly Nehru's secularism emerges from a modern understanding of the secular as "of *this* world" and marked off from a distinct supernatural world that is the domain of the religious. He believed that religion was a storehouse of superstition and prejudice, the bane of modern India. In his *Toward Freedom: The Autobiography of Jawaharlal Nehru,* he expressed this view in no uncertain terms: "[T]he spectacle of what is called religion, or at any rate organized religion in India and elsewhere, has filled me with horror, and I have frequently condemned it, and wished to make a clean sweep of it. Almost always, it seems to stand for blind belief and reaction, dogma and bigotry, superstition and exploitation and the preservation of vested interests."[47] Nehru thus echoes Voltaire's stance on religion, and in Voltairean fashion, he uses the qualifying phrase "organized religion." This is reflected in the modernizing/secularizing impulse that he instituted in the early years after independence by leading a statist reform of Hindu society through the administration of temples and *maths*, the abolishment of untouchability, and the restructuring of

Hindu personal laws, among other things. It is this kind of secularizing impulse that is perhaps too easily understood as the be-all and end-all of Nehruvian secularism—and this explains its current ill repute with a number of scholars.

But careful attention to the differences between the notion of secularism as a statist doctrine, on the one hand, and as a broader project of regulating public life (admittedly state led) with ambitions of freeing society from the "clutches" of religious tyranny, on the other, can help us to provide a more nuanced reading of Nehru's complex stance on secularism. Those who set up Nehruvian secularism in explicit contrast to Gandhian equal respect as different models for the secular state must consider Nehru's differential investments in the notion of secularism as a political doctrine and his desire for the eventual secularization of Indian (read Hindu) society. Contemporary efforts to revise, clarify, defend, or reject secularism, I argue, have not considered completely the implications of this important distinction for our current context.

As the chief architect of the postindependence Indian state's trajectory, Nehru was firmly convinced of the need for a secular state in India, but in his vision of such a state, he went to great lengths to explain that a secular state was not one that was hostile to religion. On the contrary, it would ensure "freedom of religion and conscience, including freedom for those who may have no religion."[48] In another instance, he comes close to offering a definition of secularism that echoes the Gandhian vision of *sarva dharma sambhava*, except here it becomes the basis of state policy:

> It is perhaps not very easy to find a good word in Hindi for
> 'secular.' Some people think it means something opposed to re-
> ligion. That obviously is not correct. What it means is that it is a
> state which honors all faiths equally and gives them equal oppor-
> tunities; that, as a state, it does not allow itself to be attached to
> one faith or religion, which then becomes the state religion.[49]

In contrast to Smith's formulation, Nehru articulates secularism as a principle of *impartiality*, or separation of state from any *one* religion. A secular state is first understood in its minimal sense as a nontheocratic state. Yet Nehru goes further when he suggests that it is the obligation of the state to *honor all faiths equally.* Not only does such a state not favor any one religion but it also protects all religions. It is crucial to understand, therefore, that Nehru's understanding of state secularism is one that is not antagonistic to all religious beliefs and practices in the way that his project or hope for the secularization of society may be interpreted to be.

Although it is important to reject certain *aspects* of the Nehruvian project of secularism for the ways it tends to constitute all facets of the religious as obscurantist and premodern, Nehru's notion of a neutral procedural state continues to remain crucial for ensuring individual citizens basic human rights, such as survival and life, regardless of their religious allegiances. I do not concur, therefore, with those who argue that we must reject the secular state. Among others, Ashis Nandy and Partha Chatterjee make persuasive cases, in different ways, for refuting the Indian secular state on the basis that it is not adequate for effecting religious tolerance or for preventing the marginalization of minorities, but they overlook what it is that the secular state *can* uphold.[50] The liberal secular state is essential for preventing religious violence and ensuring that groups can *live together in reasonable concord.* It can ensure a minimal level of civility and forbearance in civil society. The perceived failure of the Indian secular state (or other nominally secular states) to "protect" religious minorities in times of violence and conflict, then, does not so much have to do with the *principle* of state secularism in India but with the failure of successive regimes to sustain and uphold this principle.

The notion of neutrality itself must be reformulated in terms of its basic lexical meaning as impartiality rather than as state indifference to religion, while recognizing that an *ultimate* impartiality of the state or public sphere is not possible given the constraints of the nation-form (as I discuss in the next section). Responding to the crisis in Algeria, Derrida calls for a

> radical neutrality and a faultless tolerance which would not only set the sense of belonging to religions, cults, and thus also cultures and languages, away from the reach of any terror—whether stemming from the state or not—but also *protects the practices of*

faith and, in this instance the freedom of discussion and interpretation *within* each religion. (my emphasis)[51]

In the spirit of Derrida's injunction, I propose that the Hindi word *dharamnirpekshata*, which is often used to translate secularism, must be reformulated as the closely related yet different term *dharamnispakshata*. Often taken to mean an "objective" or impartial stance, *nirpeksha* is more accurately translated as absolute, indifferent, *without* expectation or consideration. Hence, *dharamnirpekshata* can be rendered as indifference to religion, or having no concern with religion—a fairly accurate translation of western secularism. (Translating *dharma* as religion, of course, is very problematic and relates to the difficulties of translating the Latin noun *religio* into other languages, which have very different experiences of the sacred.)[52] The term *nispakshata* is perhaps a more faithful translation of the notion of impartiality, understood as the state of not being biased, being neutral to both sides (where *paksh* is "side").[53] While the normative liberal narrative of secularism demands that such impartiality be achieved by aloofness from all religion (we are back to indifference), the Indian variant of secularism has tended to proceed through practices of intervention, proximity, and/or recognition. Rajeev Bhargava, for example, claims that the neutrality clause intrinsic to the liberal secular state in the west manifests itself in Indian state secularism, not as complete exclusion or strict noninterference between religion and the state but as a form of "principled distance."[54] However, the questions remain: How "principled" has been the "principled distance" stance the Indian state has sought to maintain? Have these practices of intervention and recognition meant different things for majority and minority religious communities?

To respond to these questions, we must grapple with the implications of the third constitutive aspect of the liberal secular state—equality.

Equality of Citizenship

The Indian Constitution provides for a number of individual rights that can be said to constitute its secularism. Articles 14, 15, and 16 of the Constitution provide for equality of all citizens before the law. Article 15 (1) in particular outlines that the state shall not discriminate against any citizen on grounds of religion, race, caste, sex, or place of birth. Article 16 (2) states that no citizen will be ineligible for, or discriminated against, with respect to any employment or office under the state on the basis of religion, caste, sex, descent, or place of birth. Similarly, article 29 (2) provides that no citizen will be denied admission into an educational institution maintained by the state or supported by state funds on grounds of religion, caste, race, or language. Clearly, the Constitution guarantees equality of citizenship under the law. The principle of secularism, specifically, is meant to ensure that *individuals* are not discriminated against because of their belonging to particular religious groups. However, uniform rights in themselves are not adequate for addressing structural inequalities in society along the lines of religion, caste, race, sexuality, language, or the like. While secular citizenship offers enfranchisement to individuals from minority religious groups, it can often serve as a mask for assimilating these groups to the hegemonic national culture. To understand the persistent marginalization of religious minorities in a liberal secular state and consequently to make the case for a deeper notion of equality than that allowed by individual rights, I make a brief detour by way of nationalism to demonstrate the limits of the third principle of the secular state and the necessity for supplementing it with other models of democratic citizenship.

Nationalism, Religion/Culture, and Minorities

Nationalism and nation-states have been the focus of sustained academic analysis for quite some time, especially within postcolonial studies. As the primary idiom of anticolonial liberation movements, nationalism emerged as a powerful concept with immense revolutionary potential for mobilizing the colonized populace. Yet the increasing emergence of ethnoreligious political movements that are either struggling for greater autonomy within an existing state or are seeking to secede to establish independent states has led to much stocktaking on the viability and success of the modern nation-state. The gap between the idealized model of the "nation-state" as comprising "a people" in a bounded territory and the reality of diverse and stratified groups inhabiting its confines with differential access to the state forces us to consider the nation-state as a totalitarian form of political community that is defined by inequalities.

In order to understand the built-in inequalities that are intrinsic to the concept of the nation-state, we must address the structural exclusions of the "nation-form."[55] In an important argument, Étienne Balibar suggests that the nation-form and nationalist ideology are articulated with a *structural violence,* which is at once institutional and spontaneous, visible and invisible:

> Nationalism is the organic ideology that corresponds to the national institution, and this institution rests upon the formulation of a *rule of exclusion, of visible or invisible 'borders,'* materialized in laws and practices. Exclusion—or at least unequal ('preferential') access to particular goods and rights depending on whether one is a national or a foreigner, or belongs to the community or not—is thus the very essence of the nation-form. (23)

At the most obvious level, these are external exclusions that serve to differentiate foreigners from nationals or citizens, but of course, these exclusions also function internally along the lines of race, gender, sexuality, religion, language, or caste, among other axes of inequality.

Following Benedict Anderson's famous formulation, modern nations have come to be viewed as "imagined communities."[56] They are powerful cultural and historical constructs that are constantly straining to represent themselves as a *horizontal community* bound to a unique territory—a unified cultural entity based on commonalities such as those of language, religion, custom, or geography—despite the actually existing diversities and inequalities within most national states. Thus, nationalist discourse seeks to constitute itself as a transcendent identity that stands above the "narrow" affiliations of culture, religion, race, or caste. This is especially true of liberal societies. In fact, as Wendy Brown points out, in liberal societies, "ardent attachments of any sort—to a God, a belief system, a people or a 'culture'—must remain private and depoliticized if they are not to endanger civilization and the autonomous individual who signifies a civilized state."[57] Culture and religion in liberal societies are construed as optional and to be privately enjoyed, more in the nature of lifestyle choices than something that is constitutive of the subject. On the other hand, organicist societies are viewed as saturated and ruled by cultural bonds; they represent the "other" of liberalism. Brown writes,

"In liberalism, the individual *has* culture or religious belief; *culture or religious belief does not have him or her*" (31). Collective identities or attachments of any sort—other than nationalism—are viewed as dangerous and regressive and can be tolerated only if they are contained within the domestic or private sphere. In this way, liberalism can project itself as at once above culture and as culturally neutral in the form of the secular state and the law. Nationalism becomes the only legitimate form of collective identity in liberal modernity.

But, in fact, nationalism works by selectively rendering certain cultural practices and institutions as national myths. Nationalisms habitually draw upon *particular* cultural identities and long-standing associations with territory to base their claims for distinct statehood and sovereignty. Thus, certain ethnic groups (more often than not the majority group) come to constitute the repository of the nation, while minority customs, traditions, and narratives are marginalized, delegitimized, and rendered as strange and foreign. Balibar reminds us that the sociopolitical concept of "minority" used to designate ethnic or religious groups living among majoritarian populations is never free of the juridical understanding of "minors" as those individuals and groups who are subjected to the more or less protective authority of the genuine citizens.[58] States play a constitutive role in producing such skewed majoritarian accounts of history and cultural identity, often supplemented in their work by institutions such as education, the family, media, and the law despite formal assertions of universal citizenship for individuals.[59]

In theorizing the deep links between (particular) cultural formations and nationalism, it is important to consider religion. Contemporary western critiques of secularism have tended largely to engage with religion as a matter of private individual faith and belief rather than as a possible basis for identitarian cultural claims in multireligious contexts. In these formulations, religion is construed as somehow distinct from "culture," which is considered to be the realm of language, food, dress, custom, and the like. Surprisingly, this notion of religion as separate from culture is also reflected in much contemporary multiculturalist discourse. Thus, current claims about the rights of immigrant groups (which are also often minority *religious* communities) in advanced liberal plural immigrant societies like Canada, the United States and Britain can be articulated only when framed under the umbrella of culture. Culture as a secular site is much more palatable as a form of ethnicity than identitarian assertions made on the basis of religious affiliations—as evinced, for instance, in the Hijab and *The Satanic Verses* controversies. For example, prominent multiculturalist theorist Will Kymlicka's work reflects this tendency to consider religion (understood as a matter of private faith) as distinct from ethnocultural affirmations of identity.[60] Liberalist discourses like multiculturalism therefore need to be located within a discourse of modernity that effectively succeeds in subsuming difficult questions about religion.

If, on the one hand, western discourses of secularism and multiculturalism have a propensity to treat religion solely as a matter of subjective belief, on the other, anthropological and sociological conceptions of religion have been inclined to consider religion as an aspect of culture (as a part is to a whole), sometimes to the extent of equating religion with culture, particularly in nonwestern social formations. One of the most influential examples of this perspective is to be found in Clifford Geertz's essay, "Religion as a Cultural System." The term culture is viewed as interchangeable with "religious tradition" or with religion per se, where both are seen as intricate and meaningful *wholes* constituted by signs and symbols.[61] Though much recent work in cultural anthropology has moved beyond this traditional construction of cultures as distinct and separate wholes, this scholarship still tends to consider religion as a part of culture. Undoubtedly, in contrast to the restricted post-Reformation Christian paradigm of religion as privatized belief, this perspective enables us to consider religion as a potential basis for affirmations of collective identity. Religion can be viewed as a form of group identity that is relational and contingent in specific multireligious contexts rather than due to some essential pre-given relationship between religion and most nonwestern contexts (the commonplace of Orientalist discourses about India, for example). Thus, religion can be understood as a significant marker of identity in the Indian subcontinent given the presence of varied religious groups in a common territory, even while there may be overlaps of ritual, language, food, and dress among these groups.

In contrast to sociological and anthropological understandings of religion, I argue that religion cannot be viewed as just another aspect of culture and ethnicity.[62] If much contemporary western secularist discourse tends to elide specific questions of religious identity, there is also the reverse temptation to see religion as interchangeable with culture, and

hence with ethnicity. Gayatri Spivak offers a more nuanced way of thinking about the imbrication of religion and culture. She proposes that the
"signs that spell 'culture' for a mobilized collectivity are often indistinguishable from signs that can easily spell 'religion.' Religion in this sense
is the ritual markers of how we worship and how we inscribe ourselves
in sexual difference. These are performative gestures of being-human,
needing no referential 'evidence,' being between nature and super-nature,
a precarious place that needs such semiosis constantly."[63] Yet, she also
cautions us that *it is neither possible nor desirable to perform a precise
identification between religion and culture,* as Samuel Huntington does,
for example, in his clash of civilizations thesis. Thus, she sees religion as
something akin to "linguistic competence" and proposes that we must
learn to grapple with this "ground-level institutionality of religion," which
is called upon to negotiate in different psychopolitical situations (104). We
cannot afford to be dismissive of pervasive religiocultural "signs."

I argue that concepts of culture and ethnicity are at once *necessary
yet insufficient* to think religion today, much like faith and belief cannot be considered as the sole "proper" terrain of religion. "Religion," or
the diverse experiences of the sacred and the holy that we have come to
call religion, *exceeds* the discourse of ethnicity even as it is preoccupied
with questions of identity, solidarity, and community that have been the
traditional terrain of ethnicity. Undoubtedly, the arguments about religion
as identity that have emerged from multireligious contexts like the Indian
subcontinent are very important in providing a shift from the often limited focus on questions of individual subjectivity, faith, or belief that tend
to dominate western academic discussions on secularism. Nevertheless,
what we name "religion" today is at once a discourse of community and
affiliation (and hence a possible source of identity in a relational context)
and a powerful subjective experience of faith, divinity, and openness to
the other.[64]

In considering the issue of nationalism and its exclusions, we must
therefore reflect on religion (or religion-based identities) as an important axis of inequality in its own right in liberal secular nation states.
Nationalism does not represent the transcendence of religious or cultural differences as it claims, but their rerouting along the lines of majority and minority religions. While majority religions are identified with
the nation and hence with secular culture as such, minority religions

are constituted as marginal and excessive to the nation. As Slavoj Žižek writes, "In short what really bothers us about the 'other' is the peculiar way it organizes its enjoyment: *precisely the surplus, the excess that pertains to it*—the smell of their food, their 'noisy' songs and dances, their strange manners, their attitude to work."[65] One could also add the other's "strange" beliefs and practices of worship to this list. The pervasive content of majority religions is thus rendered transparent and invisible, whereas minoritarian religious beliefs and practices are constructed as threatening and hyper-visible. In the Indian landscape, the Muslim becomes the site or the repository of this "excess"—and hence is constituted as the stranger within the nation. Consequently, Aamir Mufti proposes that a "post-Enlightenment genealogy of Nehruvian secularism" should entail a fundamental reconsideration of what "Indian Muslim" has meant for the secular critical temperament in India.[66] Mufti suggests that "'German Jew' and 'Indian Muslim' are names not merely of social groups but of entire cultural and political problematics and trajectories; names, furthermore, of the respective torments of European and Indian modernity" (78).[67] Although it is true that all minority communities face the burden of nationalism in a manner subordinately different from that of the majority community, the Muslims of India occupy the special place of "national minority," especially since Partition and the construction of Pakistan as the default homeland of all Indian Muslims. Secular nationalism presents Muslims with a very specific and dichotomous choice: either to merge into the nationalist mainstream or to be construed as communalist and retrogressive.

While we want to be careful to differentiate between individual nationalisms that are accommodative and tolerant, on the one hand, or inflexible and rigid, on the other, so as not to conflate all "love of country" or feelings of belonging to a group with xenophobia and racism, we should understand that these are not completely incompatible discourses. Thus, although it may be important to highlight the differences between secular Indian nationalism and Hindu nationalism, we should also be able to acknowledge the continuities between these seemingly disparate discourses. Exclusion, then, is the very nature of the nation-form.

As a result, many ostensibly secular *states* are implicitly institutionalized along the lines of the dominant majority religion. The secular Indian state is no exception. Even though a greater part of state policies are framed in language that is neutral or even indifferent to religion, its practices have never been indifferent. State practices have often entailed the strengthening of an upper-caste Hindu idiom as secular nationalism while offering periodic symbolic gestures to minority religious groups. Historically, when secularism has involved intervention, it has focused predominantly on reforming Hindu religious customs and practices (as manifested, for example, in the Hindu reformist program undertaken during the framing of the Constitution and the enactment of the Hindu Code Bill), while minority communities were rendered outside the state's realm of concern. (Thus, reformed Hinduism in the Indian context comes to function in an analogous manner to Protestant Christianity in various western countries.) And when secularism has entailed the *recognition* of different groups, it has tended to intensify the most patriarchal aspects of each religious group (for example, in the ongoing system of different personal laws). It has certainly not involved equality or *political power sharing* among different religious groups. Although this was a possibility before independence at the Round Table discussions and even during the Constituent Assembly debates, Partition ensured that these alternative political possibilities were shelved.[68] Clearly, the third constitutive aspect of the liberal secular state—the principle of equality—must be supplemented by some other project(s) in order to ensure a more substantive notion of democracy. Only when broader practices and policies of justice and equity are implemented at the level of the state and citizenship will we be able to think about possibilities of cohabitation among disparate religious groups that are unequally located with reference to the state and national culture.

Pluralism and Minority Rights

If we acknowledge that the rule of exclusion is a structural premise of the nation-form and the liberal state often serves implicitly to uphold such exclusions, the urgent task that confronts us is to come up with alternative conceptions of political community that can address the institutional inequalities of a secular nation state. Many western political theorists have come to accept the necessity for the public recognition and accommodation of ethnocultural diversity in the form of minority rights or multiculturalist policies—what Will Kymlicka has termed the "liberal pluralist approach."[69] Indeed, this theoretical discourse is part of a broader development toward the codification of minority rights in international law. The U.N. declarations on the Rights of Persons Belonging to National or Ethnic, Religious and Linguistic Minorities (1992) and the Draft Declaration on the Rights of Indigenous Peoples (1993) are only two examples of the efforts to internationalize minority rights. To be sure, the very idea of juridical and social collective rights for particular groups goes against the grain of liberal democracy with its emphasis on individual rights. Balibar's notion of a "conflictual democracy," which combines different heterogeneous constitutional principles, is useful here. In this conception, legal or formal democracy, which recognizes individuals as the true bearers of rights, must be combined with the development of "social or substantial democracy," which seeks to address inequalities and conflictual interests. This second conception of democracy attempts to make sure that "individual freedom is not pure and simply equivalent with competition, and competition with the elimination of the weakest in the city" (*We the People*, 224). Balibar also makes the case for what he calls "expansive democracy," which calls for the constant reinvention of politics in response to the "integration of new elements." In contrast to Habermas, who emphasizes the need to *conserve* the democratic achievements of the European nation-state, Balibar suggests that the history of constitutionalism has not been exhausted; therefore, we must constantly strive to transform and *reinvent* our very ideas of citizenship and democracy (190–93).

Some of the most creative and energetic debates on the reinvention of democratic politics in recent times have emerged in response to the rise of the Hindu Right in India. The threat of Hindutva, with its imperative for a homogeneous Hindu nation, has led to a substantial reconsideration and qualification of the project of liberal secularism in India. In particular, it has highlighted the limits of procedural neutrality and equal rights for addressing the marginalization of minority religious groups that are under threat of erasure. The Indian Constitution already has in place certain minimal cultural rights for religious and linguistic minorities that go beyond a commitment to individual rights. Article 29 gives linguistic and cultural minorities the right to conserve their language and culture, while Article 30 allows linguistic and religious minorities to run their own educational institutions, which are entitled to state aid like other educational establishments. Even though these are minimal rights, the provisions for minority rights do make the Indian Constitution an unusually prescient document, anticipating, as it did, many of the current debates about pluralism and the place of minorities in the nation. Significantly, minority rights in India are often defended under the umbrella of secularism and the "tolerance of minorities."

However, in a peculiar turn of events, the Hindu Right has successfully appropriated constitutional discourses of secularism and formal equality to discredit oppositional parties as "pseudo-secularists." For example, the 1990 Bharatiya Janata Party (BJP) Manifesto stated: "[T]he BJP believes in positive secularism which, according to our constitution makers, meant *sarva dharma sambhava* and which does not connote an irreligious state."[70] Gandhi's notion of *sarva dharma sambhava* is here ingeniously deployed to argue against the exclusion of *Hindu* religious idioms and symbols from electoral politics and state policies. At the same time, the principle of religious neutrality is also endorsed to argue against any kind of group provisions for religious minorities. Former Prime Minister Vajpayee, in his 1996 inaugural address to the nation, spoke of the BJP's "secular" vision and maintained that India would never be a theocratic state under the BJP.[71] L. K. Advani declaimed as early as 1990:

> The idea of a theocratic state is an anathema to the Indian mind. The BJP believes that the State in India has always been a civil institution which respects all religions equally and makes no discrimination between one citizen and the other on the grounds of language, caste or religion. It is the duty of the State to guarantee justice and security to all minorities—linguistic, religious or ethnic. The BJP considers that *it is also imperative for national integration that minorities do not develop a minority complex* (my emphasis).[72]

Within the view of the Sangh Parivar, the formal equality of all communities requires that no community should be singled out for special or supposedly preferential treatment; the argument is that this would be a violation of the principle of secularism. Any laws or policies that provide differential treatment of minorities are labeled as "pseudo-secularism" or the "appeasement of minorities." Thus, the BJP opposes the existing system of separate personal laws for the different religious communities; the goal of a Uniform Civil Code, until recently, was at the forefront of the Hindu nationalist electoral mandate. As a result, many secularists and liberal feminists found themselves in a peculiar quandary as they were placed, unwillingly, in alliance with the proponents of Hindu majoritarianism.[73]

Clearly, the question of the conflicting relationship between liberal secularism and special rights for religious minorities needs to be worked out, especially when these rights are defended under the rubric of secularism, as is often the case. In an important argument, Neera Chandhoke suggests that secularism, as a political creed, is helpless when it comes to the task of providing supportive social and political environments for vulnerable groups whose ways of life are under threat of erasure in the face of majoritarianism. While she makes a strong case for minority *cultural* rights that can ensure that minority groups will not decay or that their "identity" is not overcome by majoritarianism, she also believes that the concept of secularism does not in itself carry this precise connotation. As a doctrine underpinning the liberal state, secularism is based on the principle of *formal* equality, and it is indifferent to the presence of existing institutionalized inequalities in society; hence, secularism *"simply does not possess the resources"* to deal with the question of collective rights for minorities.[74] Chandhoke suggests that it is time to shift ground by making the case for collective rights under the rubric of secularism's antecedent moral principle—equality—and only then will we be able to enlarge the concept of secularism to accommodate minority rights.[75] We need to relocate the secular agenda within the broader context of democracy to pave the way for a more substantive notion of equality. Among the measures she recommends in her expanded version of state-sponsored cultural rights are the publication and translation of books in minority languages, the creation of special cultural sections to publicize minority cultures, agencies to promote art of minority groups, and space for minority cultures on radio and television.[76] Rather than reject secularism per se, we must move "beyond secularism."

In later work, however, Chandhoke decides to *restate* the case for secularism rather than move beyond secularism for affirming minority rights. Not only is secularism invaluable for regulating intergroup conflict in any multireligious society, but it is also expansive enough to accommodate collective rights for minority religious groups, particularly given the way the concept has taken shape in India—*sarva dharma sambhava*—which rules that "all religious groups are equal; therefore, by assumption, they should be equally treated."[77] In a small but not inconsequential shift from her previous argument, she concludes that minority rights are *not* a violation of secularism when defined as the equality of all religious groups (67).[78] It is not coincidental that this new essay is written in response to the events in Gujarat, since there is an increasing sense of urgency among (secularist) scholars and activists that we need to "name the secular."[79] I continue to assert, however, that any kind of political arrangements to redress institutionalized inequalities in society along the lines of religion must not be defended under the umbrella of secularism. The governing principle of liberal secularism is that the *individual* citizen will not be discriminated against on the basis of his/her membership in a particular group. While the case for minority rights can certainly be made by referring to the antecedent principle of democratic equality, I believe that the concept of secularism is not expansive enough to make room for group rights without losing whatever potential it may have for protecting basic individual rights—such as those of life and survival—irrespective of religious affiliation. We ask too much of the concept when we want it to take on the task of anything more than a formal equality in society.[80] I believe that secularism has to be limited and minimized if it is to be effective at all in protecting individuals from the reach of any terror based on their belonging to a particular religious group.

Concerns about the issue of inequalities and exclusions within the framework of a liberal secular state might be addressed by moving away from the liberal idioms of "protection," "tolerance," and even "recognition" of minorities to more substantial questions about equality, democratic participation, and power sharing. While Indian secular discourse has tended largely to focus on protecting minority cultural rights and the related issue of personal law, I propose we think instead in terms of reinventing the very institutions of liberal secular citizenship. Among others, Gyan Prakash and Gyanendra Pandey have suggested moving beyond the majority–minority framework to think in terms of a decentered pluralism in which everyone may live as a "minority among minorities" rather than as a permanent majority ruling over marginalized minorities.[81] Prakash asks if the language of "toleration" is adequate to meet the challenge of Hindutva when it reproduces Muslims as "minor subjects of the nation" (178). His essay is closely allied with Aamir Mufti's efforts to think and act from the marginalized location of minority, where minority itself becomes the space for cracking the majoritarian, representative, nationalist self and thus a position from which to articulate claims of an ethical, political, and cultural nature.[82] In a similar vein, Gyanendra Pandey interrogates the sanctity of nationalism and the nation-state and the hijacking of the state by nationalism. If the democratic state is complicit in perpetuating "colonial conditions within national borders" such that the Indian state or important parts of it have begun to act like "a politicized religious community themselves," then the most urgent task confronting any politics of "difference" in our present conjuncture may be an *unyoking of the pair, state and nation,* to prevent the majority community from becoming coterminous with the nation, as such.[83]

However admirable these arguments for a society of multiple minorities, it is never entirely clear how such delinking of (majoritarian) nationalism from the state is to be achieved in political terms. Transnational citizenship as exemplified by European unification provides one possible site for such an unyoking to take place: it has initiated the process of having "progressively divorced the two concepts of citizenship and nationhood that the classical state practically identified," but this new version of citizenship also risks a new "European apartheid" (the condition of non-European populations in the current space of the European Union).[84] Nevertheless, seizing upon the possibilities opened up by the process of European unification, Étienne Balibar attempts to reinvent the democratic state through a transformation in our notions of citizenship by calling for a "citizenship of residency" in competition with a "citizenship of belonging" (193). Turning to the Dutch political theorist Herman van Gunsteren's notion of "communities of fate" where heterogeneous people have been thrown together by history and economic circumstances in situations in which their interests cannot completely diverge without risking mutual destruction, he argues that the recognition of citizens' rights be instituted "beyond exclusive membership to one community." If communities are "communities of fate," the place where people are recognized as citizens must be where they live and work and bear children; Balibar further proposes that citizenship must be located at the borders "where so many of our contemporaries actually live" (132).

Balibar's work suggests that for a truly meaningful unyoking of the state from nationalism, we may have to think beyond the concept of national sovereignty and redefine the institutions of citizenship and democracy. Clearly, however, national sovereignty in the Indian subcontinent, and indeed in Europe, is not so easily dismissed.[85] In the face of this recognition, the task of constitutional discourse within nation states must, of necessity, be to think in terms of redressing the institutionalized exclusions of the nation-form. This, then, is the aporia of constitutionalism in the age of nation-states: to try to rectify the very exclusions put in place by the form of the nation and the liberal democratic state. What we can hope to achieve is the instituting of a more meaningful notion of equality that does not limit itself to questions of cultural "identity" and of protecting "differences."

I argue that much contemporary secularist discourse in India has allowed its agenda to be overdetermined by the Hindu Right. Since the very notion of Hindutva is premised on the idea of coerced cultural assimilation, the emphasis in the secularist debates has been on preserving distinct religiocultural identities, sometimes to the extent of rendering them external to democratic procedures.[86] The question of difference must be addressed very carefully so that we do not assume naturalized identities and reify religiocultural differences, as is the trend in much multiculturalist and secularist discourse of difference. If we recognize that cultural differences are contingent and historically constructed, with the modern state itself playing an important role in producing these identities at different moments, then protection is an inadequate response to the challenge of Hindu majoritarianism. It also risks fixing the most patriarchal aspects of each religious group, since claims for differences often deploy and reify norms of gender and sexuality. The important issue, then, is not how democratic societies can recognize already existing cultural group difference but rather by what means they should process the *political* claims that arise to challenge the exclusions produced, in part, by the modern state itself.[87] If religion and culture, like race, class, gender, and sexuality, are typically deployed to establish lines of inclusion and exclusion in a nation-state, then identitarian cultural claims must be brought into the democratic political process. In short, both privatization and protection are ineffective answers to the threat of Hindutva.

Politicized cultural identities in global movements for indigenous and minority rights have moved far beyond demands for the protection of language, tradition, and custom to claims for democratization, redistribution, and political participation. Writing of global movements for indigenous and minority rights, Courtney Jung reminds us that while the search for "recognition and respect" (for example, Charles Taylor's formulation of a "politics of difference") may be implicated in this kind of politics, it is by no means the most important aspect of the political stakes involved here.[88] Understanding religiocultural "differences" not as essentialized preexisting identities, but as forms of *exclusions* engendered by nationalism and the modern state will enable us to move past the multiculturalist paradigm of a "politics of difference"—to think instead in terms of power sharing and equality within the form of the nation-state.[89] This change would call for a rethinking of priorities and a shift in the secular agenda in India, one that does not serve only as a counter to Hindu nationalism's politics of assimilation.

Accordingly, I suggest that we need to set up avenues for addressing the exclusion of Indian Muslims through the democratic process. Providing compelling evidence about the widespread illiteracy, poverty, and discrimination in employment among Muslims, Zoya Hasan asks if it is enough to "recognize" minority cultures in the public arena, or should diversity also be reflected in public employment and the political institutions of representation?[90] She suggests that since the *political process* plays a central role in the distribution of education, employment, and wealth in India, Muslims need to be able to play a more central role in political power and decision-making bodies through political representation as a group. Anticipating the opposition to special representation for Muslims, she finds some hope in the experience of the empowerment of Other Backward Castes (OBCs) who have been able to find increasing political representation since 1989 through the initiative of political parties, which have started giving them a larger number of tickets. Thus, political parties could play a crucial role in addressing the imbalance of Muslim representation through a similar initiative—for example, by fielding Muslim candidates in the seventy parliamentary constituencies that have substantial Muslim populations. In the realm of economic policies, she reminds us that Muslims have been completely excluded from post-independence India's vast array of positive discrimination programs. She advocates that the more deprived Muslim groups could be included in the existing lists of "Backward Classes" rather than instituting a separate quota for the community, given the inevitable backlash one can expect from many constituencies, especially the Hindu Right.

Similarly, Yamini Aiyar and Meeto Malik point out that civil society organizations have followed the lead of constitutional discourse in prioritizing cultural rights over the everyday material deprivation faced by large sections of Muslims in India.[91] By contrast, they cite the example of organizations like the All-India Backward Muslims Morcha, which have made a strong suit for redistributive and affirmative action policies to be extended to Dalit Muslims and have gone to the extent of offering to trade the Babri Masjid issue over reservations for Muslims. Aiyer and Malik envision a crucial role for civil society organizations in pushing the state to think past the matter of personal law or other "cultural rights." Although the issue of whether reservations are the best avenue for addressing disparities in society remains an extremely contentious one, the state certainly needs to move beyond the limits it has set on minority rights and to think in terms of political and socioeconomic rights. The recommendations of the recently released high-level Sachhar Committee Report (appointed by Prime Minister Manmohan Singh) on the social, economic, and educational status of Muslims in India is an important step in this direction. Above all, the Report has worked to dispel many Hindutva-fostered myths and stereotypes about Indian Muslims, including the common misconception that a vast majority of Muslim children study at *madrasas* (religious schools)—according to the report, only 4 percent of Muslim children go to *madrasas;* notions about the rising fertility rate of Muslims—which is in fact on the decline; and the commonly held belief that Muslims are willfully "backward." In fact, as Seema Mustapha points out, the findings of the committee suggest that Muslims "are more than willing to avail of government facilities and the secular infrastructure that are, however, not always available."[92] The committee's recommendations on education and employment are of particular importance. It divides Muslims into three classes: (1) *ashrafs* (who are seen as equivalent to upper-caste Hindus), (2) *ajlafs* (along the lines of Hindu OBCs), and (3) *arzals* (similar to Dalits). It proposes that *ajlaf* and *arzal* Muslims be accorded some of the same benefits that are available to OBCs and Dalit Hindus, particularly in the spheres of education and employment.

To be sure, these measures, and what scholars like Hasan, Aiyer, and Malik propose, still function within the realm of "minority rights"; however, these models of power sharing and political participation come as close as possible to the desire for a decentered pluralism so long as we are functioning within the form of the nation-state with its intrinsic institutionalized inequalities. Moreover, since the state is not likely to lose its importance in mediating and regulating the relationship between different religious and caste communities in the foreseeable future, I believe it is crucial to work with the state in promoting coexistence and equality rather than to reject it altogether. The idea is to situate Muslims within the network of political and social structures that they share with other groups rather than render them outside these structures. The emphasis is not limited to countering Hindutva's homogenizing agenda; it includes envisioning a broader and more substantial program of justice and equality. Only by reducing the effects of stratification and inequality—often reified as naturalized and fixed differences—can we hope to work toward the living well together of disparate religious groups in society. Politicized cultural identities can therefore be used to stake economic and political claims of immense significance.[93]

At the same time, however, any agenda based on religiocultural identity risks reifying those who occupy that identity and reinforcing antagonisms between competing groups, even when the claims are not restricted to the realms of "culture" or "tradition." Ironically, just as anthropologists have come to emphasize the constructedness and fluidity of cultures in what has come to be termed as the "cultural turn," political theorists and activists have been increasingly affirming cultural rights (often based on essentialized notions of cultural differences). In pointing to the possibilities for *democratic participation* of different religious and cultural groups rather than insisting on the preservation of assumed naturalized "differences," I have attempted to move away from an idealized and atemporal notion of collective identity.[94] Nonetheless, the aporia of a minority rights discourse remains—mobilizing notions of a distinct, often bounded, cultural identity in order to stake its claims, this discourse risks fixing identities, besides denying ambiguities within the group. Moreover, minority rights formulated within the nation-state undoubtedly reinforce its sovereignty. Consequently, even as we make the case for material and political claims based on the idea of a distinct Indian Muslim identity, we cannot afford to support this project uncritically. Rather, we must be constantly vigilant about the pitfalls of this project, especially since ethical practices seek to move past identity politics (without endorsing a rupture with all identitarian belonging) in an effort to heed the call of the other.

This chapter is concerned predominantly with transforming the state and structures of citizenship in light of Derrida's notion of living well together. My effort is to narrow the gap between the ethical and the historicopolitical by formulating practices of equality and deep democracy in the realm of the state. Although I question the possibility—and desirability—of a truly secular public sphere freed of all religious citations, I also underscore the importance of the secular state in multireligious societies. I argue that we need a procedurally neutral secular state to ensure that different religious groups can live together with a reasonable degree of civility and forbearance. However, my understanding of the secular state endorses Nehru's formulation of such a state as one that honors all faiths equally rather than one that excludes religion from politics as such. Concurrently, I also draw attention to the majoritarian underpinnings of most nominally secular nation-states. Informed by Balibar's notion of "conflictual democracy," I stress the importance of the state in bringing about a more meaningful notion of equality in society through the participation of minority religious groups in the democratic political process while also acknowledging the limits of a minority rights' discourse. The state and structures of citizenship therefore remain an important horizon for enabling reasonable coexistence as well as for bringing about equality among disparate religious groups in the nation.

But if state secularism can only work to *restrain* or contain religious violence, how do we begin to imagine the living together of peace and justice? If the task before us is not just how we can live together with some minimal degree of civility, but how can we live together well, then the question of peaceful coexistence must be taken outside the realm of the state where it is most often debated. We cannot afford to *limit* ourselves to statist solutions of the kind proposed in contemporary secularism debates. This book makes the case for a critical reframing of the questions that surround secular and anticommunal discourse in India by taking this discussion beyond the domain of the state and constitutionalism to think instead in terms of an ethics of coexistence. With this aim, I turn to literary and cinematic narratives for envisioning a living together of peace and accord that is not restricted to the enforced tolerance of the liberal secular state.

But unlike the efforts of scholars such as Rustom Bharucha to expand *secularism* as an "everyday critical life practice," I argue that secularism cannot take on the burden of ethical ways of relating to otherness even if it has become imbricated with the language of tolerance among Indian elites.[95] In contrast, Ashis Nandy has proposed that we must reappropriate the conceptual domain of religious and ethnic "tolerance" from the hegemonic language of a state-sponsored secularism. Although Nandy ignores the complex trajectories of the Indian variant of secularism and rejects Enlightenment secularism altogether, I concur with him that secularism as a term cannot take on the vision of living well together (though we differ substantially on what this vision would entail)—despite its specifically "Indian" connotations—given its Enlightenment genealogy and its fraught and slippery meanings in the Indian context. However, unlike Nandy, I do believe that it must be an important *aspect* of this project.[96] As Anuradha Needham and Rajeswari Sunder Rajan note, secularism cannot be the only mantra for envisioning a violence-free society.[97] The rest of this book focuses on envisioning more ethically resonant models of peaceful coexistence that would move beyond a politics of civility and beyond reasonable coexistence.

In different ways (and to different extents), the literary and cultural productions addressed in the following chapters enable us to imagine ways of living with the other in peace and accord. The imaginative visions of these fictions open up possibilities of justice, solidarity, and coexistence that are radically different from the politics of condescension or assimilation. Responding to different moments of crisis, predominantly the Partition of India in 1947, the 1984 anti-Sikh riots in the wake of Indira Gandhi's assassination by her Sikh bodyguard, and the destruction of the Babri Masjid in 1992, these fictions variously draw attention to the fundamentalist agenda of Hindu nationalism; the limitations of secular nationalist discourse; the terrifying consequences of communal violence; the importance of minoritarian claims on national culture; and the centrality of a feminist initiative to any agenda of coexistence. All of these literary and filmic examples share an innate opposition to communal and nationalist conflict in the subcontinent and the desire for a more open and truly humane world. In the identification of such imaginative sites, we may envision the possibility of a world free of terror and violence.

2

$\vee$

For God's Sake, Open the Universe
a Little More: Cosmopolitan Fictions

Cosmopolitanism has reemerged within current cultural theory as a philosophical project for a more habitable and just world. The old sign of cosmopolitanism has come to name an ethos of mutuality and openness to others in response to contemporary conditions of increasing proximity. In the work of scholars as wide-ranging as Martha Nussbaum, Bruce Robbins, Pheng Cheah, Paul Rabinow, Anthony Appiah, Homi Bhabha, and David Hollinger, cosmopolitanism has come to signify an ethical stance of thinking beyond one's group—most typically "the nation"—in order to envision justice on a global scale.[1] It also emerged as a critical concept in Derrida's late work, one that is closely related to his call for an ethics of hospitality, where hospitality is understood as the unconditional welcome offered to all others, including the "wholly other, the absolutely unforeseeable *[inanticipable]* stranger."[2] This chapter considers Salman Rushdie's *The Moor's Last Sigh* (1995) and Amitav Ghosh's *In an Antique Land* (1992) as "cosmopolitan" narratives in light of these recent theoretical and philosophical meditations on cosmopolitanism and hospitality. By examining the attempts of these literary works to envision a more inclusive and hospitable world, I argue that a revisionary notion of cosmopolitanism can be used to infuse the project of living together in the Indian subcontinent. While *The Moor's Last Sigh* seeks to open up the idea of the Indian nation for excluded and displaced minoritarian subjects in response to Hindu nationalism's attempts to constitute India as a Hindu nation, *In an Antique Land* proffers medieval transnational— or rather prenational—trading cultures as a model of a more open and welcoming world. In their visions of a more hospitable nation or region,

Rushdie and Ghosh enable us to imagine possibilities of multireligious and multicultural coexistence beyond those of statutory convention or the contractual obligations of secular citizenship.

Typically, cosmopolitanism as a worldview or a sensibility has stood for detachment from all bonds—the Stoic ideal of the "world citizen"—or the "gendered and classed privilege of mobile observation in a world of tight borders and limited visibility."[3] If, like secularism, on the one hand, it can connote indifference to all ties, on the other, it can also signify multiple belongings and allegiances—the notion of being "at home in the world." Its colloquial connotations comprise a whole range of semantic accretions, including global mobility, class privilege, diversity, cultural hybridity, inclusiveness, and an outward-looking attitude. Timothy Brennan's proposition of a new category of highly publicized, globally mobile writer, the "Third World cosmopolitan celebrity writer," seizes upon the sense of privilege that seems to underlie most definitions of the cosmopolitan.[4] Brennan argues that writers like Salman Rushdie, Bharati Mukherjee, Derek Walcott, Gabriel García Márquez, and Mario Vargas Llosa traverse within a *world* literature that does not recognize traditional national boundaries; thus, they become "spokespersons for a kind of perennial immigration, valorised by a rhetoric of wandering, and rife with allusions to the all-seeing eye of the nomadic sensibility" (2). Besides the accidents of an itinerant biography, a shared political sensibility—an interrogation of "radical decolonization theory" and nationalism as well as an affirmation of cultural hybridity—that also translates into common aesthetic strategies constitutes these celebrity writers as cosmopolitans (7). According to Brennan, metropolitan critics are eager to embrace these writers precisely because they reinforce dominant western tastes and attitudes, even as they simultaneously chastise and speak pedagogically to the west. Thus, "the non-exilic world-travelling writer—often an aesthete, and already attuned to the metaphysical state of transculturalism—is in many respects as old as the New World conquest."[5]

Post-1980s Indian writers in English are often taken to be especially representative of Brennan's category of the globally mobile and internationally consumed "third-world" cosmopolitan celebrity writer. These writers came to prominence at a specific postindependence historical moment, marked by the 1981 publication of Salman Rushdie's *Midnight's Children*.[6] However much critics may quarrel with the politics of its representation, *Midnight's Children* was tremendously influential for a generation of Indian English writers. The sheer exuberance of the novel's self-confidence, its linguistic psychedelics, and its considerable commercial and literary success helped to create a new receptivity and confidence in international book markets in the work of English writers from the subcontinent. As a result, the 1980s and 1990s witnessed an explosion of Indian English writing.[7] Many of these post-Rushdie writers emerged from a privileged social background of upper-class affluence, metropolitan—often western—university education, and membership in influential professions. The specific material and historical formation of these writers allowed them access to other spaces in which they could live and write. The use of English as a literary medium itself became constitutive of a certain kind of cosmopolitanism not only in terms of the material configuration of class, education, and profession but also in its capacity to simultaneously reach out to a pan-Indian, admittedly upper middle-class audience and a larger international reading public.

Clearly, Rushdie and Ghosh can be viewed as paradigmatic examples of the postcolonial celebrity author: having led fairly peripatetic lives, they now live in and work out of New York and have acquired the status of public intellectuals. This mobility—mixed with the transcontinental address of their work; the sheer geographical and historical sweep of their narratives; the complex temporalities of their fiction; their transnational world-subject narrators, authorized as they are in their mastery of events—becomes constitutive of their cosmopolitan status in the specific sense that Brennan carves out.

However, even as I employ Brennan's moniker of "third-world cosmopolitan writers" for Rushdie and Ghosh, I do not endorse the commonplace dismissal of the English-language cosmopolitan writer as simply someone who is elitist and alienated. Although my use of *cosmopolitanism* to describe the sensibility of these writers acknowledges the charges of class privilege and estrangement to some degree, I also seek to recapture some of the positive valences of the term, particularly as it bears upon their visions of a more interconnected and coexistent world. Accordingly, I do not view all contemporary Indian English writers as default cosmopolitans merely by virtue of their elite status or the international reach of their work. My project thus intersects with Bishnupriya Ghosh's effort to resist lumping together *all* post-*Midnight's Children* writers as cosmopolitan writers. Ghosh deploys the label *cosmopolitan* to designate writers like Rushdie, Amitav Ghosh, Upamanyu Chatterjee, Arundhati Roy, and Vikram Chandra who, she argues, offer "critical resources for living in our contemporary globality, refocusing attention on our mutuality in speaking of many and contingent translocal solidarities."[8] Unlike Ghosh, however, I am not reflecting upon cosmopolitanism as a response to contemporary conditions of increasing globality. Rather, my interest in the notion of cosmopolitanism has to do with its relevance for engaging the specific context of rising religio-nationalist violence in the Indian subcontinent.

I thus begin by providing a brief qualification of the term in light of its appropriation within current theoretical discourse before explaining my use of *cosmopolitanism* to describe the sensibility and ethical vision of these writers.

Cosmopolitanism

As a historical concept, cosmopolitanism can be traced back to the Stoics who used the notion of *kosmou politês* (world citizen) to define someone who "refused to be defined by his local origins and group memberships," and gives "first allegiance to no mere form of government, no temporal power, but to the moral community made up by the humanity of all human beings."[9] In an essay that argues against Richard Rorty's call to Americans for a renewed patriotism, Martha Nussbaum recommends a return to this old Stoic ideal as an antidote to American self-absorption and jingoism. She proposes that "we [Americans] should not confine our thinking *to our own sphere,* that in making choices in both political and economic matters we should most seriously consider the right of other human beings to life, liberty, and the pursuit of happiness" (13–14). Nussbaum envisions the cosmopolitan ideal as a self at the center of a series of concentric circles that move through family, neighbors, local groups, fellow city dwellers, fellow countrymen, and finally the largest circle, that of humanity as a whole. Our task as world citizens, she suggests, is to make "all human beings more like our fellow city dwellers," our neighbors and our families (9). While she concedes that one does not have to give up "local affiliations" to be a citizen of the world, ultimately, she upholds the lofty Stoic ideals of detachment and indifference to endorse a transcendent cosmopolitan self able to overcome all kinds of affective identifications in favor of *a commitment to humanity as a whole* (4).

Following Nussbaum's lead, a number of cultural theorists have proposed cosmopolitanism as an appropriate ideal for an increasingly globalized world and, indeed, as the defining sensibility of our present.[10] As Brennan points out, "[G]lobalization bears on cosmopolitanism as structure to idea. It is that purportedly new material reality to which the new ethos—cosmopolitanism—responds."[11] Homi Bhabha, for example, writes of the need to take note of a world of more "complex boundaries," which compels us to "stretch our social and historical imaginations beyond our ready visualizations"—to make a "global leap," as it were.[12] Cosmopolitanism in Bhabha has to do with how we see ourselves as part of a "shared history of the present" and is a crucial aspect of the project of developing a "social ethic of proximity between self/other and the otherness of the self"—in other words, of the living together that Derrida proposes (2). The aim of much new academic discourse on cosmopolitanism is to reach beyond the nation and to engender transnational solidarities in an effort to achieve justice on a global scale. However, much of this work attempts to qualify and temper Nussbaum's ideal of primary allegiance to the circle of humanity to offer instead a range of more plural and qualified cosmopolitans such as discrepant, situated, vernacular, rooted, minoritarian, and critical cosmopolitanisms. Theorists such as Anthony Appiah, Bruce Robbins, and Pheng Cheah affirm Nussbaum's notion of a cosmopolitanism that could serve as a check to U.S. hegemony and power, but they also believe that cosmopolitanism doesn't necessarily have to take the nation-state as its inevitable antagonist. Although they are critical of nationalism as a majoritarian and territorial ideology, the "new cosmopolitans" (to use David Hollinger's phrase) do not envision the end of nation-states, or a form of world government.[13] Robbins and Cheah, for example, offer cosmopolitanism as a program of transnational justice that calls for *"thinking and feeling beyond the nation,"* but one that also does not seek to constitute a postnational politics.[14] Similarly, David Hollinger, in his survey of the new cosmopolitanism, modifies Nussbaum's notion of commitment to humanity as a whole to affirm cosmopolitanism as a "support of basic welfare and human rights of *as wide a circle of humanity as can be reached,"* while acknowledging the difficulties entailed in achieving solidarity with those we view as very different from ourselves. In his view, the objective of cosmopolitan discourse is to "maximize species-consciousness, to fashion tools for understanding and acting upon problems of a global scale, to diminish suffering regardless of color and class and religion and sex and tribe" (283). In fact, in her more recent work, Nussbaum also attempts to moderate her version of "egalitarian cosmopolitanism" that upholds the notion of "equal concern for all" and which is viewed as irreconcilable with "special attachments to kin."[15] Although she continues to hold on to the ideal of "equal concern," she recognizes that it has to be built up by means of "the imagining that is characteristic of compassion"; equal concern for all is not something that exists a priori (388).

In these formulations, cosmopolitanism is simultaneously upheld as an ethical stance—the effort "to expand the circle of the we," to use Hollinger's phrase—and as a model of a diverse, accommodative, and more just world (239). As an ethos of transnational/translocal affiliation, cosmopolitanism is offered precisely as a means of creating a more open, welcoming, interconnected—and hence cosmopolitan—world. The new cosmopolitanism's conception of cultures and nations moves away from the notion of pure and discrete cultural and ethnic enclaves to the idea of shared and interlinked cultures, religions, communities, and allegiances. It endorses multiple and discrepant affiliations and belongings rather than a detachment from all bonds.

However, another somewhat different version of cosmopolitanism also exists. While scholars such as Nussbaum, Robbins, and Bhabha invoke a transnational cosmopolitanism as a means, in part, of providing a check to U.S. power and self-absorption, others such as Ross Posnock, Jeremy Waldron, and Hollinger use the concept to designate the national specificity of the United States as a heterogeneous and hybrid nation.[16] A cosmopolitan stance is invoked by these scholars as an alternative to racial and ethnic divisions *within* America; indeed, America is often invoked as an exemplar of a cosmopolitan nation in their work. For example, Hollinger believes that the United States, as a cosmopolitan nation, can remind the world that even a racially marked society can include individuals from "different communities of descent on terms of considerable intimacy within a civic solidarity." In this, it may "provide a modicum of hope for cosmopolitans" ("Not Universalists, Not Pluralists," 246, 245). This fairly widespread view of America as a cosmopolitan nation leads

Timothy Brennan to reject the impulses of what he calls "cosmo-theory," since he believes that theories of cosmopolitanism unwittingly buttress the notion of America as a yardstick for the rest of the world even when they are promoting ideals of transnational solidarity.[17]

As Bruce Robbins astutely notes, in these two discourses, we see the term cosmopolitanism being employed on two different "scales"—the one transnational and the other national—which therefore should not be judged by the same criteria or asked the same questions.[18] Robbins's insight about scale offers a useful way of reading Rushdie's *The Moor's Last Sigh* and Ghosh's *In an Antique Land* together through the lens of cosmopolitanism: in my reading, the first offers a national version, while the second upholds a more transnational account of cosmopolitanism in order to imagine a peaceful and coexistent world. However, I do not agree with Robbins that these two different versions of cosmopolitanism cannot be asked the same questions merely because of their differences of scale. I argue that the debate on cosmopolitanism, for too long, has been limited by the national/transnational binary and that the effort to theorize a new cosmopolitanism has to get past these modernist categories. What both discourses have in common is the notion of thinking beyond one's group—whether the nation or exclusive racial and ethnic identities within the nation—in order to be responsible to other human beings in the world. (Thinking beyond one's group may range from the facile injunction to achieve a break with all identitarian belonging to more complex affirmations of multiple, discrepant, and often conflicting allegiances.) Both would be in accord with Gayatri Spivak's belief that "identity politics is neither smart nor good," since ipseity or self-sameness has something of a relationship with despotism and claiming ownership.[19] Given this commonality, could there be a more productive way of bringing together the national and transnational versions of cosmopolitanism?

I suggest that the binaries that limit "cosmo-theory" would benefit from Derrida's thinking on these issues. Theorists of cosmopolitanism have not yet been attentive to his insights on living together and the interrelated concepts of hospitality and cosmopolitanism.[20] Derrida's injunctions about thinking beyond the "ensemble" and welcoming the "stranger" as crucial conditions for the living together of peace and harmony are especially useful for resolving the binary between the national and the transnational accounts of cosmopolitanism. Derrida maintains that the authority of the whole, the ensemble—whether a natural, biological, or genetic organism or a "social body" like the family, religious/ethnic group, or nation—will always be the first threat to all living together; hence, one cannot claim that parts of the same ensemble (community) live *well* together. Living together calls for the response of an "interrupting excess" with regard to the law, statutory convention, or organic symbiosis—that is, to the *totality* or cohesiveness of any ensemble that we may have inherited.[21] It cannot be limited to living with those who have been given to us by virtue of birth, blood, soil, or the juridico-political contract. Derrida reminds us:

> For the eloquent and meticulous militants of the rights of men and of social struggles in their countries should never forget that never, in the entire history of humanity, have so many men on earth been lacking bread and drinkable water, and that indifference or passivity on this subject is the beginning of a crime against humanity, a transgression of "you shall not kill;" and whoever says "you shall not kill," if he restricts himself to my neighbor, my brother, my fellow man, man, also avows, what a paradox, the accepted murder of all living others in general, to wit, what one names stupidly [bêtement] and confusedly the animal. (39)

Like theorists of cosmopolitanism, he too seeks to envision justice on a global scale—indeed at the level of *the planet* in his extension of concern to "all living others" and not just to those designated as "human"—but he also acknowledges that one cannot give up a preference for all the forms of the proximate.[22] Thus, he avows the "aporia" of renouncing a penchant for "my own"—the ensemble of those who have been given to me, before any choice, in all the senses of "community," including family, coreligionists, countrymen, neighbors, and even other human beings—but does not seek to justify it before a "universal justice." Avowing this hierarchy for "one's own," a hierarchy that has led to many wars, crimes, and injustices, is not adequate, but he believes it must be the first step toward the living together of peace and justice.

However, it is not merely enough to interrupt the totality of the whole, according to Derrida; one must open up one's "home"—one's dwelling, one's language, one's nation, one's state, and one's self—to the other. He thus imbues the traditional concept of hospitality with a new significance.

He points out that hospitality in the "ordinary sense" is inextricably interwoven with hostility, since it requires that the host—he who offers hospitality—must be a master in his home.[23] The host, typically male, authorizes who crosses the threshold by selecting, choosing, and filtering who may or may not pass through the door. He is also the master of the household, and hence the master of the woman "who becomes the stake and essence of hospitality" (13). Hospitality thus makes claim to property ownership and authority. The law of identity or the *"being-oneself in one's own home"* becomes the "condition of the gift [another of his key late notions] and of hospitality" (4). This "despotic sovereignty" and the "virile mastery" of the host/master of the house is intrinsically related to ipseity—it is "nothing other than ipseity itself, the same of the selfsame" (15). Thus, Derrida locates a violent contradiction inherent to the concept of hospitality—the host must be assured of his sovereignty over the space that he opens up to the other—which limits hospitality at its origin. In fact, the very act of saying "I welcome you" or "I invite you" becomes a way of insinuating that one is at home here and hence of appropriating a place for oneself. This seemingly "aporetic paralysis" at the very threshold of hospitality must be overcome—thus, hospitality can only take place beyond our precomprehension of hospitality.

The absolute hospitality that Derrida calls for *"presupposes a break with hospitality in the ordinary sense, with conditional hospitality, with the right to or pact of hospitality."*[24] It requires that "I open up my home and that I give not only to the foreigner (provided with a family name, with the social status of being a foreigner, etc.) but to the absolute, unknown, anonymous other, and that I give place to them, that I let them come, that I let them arrive, and take place in the place I offer them, without asking of them either reciprocity (entering into a pact) or even their names" (25). Drawing on the work of Emmanuel Levinas and Louis Massignon, Derrida affirms a vision of hospitality in which the host becomes the hostage of the other prior to becoming the host; it calls for a relinquishment of all claims to mastery and ownership.[25] Moreover, hospitality must not be restricted to the "foreigner," the *xenos*—who is the citizen of a country and endowed with a legal subjectivity—but must be offered to all others, including those we might think of as "barbarians," to whosoever turns up before any determination or any identification, "a human, animal, or divine creature" (*Of Hospitality*, 77). Derrida diffuses and extends the very meaning of "foreigner" beyond its traditional inscription in the Greco-Roman and European discourse of hospitality to include the "wholly other," one who is not only beyond the conditional circles of language, family, or citizenship but also beyond the "its other" of dialectics ("Hostipitality," *Angelaki,* 8, and "Hostipitality," *Acts of Religion,* 363–64). The boundless hospitality he calls for transgresses all the laws of hospitality as we have known them, since hospitality in this revised sense is not about debts, calculations, duty, or contractual obligations. In fact, the experience of hospitality is coextensive with ethics itself: "Insofar as it has to do with the *ethos,* that is, the residence, one's home, the familiar place of dwelling, inasmuch as it is a manner of being there, *the manner in which we relate to ourselves and others,* to others as our own or as foreigners, *ethics is hospitality.*"[26] Hospitality is thus crucial to Derrida's understanding of ethics—our responsibility toward the other—and is inseparable from his thinking of justice. However, it is important to ask what this idea of limitless hospitality entails in terms of the political or the historical. How can we narrow the gap between the ethical and the political, between justice and the law?

In order to inaugurate a new politics of hospitality, Derrida turns to the concept of cosmopolitanism. He invokes the tradition of cosmopolitanism—from Greek Stoicism and Pauline Christianity to Kant. He recalls Kant's famous formulation in "Perpetual Peace," which makes an explicit connection between hospitality and cosmopolitanism: "[T]he law of cosmopolitanism must be restricted to the conditions of universal hospitality," where "hospitality signifies the claim of a stranger entering foreign territory to be treated by its owner without hostility . . . so long as he conducts himself peaceably." This right of hospitality "belongs to all mankind in virtue of our common right of possession on the surface of the earth on which, as it is a globe, we cannot be infinitely scattered, and must in the end *reconcile ourselves to existence side by side*" (Immanuel Kant, cited in Derrida, 21–22). In Kant's generous and expansive notion of cosmopolitanism, we find the conditions for hospitality, which is also linked to his dream of the coexistence of all peoples, of "perpetual peace." However, Kantian cosmopolitanism continues to be limiting for Derrida because it is conditional upon citizenship and state sovereignty. It restricts hospitality to the right of visitation, thus excluding a right of residence. Derrida seeks to invent a "new cosmopolitics" that would go beyond the juridicality of Kantian cosmopolitanism by reviving the tradition of the "city of refuge." Cities of refuge would be open and welcoming places where everyone may live as a stranger/foreigner, and where no one—individual or group—has prior claim. These autonomous cities would be elevated above and beyond the nation-state when dealing with questions of hospitality and refuge. Their aim would be to redefine the right to asylum beyond the traditional western solution of repatriation or naturalization. The notion of the hospitable—cosmopolitan—city becomes Derrida's attempt to give *political* shape to his treatise on hospitality. It does not represent so much the effort to make manifest an impossible hospitality as the initiative to transform existing laws of hospitality in light of the Law of unconditional hospitality.[27] Absolute or pure hospitality, while admittedly impossible, provides the inspirational horizon for a new cosmopolitanism in Derrida's thought.

Derrida's thinking on cosmopolitanism and hospitality allows us to qualify and modulate the insights of contemporary Anglo-American discourse on cosmopolitanism. In contrast to recent discussions on cosmopolitanism, Derrida chooses to advocate the related concept of hospitality. Rather than restricting ourselves to thinking, feeling, and acting beyond the (American) *nation,* he invites us to interrupt the totality and the cohesiveness of *any* ensemble that has been given to us by blood, birth, belonging, or by the juridico-political contract. What is more, he enjoins us to offer an unconditional welcome to all others to enter our ensemble, our home, especially those who have been designated as our strangers and enemies. Only then can we begin to think in terms of inaugurating the living together of justice or peace. Hospitality and cosmopolitanism thus correspond to the split between the ethical and the political in Derrida's thought. Although Derrida believes that any *historical* or *political* manifestation of ethical concepts like hospitality necessarily constrains their unconditional possibilities, he also believes that if hospitality is to be effective, such laws/political manifestations are necessary.

This imbrication of cosmopolitanism and hospitality is very relevant to our understanding of the imaginative visions of *The Moor's Last Sigh* and *In an Antique Land.* I read these works as Rushdie's and Ghosh's efforts to envision a version of Derrida's "city of refuge"—albeit at a different "scale." Both writers imagine a more open and hospitable world that is welcoming to all—hence my use of Rushdie's passionate plea as the title of this chapter: "For God's sake, open the universe a little more."[28] But where Rushdie seeks to revitalize the idea of a cosmopolitan Indian *nation,* Ghosh turns to premodern spaces of hospitality to contest the rigid boundaries of modernity. By means of their evocative accounts of a nation or a region—where all are welcome, but where no one can claim ownership—these literary works offer compelling representations of the Derridean vision of living well together.

Minority Cosmopolitanism in *The Moor's Last Sigh*

Salman Rushdie is the exemplary cosmopolite of postindependence South Asian literature in English. Born in India, having lived in London (with some interim years spent in Pakistan when his family moved to Karachi from Bombay), and now in New York, he was propelled into unprecedented fame by Khomeini's fatwa; Rushdie's biography thus amply testifies to his status as a cosmopolitan celebrity author. His literary works have never respected conventional artistic or national boundaries, neither in the sheer breadth of their literary and historical allusions nor in their transnational address. In fact, Rushdie has gone out of his way to present himself as a migrant Indo-British (and now as the newest "New Yorker") writer who is at once an insider and an outsider in both societies and whose literary forebears include Tagore and Ram Mohan Roy as much as Swift, Conrad, Gogol, Cervantes, Kafka, and Melville. As he writes in his well-known essay, "Imaginary Homelands," "[W]e are inescapably international writers at a time when the novel has never been a more international form . . . cross-pollination is everywhere."[29] The work I examine here, *The Moor's Last Sigh,* is very much in the cosmopolitan literary mode with its impressive historical and geographical sweep, moving from Moorish Spain to a contemporary India overtaken by the rhetoric of the Hindu Right. In one body, the narrative encompasses a recounting of the Sephardic Jews' exodus from fifteenth-century Spain and the politics of present-day, Shiv Sena–dominated Bombay. Rushdie's protagonist, Moraes Zogoiby (the Moor), comes to embody the accelerated pace of this swirling-bursting narrative, living as he does a high-speed life, with a body that ages twice as quickly as a normal man's.

My reading of *The Moor's Last Sigh* as a "cosmopolitan" novel, in Derrida's sense of the term, has to do with the text's effort to reimagine

India as an inclusive and hospitable nation in contrast to the Hindu nationalist vision of India—an essentially Hindu nation subject to a history
of foreign invasions from the time of the Mughals to the onslaught of
British colonialism. Like *Midnight's Children*, this novel is an allegory of
the nation: the four-generational saga of *The Moor's Last Sigh* takes up
again the national biography that was undertaken in *Midnight's Children*
and continues where the first novel drew to a close, the Emergency, with
its shadows of impending darkness. Most critical readings of the novel
tend to read it as a lament for the Nehruvian vision of a secular India
(much like the earlier work); I argue, however, that in this novel Rushdie
goes beyond the Nehruvian idea of the nation by affirming the idea of a
hospitable India *that is multiple and diverse at its very origins*. Traveling
through accelerated time, the protagonist-narrator of this novel seeks,
nostalgically, to evoke a tangible cosmopolitan India that came into existence because of the conjoining and cross-fertilizations of different races
and religions. It redefines the national community as inherently plural—
rather than the originary preserve of an upper-caste Hindu community—
by placing an emblematic minoritarian figure at the *center* of its "Indian"
narrative. Rushdie's cosmopolitanism thus resonates with Homi Bhabha's
notion of a "vernacular" or "minoritarian" cosmopolitanism that seeks
"to minoritise" or affiliate with the cause of exclusion. It identifies with
the perspective of minorities "not only out of principle but from a passion, a structure of feeling, of how the core or canonical national and
transnational myths demand to be 'peripheralised.'"[30]

The novel allies with the cause of minority, above all, by taking on the
blatantly majoritarian program of Hindu nationalism. The construction
of insiders and outsiders, natives and aliens, citizens and foreigners, has
been fundamental to the Hindu Right's program for consolidating India
as a Hindu nation. An early ideologue of the Hindu Right, V. D. Savarkar,
defines a Hindu as anyone "who regards this land of Bharatvarsha, from
the Indus to the seas as his Fatherland as well as his Holyland, that is
the cradle land of his religion."[31] The claim is that "Hindus"—a term that
elides the many differences of caste, region, and class among the majority
community—are the original inhabitants and hence the rightful owners
of India, the true guardians of its heritage and its culture. While Jains,
Buddhists, and Sikhs may also be considered "Indian," since they believe
in faiths that originated in India, Muslims and Christians do not truly

belong to the nation, as their sacred places lie outside the territorial borders of India. In this formulation, Hindu religious beliefs and practices become synonymous with national culture, while minority customs are rendered extraneous to the nation such that they become "strange" and "foreign." Muslims and Christians are welcome so long as they conform to the dominant Brahminical Hindu culture—in the more benign version of Hindu majoritarian politics. The Hindu Right's version of hospitality thus brings out the hostility that is intrinsic to the concept of hospitality, since it is *conditional* upon (upper-caste) Hindu identitarian claims—what Derrida terms "the being oneself in one's own home"—on the Indian nation. By contrast, *The Moor's Last Sigh* upholds a vision of a hospitable India where no one has prior claim and which is welcoming to all others, especially to those who have been constructed as strangers within the nation. Rushdie's novel reveals how the wholeness or totality of the nation as an ensemble can be achieved only by elevating certain religiocultural practices and institutions as representative of the nation as such, and it sets out to prise open the majoritarian underpinnings of national culture.

The Moor's Last Sigh's denunciation of Hindu nationalism is best articulated through the satiric portrayal of the character of Raman Fielding, also known as Mainduck ("the Frog"). In the figure of Fielding, Rushdie unsparingly caricatures Bombay's most prominent and notorious Hindu nationalist politician, Bal Thackeray. His party, the Shiv Sena, figures in Rushdie's text as "Mumbai's Axis," so named after Mumbadevi, the patron goddess of the city of Bombay. The novel elaborates, in frightening detail, the fascist rhetoric of a Hindu right wing politics that has now become all too familiar in India. Mainduck, we are told, is against unions and derides the Marxist analysis of society as class struggle. He affirms his belief in the eternal verity of caste and views all non-Marathi speakers—including those born in Bombay—as "immigrants" or aliens. Above all, Rushdie draws attention to the antiminoritarian—specifically anti-Muslim—agenda of the Shiv Sena. Mainduck and his party endorse the idea of returning to a golden age, "Ram Rajya," a time before the "Muslim hordes" "invaded" India's geographic sanctity. On one occasion, Mainduck declaims in typical Hindu nationalist–speak:

Let everyone see today what—what we do for minorities. . . . Is
it a Hindu who is given this honour? Is it one of our great Hindu

artists? No matter. In India every community must have its place, its leisure activity—art et cetera—all. Christians, Parsis, Jains, Sikhs, Buddhists, Jews, Mughals. We accept this. This too is part of our ideology of Ram Rajya, rule of Lord Ram. Only when other communities are usurping our Hindu places, when minority seeks to dictate to majority, then we can say that the small must also accept to bend and move before the big.[32]

In this conception of the "small" and the "big," Rushdie encapsulates the numerical logic of the majoritarian politics of the Hindu Right, which can only cede a subordinate place to minority religious groups in the nation—if at all. It is against this idea of the Indian nation as originally and primarily a *Hindu* nation that he posits his vision of a cosmopolitan India.

The cosmopolitan ideal is represented variously in the person of the eponymous protagonist who is constituted as an allegorical figure for India; a multicultural Bombay that is constituted as the repository of a hospitable India; and the invocation of Moorish Spain as an exemplarily peaceful and coexistent world through Aurora's paintings. I examine each of these figurative sites of cosmopolitanism in the novel to consider the ways in which they provide a more hospitable imagining of the Indian nation than that offered by Hindutva accounts or even by official Indian nationalism. As nationalism scholar Prasenjit Duara notes, "In present-times, the nation-state has not been able to exhaust the identifications of the individual, nor, for that matter, has it been able to confine the meaning of the nation to its [own] representations. . . . The state is never able to eliminate alternative constructions of the nation among both old and new communities."[33] Although the state may have hijacked nationalism, there often exist contending versions of the nation that contest and challenge the hegemonic, state-led narrative of the nation. Thus, the study of nationalism may find it more useful to speak of "different 'nation-views,'" as we do 'world-views,' which are not overridden by the nation, but actually define or constitute it" (10). *The Moor's Last Sigh* presents one such different "nation-view" by means of its imaginative effort to reinvent India as a hospitable and cosmopolitan nation that can be "home" to all the diverse religious and ethnic groups that comprise it.

The protagonist-narrator of the novel, Moor, stands at the center of this cosmopolitan account of the Indian nation. He is the illegitimate product of an interreligious union between a Catholic and a Jew. In what has become a familiar Rushdiean celebration of miscegenation, the narrator affirms proudly, "I, however, was raised neither as Catholic nor as Jew. I was both and nothing: a jewholic-anonymous, a cathjew nut, a stewpot, a mongrel cur. . . . Yessir a real Bombay mix." (104). He traces his lineage to the Portuguese explorer Vasco da Gama on his mother's side and a family of Sephardic Jews on his father's side, who sailed to Cochin in and around 1492, when the Catholic conquest of Moorish Spain forced Jews (and Muslims) to choose between expulsion and Christianity. Like Saleem Sinai's mixed-up ancestry in *Midnight's Children,* the Moor's hybrid genealogy is a figure for the cosmopolitan nation itself; in this later novel, however, the protagonist also represents the nation's diverse minorities in his person. Not only does he have a mixed-up "cathjew"— Catholic and Jewish—ancestry, he also claims illegitimate descent from Boabdil, last Sultan of Moorish Spain, on his father's side. While there are similar speculations about a "wrong-side-of-the-blanket" descent from Nehru himself (much like Saleem's various and diverse parental figures), the Moor's composite minoritarian lineage establishes him as a figure for all excluded minorities. By placing a hybrid Jewish-Catholic figure at the center of his "Indian" narrative, Rushdie is able to figure Indian national culture as a complex enunciation of multiple and diverse religious and cultural claims:

> CHRISTIANS, PORTUGUESE AND JEWS; . . . Spanish shenanigans, Moorish crowns . . . can this really be India? Bharatmata, Hindustan-hamara, is this the place . . . Is this not the most eccentric of slices to extract from all that life—a freak blond hair plucked from a jet-black (and horribly unravelling) plait? No, sahibzadas. Madams-O: no way. Majority, that mighty elephant and her sidekick, Major-Minority, will not crush my tale beneath her feet. Are not my personages Indian, everyone? (87).

By way of the Moor's story, Rushdie seeks to tell the stories of the myriad other communities that have also been constitutive of a cross-pollinated Indian culture, besides the majority Hindus and the "major-minority" Muslims. In many ways, the Jew in this novel functions as a symbolic figure for all minorities, especially given the conceptual apparatus that has attached itself to the figure of the "wandering Jew" as the paradigmatic marginalized figure of modernity—the original diasporic. If Rushdie's *cosmopolitan* worldview paradoxically takes the *nation* as its unlikely horizon in this novel, then this is a worldly and hospitable nation that seeks to admit the dispossessed, the persecuted, and the illegitimate.

In a recent essay on *The Moor's Last Sigh*, Dohra Ahmad makes the ingenious suggestion that the Jew in this novel is deployed as a figure for the Muslim, who has been the primary target of Hindu nationalism's project of constructing a homogeneous Hindu India.[34] She reminds us that even though Rushdie foreswore Islam as a literary subject after the fatwa, Islam lingers in the novel not only through the invocation of the royal ancestor—Boabdil—but also in a more metaphorical way: "Invisible Islam, then, is split into two components: migrant Islam, the minority religion of banished Boabdil, becomes a struggling Judaism, and fundamentalist Islam, majority religion and statist ideology, becomes a warped dishonest monotheistic Hinduism" (5). Ahmad's argument about Judaism functioning as a displaced figure for minority Islam in India is quite persuasive, especially given the way Rushdie chooses to recall his protagonist's Islamic inheritance in his very name—Moor—even though he foregrounds his Jewish-Catholic milieu. The absent-presence of Islam lingers most evidently in this novel through Rushdie's evocation of Moorish Spain—often celebrated as the golden period of Islamic history—as an exemplar of multireligious coexistence. In fact, it is no coincidence that Rushdie chooses to uphold medieval Muslim Spain as an ethical counter to the ills of contemporary Hindu nationalist–governed India in this, his first novel after the furor created by *The Satanic Verses*. It is as though he needs to establish that he is not against Islam per se, only against its fundamentalist strains (even though his recent nonfictional writing tends to equate Islam with fundamentalism, very much in the mode of liberal western opinion).[35] Likewise, the choice of Hindu nationalism as the primary antagonist in this novel appears as a conscious effort to assert that he is against fundamentalisms of all persuasions and not just the Islamic variety. To argue that Hindutva serves as a stand-in for fundamentalist Islam as Ahmad does, however, is to lose sight of Rushdie's very specific concerns about the threat posed by Hindu majoritarianism to the idea of the cosmopolitan Indian nation.

At the heart of Rushdie's cosmopolitan alternative to Hindu nationalism's vision of a homogeneous Hindu India is the city-space of Bombay, which is figured as the soul of the nation, much like Moor (the "Bombay mix") serves as an allegorical figure for the idea of India that Rushdie seeks to uphold. As Rushdie tells us in an interview: "There is only one place for every human being and always only one place that gives you the feeling of being at home. I was born in Bombay and even now going to Bombay is the only time when I have the feeling of coming home."[36] *The Moor's Last Sigh* is a profound elegy to the Bombay that once was the "great cosmopolis," the "city of mixed-up mongrel joy," now overwhelmed by the forces of the Hindu Right—specifically the Shiv Sena. In the novel, Bombay is central to India not simply as a consequence of its geographic location but also because this is where all Indias meet and merge. The city embodies Rushdie's affirmation of hybridity; like the Moor, it is the "bastard child of a Portuguese-English wedding, *and yet the most Indian of Indian cities*," where harmony emerges from cacophony (350). For Rushdie and his narrator, Bombay becomes metonymic of India's plurality and diversity of cultures. It holds out the perpetual possibility of creating bridges between cultures and communities. The jostling crowds of Bombay are celebrated for their "compacted humanity," for bringing people so close together that privacy itself ceases to exist and the "boundaries of your self begin to dissolve"—a feeling, the novel suggests, which can only come from being in love or from being in a crowd (193).[37]

Writing in the aftermath of the destruction of the mosque at Ayodhya and the ensuing communal riots and bombings in Bombay, Rushdie's distress at what has been done to his beloved city expresses itself in his narrator's lament:

> In Punjab, Assam, Kashmir, Meerut—in Delhi, in Calcutta from time to time they slit their neighbours' throats and took warm showers, or red bubble-baths, in all that spurning blood. They killed you for being circumcised and they killed you because your foreskins had been left on. . . . In Bombay such things never happened. . . . on the way to Bombay the rivers of blood were usually diluted. . . . Am I sentimentalizing? *Now that I have left it all behind, have I among my many losses, also lost clear sight?* It may be said that I have; but still I stand by my words. *O Beautifiers of the City, did you not see what was beautiful in Bombay was that it belonged to nobody, and to all. Did you not see the everyday live-and-let live miracles thronging its overcrowded streets?* (my emphasis, 350–51)

The dream of a cosmopolitan Bombay is articulated through the simultaneous experience of nonbelonging and multiple belongings. Like Derrida's "open city," Rushdie's hospitable city is one that belongs to no one and to all, where everyone may live "with and as a stranger . . . 'at home' [chez soi], in all the figures of the 'at home.'"[38] To be sure, Rushdie's cosmopolitan Bombay is an imaginative construction, but undoubtedly, it is an immensely appealing vision of the hospitable city, one that bears all the hallmarks of plurality, diversity, and heterogeneity he upholds as ideals for the Indian nation. The parallels with his own life are poignantly evident in this passage, making it impossible to read his work without addressing his life circumstances. Forcibly exiled from his beloved city at the time he was writing this book because of the Indian government's refusal to grant him a visa, his anguish is apparent here.

Nevertheless, we must ask what it means to uphold an upper-class metropolitan space as a metonym for the nation. Although Rushdie goes to some length to unveil "invisible Bombay"—the "phantom people" who comprise the laboring population of the city—it is the Moor's affluent Malabar Hill Bombay that is constructed as the site of his cosmopolitan idealism. Consequently, Rushdie's version of cosmopolitanism remains faithful to the concept's legacy of class privilege despite his well-intentioned efforts to acknowledge the subaltern populations, "the wraiths that kept the city going, building its houses, hauling its goods, cleaning up its droppings, and then simply and terribly dying . . ." (212).[39] I am reminded of Joseph Conrad's description of the African phantoms in *Heart of Darkness,* a novella that, while providing one of the earliest metropolitan critiques of the imperialist project, is unable to envision Africans as anything other than objects of pity.[40] This comparison is not meant to paint Rushdie as a neocolonialist writer in postcolonial drag, merely to draw attention to the upper-class and urban imaginary of his cosmopolitan vision of the Indian nation. In positing metropolitan Bombay as the essence of the nation, he unwittingly brings to play a class-based form of exclusion even while writing against Hindu nationalism's exclusionary vision of India.

Rushdie's dream of a cosmopolitan India is also expressed by means of the formal and thematic concerns of Aurora's paintings. Through his descriptions of Aurora's art, Rushdie seeks to evoke the "golden" past of Moorish Spain. In this novel, Rushdie deploys ekphrasis to great effect to illustrate Aurora's visual art while also providing a metafictional gloss on his own aesthetic preoccupations. Mary Lou Emery observes, ". . . Rushdie's novel portrays works of art as the visual scripts for the narratives in which they appear, opening windows within those narratives for alternate stories, multiple in direction and possibility, even taking on lives of their own, yet remaining within, while creating, the larger narrative."[41] Aurora's art provides a "visual script" for Rushdie's imaginative account of India as a diverse and hospitable nation where different religiocultural groups can coexist peacefully. Aurora uses Arab-Spain to posit a counter to the Hindu Right's vision of a homogeneous and monocultural India. The narrator provides a succinct description of her paintings: "In a way they were an attempt to create a romantic myth of the plural, hybrid nation; she was using Arab-Spain to re-imagine India" (227). In her vision of India as "Mooristan," Aurora creates a dream of an interconnected cosmopolitan nation "where worlds collide, flow in and out of one another, and washofy away" (226). She depicts a fluid and interlinked world where land and sea merge into each other, and strange, composite creatures transgress the frontiers between landscape and seascape. We are told her paintings are a palimpsest where the old "tolerant" flourishing Spain of the Moors overlays the ugly oneness of present-day India.[42] The metaphor of the palimpsest in this novel, "of one country, one dream, bumpo'ing into another, or being under, or on top of it" recalls Nehru's image of India as "some ancient palimpsest on which layer upon layer of thought and reverie had been inscribed, and yet no succeeding layer had completely hidden or erased what has been written previously" (Rushdie, 226).[43] Yet, the novel also disrupts Nehru's account of national culture, which locates Vedic society as *the* origin of Indian culture *absorbing* all "foreign" influences, particularly the disruptive—albeit beneficial—entry of Islam.[44] In contrast, Rushdie goes to great lengths in this novel to reinvent the idea of India as constituted by multiple religiocultural claims by refusing any *prior* right of upper-caste Hinduism. Aurora's painterly vision of Moorish Spain where different religious and cultural groups coexist peacefully, and where no one group has antecedent claims, exemplifies Rushdie's yearning for a more hospitable idea of the Indian nation.

In particular, the Moorish fort, the Alhambra, becomes a central trope of cosmopolitanism in this text: this "palace of interlocking forms and secret wisdom" is a "monument to a lost possibility that nevertheless has gone on standing, long after its conquerors have fallen; like a testament to lost but sweetest love, to the love that endures beyond defeat, beyond annihilation . . . to the defeated love that is greater than what defeats it, to that most profound of our needs, to our need for flowing together, for putting an end to frontiers, for the dropping of the boundaries of the self" (433). Rushdie's description of love has something like a relationship with Derrida's notion of hospitality as the welcome offered to all others—to every other—to enter my self. The narrator expresses a profound longing for a self that is porous and permeable, a desire for the capacity of that individual self to merge and flow into others. Love becomes Rushdie's preferred term for something akin to an ethics of hospitality. Love is understood as "the blending of spirits, as mélange, as the triumph of the impure, mongrel, conjoining best of us over what there is in us of the solitary, the isolated, the austere, the dogmatic, the pure" as an alternative to the "clean, mean, *apartheiding* Ones" (289). Significantly, Derrida also invokes the word "love" in his discussion of an absolute hospitality where the host would abandon himself to the other: "This is also what one calls love, and first of all, mystical love, which gives itself without giving anything else but itself" ("Hostipitality," *Acts of Religion*, 389). Yet, we must also ask what it means to yearn for a world without any boundaries at all, to merge into the other to the extent of effecting a communion with the other. However appealing Rushdie's dream of a borderless world may be in contrast to the segregationist visions of fundamentalists, it is important to see the pitfalls of this vision in its desire to negate the alterity of the other.[45] Absolute hospitality in the Derridean sense demands the interruption of the ensemble—including that of "the secret, of separation, of solitude, of silence and of singularity"—but it also takes this singularity, this separation, to be the very condition from which "a stranger accords himself to a stranger in hospitality."[46] In contrast, Rushdie's vision of mélange and blending tends to dissolve singularity altogether in its desire to become one with the other.

What is more, Rushdie's ideal cosmopolitan subject can only be articulated through the figure of the transcendent human who is able to effect a rupture with all identitarian belonging. This view is expressed most clearly in Moraes's dreamlike yearning to peel off his skin and go forth naked into the world, "like an anatomy illustration from *Encyclopedia Britannica*, all ganglions, ligaments, nervous pathways and veins, *set free from the otherwise inescapable jails of colour, race and clan"* (136, my emphasis). For Rushdie, these lived identifications are no more than prisons that confine and constrain you; they are not seen to hold any positive potential of affect or solidarity.[47] Thus, the narrator wistfully muses: "In Indian country, there was no room for a man who didn't want to belong to a tribe, who dreamed of moving beyond; of peeling off his skin and revealing his secret identity—the secret, that is, of the identity of all men—of standing before the war-painted braves to *unveil the flayed and naked unity of the flesh*" (414). In this passage, Indians from the India Columbus set off to "discover" are conflated with the American Indians he in fact encountered; both become congruous within Rushdie's ethos in their incomprehensible need to belong to groups. In a classic reiteration of the liberal paradigm, group identities are thus pathologized as "tribal identities." Clearly, the ideal cosmopolitan subject is, for Rushdie, the abstract figure of the human who transcends and stands beyond all communal identifications rather than a subject who goes towards the other by *interrupting* the totality of his identitarian claims.

It is hardly surprising, then, that Rushdie also upholds the idea of the transcendent citizen-subject, one who would be a citizen before and above all other forms of collective identification. Historically, the notion of the autonomous human—the subject of the "rights of man"—emerged in tandem with the abstract figure of the citizen. This moment is often traced back to the French Revolution and the "declaration of rights," which, paradoxically, could only promote the idea of the "unity of man" *within* the framework of *national* sovereignty and citizenship.[48] As Ian Balfour and Eduardo Cadava observe, "If in principle, human rights therefore would seem to pertain to all humans, the earliest declarations articulated a tension between man and citizen that continues to haunt discussions of who has the right to be protected and who does not."[49] Replaying this fundamental paradox at the core of human rights discourse, Rushdie simultaneously upholds a vision of human unity as well as the blank secular citizen-subject who is able to rise above divisive group affiliations within the nation. The novel laments the damage done to Nehru's vision of an India that would be in Moor's grandfather Camoens's paraphrase, "*above* religion because secular, above class because socialist, above caste because enlightened, above hatred because loving, above vengeance because forgiving, above tribe because unifying, above language because

many-tongued, above colour because multicoloured" (51). The repeated
use of the word "above" gestures to the author's belief in the modernist
(Nehruvian) ideal of transcendent citizenship, even as he seeks to make
room for minoritarian identities within the space of the nation. Thus, there
is a certain contradiction in *The Moor's Last Sigh,* and indeed in much of
Rushdie's oeuvre: while reveling in the abundance of a mixed-up mongrel
cultural plurality, he also affirms the idea of the unified and autonomous
human who can shed all forms of collective identity at will, other than allegiance to the nation. National identity must override all other identities
in society, including religious, regional, and linguistic allegiances. Group
identifications, then, are at once accommodated and denied in Rushdie's
work. He valorizes plurality and diversity, but he is unable to recognize
the particular beliefs, practices, and mores that give rise to this plurality in
the first place. Thus, "Jews, Christians, Muslims, Parsis, Sikhs, Buddhists,
Jains" all crowd into the canvas as "a miraculous composite of all the
colours in the world" in Aurora Zogoiby's vision of Moorish Spain (227,
my emphasis). In this execution of an idealized nation-space, tangible
differences of belief, identity, and location may be accommodated only
so long as they contribute to the aestheticizing "colors" of a plural and
composite world, not if they were to make political claims based on their
contingent differences.

Above all, there is no room for religion or religion-based affinities in
Rushdie's vision of a cosmopolitan nation. In order for his vision to exist,
it would appear that his world cannot have any place for religion. Thus,
the narrator longs for his parents' secret recipe, the "priest-poison-beating
anti-veneme" that had "cured" them of religion (55). Refusing to acknowledge the tangibility of religion as culture in the lives of people, Rushdie's
particular brand of liberal secularism in this novel is of the kind Spivak
refers to as "sanitized"—it is irreverent and dismissive of all aspects of the
religious. In contrast, Sara Suleri has commented on his remarkable ambivalence toward religion in earlier works such as *The Satanic Verses.*[50]
This later novel, however, is fairly unequivocal in its condemnation of
any form of religious faith or practice. The endearing deity of *Midnight's
Children,* the elephant-god Ganesh, appears in this text as Aurora's op-
ponent. Every year, Aurora performs her "profane gyrations" on the day
of the religious festival of Ganesh Chaturti in defiance of the "perversity
of humankind, which led these huge crowds to risk death-by-trampling"

(123–24). Although there are some interesting moments in the text when characters such as Zeenat Vakil (reappearing after *The Satanic Verses*) bemoan the ways in which Hindu nationalism is transforming Hinduism into a monotheistic Abrahamic religion converging around the figure of a martial Ram, by and large, the novel seeks to do away with religion altogether. In my view, this complete dismissal of religion appears as a serious faultline in Rushdie's vision of a cosmopolitan nation.

In an important episode, a precursor of darker times to come, Camoens goes to the (fictional) town of Malgudi to hear Gandhi speak and announces his prophecy of doom for India:

> In the city we are for secular India but the village is for Ram. And they say *Ishwar and Allah is your name* but they don't mean it, they mean only Ram himself, king of Raghu clan, purifier of sinners along with Sita. In the end I am afraid the villagers will march on the cities and people like us will have to lock our doors and there will come a Battering Ram. (56)

Rushdie clearly validates a secular and plural public-sphere against the forces of fundamentalist majoritarianism; however, in this simplistic dichotomy between the "rural" and the "urban," the "religious" and the "secular," he effectively makes secularism the sole provenance of a westernized, urbanized Indian elite and risks validating the Hindu Right's construction of secularism as essentially a "western" ideology unsuitable for the Indian context (even as they may uphold the idea of a secular state). In the classic tradition of a certain kind of Enlightenment secularism, Rushdie constructs religion as backward and irrational; secularism, concomitantly, serves as a figure for a fetishized reason.

To be sure, in this novel more than in any other work, Rushdie also interrogates the concept of secularism. Consider, for example, the dystopic rendition of a certain kind of secularism toward the end of the novel:

> It occurred to me that my father's pre-eminence over Scar and his colleagues was a dark, ironic victory for India's deep-rooted secularism. The very nature of this inter-community league of self-interest gave the lie to Mainduck's vision of a theocracy in which one particular variant of Hinduism would rule, while all India's other peoples bowed their beaten heads.

Vasco had said years ago: corruption was the only force we had that could defeat fanaticism . . . a godless crooked army that could take on and vanquish anything that the god-squad had sent its way. (332)

Writing about Rushdie's affirmation of hybridity, Dohra Ahmad suggests that he self-consciously points to the underside of hybridity to take "ownership of all possible interpretations." For example, Aurora herself concedes that the notions of impurity, cultural admixture, and mélange "were in fact capable of distortion, and contained a potential for darkness as well as for light" (303). Similarly, I argue that moments such as the above passage represent the writer's attempt to think secularism at its limits and to acknowledge the possibilities of perversion that always threaten it from within. However, the notion of secularism continues to be crucial to his vision of multireligious coexistence and a cosmopolitan India, even as he mourns its "last sigh" in this novel.

Part of the early postindependence generation that believed firmly in the Nehruvian vision of a secular-democratic India, Rushdie uses the bodily degeneration of his sorry narrator to express his profound disappointment with the failure of this vision to realize its promise. This disappointment is expressed allegorically through the transformation in the figure of the Moor in the novel, who moves from being a "unifier of opposites, a standard-bearer of pluralism, . . . a symbol—however approximate—of the new nation" into a "semi-allegorical figure of decay" (313). The narrative trajectory of the Moor thus comes to stand in for the disintegration of the national idea he embodies. As a result, the novel has often been read as a lament for the Nehruvian vision of India. Rustom Bharucha, for example, in his reading of the text, concludes, "For all his irreverence, Rushdie remains almost dutifully stuck, like an old gramophone record, to his very privileged reading of the Nehruvian legacy of secularism. . . . Rushdie's critique of contemporary India is cast in a timewarp, and as such, is almost as redundant as that stuffed old dog-on-wheels 'Jawaharlal,' who is trundled through the last pages of the novel, an object of pathos rather than derision."[51]

Although I agree with Bharucha about the novel's commitment to the Nehruvian idea of a *secular* nation—one that has been emancipated from all religion—my reading has also underscored how this text offers an implicit critique of Nehruvian notions of nationalism. In making its minoritarian protagonist—the "Jewholic anonymous" Moor—the repository of his vision of a cosmopolitan Indian nation, *The Moor's Last Sigh* not only seeks to imagine a more inclusive nation but also redefines national culture as inherently plural and diverse. In my view, Rushdie's attempt to reimagine India as a hospitable nation by opening up the totality of the Indian nation for those who have been rendered "strangers" *within* the nation remains the most important contribution of this ambitious novel toward the ethics of living well together.

Yet *The Moor's Last Sigh* is unable to think past the modernist category of the "nation" in its vision of a more hospitable world. Although the novel makes a persuasive case for not ceding the conceptual territory of the nation to Hindu nationalists, its version of hospitality is limited by the bounds of the nation-state. This is even more evident in an earlier work, *Midnight's Children,* in which Saleem Sinai's thought processes and magical powers are jammed once he moves to Pakistan—that "other" country across the border. As Derrida points out, "[I]f there is a door, there is no longer hospitality" (Derrida, "Hostipitality," *Angelaki,* 14). Thus Rushdie's version of cosmopolitanism reiterates some of the very boundaries it sets out to question in its inability to move beyond the binaries of "Indian" and "Pakistani." The work I now turn to, Amitav Ghosh's *In an Antique Land,* enables us to think past the nation-state by evoking a premodern cosmopolitan area where "anyone can come in at any time and can come in without needing a key for the door" (Derrida, 14).

Displaced Encounters in *In an Antique Land*

If Salman Rushdie turns to Moorish Spain to revitalize the idea of a cosmopolitan nation, Amitav Ghosh invokes medieval Indian Ocean trading cultures to offer a more transnational model of cosmopolitanism that is not limited to the imagined community of the modern (Indian) nation-state. Ghosh belongs to the group of emergent writers who rose to prominence in the 1980s in the wake of Rushdie's success. The text that I examine here, *In an Antique Land,* is a work of stupendous research, centered on a quest for genealogies, historical evidence, archival material, and empirical records. Yet it is also a speculative, imaginative, and conjectural work, very much in the genre of the literary narrative, which constructs and imagines a past world. Part travel narrative, part anthropology, part historical account, and part literary narrative, this work has been widely celebrated for its ability to straddle different disciplinary boundaries as well as its expansive geographical and historical span. *In an Antique Land* features two interwoven narratives far removed from one another in space and time. The first narrative is the author's attempt to write a self-reflexive anthropology based on his ethnographic encounters in an Egyptian village in the early 1980s. It allows *In an Antique Land* to be read as an immensely self-reflexive work, one finely attuned to the many ironies at play when an Indian anthropologist studying at Oxford seeks to write about another nonwestern culture. The second central narrative of the text is at once historical, speculative, and literary in its attempt to imaginatively reconstruct the precolonial mercantile past of the Indian Ocean as a hospitable, cosmopolitan world. This second narrative revolves around the stories of Abraham Ben Yiju, a Jewish merchant of North Africa who traveled between India and the Middle East in the twelfth century, and his Indian slave, Bomma. Confronted with a divided present, Ghosh imaginatively retrieves these overlooked histories to remind us that hospitable areas and regions did exist at some point—they are not just a utopian ideal.

But what could a narrative about the medieval Indian Ocean trade have to do with contemporary religio-nationalist conflicts in the subcontinent? I read *In an Antique Land* as a displaced intervention in the context of present-day Hindu–Muslim/Indian–Pakistani conflicts. In my reading, Ghosh transplants his concerns about religio-nationalist violence in the subcontinent onto the terrain of a transcontinental Indo–Egyptian encounter that spans centuries. I explore his fascinating construction of the category of the "medieval"—in opposition to the usual derogatory connotations associated with the "dark" pre-Renaissance middle ages—as a flexible, porous, and accommodative culturo-temporal space that is hospitable to everyone. I argue that Ghosh's evocation of the premodern past directs us toward possibilities of multireligious and multicultural coexistence in the present—specifically by enabling us to think outside the frame of modernity and its identitarian territorial divisions. However, while attesting to the immense appeal of Ghosh's cosmopolitan vision, I trace the ways in which the book's facility at straddling different temporalities and cultural contexts can also serve as its limitation in terms of the sometimes sweeping conflations it renders between widely divergent contexts and the consequent evasions it effects of minoritarian identities in a post-Partition subcontinent. I also interrogate Ghosh for his inability to question his own secular universalist positioning in his account of his ethnographic encounters.

In an Antique Land is part of the growing field of Indian Ocean studies, which has expanded ever since Alan Villiers published his 1952 study *The Indian Ocean.*[52] What sets Ghosh's work apart from similar historiographical projects, despite the rigorous empirical research he undertakes to reconstruct the intertwined stories of Abraham Ben Yiju and Bomma, is the imaginative nature of this endeavor. Indeed, Ghosh discovers there is very little empirical or archival material available on Ben Yiju and Bomma, even though he travels between Cambridge, Cairo, Mangalore, and Philadelphia to reconstitute their stories. As Leela Gandhi notes, "[T]o flesh out these slim pickings, Ghosh must continually imagine a narrative plenitude"; he is constantly envisioning, assuming, and speculating about the lives of his medieval protagonists to weave together a coherent narrative from fragments and traces.[53] What interests me, then, is not so much the historical accuracy of his attempt to locate a cosmopolitan world in the mercantile past of the Indian Ocean's trading cultures (which has been amply testified to in the burgeoning historical studies of the region), but the ways in which Ghosh posits this world as a counter to the rigid—national and religious—boundaries of modernity. The medieval past is almost always set up in dialectical relation to a fragmented Hindu–Muslim and Jewish–Muslim present in the hope of shaping a different, more habitable future. What the contours of this vision of the past are and how tenable it is as a model of a mutually coexistent world concern me here.

Writing of Ghosh's work, Clifford Geertz praises it for its evocation of a:

mobile, polyglot and virtually borderless region, *which no one owned and no one dominated,* Arabs, Jews, Iberians, Greeks, Indians, various sorts of Italians and Africans pursued trade and learning, private lives and public fortunes, bumping up against one and another . . . but more or less getting along, or getting by, within broad and general rules for communication, propriety and the conduct of business. It was, we might say, a sort of multicultural bazaar. Today this part of the globe is divided, like the rest of the globe, into singular and separated national States.[54]

In particular, the hospitable manner of these interactions—what Ghosh calls the "shared enterprise" of transcontinental trade—stands in sharp contrast to the later mode of European colonial expansion and is especially appealing to the anthropologist-historian.[55] Thus he writes, "In matters of business, Ben Yiju's networks appear to have been wholly indifferent to many of those boundaries that are today thought to mark social, religious and geographical divisions" (278). Reflecting the current anthropological move away from a notion of discrete and bounded cultures, Ghosh creates an appealing picture of a porous and hospitable world marked by an ease of mobility between different cultures, religious traditions, and regions. His account of Qus, an oft-frequented resting place along the Nile used by travelers between Egypt and India, for instance, revels in the abundant diversity of the place. Emphasis is placed on Ben Yiju's description of this "admirably cosmopolitan town" with many Yemeni, Ethiopian, and Indian traders as "'a station for the traveller, a gathering place for caravans, and a meeting-place for pilgrims'" (174). Similarly, Ghosh describes geographically distant Calicut as one of the most "cosmopolitan" places on the coast, frequented by regular visitors from "'China, Sumatra, Ceylon, the Maldives, Yemen, and Fars (Iran)'" (243).

Ghosh the historian is also drawn to Ben Yiju's mercantile congregation and the several centuries of travel history that took these Jewish-Egyptian traders across the Mediterranean to the Indian Ocean. If Rushdie's Moor lives in accelerated time, characters in Ghosh's cosmopolitan world, as James Clifford so aptly puts it, "have been for centuries dwelling-in-travel."[56] Ben Yiju belongs to a renowned community of Jewish merchants and traders originally from Ifriqiya (in what is now Tunisia), who went on to live in Fustat, Egypt, and who traveled constantly across the Indian ocean; Ben Yiju himself lived in India for close to seventeen years as an expatriate until his eventual return to Northern Africa. In another example, Ghosh cites two men in Ben Yiju's circle of acquaintances "whose dates and places of writing bear witness to a pattern of movement so fluent and far-ranging that they make the journeys of later medieval travellers, such as Marco Polo and Ibn Battuta, seem unremarkable in comparison" (157). *In an Antique Land* consistently bears witness to a "group of people whose travels and breadth of experience and education seem astonishing even today, on a planet thought to be newly-shrunken" (55). Ghosh's celebration of these interlinked travel histories calls into question what Clifford has described as "the classic anthropological quest" for discrete

traditions, highly localized and bounded cultures (8). This shift from traditional anthropological assumptions about tightly marked-off cultures
is also evident in Ghosh's account of contemporary Egyptian villages,
which seem to be "possessed of all the busy restlessness of an airport's
transit lounge . . . some men had passports so thick they opened out like
ink-blackened concertinas" (173). Thus, the anthropologist can no longer
position himself as a global traveler visiting rooted natives: "His 'ancient
and settled' fieldsite opens on to complex histories of dwelling and traveling, discrepant cosmopolitanisms."[57]

It would be only too easy to take to task a cosmopolitanism that rests
upon an ideology of a traveling culture in which only certain (elite) classes
of people can be called cosmopolitan. If we consider Bomma's life story,
however, it is clear that the Indian Ocean world was not restricted to affluent merchants and traders.[58] Writing of Bomma, Ghosh emphasizes his
subalternity:

> . . . the reference comes to us from a moment in time when the
> only people for whom we can even begin to imagine properly
> human, individual, existences are the literate and the conse-
> quential, the wazirs and the sultans, the chroniclers and the
> priests - the people who had the power to inscribe themselves
> physically upon time. But the slave of Khalaf's letter was not of
> that company: in his instance it was a mere accident that those
> barely discernible traces that ordinary people leave upon the
> world happen to have been preserved. It is nothing less than
> a miracle that anything is known about him at all. (17)

In accord with the agenda of the subaltern studies project, Ghosh seeks to
imagine the subjectivities of those who have been relegated to the margins
of history and hence to recuperate a different history of cosmopolitanism,
one that is not limited to the exploits of the wealthy and the affluent.[59]

Indeed, Ghosh makes clear that his affirmation of travel doesn't necessarily entail physical movement across vast vistas of space. Travel is
deployed as a trope for the worldly cosmopolitan *imagination,* one that
is able to think beyond the self and go toward the other. Invention and
imagination, key words in the cognitive vocabulary of the narrator of his
earlier novel, *The Shadow Lines,* suggest a belief that travel does not

merely mean living in many places; rather, it has to do with our ability to access the other in the imagination.[60] In *The Shadow Lines*, the narrator's uncle, Tridib, plays an essential role in shaping this vocabulary; he teaches the narrator to use his "imagination with precision." Tridib believes that we cannot see without inventing what we see, so we must use our imagination, or else we will always live in other people's inventions.[61] Thus, the narrator has lived in Tridib's stories about London during the Blitz long before he ever went to London. And when he does visit London, his "cartographic imagination" allows him to lead other characters through places he has never actually visited.[62] Likewise, in the present-day world of *In an Antique Land*, Ghosh finds the amazement and curiosity of the Egyptian fellaheen, Zaghloul and Khamees, especially attractive: "[F]or them the *world outside* was still replete with the wonders of the unknown" (174). A particularly evocative instance of Ghosh's validation of the traveling imagination is provided by the narrator's friend Nabeel who tries to imagine the narrator's loneliness when he makes tea for himself: "It must make you think of all the people you left at home . . . when you put that kettle on the stove with just enough water for yourself" (152). The narrator muses to himself, "Nabeel's comment stayed in my mind; I was never able to forget it, for it was the first time that anyone in Lataifa or Nashawy had attempted an enterprise similar to mine—to enter my imagination and look at my situation as it might appear to me" (152). Ghosh's emphasis on the imagination resonates with Spivak's belief that "the imagination, which is our inbuilt capacity to other ourselves, can lead perhaps to understanding other people from the inside."[63] Ghosh uses travel as a metaphor for the (worldly) imagination, which becomes the means to "coming as close as possible to accessing the other as the self" (Spivak 230).

The many forms of exchange and meeting between (and within) different linguistic and religious traditions in the Indian Ocean world also provide an example of a more hospitable and coexistent way of life that does not exist in postcolonial modernity. For the ethnographer-historian, this great mercantile civilization corroborates a vision of a flexible and interconnected world that is not rent asunder by linguistic, religious, or national cleavages. For example, the language used by Ben Yiju and his contemporaries is the hybrid Judaeo-Arabic, a colloquial dialect of medieval Arabic written in the Hebrew script. Similarly, although Ben Yiju and his friends were all observant Jews, Ghosh suggests that the everyday world of their religious life was one they shared with the Muslims of the area: "[W]hen they invoked the name of God in their writings it was usually as Allah, and more often than not their invocations were in Arabic forms, such as insha'allah and al-hamdul-illah. Distinct though their faith was, it was still part of the religious world of the Middle East" (261). Significantly, this hospitable trafficking of idioms and ideas is represented as taking place not only between different religions and cultures but also *within* a tradition and is central to Ghosh's formulation of a cosmopolitan world. Thus, he consistently draws attention to "the beliefs and practices that have always formed the hidden and subversive counter-image of the orthodox religions of the Middle East: the exorcism cults, the magical rites, the customs of visiting saints' graves and suchlike" (263). For educated and salaried Egyptians like Ustaz Sabry, these practices are not part of "the true practice of Islam"; they are mere superstitions (141). For Ghosh, on the other hand, they are ample testament to the immense diversity, heterogeneity, and permeability *within and between* different religions and cultures in the region. This fluidity of movement between different regions and religions that comprised the Indian Ocean mercantile civilization is central to Ghosh's invocation of it as a model cosmopolitan world—of the kind that Derrida envisions. It is a world that has not yet been clearly demarcated into territorial national states and one where no one claims ownership or mastery.

However, *In an Antique Land* has come in for some criticism for its invocation of the past, most notably in a provocative and insightful essay by Gauri Viswanathan.[64] She argues that Ghosh finds a model of syncretism in the history of the Indian Ocean trade and the hybrid identities it engendered that is no longer available in the present. The notion of syncretism as the synthesis of different religious forms has undergone many transformations and mutations in meaning, from its use as a nineteenth-century term of disapprobation to its more contemporary connotations of tolerance and peaceful coexistence in multireligious societies. Charting this shift, Viswanathan interrogates the place of syncretism in a post-Orientalist project that seeks to promote noncoercive ways of knowing and studying "other" cultures. She cautions that if inadequately historicized, syncretism can become a "code word for the incorporation and assimilation of 'minority' cultures into the culture of the dominant group"

(7, 2). It can obscure the varied ways by which unequally empowered groups have negotiated their differences in specific historical contexts. Further, she suggests, the rituals and practices seen as syncretic by the outside anthropological observer may not necessarily be subjectively experienced as such by their practitioners.

Although Viswanathan's critique of an unqualified valorization of syncretism is very pertinent, her reading of *In an Antique Land* is too strongly determined by the theory of syncretism. Ghosh creates an admittedly idealized portrait of a hospitable world in the medieval past, but he is also attentive to the importance of cultural and religious differences in the medieval Indian Ocean world. For example, he notes that Ben Yiju and his friends were all "orthodox, observant, Jews, *strongly aware of their distinctive religious identity.* But they were also part of the Arabic-speaking world, and the everyday language of their religious life was one they shared with the Muslims of the region" (261). Elsewhere, writing of the region of Tulunad in India, he observes, "[L]ike so many other parts of the subcontinent, it forms a cultural area which is *distinctive and singular,* while being at the same time closely *enmeshed with its neighbors in an intricate network of differences*" (244). What emerges, then, is not so much "an undivided community" (as Viswanathan suggests) characterized by the dissolution of differences in a condition of happy hybridity of the kind to be found in *The Moor's Last Sigh,* but a more complex picture of interconnection and affiliation between different cultures and religions that are brought together through history or geography.

If Ghosh does feel the need to hold on to some notion of syncretism, it is only in his profound desire to find remnants of the shared past in the conflict-ridden present—in his account of the shrine of the Jewish–Muslim saint Sidi Abu-Hasira, for example, which still draws both Jewish and Muslim followers, or the story he recounts of the Muslim mariner worshipped in the form of a deity called the Bobbariya Bhuta in a Hindu shrine in Tulunad, India. Viswanathan's critique of syncretism is helpful here, reminding us that it is naïve to celebrate such practices as an example of "tolerance." While Ghosh's narrator may celebrate the irony of finding the Bhuta deity in the now Sanskritized shrine, the followers of the deity do not share his perspective and indeed want to deny any link with the past. Ghosh's informant, the young student who belongs to the Magavira fishing community that had once worshipped the Muslim trader, proudly tells him that this is no longer a Bhuta shrine, but a "real Hindu temple" (274). The complex account of an enmeshed world of differences we get in Ghosh's invocation of the past can find articulation in the text's *present* only in such examples of a compromised syncretism. The author's longing to discover some remnant of the precolonial past in the divided present leads him to a somewhat forced quest for surviving Jewish–Muslim and Hindu–Muslim syncretic practices, often identified in shared religious shrines or figures. This is not to suggest that these figures or places do not exist, only that we cannot afford to celebrate them uncritically or even ironically as subversive countercultures.[65]

Like *The Moor's Last Sigh, In an Antique Land* is also a profoundly elegiac narrative bemoaning the destruction done to the multiple entangled histories of the medieval Middle Eastern and Indian pasts. Ghosh makes his appeal for a more hospitable world on the basis of his imaginative historical work, which grounds his belief that cultures and religions were intertwined long before the territorial and identitarian divisions brought about by the onslaught of modernity. He lays the blame for this damage on European colonialists who were unable to comprehend the pacifist modes of a "culture of accommodation and compromise":

> Unable to compete in the Indian Ocean trade by purely commercial means, the Europeans were bent on taking control of it by aggression, pure and distilled, by unleashing violence on a scale unprecedented on these shores. As far as the Portuguese were concerned, *they had declared a proprietorial right over the Indian Ocean:* since none of the peoples who lived around it had thought to claim ownership of it before their arrival, they could not expect the right of free passage in it now. (my emphasis, 288)

To recall Derrida's metaphor of the door, in Ghosh's account, the Europeans introduce the notion of thresholds and boundaries by claiming ownership of the Indian Ocean region. With the landing of Vasco da Gama in India, the author laments, "[T]he knell had been struck for the world that had brought Bomma, Ben Yiju and Ashu together, and another age had begun in which the crossing of their paths would seem so unlikely that its very possibility would all but disappear from human memory" (286). Gauri Viswanathan suggests that the text cannot get beyond a "disquieting nostalgia" in its attempt to grapple with contemporary divisions. Nostalgic narratives are often dismissed as escapist—the longing for an idealized past is seen to undermine political action and social transformation in the present. I argue, however, that desirable constructions of the past *can* play a powerful role in shaping the contours of a different present and a future "to come." Above all, Ghosh's imaginative narrative about a cosmopolitan past is an act of memory that points to possibilities of living together in the present.

Juxtaposing many histories and time frames in his narrative, Ghosh writes: "[T]he remains of those small, indistinguishable, intertwined histories, Indian and Egyptian, Muslim and Jewish, Hindu and Muslim, had been partitioned long ago" (339). The displaced nature of his concern with post-Partition *subcontinental* schisms (both transnational and intranational) is evident here in the very use of the word "partitioned" with all that it evokes for a South Asian readership. The immense geographical sweep of this narrative and the generic synthesis of anthropology and history allow him to bring together his concerns around contemporary subcontinental violence with the dilemmas of his Egyptian ethnographic encounter as well as with the contentious issue of Arab–Jewish cleavages in present-day Israel/Palestine. History, then, in *In an Antique Land* is not just "the arena of displaced desire" for the "anxieties of participating in a potentially coercive anthropology" (as Viswanathan suggests), but it also provides a site for working over contemporary Indian–Pakistani/Hindu–Muslim divisions.[66] Displacement in this narrative functions not just across time but also across space.

In fact, the ethnographic narrative of *In an Antique Land* can also be read as a persistent, conscious, and sympathetic effort at understanding, interpreting, and getting to know the figure of the Muslim other of post-Partition India, but only as a displaced venture in another land. A particularly illustrative example of this displacement is the episode in which Ghosh's persona is asked quite directly if he has been circumcised; unable to confront his subjects-turned-interrogators, he stumbles out of the room. When asked why by his friend, Nabeel—"they were only asking questions just like you do"—the knowing voice of the narrator inevitably takes over and recounts a story of childhood trauma emerging from his memories of a communal riot in Dhaka, East Pakistan (present-day Bangladesh) in 1964:

> The stories of these riots are always the same: tales that grow out
> of an explosive barrier of symbols—of cities going up in flames
> because of a cow found dead in a temple or a pig in a mosque;
> of people killed for wearing a lungi or a dhoti, depending on
> where they find themselves; of women disembowelled for wear-
> ing veils or vermilion, of men dismembered for the state of their
> foreskins. (210)

The frightening images of flames, mobs, and people rioting are meant
to explain the avowedly "secular" anthropologist's unease with bodily
marks of difference such as circumcision (or the lack of it). He remarks,
"I could not have expected them to understand an Indian's terror of symbols" (210). Neelam Srivastava offers a sympathetic gloss of Ghosh's explanation: "The fact is that he has known a previous incarnation of the
Hindu–Muslim encounter in another period, in another country—which
colours, affects, shapes, determines the development of the present incarnation, that between an Indian anthropologist, apparently secularized,
and Egyptian Muslim fellaheen."[67] One might ask, however, if the present ethnographic Indo–Egyptian encounter should be read as yet another
incarnation ("repetition") of eternal "Hindu–Muslim" conflict that takes
the same form everywhere—across time and space. What is it that Ghosh
has to fear from Egyptian villagers who have nothing in common with
Indian Muslims other than a shared religious identity? They certainly do
not carry the burden of collective memories of religious conflict and the
Indian Partition.

Despite its powerful appeal, then, there are also pitfalls to Ghosh's
synthetic cosmopolitan imagination, which lead him to collapse the
differences between the different contexts and temporalities he engages.
Ghosh's transnational imagination is clearly limited by his constant need
to bring together his various concerns, to the extent of amalgamating
them, and thus effacing differences between disparate intersubjective encounters and contexts. This grafting of Hindu–Muslim divisions onto the
terrain of his current Indo–Egyptian encounter unwittingly obscures the
unequal location of Hindus and Muslims in *post*-Partition India. While
Ghosh is very aware of the hierarchies implicit in the ethnographic situation, his transnational imagination tends to eclipse the ways in which
groups are unequally authorized within a bounded nation-state. In other

words, there is no attempt to consider the complex minoritarian position that Muslims occupy in contemporary India.

Further, the threatening image of the senselessly rioting crowd disguises the authorial persona's own discomfort with bodily markers of religious identity. This is not to deny that communal violence in the Indian subcontinent quite often centers around visible markers of difference (what Ghosh calls "symbols") between groups, but these "symbols" and practices are also ways of being and living in the world, what Spivak describes as a form of "linguistic competence." They are not just "regressive" or "backward" religious rites that are always already threatening to the stability of a secular world, as Ghosh's narrator's unease implies. The authorial persona is unable to reflect critically on his own secular universalist positioning. Thus, the ethnographic narrative of *In an Antique Land* is persistently *staged* as an (unequal) encounter between an avowedly "secular" Ghosh and the "faithful" Islamic fellaheen of Egypt. Only at one point in this account does the narrator reluctantly concede that he was born a Hindu, observing that "if I had a religious identity at all, it was largely by default" (47). Yet, despite his own avowal of a nonreligious secular identity, the subjects of his ethnography constantly cast him as "Hindu" and "other," especially given the concrete differences in bodily markers of identity. Indeed, the narrator feels his alterity most deeply in those moments when he is counter-questioned about Hindu practices concerning birth, marriage, or death, despite his best efforts to resist being cast as a Hindu. As a result, even though this is an exemplary ethnographic account that re-creates many encounters in which the interrogator becomes the interrogated, the authoritative, ostensibly dispassionate, and neutral voice of the narrator drowns and submerges the many voices within the text that may have the potential to reveal the chinks in his liberal-secularist stance. For example, although he does make room for Nabeel's counter-questions in his discursive account (the text itself) in the circumcision episode, he overwhelms them by retreating to this position of inexplicable cultural difference. He is unable to acknowledge that it is the jolting awareness of his Hindu identity in a relational context that leads him to run away from his interlocutors.

The differences, however, from Rushdie's defiant and loud secularism are evident. In Ghosh's text, the nonjudgmental ethnographer makes an attempt to understand what constitutes *belonging* to a community of believers rather than endorsing a complete break with all identitarian ties. For instance, during the month of Ramadan, Ghosh's persona wants to join in the fast in order to be part of what is happening in the village, but as he is reminded, participant-observer non-Muslim anthropologists cannot quite belong. He concludes that "the breaking of the fast was the beginning of a meal of communion that embraced millions of people . . . to belong to that immense community was a privilege which they had to re-earn every year, and the effort made them doubly conscious of the value of its boundaries" (76). He could not simply "participate" once and know what it means to be a part of a community or to belong to that community. Perhaps, he concludes, it is more important to respect the boundaries of inclusion and exclusion set up by the community and not to intrude as an outsider. In Ghosh's work, religion is never dismissed; as I have already discussed, this cosmopolitan writer is persistently drawn toward the many local traditions and beliefs that are constitutive of a shared culture. The text is littered with accounts of *mowlids* (fairs) and legends of saints who continue to be held in reverence by his rural Egyptian subjects despite their current disrepute with emerging orthodox Islamist movements. *So long as religion and culture can be viewed interchangeably,* Ghosh the anthropologist is comfortable with everyday beliefs and practices; however, he is unable to acknowledge the ways in which identities—*including his own*—get constructed in contexts of proximity to religious and cultural others.

While Rushdie affirms the idea of the abstract secular citizen-subject, Ghosh feels the need to position his own narratorial persona as somehow above and beyond religion even as he is respectful of subaltern religious traditions. One might ask what it would mean to acknowledge and avow a *Hindu* identity rather than to deny it, especially in light of the recent anti-Muslim violence in India. A number of secular Hindu activists who went to Gujarat after the carnage in 2002 spoke of their feeling of shame and their desire for atonement. Writing of this experience, Nivedita Menon acknowledges, "The horror has been perpetrated in our name—in the name of Hindus. We are responsible. For many of us who never considered ourselves to be 'Hindu' it is a difficult process of coming to terms with this identity. . . . this is not an identity we can choose to take on or deny—this is an identity that we bear for better or worse, and all the more so if we are believing and practising Hindus."[68] A secularist stance that wants to deny or transcend all identitarian belonging is no longer possible in contemporary India. Rather, "Hindus" must learn to reclaim their identity from those who perpetrate violence in their name.[69] The narrator of *In an Antique Land* is unable to do so; he can only affirm a "tolerant" liberal secularism, admittedly one that does not disrespect the other's beliefs and practices.

Through his imaginative construction of a more open and hospitable world in the Indian Ocean's trading cultures, Ghosh the literary-historian is able to gesture toward modes of coexistence that do not demand the absorption and assimilation of religious and cultural others even as he firmly opposes a xenophobic culture of distance. Although there is no going back to the cosmopolitan past that *In an Antique Land* nostalgically recalls for us, I believe that Ghosh's account of regions, religions, and cultures as *enmeshed* and intertwined in a network of differences continues to be relevant to reimagining Hindu–Muslim divisions within the nation-state and the partitioned subcontinent at large. He enables us to see how the thorny issue of Hindu–Muslim conflict in India has to be addressed on a subcontinental scale and not merely as an "Indian" dilemma. By means of its vision of a hospitable region that is not bound by the sovereign nation-state, *In an Antique Land* allows us to think past the conceptual categories of modernity we take so much for granted.

In different ways, the literary works I examine in this chapter posit a cosmopolitan vision that seeks to open up the ensembles of nationality, religion, language, history, or territory. Both narratives uphold the idea of a hospitable world where all are welcome and where no single group can place itself in the position of the host who asserts proprietorship. Where Rushdie's *The Moor's Last Sigh* reinvigorates the idea of the Indian nation as a hospitable community that is open to all—especially those who have been rendered as strangers within the nation, Ghosh's *In an Antique Land* imaginatively retrieves the medieval Indian Ocean world as a possible model of a cosmopolitan area that is not limited by the bounded territorial imaginary of the modern nation-state. The cosmopolitan visions of these fictions make poignant and deeply felt poetic pleas for a truly open, hospitable—and hence just—world. If this be cosmopolitanism, it is one of "stepchildren" and not of the "ruling kind."[70]

The Moor's Last Sigh and *In an Antique Land* provide compelling representations of what a living well together might look like—in Derrida's sense of the term. Both literary narratives thus open up an important doorway for us, but the question remains: how does one go toward the other in order to inaugurate the hospitable world they envision? What might an "ethics of alterity" (to use Spivak's phrase) look like in the specific context of the partitioned subcontinent? To begin to respond to this question, we must engage the fictions of memory I examine in the next chapter, which return to the moment of Partition in an effort to heed the call of the other.

3

$\vee$

Acts of Return: Literature and Post-Partition Memory

The year 1947 saw the formal end of the British Raj in India, but independence simultaneously brought with it the division of India into the two new postcolonial states of India and Pakistan. A subcontinental holocaust of tremendous magnitude, Partition was attended by immense dislocation and devastation for millions of people as they crossed the newly drawn borders of the two nation-states. In this chapter, I sketch out some of the historical, imaginative, and affective reasons for considering Partition as a moment in history that has come to shape and confirm India's very sense of nationhood in formative ways, especially in terms of marking its difference from a Muslim Pakistan. The divisive legacies of that moment of truncation, violence, dislocation, and suffering are crucial to understanding contemporary religio-nationalist conflict in the subcontinent. I view Partition as a spectral presence that continues to inform and haunt both Hindu–Muslim relations in India and contemporary international relations in the subcontinent. To speak of the *moment* of Partition violence and suffering, then, is to use a problematic construction, a "linguistic oxymoron," for such "moments" can often constitute an emotive and affective framework for a virtually infinite continuum of violence in collective and generational memory.[1] I argue that an alternative understanding of Pakistan—and the very demand for Pakistan—has to be at the forefront of contemporary efforts at envisioning multireligious coexistence in the subcontinent.

Drawing on recent scholarship about amnesia, cultural memory, and mourning, I begin by asking, what might it mean to remember and memorialize a traumatic event in the history of a nation?[2] What could it

mean to return to the silences of a nation, or in this instance, three nations, while recognizing that Partition meant very different things for
India, Pakistan, and Bangladesh?[3] What is at stake in such a return from
our present historical moment at the turn of the twenty-first century and
from a generational remove from this originary violence? Informed by
Derrida's proposition that "there can be no 'living together' that is not
devoted to this return, this going back upon oneself or back over one's
steps, this repetition of inaugurality," I argue for the critical significance
of returning to and *avowing*—admitting, acknowledging—the impossible
past of Partition for the three successor nations of British India.[4] Derrida
notes that what we are witnessing today is a globalization of the scene of
avowal—an almost theatrical process of returns to a proximate or distant
past, which may or may not be accompanied by repentance, forgiveness,
reparation, and reconciliation. Examples of such scenes of avowal or acts
of public repentance include the Nuremberg trials, the declarations by the
Japanese government toward the Koreans, and the South African Truth
and Reconciliation Commission in the aftermath of apartheid, among
others. While there are many aporias and risks that attend these returns
to difficult and shameful moments in national pasts—such as their appropriation as alibis by powerful states or economic powers—they mark an
"undeniable rupture" in the history of the political, juridical, and ethical,
including the relations between civil society and the state and between
states and international law. What is especially significant about contemporary scenes of return and avowal is the notion of "imprescriptibility"
that underlies them, a notion which indicates that "there is no longer an
end to responsibility that the guilty can assume" (37). The concept of a
"crime against humanity" is the juridical mechanism of this global scene
of avowal. Despite the problems and insufficiencies of this concept, in
marking a *beyond* of the sovereignty of the nation-state, it marks an "ir-
reversible progress" in international law—as the "horizon of all progresses
to come of international law" and as "the practical setting to work of any
declaration of the rights of man" (29–30). Consequently, Derrida believes
that avowing the unavowable, often through returns to a "founding violence," must be the very condition of a new living together, one which
exceeds the compulsory tolerance of the juridical contract. (The corollary
of this injunction would be a pure forgiveness that asks us to forgive the
unforgivable, which, he argues, is as important to the task of a new living
together.)[5]

Indeed, the founding of any state or of a constitution—therefore of a "living together" according to a juridical or political contract—is premised upon such an originary violence, since it establishes a law where the law did not exist (23). The inauguration of the modern subcontinental states of India and Pakistan—and subsequently Bangladesh—therefore can be viewed as no more than examples of this originary violence that underlies the foundation of all modern states. However, since independence and the instituting of sovereignty in the subcontinent were also attended by unimaginable brutality, displacement, and anguish for millions of people in 1947 (and once again in 1971), I consider Partition to be the "founding trauma" of Indian nationalism, one which continues to remain intrinsic to the trajectories of contemporary geopolitics in South Asia. I derive the term "founding trauma" from Dominick LaCapra, who uses it to describe limit events like the Holocaust, slavery, and apartheid as *the* traumas "that paradoxically becomes the basis for collective and/ or personal identity"[6] Such traumas become "typical of myths of origin and may perhaps be located in the more or less mythologized history of every people."[7] I argue that any effort to imagine a "living together" of peace and accord in the subcontinent must return to—acknowledge, reflect upon, and avow—this founding trauma of the Indian subcontinent. Partition must not be viewed as a horrific aberration in the history of the Indian nation, since the division of the country is the very condition of the establishment of sovereignty in the subcontinent.

This chapter addresses three literary narratives that undertake such a project of return to the Partition from a near present. The literary fictions I consider here are Amitav Ghosh's *The Shadow Lines* (1988), Mukul Kesavan's *Looking through Glass* (1995), and Shauna Singh Baldwin's short story "Family Ties" (1996). In each narrative, a post-Partition narrator from the second generation meditates and reflects upon the difficult past of Partition either through a gradual unveiling of familial and national secrets (Ghosh and Baldwin) or through a magical transposition into the past (Kesavan). Always refracting events for us, the narratorial subjectivities in these accounts are akin to those of the "secondary witness," the historian, or the literary critic whose response might entail "empathetic unsettlement" or even "muted trauma" but who are ultimately distanced from the pain of victims.[8] By means of their literal or metaphorical journeys to the past, the protagonist-narrators of these fictions attempt to grapple with the multiple and fraught meanings of

Partition. These literary narratives underscore the importance of remembering Partition, especially for those who did not experience it first hand, but whose subjectivities have been shaped by the legacies of this historic trauma through familial, group, and national mythologies.

What form should remembering take and what might be some of the risks entailed in such projects of memorialization are the questions that concern me in the next section, specifically in light of recent Holocaust scholarship that is often deployed as a model for current work on the Partition.

The Holocaust as a Paradigm for the Partition?

The Holocaust has come to shape much contemporary scholarship on trauma, memory, and memorialization not only as a recognizable model for a limit event but also in terms of the trajectories and responses that it has spawned. It is not surprising, then, that Holocaust scholarship should also provide a paradigm for much recent thinking about the Partition (including my own earlier work).[9] The Holocaust and the Partition are very different kinds of founding traumas: the first is the genocide of a people by a bureaucratic rationalist state, the second, a terrifying violence of mutuality (albeit one from which the state is not an innocent bystander). Nevertheless, the sheer volume of scholarly work on the Holocaust makes it a very useful model for engaging Partition as a limit event. Holocaust scholarship provides us with a series of concepts such as witnessing, victim testimonials, memorialization, and mourning that are undeniably useful for contemporary efforts to come to terms with the historic trauma of Partition in the interest of thinking peaceful coexistence in the present. The attempt to open up a comparison between the two disparate events also helps to contest the still widespread assertions about the uniqueness of the Holocaust as a kind of mysterious and ontological event that is "beyond understanding"—as Elie Wiesel famously claimed—and as one that is unrepresentable.[10] Peter Novick, one of the most provocative critics of the "talk of uniqueness and incomparability" surrounding Holocaust discourse in the United States, contends that it "promotes evasion of moral and historical responsibility" for the United States' own complicity in perpetuating historic traumas like slavery or the extermination of Amerindians over centuries.[11] Indeed, the emergence of new fields like comparative genocide studies challenges claims for the Holocaust's uniqueness and invites us to consider events and histories of devastation, such as Hiroshima, the Partition, and the Armenian and Rwandan genocides, among others.[12] I argue, however, that we cannot simply *apply* Holocaust studies' models such as witnessing and the obligatory imperative to remember limit events through repeated telling to such historical contexts as the Partition without attending to their social and cultural specificities. In this section, I address some of the pitfalls that might attend projects of cultural memorialization—such as the remembering of grief as an incitement to war and revenge and the reification of victimhood as a kind of ontological and unchanging status—before positing the notion of an uncanny practice of remembrance that would enable us to go toward the other.

Only in the last two decades has scholarship from the humanities and social sciences begun to address this historic trauma and its continued impact on social and political formations in the subcontinent. Historiographies of nationhood, for instance, in each subcontinental country have been conspicuous in their failure to acknowledge and claim this cataclysmic history, although, invariably, the attention that Partition has received in academic histories in India has been considerably greater than in Pakistan and Bangladesh. It is the loss of territory, however, that has been instituted as national trauma in the official Indian national consciousness, and not the more (im)palpable loss of lives, homes, communities, and selves. Historian Gyanendra Pandey, whose work has been at the center of contemporary Indian rethinking on the events of 1947, argues that this originary moment of division has either been suppressed in colonialist and nationalist historical writing, or it has been narrativized as aberrational and extraordinary. Those who have addressed Partition have spoken primarily of the high politics and constitutional debates involving Nehru, Gandhi, Jinnah, and Mountbatten. As Pandey notes, "[T]his is not a history of the lives and experiences of the people who lived through that time, of the way in which the events of the 1940s were constructed in their minds, of the identities or uncertainties that Partition created or reinforced."[13]

Since the mid-1980s, however, there has been a proliferation of retrospective historical, journalistic, autobiographical, ethnographic, and imaginative materials that attempt to address Partition from the present

historical conjuncture. These belated efforts include commemorative issues in academic journals and popular magazines; English translations
of Indian-language Partition narratives written in the two decades following independence;[14] recently published or resurrected memoirs of
social workers who worked with the newly constituted citizen-refugees
of the two new nations (Anis Kidwai's *In the Shadow of Freedom* and
Kamlaben Patel's *Torn from the Roots*); films like Deepa Mehta's *Earth,*
Pamela Rooks's *Train to Pakistan,* Sabiha Sumar's *Khamosh Pani,* along
with more mainstream Hindi films like *Pinjar* and *Gaddar;* and some
seminal feminist compilations of oral histories of survivors (Ritu Menon's
and Kamla Bhasin's *Borders and Boundaries* and Urvashi Butalia's *The
Other Side of Silence*).[15] As a new and prominent phenomenon in contemporary India, this return to Partition demands to be read in terms of
the politics of the present.

Undoubtedly, renewed academic interest in the Partition has emerged
in response to particular moments of crisis marked by religious conflict.
Many scholars have attested to returning to the events of 1947 only when
prompted by the 1984 anti-Sikh riots—three thousand Sikhs in Delhi were
massacred in the wake of Prime Minister Indira Gandhi's assassination
by her Sikh bodyguard. Until then, Partition had largely come to be ratio-
nalized and accepted as a single, perhaps necessary, act of division that
could never recur, an event from a distinct and discrete historical epoch
increasingly removed from the present moment. Yet, the visceral tangibility of the violence of 1984 forced activists providing food, shelter, and
relief to survivors to confront the looming presence of Partition and its
living ghosts in their present. Ritu Menon movingly describes this experience: "But here was Partition once more in our midst, terrifying for those
who had passed through it in 1947. . . . Yet this was our own country,
our own people, our own home-grown violence. Who could we blame
now?"[16] More recently, the ascendance of the Hindu Right and the destruction of the Babri masjid have resulted in repeated and increasing
violence against Muslims throughout India. Strikingly, the riots sparked
off by Ayodhya were not restricted to India alone but spread across the
borders to Pakistan and Bangladesh as well. Horrified by this resurgence
of religious violence, secularists and anticommunalists of all persuasions
were impelled to return to the violence of Partition in the hope that this
watershed in the history of the subcontinent might have some moral and
political lessons for our times.[17]

Warning us against the perils of amnesia, scholars ask if the disruptive inheritances of Partition can ever be disentangled from the narrative of independence. They remind us that what a culture chooses to remember or forget is inextricably tied to issues of power and hegemony; hence, they contend that forgetting and suppression must be contested by active remembrance.[18] The argument maintains that acts of remembering may prove useful in countering the destructive effects of repression and amnesia. The hope is that such acts may prevent similar instances of violence in the future and enable reconciliation and healing between Hindus, Muslims, and Sikhs.[19] Clearly, these efforts stem, in part, from concern about the imminent loss of the generation that witnessed Partition first hand—thus, Partition scholars have collated valuable survivor testimonies to counteract the official forgetting of Partition suffering in nationalist accounts. Feminist historical work on Partition is part of this broader memorializing imperative, but there are also some marked differences in their aims: feminist scholars such as Ritu Menon, Kamla Bhasin, Urvashi Butalia, and Veena Das also seek to reveal the patriarchal underpinnings of modern nationalist projects and to reclaim women's subjectivities from the margins of history. While my argument about avowing and working through the past of Partition takes its departure from these groundbreaking historical returns to Partition—and indeed it aligns itself with them—I also want to point to some of the risks entailed in projects of memorialization. Memory projects can be (and have been) used to incite violence and revenge in the interest of *consolidating group identities.* Partition stories in particular have been repeatedly deployed in the narratives of Hindutva, particularly by the Rashtriya Swayamsevak Sangh (RSS), to create a narrative of unremitting victimization of "Hindus." In these accounts, the past is figured as a burden for present-day Hindus who must overturn and avenge it in the present. How, then, do we differentiate "our" acts of "cultural memory" from "theirs"?[20] Acknowledging the dangers of memory projects like his own, Gyanendra Pandey nevertheless cautions us about "surrender[ing] the entire field of the history of Partition . . . simply to those right-wing historians."[21] Pandey is undoubtedly right to suggest that we cannot afford to cede the memory of Partition to fundamentalist groups and individuals who seek to provoke hostility and conflict, but we cannot continue to endorse an uncritical mode of remembrance that affirms all such acts of cultural memory without trying to theorize differences in modes of remembrance beyond those of intention. The imperative to return to Partition therefore needs to be elucidated more clearly—to what end and how should those of us who envision the peaceful living together of disparate religious groups and nations in the subcontinent grapple with the memories of Partition?

Recently, these belated historical endeavors to remember Partition have come in for some interesting criticism. In a thought-provoking conversation, entitled "Remembering Partition," political scientist Javeed Alam and historian Suresh Sharma contend that the new oral-historical projects around Partition, which seek to expand the domain of traditional history by excavating the memories of the victims of Partition violence, raise some contentious issues about the "ethics of remembrance."[22] Alam insists that because Partition, unlike the Holocaust, does not allow for a clear distinction between perpetrator and victim (this was not the violence of a fascist state, but a violence of a people killing each other at a moment of a "loss of sanity"), it does not require the kind of institutional memorialization that the Holocaust warranted. Taking as his premise writer Krishna Sobti's statement that "the Partition is difficult to forget, but dangerous to remember," Alam argues that these recent memory projects—50 years after the event—are "morally indefensible" since historians are coercing victims to relive their painful and traumatic pasts in order to fill in the gaps in the historical record without taking into account the cost inflicted anew upon the victims. Unlike in a therapeutic situation in which the survivor presents him/herself to the analyst, these new oral historical projects necessitate a process whereby the interviewer "chases the victim" and elicits a "forgotten memory" (101). The purpose of therapy, by contrast, is to help the traumatized person to "forget the impact of trauma so that it doesn't remain central to his consciousness" (101). Moreover, at a collective level, if "Muslims, Hindus, and Sikhs have to live together in peace and harmony and amity, it is important they *leave behind* these events as something most traumatic, something tragic but something most unfortunate which ought not to have happened" (101). Alam believes that a new generation has emerged for whom Partition is a distinct historical event, a faint memory relegated to a bitter and divisive past, which is where it belongs. In his view, *such a forgetting* is crucial to our politics, to the everydayness of life, and to future peaceful social interaction between communities.

Although his fellow conversationalist, Suresh Sharma, does not share

Alam's belief that the memory of Partition should be forgotten completely, he proposes that since memory itself subsumes both forgetting and remembrance, it must not be viewed as an act of "total remembrance" (100). Everything need not be remembered all the time, and the quest for "total recovery" is dangerous and misplaced, since it might end up "eroding equations of sanity" (102). Sharma recognizes the perils of official amnesia but cautions that Partition's memory "has to be recovered with a sense of deep responsibility and compassion because the very people who indulged in this killing have subsequently worked out equations of coliving, certain norms of more or less sane interaction" (101).

This dialogue about memory raises many crucial questions about the dialectic between remembering and forgetting the historic trauma of Partition, and it compels me to clarify my own argument. While I share Alam's and Sharma's concerns about the ethics of testimonial work, I also believe there are two basic assumptions in their conversation that need to be interrogated. First, the argument that people have worked out norms of coexistence post-Partition ignores the sense of an increasingly beleaguered Muslim minoritarian identity in India, particularly after the destruction of the mosque at Ayodhya, even if everyday life within a community must inevitably revert to an uneasy "normality" following an incident of violence. Thus, we cannot afford to confuse the troubled coexistence of adversaries with the living together of peace and harmony that Derrida envisions. Second, Alam's claim that the traumatic memories of Partition have been "forgotten" is especially problematic. I argue, to the contrary, that Partition must be understood as simultaneously absent and present in postindependence India. While no memorials and monuments have been erected to institutionalize the memories of Partition, the specter of Partition as (literally) the truncation of the nation has always functioned as displaced threat and anxiety within the dominant narratives of the Indian nation. It haunts every instance of separatism in the present; consequently, the Indian state's policies toward peripheral regions like the North East and Kashmir—where a separatist discourse continues to flourish—have been governed and dictated to a large extent by the specter of 1947. Furthermore, the ghosts of Partition persist in the collective memories of families and groups, as evident during both the 1984 and 1992 riots. The traumatic testimonies of survivors, many of whom continued to return to the disturbing memories of Partition as they sought to narrativize their present experience of hurt and violation—"this is Partition all over again"—confirms that even though nationalist histories may have marginalized the event, it continues to linger in the memories of those who lived through the violence.[23]

While it is true that subsequent generations may remain abysmally ignorant about the actual history of Partition—about, say, dates and places involved—memories of Partition violence have inevitably seeped into their consciousnesses, shaping and informing their self-definitions and ways of being in the world, especially for the populations of those regions that were directly impacted by the event. Indeed, the very existence of Pakistan continues to be experienced as a trauma in the popular Indian imagination. Correspondingly, Indian Muslims, invested with the unfair burden of Partition's legacies, are often held accountable not only for the past of Partition but also for the ongoing actions and policies of the Pakistani state. Routinely constructed as "strangers" or as the "enemy within" who must be watched or expelled across the border, Muslims are viewed as coterminous with the Pakistani other and are constantly under pressure to prove and affirm their patriotic credentials. Consider, for instance, the recent pogrom of Muslims in Gujarat, where perpetrators repeatedly referred to Muslims as Pakistanis and terrorized them by horrific and inhuman acts of brutality that were intended to literally wipe out the other. Anthropologists Deepak Mehta and Roma Chatterji provide an especially evocative instance of such an identification of Muslims with Pakistanis in the reorganization of space and territorial boundaries in particular localities. In their ethnographic work with people in Dharavi, a local slum in Bombay, they found particular areas or landmarks being designated as the India–Pakistan "border" in the aftermath of the 1992–93 riots.[24] To argue, therefore, that new generations have successfully "left behind" the traumatic memories of Partition is to ignore the intergenerational transmission of memory within families and groups. My point is not to equate the impact and significance of memories recalled from personal experience and those acquired secondhand but merely to point to the power and hold of second-generational traumatic memory—what Toni Morrison has so evocatively called "rememory" in *Beloved*, her moving novel about slavery.[25] Thus, it is crucial that subsequent generations come to a radically different understanding of this founding trauma rather than rely on sanctioned nationalist histories and familial and group memories.

What I want to retain from Javeed Alam and Suresh Sharma's dialogue on the ethics of memory work is the crucial reminder that such projects should be undertaken with a deep sense of responsibility and compassion. Hence, I interrogate the need for endless testimonies from survivors of traumatic events, be it as a means of completing the historical record or as a mode of "healing" for the individual and the collective.[26] As Ana Douglass and Thomas Vogler note, the current "trend" for representing collective traumatic events through the compilation of individual personal testimonies has become a "flourishing industry" that rests on the problematic assumption that somehow the totality of an event can be grasped through the massive accumulation of survivor testimonies.[27] This is by no means to suggest that witness testimony does not have a crucial role to play in the avowal of historic traumas or in the establishment of past injustices (for example, by human rights groups) but rather to recognize that the project of "total" recovery is one doomed to failure. Undeniably, the work of Pandey, Butalia, Menon and Bhasin, and Das has paved the way for considering the enduring legacies of Partition—and the task is certainly not over—but for those of us who follow in their wake, I suggest the goal should not be to add to the compilation of barbarities by means of still more testimony in some sort of misplaced effort to "complete the historical record." Survivor testimonies are not transparent accounts of reality; they are mediated and partial narratives shaped by their current social and cultural contexts, especially when they are recorded so many years after the event. Since historic events of such complexity are always under construction and continually modified and redescribed in light of contemporary concerns, we can never hope to come to a complete knowledge of the past. Recognizing the irreducible alterity of the past even as we acknowledge its deep influence on the present is therefore crucial to projects of cultural remembrance like my own. This mode of cultural memorialization stands in sharp contrast to Hindutva projects of memory that affirm an enduring narrative of perpetual victimization of "Hindus" by an undifferentiated collectivity of "Muslims" that stretches all the way back to the medieval past.

Sharma's insight that memory is as much about forgetting as it is about remembering is also worth reflecting upon as we take on the urgent task of avowing and working through the Partition. The peculiar dilemma that confronts memory work is that although we must work against the closure of amnesia that is so typical of hegemonic nationalist accounts, we also must contain and seal off memories of violence that might contaminate the subjectivities of future generations (as Partition memories have in the context of the Indian subcontinent). Partition scholars therefore must work toward enabling subsequent generations to put an end to the violence. The assumption that endlessly rehearsing the past is the only path to "healing" for the individual survivor or the collective ignores the ways in which a deliberate "forgetting" of the past—even as it is never really forgotten—may be necessary in order to cope with the aftermath of violence. For example, on the basis of their ethnographic work with survivors of the Bombay riots, Mehta and Chatterji conclude that "reparation cannot take the form of justice [by means of the law], that coexistence is possible only if the past is deliberately put aside," where forgetting is a self-conscious and deliberate choice (238). Such a view of "forgetting" may allow for the resumption of everyday life within communities divided by violence, especially in social contexts where it is difficult to separate perpetrators from victims. This is the living together of the social contract, of pragmatism, and of a compulsory tolerance—for, as Derrida asks, how can one live otherwise? Yet undoubtedly, those who belong to minority and marginalized communities must necessarily engage in a more active forgetting to enable such living together. How, then, can we acknowledge the concerns of minority groups and think beyond the living together of pragmatism? I agree with Veena Das and Arthur Kleinman that a *double movement seems necessary* for remaking worlds shattered by violence.[28] On the one hand, at the macro level of nation and state, we must work toward the creation of alternate public spheres that can recognize and acknowledge the suffering of victims of mass violence or genocide; on the other, at the micro level, we must also allow for the rebuilding of interpersonal relationships and the establishment of new ways of inhabiting the world together for communities and survivors. In the spirit of this insight, I argue that a living together of peace and amity that exceeds the uneasy tolerance of adversaries will be possible only when attended by an avowal of Partition at the macro level of the nation, even as we must respect the need of survivors and communities to deliberately "put aside" their painful memories. In what follows, I take up the question of the place and relevance of literature to this enterprise.

Literary narratives, like recent historical work, contribute to the creation of alternate public spheres that acknowledge the impossible past of Partition. However, literary and cultural accounts also provide a valuable form of "working through," particularly in contexts in which there has been silence and erasure of traumatic pasts that are threatening to the precarious stability of the national order. LaCapra points out that "working through," while never completely transcending a traumatic collective past, is essential to the project of imagining alternative futures and effecting more desirable social and political institutions.[29] The fictional narratives I examine in this chapter are second-generational acts of remembrance that return to Partition from the late 1980s and 1990s in an effort to work though its ongoing ramifications. They are recounted by narrators who are at a generational remove from the events of 1947 but whose subjectivities have been deeply affected by the legacies of Partition. Characterized by belatedness, secondariness, and distance, these fictions direct us to what I call an "uncanny practice of remembrance" in an effort to envision a living together of peace and justice in the subcontinent.

Marianne Hirsch's work on "postmemory" in the context of the Holocaust offers a useful point of departure in thinking about the significance of second-generational acts of memory for engaging contemporary religio-nationalist conflict in the subcontinent.[30] Hirsch is concerned with the ways in which writers and artists of the second generation bear witness to events they didn't experience but whose effects they have received belatedly through the intergenerational transmission of trauma. She defines postmemory as "retrospective witnessing by adoption" whereby the children of survivors attempt to grapple with the traumatic memories they have inherited through "a consciously and necessarily mediated form of identification," one which acknowledges the alterity of the past. In Hirsch's definition, postmemory is a form of *identification* and empathy, but one that resists the appropriation of the other or the compulsive reenactment of the past as "rememory."[31] Although she allows that postmemorial practices or narratives need not be limited to the family or to an ethnic or national group—that is, *they need not necessarily be linked to an identity position*—her examples tend to focus on the transmission of memory as an intersubjective practice within the family, particularly between mothers and daughters.

In contrast, the novels of second-generational remembrance I examine in this chapter take up memory work as an "ethics of alterity."[32]

Interrogating both familial and group mythologies, these literary narratives exemplify Spivak's understanding of ethics as the effort to go toward the other by rendering our home *unheimlich* or uncanny.[33] Spivak draws on Freud's notion of the uncanny, which signifies "the turning of what is homey into something *unheimlich*"—the transformation of the familiar into something unfamiliar and frightening—to elaborate her understanding of ethics (74). In Freud, the normative definition of the uncanny is to be found in certain "neurotic men" who experience the female genital organs as anxiety-provoking: "This *unheimlich* place, however, is the entrance to the former *Heim* [home] of all human beings, to the place where each one of us lived once upon a time and in the beginning." (Sigmund Freud, cited in Spivak, 74). Spivak deploys Freud's "European male notion of the type of the uncanny as an allegory of reading" to trace the (different) figuration of the uncanny in three literary texts: Joseph Conrad's *Heart of Darkness,* Tayeb Salih's *Season of Migration to the North,* and Mahasweta Devi's *Pterodactyl, Puran Sahay and Pirtha* (78). While she reads *Heart of Darkness* as a classic figuration of the *unheimlich* in its representation of the angst produced by the familiar humanity of the African—specifically by the figure of the African woman—she suggests that *Season of Migration to the North* undoes the polarizations of colonizer and colonized in its narrator's endeavor to imagine the European other as human (and by undoing stereotypical notions of gender). However, the experience of colonialism transforms the "familiar shared humanity of that strange and unfamiliar country called England into a source of fear and anxiety" in Salih's novel as well (58). Similarly, I examine the ways in which *The Shadow Lines, Looking through Glass,* and "Family Ties" turn what is homely and familiar—the homogenous and unified (Indian) nationalist subject—into something *unheimlich* and unfamiliar by means of their literal or metaphorical journeys into the past. While *The Shadow Lines* radically calls into question the very concept of separate nation-spaces by reminding us of the permeability of national borders on the subcontinent, *Looking through Glass* reveals the majoritarian—Hindu—underpinnings of the "neutral" and "secular" post-Partition Indian citizen-subject. And, although Baldwin's short story "Family Ties" offers a secondary act of identificatory witnessing within the matrilineal family along the lines of Hirsch's notion of postmemory, it, like the two novels, also renders *unheimlich* and frightening the normative *male* nationalist self from a specifically gendered perspective. Together, these fictions, in their return to Partition, direct us to an uncanny mode of remembrance that defamiliarizes what is home—what it means to be "Indian"—from various peripheral subject positions. Such a radically different understanding of Partition—and of the nationalist subject that it inaugurated—I argue, is crucial for thinking about ethical possibilities of coexistence in the present.

Amitav Ghosh's *The Shadow Lines*

Amitav Ghosh's *The Shadow Lines* exemplifies the imperative to grapple with the traumatic legacies of Partition retrospectively through its second-generation narrator. It seeks to remember and memorialize some of the gaps and silences that underlie the origin and making of the modern Indian nation-state—silences around specific moments and events, which, if articulated, would throw the "imagined community" of the Indian nation into disarray and which thus cannot be acknowledged in the national memory. In the process, this narrative obliges us to differentiate between official memory as the permissible and legitimate recollection of our national pasts and other kinds of cultural memories that get transmitted across generations. Although the novel is not set during the Partition or in the years leading up to it, it bears eloquent witness to the trauma of Partition by testifying to its ongoing legacies. Ghosh has written of how *The Shadow Lines* emerged as a response to the anti-Sikh riots that he witnessed in Delhi in the aftermath of Indira Gandhi's assassination. Like many in his generation, he had considered Partition as an event in the distant past that could never happen again, but 1984 shattered that comfortable sense of detachment. He explains how *The Shadow Lines* became a book not about any one event (though the novel is preoccupied with the 1964 riots that he experienced as a child) but about the shifting meanings of such events and their effects on the individuals who lived through them.[34] The novel traces its post-Partition narrator's gradual realization that borders between nations are at once a source of immense violence and an absurd illusion, especially in the context of the partitioned subcontinent. By impelling into public memory the transnational violence that paradoxically ties together the people of the region—even as they may forge their identities precisely by insisting upon their permanent and essential difference from the other across the border—the novel seeks to repudiate the cartographic, political, and psychic borders instituted at Partition as ephemeral "shadow lines." It undoes the polarizations of "Indian" and "Pakistani" by challenging the spatial imaginary of Indian and Pakistani nationalisms and their concomitant territorializations of identity. *The Shadow Lines* thus renders uncanny the concept of distinct and autonomous—Indian and Pakistani—nation-states that were inaugurated with independence/Partition.

The narrator's grandmother, Tha'mma, serves as the representative figure for an exclusionary nationalism that seeks to demarcate fixed differences between the Indian self and the Pakistani other in the novel. Tha'mma belongs to the generation that was brought up on the nationalist dream for independence from colonial rule, and she is willing to kill for her freedom. Her validation of violence in the service of the nation's freedom is especially apparent in the story she recounts to her young grandson and her nephew, Tridib, about her encounter with a "terrorist." Tha'mma was in college in Dhaka in the early 1920s when armed anticolonial resistance movements were at their peak. The colonial government had responded predictably with all the coercive mechanisms of an authoritarian state, including such measures as arrests, deportations, and executions. When the police arrested one of her classmates, a shy quiet boy, during a raid, Tha'mma was taken by surprise because he was most unlike her image of a valorous nationalist. She speaks nostalgically of the event and wishes, "if only she had known, if only she had been working with him, she would have warned him somehow . . . she would have gone to Khulna with him too, and stood at his side, with a pistol in her hands, waiting for the English magistrate."[35]

Tha'mma is a firm believer in the necessity of war and bloodshed for forging an internally coherent unity within the geographical confines of the nation-state. She cites Britain as a paradigm of successful nationalism because "it took those people a long time to build that country; hundreds of years, years and years of war and bloodshed. . . . War is their religion. That's what it takes to make a country" (77–78). She is convinced that India also needs to draw its borders in blood before it can achieve that state of exalted nationalism; only once that happens will "people forget they were born this or that, Muslim or Hindu, Bengali or Punjabi: they become a family born of the same pool of blood" (78). Like most good citizens of modern states, Tha'mma has internalized the language of modernity, which demands that the nation be the privileged site of collective identity and the state be the sole legitimate purveyor of violence. She can only endorse a vision of living together that is limited to those who have been given to us by blood, soil, and statutory convention.

However, the gaps and fissures in Tha'mma's notions of blood and belonging are laid bare in one of the most poignant sections of the novel. Born in Dhaka, Tha'mma suddenly discovers home and nationality to be at odds with one another, with Partition. Although she refuses to call herself a "refugee," since she had left Dhaka before Partition, the division of the country along religious lines ensured that she, as a Hindu, had been unable to return to her natal home until her final fateful trip in 1964. That year, she returns to Dhaka to rescue her senile old uncle who, in spite of the danger to his life as a Hindu in predominantly Muslim East Pakistan, has stubbornly refused to move from the place of his birth. Tha'mma decides she must bring him "home" to Calcutta to save him from what has now become "that country" in her vocabulary (136). The nation is viewed as synonymous with home at this point in Tha'mma's narrative. In fact, Tha'mma's spatial conceptualization of nationalism requires a tangible border between India and Pakistan in the form of trenches or soldiers pointing guns that would clearly demarcate the territory of the two nations. Thus, she is troubled by the apparent lack of physical borders between the two new nations:

> But if there aren't any trenches or anything, how are people to
> know? I mean where's the difference then? And if there's no difference, both sides will be the same; it will be just like it used to
> be before, when we used to catch a train in Dhaka and get off in
> Calcutta the next day without anybody stopping us. What was it
> all for then—Partition and all the killing and everything—if there
> isn't something in between? (151)

Yet there is something "in between": as her son informs her, "the border isn't on the frontier; it's right inside the airport" (151). The logic of modernity and its corollary nation-statehood work in more subtle and coercive ways—Tha'mma now needs a visa to visit her place of birth. As she considers the possibility of filling in bureaucratic forms on which she

will have to list her place of birth as Dhaka despite her Indian nationality, she is faced with the disturbing knowledge that nation and home
are not always identical. Her ambivalence about "home" is further under-
lined when, in an interesting slip, she speaks of *"coming* home" to Dhaka
(152). Her grandson, the adult narrator, who at the time had seized the
opportunity to correct his schoolmistress grandmother, understands, in
retrospect, that people like her—who were granted nation-statehood at
the same instant as they were irrevocably dislocated from their homes—
were continually looking for a language that would allow them to come to
terms with this tragic irony of history.

Tha'mma's unwavering faith in creeds of nationality is finally shaken
when she is confronted with the tenacious resistance of her old uncle to
the newly invented national identities of the subcontinent. Refusing to
leave Dhaka, he tells her, "Once you start moving you never stop. . . . I
don't believe in this India-Shindia. It's all very well, you are going away
now, but suppose when you get there they decide to draw another line
somewhere? What will you do then? Where will you move to? . . . As
for me, I was born here, and I'll die here" (215). Ironically, however, her
nephew Tridib is killed during the same visit, a victim of the communal
violence that has percolated from Kashmir, India, to Dhaka, East Pakistan,
thus ensuring her eternal hatred and bitterness for that "other" country,
once her home. A year later, as India and Pakistan fight each other in the
1965 war, she donates her treasured gold chain—her husband's first gift to
her—to the war fund. She informs her frightened grandson that she did
it for his sake: "We have to kill them before they kill us; we have to wipe
them out. . . . This is the only chance. . . . We're fighting them properly at
last with tanks and guns and bombs" (237).

But her grandson, the secondary witness of this novel, comes to a very
different understanding of the borders that were ratified at Partition as he
undertakes an imaginative journey into the past. This is not to say that
mapping the contours of this repressed past is easy: "[It] is a struggle with
silence" he writes, for silence marks the site of both familial and national
trauma in this text. His uncle Tridib's death at the hands of the Muslim
mob in 1964 stands as the central traumatic event of the novel. To return
to the events that led to Tridib's death, however, entails not only an ex-
cavation of a painful familial history but also the unveiling of a national
silence, an unspoken collective agreement to forget those moments in his-

tory that might contest the representational claims of nationalism. What is it, the narrator wonders, which makes us chronicle events like wars but forget the millions who die in religious riots? He muses that even though the same number of people died in the riots of 1964 as died in the Indo-China war of 1962, the riots quickly vanish from public memory and leave no trace of their devastation within historical accounts. "What is it that makes all those things called 'politics' so eloquent and these other unnameable things so silent?" he asks (228).

Consequently, the narrator embarks on a voyage of discovery to trace and uncover some of the silences that shroud sites of personal and national trauma. The journey takes him to a land outside of physical space and tangible distances as he attempts a piecemeal reconstruction of the past through old newspapers, the stories of such characters as Robi and May, and his own childhood memories. An exploration that interweaves the public and the private, it finally enables him to make the connections, all these years later, between Tridib's death in Dhaka, his own terrifying experience of religious conflict as a child in Calcutta, and the disappearance of a sacred relic: a single hair of the Prophet Mohammed from a mosque in Srinagar, Kashmir. The narrator discovers that in December 1963 the Mu-i-Mubarak vanished from the famous Hazratbal mosque in Srinagar. Although people from different religious communities in Kashmir gathered to mourn this collective loss and protest against the theft of the relic, many in Pakistan condemned this incident as an attack against "Muslim" identity. Subsequently, a demonstration in Khulna, a little town in East Pakistan, turned violent, and the riots spread to the capital Dhaka, forcing the minority Hindu community to flee across the border to Calcutta. As the incoming refugees brought rumors of violence against Hindus in Pakistan, Indian Muslims in Calcutta were assaulted in turn to avenge the perceived attacks on "Hindu" identity.

As he uncovers the chain of events that led to Tridib's death, the narrator begins to comprehend how nationalism is a deeply spatial and geographical construct that territorializes identities through primordial claims of blood and belonging tied to particular spaces. Liisa Malkki points out that in this "national order of things," the world is conceived as a multicolored school atlas wherein different colors represent different nations—one country cannot simultaneously be another. The world of nations is thus conceived as a discrete spatial partitioning of territory" where there can be no "bleeding boundaries."[36] The post-Partition narrator of *The Shadow Lines* had grown up with the certitudes of essential and fixed differences across national boundaries "simply because Dhaka was in another country" (219). In retrospect, he realizes, "I grew up believing in the truth of the precepts that were available to me: I believed in the reality of space; I believed that distance separates, that it is a corporeal substance; I believed in the reality of nations and borders; I believed that across the border there existed another reality" (219). But as he traces the sequence of events that caused Tridib's death, he is able to undo the polarizations of Indian and Pakistani by recognizing the "looking glass" nature of the borders that were an inheritance of both colonialism and independence. He understands that while the people of East Pakistan had little interest in the fate of mosques in Vietnam and South China, which were much closer in terms of physical distance, reports of the disappearance of a religious relic from a shrine in far-away Kashmir, India, could lead them to attack the minority Hindu community in their own country. The narrator's "voyage to a land outside space" forces him to confront "this other thing" that continues to yoke the denizens of the subcontinent regardless of the distinct national borders etched to separate them (224). Ghosh thus endorses the notion of a subcontinental collectivity, something that "sets apart the thousand million people who inhabit the subcontinent from the rest of the world—not language, not food, not music—it is the special quality of loneliness that grows out of the fear of the war *between oneself and one's image in the mirror*" (my emphasis, 204). That which has been deemed "other"—the Pakistani—now appears as a mere reflection of the familiar, homely nationalist self.

While the cosmopolitan idealism of the narrative also speaks nostalgically of a time when Europe was a better place without borders and observes how London and Berlin seemed to become mirror images during the Second World War, it is apparent that the metaphor of the shadow lines is used specifically to refer to the entangled relationships of partitioned nations within the subcontinent. This metaphor is abundantly clear in the instance when the adult narrator draws two circles on Tridib's old Bartholomew's Atlas: the first with Khulna at its center and Srinagar on the circumference and the other with Milan at its center and the region within the same 1,200-mile radius. The narrator realizes that all it took was a week for the violence to spread from Srinagar to Khulna within his first circle, but he cannot imagine an event that could connect the people of Milan to the cities on the periphery of the second circle—Stockholm, Dublin, Casablanca, Alexandria—except war. He concludes that within this second circle, "there were only states and citizens; there were no people at all" (233). By taking us to the transnational violence that makes a mockery of separate nation-states on the subcontinent, *The Shadow Lines* suggests that although the inhabitants of this region may have come to believe in the "special enchantment of lines" and borders, nevertheless, they continue to be bound to one another in a specular relationship of animosity and violence (233).

The Shadow Lines thus reveals the futility of any attempt to grapple with contemporary Hindu–Muslim violence in India in isolation from the shadow of Pakistan. Those who anxiously affirm the patriotic credentials of Indian Muslims by marking their difference from the Pakistani other risk reiterating boundaries that continue to be questioned by border-crossing violence, including that manifested post-Ayodhya and powerfully memorialized in Ghosh's novel. Only by undoing narratives of essential-ized differences between a "secular" India and a rabidly "fundamentalist" Islamic Pakistan, as the narrator learns, can we begin to think about pos-sibilities of multireligious coexistence in the subcontinent. While Ghosh is also careful to invoke the flip side of the transnational subcontinental collectivity—"the madness of a riot is a pathological inversion, but also therefore a reminder, of that indivisible sanity that binds people to each other independently of their governments"—it is evident that the affect of violence overwhelms all other affective ties of solidarity between the people of the subcontinent in this text (230). Only once does the novel point to the deep genealogical affiliations, the shared history and geog-raphy of the subcontinent. Reflecting on Tridib's death fifteen years later, after a chance encounter with a Bangladeshi restaurant owner in London, his brother Robi asks in anguish: "Why don't they draw thousands of little lines through the whole subcontinent, and give each little place a new name? What would it change? It's a mirage; the whole thing is a mirage. *How can anyone divide a memory?*" (my emphasis, 247). "Memory" here serves as shorthand for the shared past and common culture of the sub-continent. But the dense texture of these mutual memories is never really delineated in this text.[37]

The narrator can only express a *"longing* for everything that was not in oneself, a torment of the flesh, that carried one beyond the limits of one's mind to other times and places, and even if one was lucky, *to a place where there was no border between oneself and one's image in the mirror*" (29). In this passage, the narrator articulates a profound yearning for accessing the other as a self by means of the imagination, which, as Spivak argues, is crucial to the experience of ethics.[38] However, alterity in this novel functions merely as a reflection of the self. The trope of the mirror image is used repeatedly in the novel to designate the other. For example, Nick serves as the narrator's reflection, only better and more desirable as seen through Ila's eyes, much as Dhaka and Calcutta come to function as each other's images during the 1964 riots. As Spivak points out, it is not enough to recognize the "self-consolidating other as the self's mere negation."[39] Alterity must remain underived from us; it is not just our dialectical negation. If we grasp ethics as a problem of relation rather than of knowledge, then, we must learn to imagine the other as an other as well as a self.[40] Although Ghosh's novel serves to undo the binaries of Indian and Pakistani, in figuring the Pakistani other as a mere reflection of the Indian self, it runs the risk of subsuming the other into the self (much like Rushdie's vision of love in *The Moor's Last Sigh*).[41]

However, the novel does provide a more nuanced account of the alterity of the past. By way of its second-generational act of memorialization, *The Shadow Lines* enables us to understand the significance of Partition as a living history that endures in the present of the subcontinent. But if the past in this novel is viewed as intimately related to the present, it is also understood as irreducibly different. Unlike Ila, who lives so intensely in a present shut away "from the tidewaters of the past and the future by steel floodgates," the narrator seeks to envision the contours of the past through his imaginative ability to travel to other times and places (30). For example, he is able to evoke his grandmother's visit to Dhaka through his empathic imagination: "I tried then to see Dhaka as she must have seen it that night, sitting by her window. But I hadn't been to Dhaka, and in any case her Dhaka had long since vanished into the past. I had only her memories to go on, and those put together could only give me a faint sepia-tinted picture of her other arrivals in Dhaka, decades ago" (193). Yet, he is also aware that his desire to imaginatively access his grandmother's visit cannot substitute for her visceral and concrete experiences of Dhaka in the 1960s: "I can only guess at the outlines of the image that lived in her mind, but I have no inkling at all of the sounds and smells she remembered" (193). Similarly, even as he attempts to reconstruct the lives of Alan Tresawsen and his friends in wartime London—through Tridib's stories about his visit to London and through old photographs—he also understands that "there are moments in time that are not *knowable:* nobody can ever know what it was like to be young and intelligent in the summer of 1939 in London or Berlin" (68).

The Shadow Lines invites us to consider the past as intimately linked to the present, often haunting it, yet it is also careful to grant the pastness of the past and its irreducible alterity. The post-Partition narrator of this novel does not presume that acts of cultural memory like his own can replicate different moments in the past simply by attempting to memorialize them—hence his astonishment at Ila's easy arrogance when she quickly and glibly equates her life in present-day Stockwell with that of Tresawsen and his friends in the 1940s. Indeed, in its very form, *The Shadow Lines* underscores the difficulties of remembrance: the fragmented and piecemeal form of the narrative emphasizes that the past can only be recuperated through narratives and stories, acknowledging thereby the unavailability of the original experience and the mediated nature of acts of cultural memorialization, especially when they take place from a generational remove. Ghosh's nuanced perspective on different temporalities has something important to teach current projects of memorialization that often view present-day riots as compulsive reenactments of the original trauma of Partition. While subsequent generations must recognize the perils of amnesia, second-generational acts of cultural memory cannot afford to collapse the differences between past and present, as is often the case with survivor accounts that experience each new instance of violence as a repetition of the first originary trauma or with the collective memories of groups that deploy past traumas in the interest of identity politics.

In contrast to memory projects that serve to consolidate the identities of groups, *The Shadow Lines* directs us to an uncanny mode of remembrance that enables us to go toward the other. The novel attests to the importance not only of avowing the founding trauma of Partition but also of coming to a radically different—defamiliarized—understanding of Partition and the separate and autonomous nation-states it is said to have inaugurated.

Mukul Kesavan's *Looking through Glass*

If *The Shadow Lines* highlights the power and the limits of the empathic imagination in accessing other times and places at which one was not physically present, Mukul Kesavan's debut novel, *Looking through Glass,* has its narrator literally transported to the pre-Partition past through the device of time travel. Kesavan's second-generation narrator, a photographer in contemporary India, is on his way to Banaras to bury his grandmother's ashes when he falls through a time warp and finds himself in 1942, one of the most politically charged years in the history of Indian nationalism. As the narrator attempts to use his new zoom lens for the first time from a bridge just short of Lucknow, training it on a man with a telescope looking up at his train, he loses his balance and falls into the frame of the picture. Reminiscent of Alice walking through a mirror in Lewis Carroll's *Through the Looking Glass,* the unnamed narrator steps across the glass of the camera lens into the space of the photographic image—and into a different time. *Looking through Glass* invites us to step across the boundary that ostensibly separates past from present and to reconsider Partition from a minoritarian perspective through its protagonist's encounter with a Muslim family of Lucknow. Once he steps into the frame of the image, history can no longer be viewed from the comfort of distance provided by the camera or by a detached second-generational point of view. The narrator's initial response to his displacement in time is to insulate himself from this world as much as he can: "If I stayed indoors as quietly and indifferently as possible, I would return to a present unchanged by its past."[42] As the story unfolds, however, it maps a shift in the "secular" Hindu protagonist who moves from wanting to be a disengaged "accidental tourist" in the "alien" time of 1942 to someone whose most intense desire is to *belong* to his adopted Muslim family and to make a home with them.

Always and already aware that Partition was an earth-shattering event in the history of the subcontinent that forever transformed the lives of millions of people, the narrator lives in constant fear that Ammi, Masroor, and Asharfi—the Muslim family that has offered him refuge following his fall into their time—will either die or make their way to the newly constituted Islamic nation, Pakistan, leaving him alone and bereft in this unfamiliar time. Forced to inhabit a different subject position by virtue of his relationship with his adopted family, the second-generation (upper-caste) Hindu narrator comes to a very different understanding of Partition. In staging its protagonist's encounter with the Muslim other of pre-Partition India, the novel renders unfamiliar the representative nationalist subject of postindependence India. It reveals the majoritarian presuppositions underlying the concept of the blank "secular" Indian citizen.

The novel traces the ways in which the figure of the Muslim has come to be constituted as the self-consolidating other of the representative (Hindu) nationalist self. Muslims are viewed as "circumcised monsters" who are radically different from, and therefore qualitatively subordinate to, a normative upper-caste Hindu self that seeks to represent itself as culturally neutral—and hence "secular." This narrative of enduring and fixed differences between the Hindu self and the Muslim other is most clearly enunciated in the narrator's and Haasan's childhood perceptions. Haasan, the family friend and confidante of Masroor's family, is an upper-caste Iyengar Brahmin from Mysore raised to believe that a mosque is a "Turka (Muslim) hatchery, and its dome a mother egg, which went to work once a week on Fridays, and produced hundreds of freshly laid Turkas" (73). He is taught that one in every six persons is a Turka and that one in six is too many. Although his father's Muslim friend, Mirza, is allowed to visit them at home and is even served coffee, the glass he uses must be cleaned with burning coals before it can be used again. Similarly, the narrator realizes how he himself was raised on stories of "Muslim mischief" and came to believe in the figure of the sinister, plotting, and menacing Muslim despite growing up "like other secular people in independent India" (175). Clearly, the Muslim in this discourse becomes the site of excess—everything that is deemed as extraneous to the nation—so that the (Hindu) nationalist subject can consolidate its own subject status.[43]

While the novel interrogates the notion of essential and fixed differences between Hindus and Muslims, it also contests the homogenizing discourse of Indian secular nationalism, in which the unbearable pressure to conform to a blank humanity divorced of all identitarian claims and affiliations falls unfailingly on the Muslim. This is especially evident in the caricatured portrait of the dilettantish Congresswoman, Madam Bose, who makes the typical claims about the Congress party being a "secular" organization with neither Muslims nor Hindus:

You must have heard them say that the Congress doesn't speak for
the Muslims, that our Quit India movement is a Hindu plot. . . .
But I cannot prove to you that this freedom will mean freedom
for Muslims. . . . I cannot prove that the Congress is secular; I
don't know if there is a single Muslim among my comrades. But I
will not apologize for this because I know that there isn't a single
Hindu either; *there are only nationalists.* (98, my emphasis)

As the spokesperson for the Indian National Congress, Madam Bose articulates a vision of the transcendent nationalist subject, one who stands
above the ties of religion, culture, language, or caste. The Congress seeks
to uphold and privilege national identities over and above all others, as
evinced in her belief that "we are Indians first" (99). But, as the narrator
quickly realizes, it is not insignificant that this speech is delivered to a
predominantly Muslim audience. The test of nationalism is always made
before a minoritarian constituency; Hindus are never asked to authenti-
cate or prove their nationalist credentials. Thus, the novel underscores
the limits of secular nationalism in its desire to create a homogeneous
and uniform national identity that would render all differences of belief,
practice, and history unimportant or insignificant.

However, through his friend Masroor, the narrator encounters a
very different narrative of the nation, one that contests the hegemonic,
Congress-led version of the nation. In the novel, Masroor is the most eloquent spokesman of a Muslim viewpoint that desires a united India, but
not at the cost of rendering invisible what was, at the time, the largest
Muslim polity in the world:

The whole truth is that there are eighty million Mussalmans in
this country, who are invisible. . . . Not invisible to everyone. . . .
Not to the British who count us. Not to those Hindus who hate
us, who see us everywhere—circumcised monsters who bathe
once a year and breed all the time. It is the Congress which can't
see us. It is the party of the nation that is blind.
    *It first bleaches us with its secularism till we are transparent
and then walks through us, as you and I would walk through
jinns and ghosts. For Nehru's Congress, we are permanently invisible.* When we're for it we aren't Muslims, we're human beings

transparent in our humanity. When we're against it, we still aren't Muslims, because then we are feudal or bourgeois, some abstract sort of anti-social villain. (my emphasis, 189–90)

Masroor points out the peculiar predicament of Muslims in the India of the 1940s caught, as they are, between the dialectic of hyper-visibility (from the British who enumerate them and those right-wing Hindus who hate them) and invisibility (from the Congress that claims to represent all Indians). It is evident that the choice that modern nationalism grants its religious and ethnic minorities is either to assimilate into the dominant nationalist culture or to be charged with the familiar accusations of treachery or disloyalty. According to this discourse, Muslims can only become "true" Indian nationalists if they disavow all claims to being Muslim. As a former ticket-bearing member of the Congress, Masroor is bitter and disillusioned at the treatment that the Congress has meted out to its Muslim members. Subsequently, in a classic magical realist gesture, the author allegorizes this effacement of Indian Muslims by the Congress: thousands of Congress Muslims, including Masroor, literally disappear after the Congress proclaims its resolution that the British must "quit India."

The Quit India movement of 1942 becomes a historical watershed in this text, above all for the ways in which it intensifies the political rifts between Hindus and Muslims. It is not the political agenda of the Quit India resolution that is opposed by Masroor and others like him as much as it is the timing of the declaration. The Muslims who disappear are those who share in common a resistance to the League's demand for a separate Muslim state: Pakistan; in fact, they are all committed to the ideal of an undivided India. But it is the Congress's refusal to understand their perspective that leads Masroor—the strident anticommunalist who would do anything to prevent communal conflict, including forestalling a Hindu–Muslim cricket match—to boldly and visibly proclaim his Muslimness. His response to the Congress's blindness, its "bleached secularism," is to propose that the Muslims of India "simplify themselves" and become opaque in the name of Islam by embracing every visible marker of Muslim identity beards, skullcaps, and burqas (191–92). His objective: to force the Congress to acknowledge that Muslim perspectives and situations may differ from the monolithic nationalist version.

In keeping with his interrogation of official secular nationalism, Kesavan, by means of his protagonist's encounter with the Muslim other, also turns the apparent neutrality of the narrator's initial "secular" outlook into a source of anxiety and unfamiliarity. As Spivak argues, something must come forth into the new and unfamiliar in order for it to become *unheimlich*.[44] In the beginning, the ostensibly secular post-Partition narrator makes numerous erroneous presumptions about Muslims (despite having grown out of his fears of the threatening Muslim). One of the most explicit instances of this ignorance is demonstrated in the narrator's belief that Haasan is a Shia Muslim from South India, given his name and its apparent connection with Shia belief. This presumption leads him to another—that Muslims are liable to believe in the myth of Mahdis or Redeemers in hiding—hence Haasan's conviction that the untraceable Masroor is incognito. But when Haasan divulges that he is an Iyengar Hindu named after his ancestral town—Haasan, not *Hasan,* the grandson of the Prophet—the presumptuous narrator is rendered speechless and forced to confront his majoritarian assumptions. Gradually, however, the narrator learns to be more sensitive to tangible Muslim beliefs and practices that are different from his own. In a significant instance, he wonders why his adopted Muslim family use a kettle with a curving spout to wash their bottoms instead of the "usual" mug:

> [L]ike other secular people in independent India I had been brought up to believe that religion was a private matter, confined to the inner space between brain and bowels, so it couldn't possibly make a difference to arse-washing techniques which fell outside its scope in the secular realm. I was also taught that differences were unimportant since we were all identical in our essential humanity. So I never asked and I still don't know what the kettle was for. (175)

For the first time, the narrator is able to acknowledge to himself that his "secularism" may be the product of his particular Hindu upbringing, which takes upper-caste Hindu beliefs and practices to be normative. Kesavan indicates that liberal formulations of secularism—now in their postcolonial incarnations—are able to deal with religious differences only by dissolving such differences to a homogenizing narrative of an essential humanity. The novel interrogates this kind of enlightenment narrative of the oneness of all religions—where those religions that have been deemed "other" or "minor" can never quite be the same as the original (post-Reformation Christianity or reformed Hinduism in the case of post-Partition India). It points to the profoundly imperial universalism underlying such claims, whereby all differences of culture and religion are rendered irrelevant. It makes clear that the discounting of difference itself can be done only from privileged majoritarian positions secure in their own authority.

In this passage, Kesavan also questions the paradigmatic liberal dictum about the private status of religion, a construction that works to render religion irrelevant to worldly concerns, in keeping with the work of scholars like Talal Asad, Jose Casanova, and Gauri Viswanathan.[45] Interrogating the modern demarcation of the religious and the secular, he demonstrates how those religions—such as Islam—whose scope and teachings *visibly* extend to the domain of the social and the cultural (to "arse-washing techniques," as he so succinctly puts it) are rendered rigid and fundamentalist and therefore inferior to majority Hinduism in Indian secular nationalism. Hinduism, by contrast, is construed as inherently secular (read tolerant), inclusive, and open to change. What proponents of such ideologies ignore—as evinced in the discourse of the Hindu Right—are the ways in which their own embodied religious practices become transparent and neutral, as they are all-pervasive in a majoritarian Hindu context. From a traditional Enlightenment perspective, Hinduism would still be considered far removed from the deistic idea of divinity associated with an abstract set of beliefs and exemplified in post-Reformation Christianity. Like Islam, it is more likely to be viewed as a religion that is completely entrenched in the perfection and development of correct bodily practices.[46] The post-Partition secular nationalist subject is thus forced to confront his own majoritarian assumptions by means of the narrative device of time travel and by the encounter with the Muslim other.

Kesavan's uncanny mode of remembrance also extends to a historical revisioning of Congress-League politics in the turbulent era of the 1940s. In most nationalist historiographies of India, Jinnah and the Muslim League are held entirely culpable for Partition. Kesavan calls into question this singular politics of blame by drawing attention to the failed alternative solutions and moments that were rejected by the Congress, including the deadlocked Simla conference of 1945, as well as the Cabinet Mission plan for a confederal India. He attempts to devilify the much-maligned Jinnah, who appears twice in the text. In an unusual episode, the protagonist, in his capacity as a waiter at the Cecil Hotel in Delhi, audaciously asks Jinnah if he really wanted the country to be partitioned. The answer that Kesavan attributes to Jinnah—"Leading question. Barristers do not have opinions—they have briefs"—is in keeping with Jinnah's famous reticence to express what he actually wanted (177). Ultimately, the author is concerned to recuperate Jinnah as a fair and constitutional leader who was driven to demand a separate Islamic nation because of the unyielding stance on various issues of the Congress.

The novel's vision of the alternative possibilities available in the 1940s that were eventually abandoned is best encapsulated in the figure of Masroor's mother, Ammi, who supports neither Nehru's Congress nor Jinnah's League. Unlike Jinnah and Nehru's shared dreams of establishing "new" nations, Ammi's concern is to preserve the present of the world she inhabits. Consequently, she contests the elections as an Independent candidate from Lucknow and launches a party called *Anjuman Bara-I-Tahaffuz-I-Haal* (Society for the Defence of the Present) in response to her impatient son's challenge to do something concrete other than wait for her husband. Her unusual election manifesto comprises a litany of negatives that outline all the things that must *not* be done once the British depart, including the renaming of roads, the instituting of laws, the writing of a Constitution, and the erasure or creation of boundaries and frontiers. Ammi's rationale is simple: "Why should you want to wreck the only world you have for some day-after-tomorrow? You'll never get there—there's no such place. . . . You I can understand: the young always want to change the world. But Gandhi and Jinnah and Nehru? Experienced old men who want to sweep their lives away and live like strangers in brand new countries" (326). In an insightful essay on the novel, Padma Challakere notes that Ammi's unusual election manifesto may be read as a call "to slow down the acts of nation-making": "It is a call to suspend our relation to the space of the new nation until we inhabit imaginatively the time-space of the present and the irreducible presence in it of the past."[47] When a journalist from the *Dawn*, the Muslim League newspaper, asks Ammi why as a Muslim woman she has chosen to launch another Muslim party, she chastises him sharply, saying, "You've got Islam on the brain" (330). Ammi does not desire to live in some Muslim homeland; "home," for her, is Lucknow, where she has spent long years waiting for her missing husband, Intezar (the name literally means "the waiting"). Through Ammi's narrative, Kesavan reminds us of the alternate possibilities that lay between the two poles of Congress's secular nationalism and the Muslim League's separatism, but that were defeated with Partition.

Eventually, once Partition become irrevocable, Ammi and her family—including the narrator—end up in the makeshift refugee camp for Muslims at the Old Fort in Delhi. Forced to dwell in a different subject position, the (Hindu) narrator witnesses the plight of innumerable Muslim families who were displaced and sundered by Partition. Thus, he observes ironically: "a single species, *Homo islamicus,* had been corralled for its own safety and well-being" in the Old Fort until they "could be released into their natural habitat [Pakistan], which was then being fenced a few hundred miles away" (216). If Ammi's family manages to find its way back to Lucknow, it is only because the fraught question of "home" is resolved for them with the serendipitous return of Inetzar. Although the displaced narrator finally gets his way with his adopted Muslim family "choosing" India over Pakistan, his futuristic hindsight leads him to believe that perhaps they would have been better off in Pakistan, for *"at least no one there had died for being Muslim"* (376, my emphasis). The narrator's second-generational positioning is made apparent through this interesting use of hindsight: it allows Kesavan to foreground the sense of a beleaguered Muslim identity in the 1980s and 1990s in India.

Strikingly, the narrator does not find his way back to his own time at the novel's conclusion. Eschewing the circular structure of time-travel narratives—and travel narratives in general—which often conclude with the traveler's return to his own space and time to tell the story to a home audience who shares his worldview, *Looking through Glass* keeps its protagonist in the past. How does one read the text's overturning of generic conventions while working within the conventions of time-travel narratives? Should it be read as a failure to integrate past and present to the extent that the narrator remains unnamed until the very end? I argue that Kesavan subverts the genre precisely in order to allow his second-generational upper-caste Hindu protagonist *to make a home in the past with his adopted Muslim family.* The novel thus stages the relinquishment of the normative Hindu self into the Muslim other in direct opposition to the Hindu Right's demand that Muslims assimilate into the dominant Brahminical Hindu culture if they want to live in India. (This is also evinced in the narrator's circumcision, albeit performed for very mundane and secular reasons.) Yet despite the apparent sacrifice of his Hindu identity, the narrator remains continually aware of his alterity, especially once they find themselves in the Old Fort and Masroor appears to become part of a "larger Muslim something" (367). The text does not presume, then, to annihilate the distance between self and other, even though its displaced Hindu protagonist finds a home with the Muslim other.

The novel ends with the image of its secondary witness, the photographer-narrator, finally finding his way into the frame of the photographic image. Until then, charged with the responsibility of taking pictures, he has not been able to become a part of his photographs. In the end, however, even if it is only as a "swirling blur," he is able to leave his trace upon the past, thus eschewing the comfort of distance provided by the camera and history.

Shauna Singh Baldwin's "Family Ties"

If Kesavan's novel reveals the majoritarian (Hindu) underpinnings of the representative nationalist self by means of its narrator's encounter with the Muslim other, the story I now turn to, Shauna Singh Baldwin's "Family Ties," uncovers the paternalistic foundation of the normative nationalist subject. "Family Ties" is part of an anthology of short fictions, *English Lessons and Other Stories* (1996), which attest to women's experiences of migration and displacement—predominantly within the Indian diaspora. This story stands apart from others in the collection for its treatment of the issue of gendered displacement through the traumatic history of Partition. In many ways, "Family Ties" foreshadows a number of Baldwin's concerns in her later magnum opus, *What the Body Remembers*, a novel that tells the story of Partition from a feminist and Sikh perspective. In this chapter, I focus on "Family Ties" because, like Ghosh's and Kesavan's narratives, it represents an act of cultural memory from the second generation, one that is at a remove from Partition. Yet "Family Ties" also differs from the two male-authored texts in foregrounding the importance of a feminist mode of cultural remembrance that transforms the normative male nationalist subject into something *unheimlich* and frightening by recalling women's traumatic experiences during Partition.[48] The story invites us to consider how the concerns of the female witness or agent of intergenerational transmission may differ from that of her male counterpart. Recounted by a ten-year-old Sikh girl, "Family Ties" resonates with Marianne Hirsch's notion of postmemory in its figuration of the intergenerational passing on of trauma—by means of a process of empathic identification—between an aunt and a niece. The female narratorial perspective of the story allows Baldwin to focus on gender and its centrality to the selfhood of religio-nationalist groups.

"Family Ties" opens in 1971 as India and Pakistan are waging war over the secession of Bangladesh, an event that becomes the catalyst for remembering the trauma of Partition. As a young Sikh girl, the narrator has been brought up on stories of Sikh valor against oppressive Mughal rulers. For instance, she and her brother, Inder, recall the story of Guru Gobind Singh's sons interred alive in a brick wall for their refusal to convert to Islam and the legend of Guru Nanak challenging the *qazis* who wanted him to sleep with his feet pointing away from Mecca. In all these tales of familial and group mythology, the figure of the Muslim serves as the eternal antagonist of the Sikhs. Thus, when the narrator hears the declaration of war against Pakistan on the radio, she imagines her father in the mold of the tenth Sikh guru, wielding his sword against an eternal Muslim enemy. Only now the scene is transformed into the legitimate terms of nationalist conflict: she pictures him as "leading the 61st Cavalry."[49] The timeless Muslim enemy and the Pakistani other become identical in her memory. Baldwin stages the ways in which collective memory establishes a continuum of violence and hostility between Sikhs and Muslims, ranging from the distant medieval past to the more proximate trauma of Partition.

Each new instance of violence between Hindus and Muslims/Indians and Pakistanis can be experienced only as a repetition of the originary trauma of Partition. Thus, the narrator's father, who lost his parents to a marauding Muslim mob in 1947 and whose sister was abducted by a Muslim man, instructs his son to defend his sister at any cost: "If the Muslims come and your sister is in danger, you must shoot her rather than let her fall into their hands." (26). An idealized masculinity demands that men kill their women rather than allow their "honor" to be compromised; it also demands that women voluntarily sacrifice their lives rather than endure the shame of rape and/or abduction by the enemy. With family and group honor inscribed upon their bodies, women cannot be allowed to transgress the boundaries that demarcate groups. Inder's response is even more frightening, since he willingly acquiesces in this patriarchal consensus about the regulation and control of female sexuality as intrinsic to the group's selfhood. The terrified narrator realizes that her brother—the same brother who always asks "why"—has not even hesitated before saying "I will" to his father's injunction. However, the young narrator silently questions the continuum of violence that instills and naturalizes this patriarchal logic. She wonders, "Is it worse to be caught, converted, killed or raped by Muslims than to be killed by a brother?" and concludes that there was no need, after all, for her to fear the Muslim/Pakistani other—*"far more is the danger from those within."* I read "Family Ties" as a classic figuration of the uncanny. The story traces how what is homely—the familiar protective figures of the father and brother, the representative nationalist subjects—turns into something fearful and frightening. The narrator realizes that her brother has been given permission to claim ownership of her selfhood: "He was told I belong to him, that he had the power to will me to live or to die" (31).

The narrator's awareness of her gendered vulnerability leads her to start asking difficult questions about her aunt, Chandini Kaur, whose name has never been mentioned by their father until the 1971 war prompts him to remember her—but only to make sure that his son can fulfill his patriarchal obligations. Given her father's willingness to kill her ostensibly to "protect" her from the enemy, the young narrator initially believes that her aunt has also been murdered by him. But the discovery of an old letter from a social worker helps her to understand that Chandini Kaur had suffered what was perhaps an even greater trauma—a form of social death. She discovers that her aunt—renamed Jehanara Begum—was abducted by a Muslim man during the Partition riots and has been "dead" to her brother ever since. The narrator learns that Chandini Kaur had repeatedly tried to return to her natal family—she had even drowned her illicit half-Muslim child in desperation—but her brother refuses to accept her as his sister, since he views her as a "tainted" woman who has transgressed the patriarchal threshold. As her father's old servant Nand Singh informs the narrator, "[A]ny sister of your father would have died before allowing herself to be called Jehanara Begum. . . . no woman of your father's family would have allowed herself to become a Musalmaan and then to have a Musalmaan's child" (29). What is most chilling is the matter-of-factness with which male characters across the spectrum of class internalize this patriarchal rhetoric of masculinity, which teaches men that women "belong" to them and that they have the power to will women's lives or deaths.

"Family Ties" interrogates the silence that shrouds women's traumatic experiences during Partition, calling for a history that could articulate in some manner the pain and suffering of thousands of women. Chandini Kaur's repressed story points to the particularly gendered forms of violence that were administered and suffered during Partition. For its female victims, Partition was an experience of violence that knew no boundaries: it was not only mobs of the other community that they had to fear, but very often, their own fathers, brothers, and uncles turned into perpetrators in the guise of protectors. In some instances, immersed within patriarchal norms, women even offered themselves up as sacrifices to protect the honor of the community.[50] "Family Ties" uncovers the patriarchal narratives of community and nation that mark women's bodies as the repositories of the group's selfhood. Chandini Kaur is the victim of an all-pervasive patriarchal order that first circumscribes her as a *Sikh* woman in this attack by the Muslim other and then leaves her homeless and unmoored because she has been marked by the other.

Mirroring the lives of many of her historical counterparts, Chandini Kaur disappears across the story into silence, leaving forever a question mark about her life for the narrator and the readers. In the absence of any further entreaties from her, all we are told is that she probably went "mad." Echoing the concerns of recent feminist historiographies of Partition, the narrator comes to realize that "after all, there is nothing in my history book about one Chandini Kaur who became Jehanara Begum and who is dead for my father and mad besides, nor any woman like her" (34). She learns an important lesson: "To be part of a family you have to agree to keep its secrets" (34). Thus, when her father anxiously reiterates that they have never had any madness in their family, she instructs herself: "This is what I must remember if ever I am asked. We have never had any madness in our family" (36). It appears that the narrator has internalized the nationalist and patriarchal lesson of suppressing difficult and shameful histories. However, the conclusion of this short story is reminiscent of

Toni Morrison's *Beloved* in which the narrator ends the story of slavery with the oft-reiterated phrase, "[I]t was not a story to pass on."[51] Much like in Morrison's *Beloved,* the narrator of "Family Ties," in her imaginative effort to re-create her aunt's story across the distance of time and generation that separates them, has in fact passed the story on to us—the readers. Drawn to her aunt's trauma by their shared gendered vulnerability, she becomes the mediating secondary witness who takes in and communicates her tragic story. "Family Ties" thus shows us how the matrilineal family—in this case aunt and niece—can become a privileged site for the passing on of traumatic memory through a process of empathic identification and solidarity that bridges the gap of time. In this way, Chandini Kaur's story is narrativized and integrated into a historically different present. In a similar instance from her more recent novel, *What the Body Remembers,* Baldwin's protagonist Roop, upon hearing a horrific account of her sister-in-law Kusum's death and mutilation at the hands first of her father-in-law (remembered as her martyrdom by him) and then by a Muslim mob, tells herself: "But I must remember . . . I must remember Kusum's body . . . Roop will remember Kusum's body re-membered" (451). The incantatory effect of the repeated phrase "I must remember" highlights the crucial importance of a feminist mode of cultural recall in defamiliarizing and rendering uncanny our sanctioned group memories and national mythologies.

Baldwin's "Family Ties" underscores the ways in which women's subordinate position in religious groups and nations is a crucial impediment to any ethics of coexistence. It provides a valuable point of departure for exploring feminist concerns about the dangers attendant upon positioning the female body in the privatized space of the religious community and the "home." Invested with the burden of "home"—in all the senses of self, nation, community—women become the worst victims in the war between different groups. Thus, the story also enables us to see the limits of liberal secularism—understood as the privatization of religion—by bringing out how religious practices, when viewed as "private," can become a source of tremendous violence for women.

In their return to Partition, the fictional narratives I examine in this chapter exemplify Derrida's injunction that "going back upon oneself or back over one's steps" must be the very condition of a new living together—

one that would go beyond the "must well live together" of pragmatism and the juridical contract. In different ways, these literary narratives enact an uncanny mode of remembrance that allows us to come to a radically different understanding of Partition. If Ghosh's expansive novel deconstructs the very idea of autonomous nation-states on the subcontinent by bearing witness to a cumulative border-crossing violence, even years after Partition, Mukul Kesavan's *Looking through Glass* reveals the majoritarian Hindu underpinnings of the representative secular nationalist self by staging an encounter with the Muslim other. Furthermore, Baldwin's "Family Ties" underlines the importance of a feminist approach for desanctifying our familiar group and national mythologies and for revealing the paternalist underpinnings of the normative nationalist subject. All three narratives, then, contest and challenge the nationalist subject inaugurated by Partition. Significantly, the narratorial positioning of each of these texts at a generational remove from the original trauma highlights the importance of working through the divided meanings of Partition for subsequent (Hindu and Sikh) generations who may not have experienced Partition directly but who have been deeply affected by its legacies of enmity and antagonism toward the Pakistani and Muslim other. I have argued that such an uncanny understanding of Partition is crucial for thinking about religious and inter-national coexistence in the present of the subcontinent. Although my literary examples focus on rendering the "Indian" nationalist subject unfamiliar, the implications of this practice of remembrance are much broader. It calls for very different imperatives from the official nationalist narratives of Pakistan and Bangladesh.[52]

4

$\vee$

Fictions of Violence: Witnessing and Survival in Partition Literature

Although contemporary discussions of secularism and coexistence in India have emerged largely as a response to the Hindu Right–orchestrated ascendance of religious violence in the last two decades, rarely, if at all, do these debates address the issue of violence itself in its terrifying impact on people's lives and everyday worlds. If state authorities are guilty of effacing or ignoring stories of individual pain and suffering, secular academic discourse also, in large part, has been unable to address the effects of communal violence in its disciplinary narratives, perhaps because violence in its very viscerality demands a different kind of telling. Women's experiences of violence and violation, in particular, are rendered invisible in both political and academic discourses, even though sexual violence against women is a constitutive element of religious riots. But what good can it do to recall and enumerate stories of violence? In this chapter, I argue that the recognition and acknowledgment of survivors' experiences is crucial to the living together of diverse religious and ethnic groups. Indeed, stories of violence and torment—the forms of repression and cruelty we call "inhuman"—have long been central to human rights discourses. Such stories play a crucial role in imagining and inaugurating a world without hatred, racisms, xenophobia, communalism, and patriarchal oppression. However, we must also ask: what might be some of the pitfalls that attend the telling of these tales?

Typically, the camera and the witness have served as the traditional allies of human rights discourse by helping to "mobilize shame" in perpetrators through the exposure and publicity of human rights violations.[1] Yet in an age when the mediatized exposure of acts of violence and injustice do not necessarily ensure their cessation and prevention, it is important to acknowledge the risks involved in the deployment of graphic images or accounts of violence. Thomas Keenan provides the disturbing example of Serbian policemen who looted and destroyed the village of Mijalic during the war over Kosovo in full knowledge of the camera recording them—and indeed brazenly waved to the camera. Human rights activists therefore must recognize that their predominant practices—exposure and publicity—are under crisis, as photographs and television are increasingly being used as opportunities for performances, media events, advertising, and exhibitions of all kinds. The delicate and risky nature of such enterprises must be acknowledged at the outset. Hence, we cannot continue uncritically to affirm the value of public scrutiny and the discourse of shame—the belief that "if mass violations become known the world reacts."[2] Furthermore, merely recapitulating the details of violence renders violence external to the survivor and could well operate as a way of gazing, voyeuristically, into her world. Enumerating a litany of horrors can often achieve the opposite of the desired goals of human rights projects. How, then, can we map the effects of violence without re-entrenching it in our narratives—without recalling violence for its own sake? To write of violence in ways that do not necessarily efface the survivor's subjectivity, perhaps, calls for a different kind of telling, one that does not necessarily sublimate violence or induce a voyeuristic reading but that is able to imagine what it might mean to dwell in the survivor's world: a world often constituted by paranormal experiences and altered states of being.

This chapter considers these complex questions through an examination of fictional accounts of Partition written in the early years after division. I focus on a select set of fictions that treat the difficult topic of sexual violence in order to ask what happens to a woman in a scene of religious conflict. I argue that literary fictions of inhuman sexual violence in times of mass conflict do not serve merely as exposés or testimonies but that they also have a crucial role in imagining a way of living together in peace and accord with the other. By allowing us to envision the tremendous impact of mass sexual violence on male witnesses, on female survivors, on heterosexual relationships, and on local worlds, these literary fictions make powerful and poignant pleas for a lasting peace.

It is an incontestable fact that violence and displacement of a scale that is unimaginable and incomprehensible accompanied the division of India into the two sovereign states of India and Pakistan. British India's partition brought with it the territorial, psychic, and emotional dislocation of millions. From all accounts, it is evident that there was a staggering loss of life and incalculable devastation for millions of people.[3] Still others were divested of their lands, homes, and livelihood or were abandoned and left destitute. The Hindustan–Pakistan plan for the division of the country was announced on June 3, 1947, according to which a new geopolitical entity called Pakistan ("land of the pure") would soon be carved out of colonial India's territory. The Muslim majority provinces of Punjab and Bengal were to be divided, and two disconnected wings—West and East Pakistan—on two opposite ends of the territory of India would constitute the territory of the new Muslim nation. Inevitably, the exact geographical pinpointing of these borders became a highly contested issue, as each community—Hindu, Sikh, Muslim—clamored for possession of places and religious shrines with which they felt they shared a deep-seated genealogical and historical connection. Significantly, the Boundary Commission, headed by the Englishman Cyril Radcliff, did not announce its decision until after the transfer of power had taken place. The Commission was given barely three months to complete its difficult task once Mountbatten decided to hasten the date for the transfer of power from June 1948 to August 1947. On August 16, 1947, the Commission declared its awards in what turned out to be a random and arbitrary division of land between India and Pakistan. The political instability and conflict of the previous decade, especially of the year before independence, had made the situation very volatile and led to the outbreak of violence. Murder, arson, looting, and sexual assault quickly became commonplace as individuals and communities responded with fear and violence to the imminent loss of their homes and lives. Minority communities on either side became particularly vulnerable to violence and reprisal. Jason Francisco observes of this time of terror: "The number of persons beaten, maimed, tortured, raped, abducted, exposed to disease and exhaustion, and otherwise physically brutalized remains measureless."[4] In the space of a few traumatic months, millions of refuges crossed the borders between a newly truncated India and the East and West wings of a newly demarcated Pakistan in what has been termed the largest "peacetime" migration in history.[5] Muslims traveled west to Pakistan, while Hindus and Sikhs moved east toward India in huge foot columns called *kafilas*, to escape the violence that had erupted on either side.

In instances of war and mass violence, women's rape routinely becomes an equalizing and retaliatory act between the communities involved, and Partition was no exception. Forced migration was often accompanied by the widespread conversion, abduction, and rape of women by men of both communities—Hindu and Sikh, on the one hand, and Muslims, on the other. Recent research has revealed that the circumstances of these abductions varied widely: some women were left behind as hostages for the safe passage of their families, others were separated from their group or families while escaping, while still others were initially given protection and then incorporated into the host family. An early estimate of the number of abducted and raped women puts the figure close to 100,000.[6] How does one seek to enter this realm of carnage and desolation, to understand it, to inhabit it, even in some small way to represent it? How does one write or tell of such tremendous violence and pain? How can we map the mutilating effects of violence and trauma on the bodies and memories of survivors in ways that do not risk voyeurism?

Traditional historiography has been conspicuous in its inability to enunciate collective traumas of the scale and magnitude of Partition, since such painful experiences can be comprehended only by taking their affective dimensions into account—dimensions of pain, shame, guilt, revenge, nostalgia that history has traditionally chosen to excise and exorcise from its tellings and retellings. Partition, in effect, gets edited out of history. However, much present-day historiography has become alive to the dangers of writing a monolithic and "objective" history; this development has resulted in the inclusion of nontraditional material like memoirs, testimonies of survivors, and literary narratives as valid sources for writing a new "history from below." Partition fictions, in particular, have received attention as "the only significant non-official *contemporary* record we have of the time, apart from reportage."[7] Thus, sociologists, historians, and feminist critics have played a key role in revivifying interest in Partition fictions. However, despite gains in understanding permitted by these scholars, they tend to offer merely incorporative and inclusive gestures toward the literature of Partition.[8] In their efforts to reclaim marginal histories and subjectivities, subaltern and feminist historical ventures turn to literary and imaginative material in order to provide an addendum to the historical archive, but they obscure the many ways in which literary artifacts may help to open up, articulate, argue, and work through crucial ethical questions. In contrast to recent turns to literature from history and anthropology, I read literary and cultural productions as modes of thinking and dreaming that can offer powerful models for the transformation of societies.

Fictional narratives depict the mass killings, the looting, the riots, the slaughter, and the camps of milling refugees that overtook cities like Lahore and Delhi at the time of Partition. Indeed, the vast majority of literary writers in the decades following Partition register the event with profound sorrow, despair, rage, or disillusionment whether they write in Urdu, Hindi, Punjabi or Bengali—the language groups most directly impacted by Partition.[9] The traumatized female subject of sexual violence, in particular, seems to have captured the literary imagination, invoking a tremendous response in the literature of the time. It was Urdu literary writers in the main, however, who took on the responsibility of attempting to pull together the fragments of culture in the aftermath of the disaster. It is no coincidence that Partition and its repercussions were such a major preoccupation of Urdu fiction in the decades following independence. Aijaz Ahmad, in his impressive survey of postindependence Urdu literature, points out that the thematics of this literature, as well as its reading and writing communities, were fragmented and recomposed drastically by the division of the subcontinent.[10] While the Partition of the country ruptured other linguistic communities as well—most notably, Bengali, Sindhi, and Punjabi speakers—leading to the redistribution of linguistic populations along religious lines, Urdu came to occupy a special place in this division of land, communities, languages, and selves. Ever since the Hindi–Urdu language debates of colonial India—which revolved around the question of what should be the "national language" of postindependence India and eventually culminated in the Indian Parliament's decision to adopt Hindi as the preferred national language—Urdu increasingly came to be identified solely as a Muslim minority language in India. With its simultaneous institutionalization as a state-imposed national language in Pakistan, it gradually lost its previous importance in systems of education and administration in India and came to be cast merely as a matter of Muslim "minority rights."[11] What is more, as Ahmad notes, besides Bengal, Partition violence manifested itself most brutally in the regions where the great majority of the Urdu-writing intelligentsia lived—regions such as Punjab, United Provinces, Bihar, Madhya Pradesh, Kashmir, Andhra, and Delhi (194). Thus, Urdu-speaking communities were affected in very specific ways by the division of the country, and Partition became a major pre-occupation of much Urdu literature in the years following division.

What is especially notable about this literature is that even as debates about the status of Urdu increasingly became entangled in the religio-nationalist conflicts of the 1930s and 1940s, Urdu fiction and poetry of the time were marked by their stridently anti-Partitionist stance. Although Partition led to the almost complete departure of Sikh and Hindu Urdu writers from Pakistan, as well as of many Muslim Urdu writers for Pakistan, Urdu remained a "border-crossing" literature until as late as the early 1960s.[12] This is evident not just in the mobile and undecided nationality of a number of Urdu writers or in the constant circulation of texts across borders but also in the commonality of concerns that shaped this literature on both sides of the new state boundaries.[13] Accordingly, the Urdu fictions I address in this chapter resist categorization as solely Indian or Pakistani. They occupy an interstitial imaginative space between the rigid territorialities of nation-states.

Unlike the magical and transformative possibilities of "midnight" envisioned by a later cosmopolitan English writer, Salman Rushdie, in that early moment of independence in his *Midnight's Children*, these Indian language fictional writers could only express their deeply felt horror and grief at the breakdown of their worlds, witness as they often were to terrifying brutalities. Written and mobilized as an urgent response to the trauma of Partition, particularly the quite often extreme and excessive forms of bodily violence that were such a visible and intrinsic part of the event, this "testimonial" fiction resounds with the exigency of being summoned by its social context and attests to the impossibility of standing outside an all-pervasive trauma. My use of the term *testimony* to describe these literary fictions draws upon Shoshana Felman's and Dori Laub's effort to understand the relationship between art and the traumatic events of our times—such as the Holocaust, the Second World War, and the nuclear bomb—as one of "conscious or unconscious *witnessing*."[14] Examining the relationship between acts of writing, reading, and witnessing, particularly in relation to the history of the Holocaust, Felman and Laub propose that "testimony is the literary—or discursive mode par excellence" of our (post–Second World War) era (5). Contemporary writers often bear witness—whether consciously or inadvertently—to a "horror or an illness whose effects explode any capacity for explanation or rationalization"; concomitantly, the act of *reading* literary texts becomes related to the act of confronting horror (4). In their collaborative work, they provide an account of how "literature becomes a witness, and perhaps the only witness, to the crisis within history" that the Holocaust has been (xviii). Like the literature on the Holocaust, the prolific fiction written in response to Partition bears eloquent witness to an unspeakable and painful history. However, in contrast to Felman and Laub's somewhat straightforward understanding of witnessing—or to be more precise, of the act of *bearing witness*—I do not consider testimony as a mode of "accessing reality" or that which establishes the "truth of what happens during an event" (xx, 80).

Once again, Derrida can instruct us about the entanglement of fiction and testimony. In a wide-ranging essay, "Demeure: Fiction and Testimony," Derrida disturbs the conventional distinctions between these seemingly opposed terms by indicating how testimony as a "promise to *make truth*" is always susceptible to fiction.[15] In the European juridical tradition, testimony is irreducible to the fictional; it is demarcated from fiction by its claim to truth value. As a first-person narrative that claims to tell the truth about a unique and irreplaceable experience, testimony is typically opposed to literature—"to what presents itself as fiction" (29). However, since testimony, *without being obligated to prove anything, appeals to the faith of the other,* "there is no testimony that does not structurally imply in itself the possibility of fiction, simulacra, dissimulation, lie, and perjury—that is to say, the possibility of literature, of the innocent or perverse literature that innocently plays at perverting all these distinctions" (29). If the possibility of fiction were to be effectively excluded from the realm of testimony, "it would lose its function as testimony" (29). Much like literary fiction, testimony too relies on the "order of the miraculous" in its appeal to an "act of faith beyond any proof" (75)—to what Coleridge famously termed the "suspension of disbelief." While never ceding the effort to establish truth and veracity, and to offer an account of what it knows and remembers, testimony can never hope to pass the test of empirical proof or certainty. The possibility of fiction therefore haunts so-called truthful or "real" testimony.

If I view fictional narratives as "bearing witness" to the inhuman violence of Partition, it is not because they serve as proof or evidence in the absence of historical archives but because they, like survivor testimonies, contribute to the effort of making public a singular, unique, and irreplaceable experience. As Derrida writes, "In principle, to testify—not being a witness, but testifying, attesting, 'bearing witness'—is always to render public. The value of publicity, that is, of broad daylight (phenomenality, openness, popularity, *res publica* and politics) seems associated in some essential way with that of testimony" (30). This act of "making public" is central to the task of acknowledging and recognizing survivors' experiences of brutality and violence. And yet, the act of bearing witness can only attest to a secret even where it makes manifest an experience—"I can only testify . . . from the instant when no can, in my place, testify to what I do" (30). In fact, the moment one is a witness, the instant one gives testimony in language to another who understands the same language, one destroys the ocular, auditory, and tactile experience to which one attests. Survivor testimony can therefore serve as only a "supplementary substitute" for the unique and irreplaceable experience, which it "replaces without replacing" (100). Like nonliterary testimonies, Partition fictions also attest to experiences that are at once singular and exemplary and are thus both "infinitely secret and infinitely public" (41). Literary narratives serve an important testimonial function wherein the singular experience of a character also becomes exemplary in attesting to the pain and suffering of millions of people as a consequence of Partition.

To read Partition literature solely as testimony, however, is to do injustice to the complexity of its concerns, much like the fictions of memory I examined in chapter 3 should not be read merely as contributing to the creation of alternate public spheres. The fictions of inhuman violence I address in what follows stretch well beyond the domain of what Avital Ronell has called the "testamentary whimper," not only in terms of literary borrowings and narrative form but also in their efforts to imagine ways out of violence.[16] While these fictions undoubtedly bring to light the horrors of Partition, they also point to ways of reinhabiting and domesticating worlds shattered by violence. Thus, they enable us to imagine a world beyond violence. I attend to two kinds of fictional narratives that emerged in response to the plight of the abducted women of Partition. In the first section, I examine a set of fictions that stage a crisis of masculinity in their male protagonists through a graphic encounter with the mutilated female body. The three Urdu literary narratives I consider include two well-known short stories by noted writer Saadat Hasan Manto:

"Open It" and "Cold Meat" (1949), as well as a lesser known short fiction, "Revenge," by journalist-writer Khwaja Ahmad Abbas.[17] I read the drama of masculinity enacted in these narratives as the beginning of an effort to imagine ways of inhabiting the world together for men and women in the aftermath of the widespread sexual violence of Partition. I argue that a reframing of masculinity and heterosexual relationships is vital to the living together of different religious groups whose identities rest upon the regulation and control of (a privatized) female sexuality.

In the second section, I explore four post-rape/abduction narratives that focus on the female survivor's response to such violence. Although survival has been a known literary topos in much fiction of violence and trauma, there are remarkably few fictions, in the specific context of Partition violence, that are able to envisage a beyond for the female subject of rape and abduction. The fictions I address are Rajinder Singh Bedi's "Lajwanti," Jamila Hashmi's "Banished," Jyotirmoyee Devi's Bengali novella *The River Churning* (1967), and Lalithambika Antherjanam's Malayalam short story "A Leaf in the Whirlwind" (1947).[18] What I find especially compelling about these fictions of survival are the ways in which they attempt to constitute the subjectivity—fragmented, liminal, othered—of raped/abducted women in a cultural context in which a woman's silence is the very condition of her survival. These fictions make evident that sometimes there is no "healing" after violence, at least not in the usual sense of a complete recovery or cure; they allow us to envision healing as something more akin to a kind of competence or management for the survivor.[19] Healing is redefined as the power to endure and live on—attending to the very aspects of life that violence obliterates—as opposed to the *overcoming* of pain and grief after a body experiences such life-altering violence.[20] Thus the path to survival that is presented in each of these narratives is never easy: the female survivor of mass violence is invariably condemned to carry her pain within her body. I argue that in taking us to the *enduring trauma* of the female survivor of communal violence, these fictions make powerful and poignant pleas for a lasting peace.

Fictions of Masculinity

In an important essay on the violence of Partition, Veena Das poses the crucial question: what could men do to witness the truth of women's violation when they were among those who had inflicted this violence on women, "not only strange men but also men known and deeply loved?"[21] Invoking Wittgenstein's query in *The Blue and Brown Books* about the possibilities of one's pain living in another's body, Das speculates about the prospect of the pain of the traumatized female body finding a home in a male body.[22] She finds a culturally specific model for the further work of transformation in subcontinental societies in the gendered division of labor in everyday mourning practices of Northern India.[23] If men emerged as "monsters" during Partition, she argues, they also longed to "humanize the enormous looming images of nation and sexuality" in the aftermath of the disaster (87). Since women had no recourse but to remain silent in the face of such destructive violence visited on the self—to take in their pain and to conceal it in order to survive—thereby reversing their usual vocal role in everyday mourning practices, Das believes it fell upon the men to hear their silence, to mould it by their presence, and *to create a home* for these traumatized subjects of Partition violence. Das's hopeful scenario in which men take women's suffering into their own bodies allows us to envision men in roles other than perpetrator of violence or complicit bystander. This is an important theoretical move with significant ramifications for a male feminist politics. It resonates with Derrida's notion of an unconditional hospitality toward the other, only Das envisions hospitality in gendered terms—as a scenario of male hospitality toward the female other—in thinking about the specific situation of the female survivor of Partition. I use Das's transformative scenario as a framework for my analysis of Partition fictions of inhuman sexual violence.

The fictions I address in this section take up the crucial question of what could men do when confronted with the visceral consequences of patriarchal violence on oppressed female bodies. Aijaz Ahmad notes that much Partition fiction was preoccupied with "documenting the detail, as if what happened needed now to be retrieved by transcription, and as if the act of writing itself may perhaps exorcise the ghostly memories of what had been seen far too vividly, suffered much too viscerally."[24] A number of writers, such as Krishan Chandar, Ramanand Sagar, Kartar Singh Duggal, Sant Singh Sekhon, Kulwant Singh Virk, S. H. Vatsayan, Ibrahim Jaleez, have attempted to delineate the mass rapes, abductions, or the general carnage that accompanied Partition.[25] Although the short stories I examine here are paradigmatic of much early testimonial literature of Partition in their attempts to provide chilling accounts of a terrible and catastrophic violence, they are also distinctive in their efforts to stun and shock readers out of apathy or complicity by staging a crisis of masculinity within their fictions. This crisis is brought about by the intimate encounter with the violated female other—an encounter that disallows their male protagonists or witnesses the comfort of distance or detachment.

The first writer I address, Saadat Hasan Manto, is considered to be one of the most vivid and powerful chroniclers of Partition violence. His stories have been widely anthologized in various literary journals as well as in most recent collections of translated Partition fictions. Ritu Menon befittingly encapsulates the centrality acceded to Manto in Partition revivals: "Partition and Manto have become so synonymous that in general perception, the two go together."[26] The events of Partition had a profound impact on Manto; witnessing its cataclysmic violence became a haunting and oft-recurring concern in his later writing. His vignettes and stories about the unimaginable terror, the inhumanity, and the sheer violence of Partition are a passionate and stinging denunciation of India's national vivisection. He often relied on a fragmented style and a detached irony to represent the excess that marked Partition violence. For example, the ironic juxtaposition of inhumane events like murder, rape, castration, and plunder with the mundane, indifferent, surreal, or absurd responses to these events creates a chilling effect in his collection of powerful sketches on the Partition, *Siyah Hashiye (Black Margins)*.[27] From all accounts, it is also evident that Partition and its attendant repercussions destroyed him. Having grown up in Amritsar, Manto moved to Bombay in the 1930s where he was associated with the film industry as a screenwriter. But after Partition, he found himself a refugee in Lahore, Pakistan, where he died of alcoholism at the relatively young age of forty-three. Writing of Partition and Manto, Aijaz Ahmad concludes, "It is at least arguable that the Partition broke Manto's sturdy heart, and the ensuing sufferings then drove him first to drunkenness, then to death."[28] In a similar vein, Ritu Menon writes, "Manto of the apocalyptic imagination was undone by the very event he so passionately documented."[29]

If today Manto is being resurrected as part of a Partition revival, we would also do well to remember that it was precisely some of his 1947 stories that provoked the most strident accusations of "obscenity" and sensationalism. While well established as an Urdu short story writer at

the time of his death, he was also a very controversial figure due both
to the content of his fictions and to his personal lifestyle. With a reputa-
tion for excessive drinking and frequenting brothels (a much elaborated
space in his short stories), Manto seems to have reveled in his role as the
"enfant terrible" of Urdu literature.[30] Often reviled by right-wing organizations for the explicit treatment of sexual violence in his writing, he was
charged with obscenity for five of his stories, including one I examine
here ("Cold Meat"). He also shared an ambivalent relationship with the
All-India Progressive Writers' Association (AIPWA), the pan-Indian organization of nationalist writers founded in 1935–36 whose proclaimed
agenda was to write about "the problems of hunger, poverty, social backwardness and slavery."[31] Although Manto was initially welcomed into
this leftist-nationalist organization, later, he was often accused of being
a reactionary and a sensation-monger. He himself tells of a friend who
alleged that he (Manto) "robbed the dead of their possessions to build a
personal collection."[32] To read Manto today entails taking into account
this controversial life history. The two short fictions I read here, *Khol
do* ("Open It") and *Thanda Gosht* ("Cold Meat"), arguably two of the
most famous fictional attempts to represent the sexually assaulted subject of Partition violence, allow me to consider the power and impact of
Manto's sensationalist story lines. I argue that Manto deploys inhuman
stories of patriarchal brutality in order to bring about a far-reaching crisis
in his male protagonists, one that paves the way for new forms of masculinity. Such a reconceptualization of masculinity is central to the living together of diverse religious groups, since the very selfhood of these groups
is predicated on the "despotic sovereignty" of female sexuality.[33]

"Open It" is a tightly compressed rape narrative that testifies to the
ways that the traumatic experience of sexual violation may lead to a complete breakdown of language and meaning for the survivor-victim. Set
during the riots of 1947, this extremely powerful short story is a searing account of the Muslim Sirajuddin's separation and subsequent reunion (of
sorts) with his daughter, Sakina. The story opens with the densely packed
statement: "The special train departed from Amritsar at two in the afternoon, and arrived at Mughalpura (Lahore) eight hours later. Many were
murdered on the way; a number of people were injured while others were
lost."[34] Much is left unsaid, but the opening line immediately establishes
the grim tone of the story, recalling the great train massacres of Partition

when entire trains carrying fleeing refugees from one side of Punjab to the other arrived at their destinations full of mutilated bodies. The period between August 9 and September 30 seems to have been particularly hazardous until the Refugee Specials were eventually arranged. During this time, most trains were derailed en route, and passengers were subjected to mass slaughter, looting, and rape.[35]

Within the interim of a paragraph, the text next moves us into the space of a refugee camp on the Pakistani side of the newly drawn border, where old Sirajuddin is trying to recall what happened to his wife and daughter during the rioting but initially can only encounter traumatic amnesia. Eventually, through flashes of memory, he is able to remember the dreadful image of his wife's dead body with her entrails ripped open, but he is completely unable to bring to mind the circumstances of his separation from his daughter. Unable to rely on his memories of that night, the old man turns to a group of eight young self-appointed male social workers from the "right" side of the border, who are engaged in "recovering" Muslim women and children from India, to help him locate his missing daughter. Day after day, he prays for their success, until one day these men come across a scared young girl on the streets of Amritsar with a mole on her right cheek, the bodily mark of identification that Sirajuddin had indicated to them. Although the girl runs away in fright, the men reassure her by invoking her father's name.

The narrative shifts once again to the confined space of the refugee camp where Sirajuddin finally encounters his daughter in the environs of the camp hospital. The father is able to identify the corpselike body as that of his daughter only by the mole on her right cheek. In a climactic closure, the author brings to life the horrors of collective sexual violence, especially as they get etched upon the bodies of women.[36] Interestingly, Manto never takes us to the brutal moment of sexual assault; rather, he evokes the traumatic history that has been inscribed inside Sakina's body by a complete rupture between language and meaning. When the doctor who sets out to examine Sakina asks Sirajuddin to open the window, the lifeless body of the mutilated young girl stirs in response to the doctor's injunction and she unties the cord that ties her *salwar*. Sakina has become so conditioned to the command "open it," that the imperative to open anything can only take her back to the past-in-presentness of her trauma, her multiple rapes.

Through a single gesture, Manto changes the focal point of the story: until now, it has been Sirajuddin's trauma to which we have had access, but through this one shockingly revealing moment, the writer shifts the focus to Sakina's impossibly traumatic past. We, as readers, can only imagine the profound and repeated violation that she must have been subjected to for such a complete rupture between language and signification to be effected. The story bears striking witness to the impact of trauma and the interminability of a posttraumatic moment whose hold can be so compelling that the survivor is unable to differentiate between past and present. As Dominick LaCapra notes, "In post-traumatic situations in which one relives (or acts out) the past, distinctions tend to collapse, including the crucial distinctions between then and now wherein one is able to remember what happened to one in the past but realize one is living in the here and now with future possibilities."[37] The blurred temporalities of Sakina's traumatized consciousness attest to the ways in which she continues to remain possessed and haunted by an unbearable past whose ghosts defy the crucial distinctions between then and now.

At the very moment that Sakina's body attests to her ongoing violation through this disjuncture between language and communication, her father shouts with joy: "She is alive—my daughter is alive!" As in *Siyah Hashiye (Black Margins),* Manto makes very effective use of irony in this story—the gap between the father's inability to register the significance of his daughter's shattering response and the painful past that refuses to let go of her body renders her trauma even more poignant. However, Manto chooses not to end this story with the black humor and the pervasive irony that is the signature of *Siyah Hashiye.* The last sentence of the narrative provides a crucial shift in focalization yet again, making this a story of male trauma around a female experience of sexual violation—"From head to toe, the doctor was drenched in sweat." It is the doctor, the third—the external, objective, detached viewer—who is able to register the implications of Sakina's involuntary bodily reaction and unknowingly gets drawn into her traumatic experience. He becomes the witness to her story. The reader is thus split between the incomprehension of the father and the realization of the doctor. The doctor's visceral and bodily reaction to Sakina's unconscious response demonstrates the impossibility of not being affected, infected, or invaded by proximity to the other's trauma even as those to the side of it may want to remain detached or alienated.

Most critical analyses of the story have limited themselves to Sirajuddin's response or to the implications of Sakina's trauma. By emphasizing the multiple shifting focalization within this brief yet immensely powerful story, I underscore the significance of the doctor's crisis even if it is only expressed in the last sentence of the text. As a result of this last sentence, the text disallows its readers the comfort of distance, neutrality, or voyeurism.

The second fiction I examine, Manto's "Cold Meat," is also a narrative of male trauma triggered by female sexual violence, but this story is recounted from the perspective of a perpetrator who is confronted with an unforeseen and undesirable knowledge about the object of his violence. By means of this narrative, Manto powerfully bears witness to a world lost in the midst of anomie and violence—a time when the boundaries between victims and perpetrators often became blurred. "Cold Meat" is the deathbed testimony of a rapist who is belatedly rendered impotent in a potent instance of the visceral transmission of trauma from victim to perpetrator. In a gruesome and shocking confession, Ishar Singh, a Sikh man, recounts his active participation in the brutalities of Partition to his lover Kulwant Kaur. The story opens with Ishar Singh's entrance into a room where an impatient Kulwant awaits his arrival. From the very beginning, the text establishes his anxiety and her impatience. Despite all her efforts to question him, he does not explain the reason for his anxiety. Ultimately, in a desperate bid to steer the conversation away from his concerns, Ishar Singh initiates sexual foreplay but discovers to his consternation that he is unable to perform adequately. When his jealous lover, convinced that he had betrayed her for another woman, stabs him with his own *kirpan* (dagger), he sees it as just punishment for his misdeeds.

Amid many graphic images of blood sputtering from of his neck, he relates his horrifying story. For eight days, he participated in the rampant pillaging and looting of Muslim property, after which he went on to murder six Muslim men of a single family. He sexually assaulted the sole remaining "beautiful" woman only to discover that she was a corpse— "completely cold meat."[38] The dreadful realization that he attempted necrophilic rape traumatizes him, while the *coldness* of the female corpse passes into his own body, rendering him sexually incapable. The chilling last line of the narrative encapsulates the invasion of trauma from victim to perpetrator: "Kulwant Kaur placed her hand on Ishar Singh's hand which was even colder than ice" (124). If in "Open It" we witness the paralysis and powerlessness of the watching doctor in the face of the traumatized female other, in "Cold Meat" we are faced with a physical crisis of masculinity in the form of sexual impotence. Strikingly, the crisis of masculinity enacted in this story is not brought on merely by an encounter with the raped woman but by an encounter with a dead woman. The subject of inhuman violence in the first story—the traumatized survivor of rape who bears a fragmented relationship to language—is literally transformed in this narrative into irreducible otherness in the form of the *dead* woman. Ishar Singh's sense of himself as male and human is shaken through this intimate encounter with the dead female other—in dying, the female and Muslim other refuses to acknowledge his masculinity and, indeed, his humanity.

Writing of *Siyah Hashiye (Black Margins)*, his collection of sketches on the violence of 1947, Manto observed:

> For a long time, I refused to accept the consequences of the revolution which followed the Partition of the country. I still feel the same way; but I suppose in the end, I came to accept this nightmarish reality without self-pity or despair. In the process, I tried to retrieve from this man-made sea of blood, pearls of a rare hue, *by writing about the single-minded dedication with which men killed men, about the remorse felt by some of them, about the tears shed by the murderers who could not understand why they still had some human feelings left* (my emphasis).[39]

In "Cold Meat," Ishar Singh's traumatic encounter with the dead woman leads to a similar moment of remorse and recognition. When Kulwant stabs him, he realizes that he had used the same *kirpan* to kill the six Muslim men. Priyamvada Gopal reads Ishar Singh's realization as a turning point in the story when "the potential in him for a regenerative transformation into a decent human being becomes evident."[40] She writes, "The story of the death of Isvar Singh, the man, and the birth of Isvar, the human being, signals an imaginative act of faith on Manto's part, one in which the reconstitution of masculinity and the rediscovery of humanity become preconditions for each other" (106). Although my reading of the story is largely in agreement with Gopal's incisive analysis, I finally depart from her hopeful reading of the conclusion because there is no escaping the fact that Ishar Singh is near death at the end of the story. What is fascinating about this narrative is the peculiar moral underlying its denouement, evident in the strict symmetry that structures it—the just punishment for an act of sexual violence is sexual impotence and then deathly spearing by a woman. It is not enough that Ishar Singh be traumatized by his participation in near necrophilia; he also must die. The "potential for transformation" is confined to a *moment* of cognition before his inevitable death, with Kulwant (another woman) serving as the accidental catalyst. It seems as if Manto can only reiterate the strict symmetry of cause and effect that propels all revenge narratives in the form of a seemingly just nemesis for the perpetrator of violence.

In order to understand the denouement of "Cold Meat," we must examine Manto's deployment of the melodramatic mode. In fact, both Manto and Abbas (as I will show) adapt melodrama to their own purposes. As an art form characterized by a seemingly archaic excess of sensation, melodrama is often taken to task for its crude and unrefined displays of emotion and sentiment, its contrived plotting usually leading up to a happy ending, and its employment of a Manichean moral universe. But it is important to ask: why is melodrama so effective and popular as a fundamental mode of narrative in literature, theater, film, and television? What is it that melodrama is able to achieve through its unapologetic appeals to the emotions? In a far-reaching thesis, Linda Williams argues that melodrama is not just a genre, an excess, or an aberration that is opposed to the norms of realism, but it is a "broad aesthetic mode existing across many media" that moves us to "feel for the virtues of some and against the villainy of others."[41] The sensationalism, or what gets termed as excess—"the emotional content and vivid style"—of melodrama is the means to the "achievement of a felt good" (23, 21). Thus, invariably, much melodrama—like "sentimental politics"—tends toward climaxes "that offer a feeling for, if not the reality of, justice" whereby the suffering of victims is recognized and villains are duly punished (24). I argue that the climax of Manto's "Cold Meat" at once partakes of the melodramatic mode and yet simultaneously subverts it. By establishing an underlying structural symmetry of wrongdoing and "just" punishment, "Cold Meat" makes use of a common convention of melodrama. However, as both perpetrator and victim, the figure of Ishar Singh blurs the Manicheanism that is such a key feature of melodrama. Hence, his death cannot offer the "feeling for justice" that is typical of the conclusion of most melodramas. Manto thus eschews the "feel good" solutions of melodrama that often simplify and obfuscate the complex social problems that it takes up. Although he deploys the conventions of melodrama, he refuses to take them to the typical resolutions that seek to assert moral certitudes in a world gone horribly wrong.

At once melodrama and not quite melodrama, "Cold Meat" is eventually unable to gesture to a beyond of violence, even though it does allow for a significant *moment* of transformation within the perpetrator through its dramatization of his crisis of masculinity. Manto's fictions of violence therefore do not offer much *narrative space* for emerging out of an endless and iterative cycle of brutality and death. Gripped by the horror of what he seeks to chronicle, there is no possible reprieve in his fundamentally "noncathartic literature"—at least not within the narrative itself.[42] It seems as if the ethical imperative for transformation must lie outside the text—with the reader who is positioned in a witnessing relation vis-à-vis the story. Manto's literary fictions leave his readers with a question and a choice: what will we do now that we are confronted with these scenarios of inhuman sexual violence?

By contrast, Khwaja Ahmad Abbas's aptly titled story, "Revenge," deploys the melodramatic mode to effect a change in the would-be perpetrator. This fictional narrative brings to light the futility of patriarchal practices of retribution by tracing the trajectory of one man's confrontation with extreme sexual violence followed by his ensuing melodramatic transformation. Like "Open It," Abbas's "Revenge is a harrowing father–daughter story about a Hindu man, Hari Das, forced to witness his seventeen-year-old daughter Janki's multiple rapes by a group of Muslim men. Consumed by the desire for vengeance, Hari Das seeks revenge by enacting a similar act of patriarchal counterviolence upon the body of a Muslim woman. The text's opening line, "Red and Yellow, yellow and red—these two colours haunted him day and night," sets the hallucinatory tone of the story.[43] The red and yellow colors of the flames to which he consigns his daughter's body metamorphose into a passion for revenge to such an extent that it permeates his entire being. Through a series of flashbacks, the story revisits and re-enacts the horrific experience of his traumatization. He remembers: he is tied to a tree and deliberately kept alive so that he can witness his daughter's violation. Unable to bear the sight, the helpless father closes his eyes, but finds himself powerless to block off the disturbing and haunting sounds of his daughter's pain, "till even those helpless sobs died away into a silence that was more frightful than those blood-curdling screams" (17). Finally, when he opens his eyes, he sees the silent body of his daughter "without colour, without fragrance, without life" (17). Abbas draws on the conventions of melodrama to evoke the pathos of the situation and to establish Janki's suffering: she is young, beautiful, "flower-like," and innocent, while the men who rape her are lustful, bestial, monstrous, and merciless.[44]

Hari Das desperately seeks to erase his traumatic witnessing of his daughter's rape, but like most survivors of violence, he is haunted by the disturbing images of his past. In a twisted logic of egalitarianism, he convinces himself that only the gruesome retributive act of stabbing a Muslim girl in the breasts will allow him to make peace with himself.[45] The Muslim men who have raped his daughter assume the form of *all* Muslims within his scheme of compensatory justice, and the Muslim woman's body crystallizes into the specific site for his fantasies of vengeance. However, it is not so easy to "find" Muslims in the carnage of post-Partition Delhi when large numbers of the community have been killed or have left for Pakistan. Those who remain are too scared to venture out of their homes. Eventually, Hari Das unwittingly finds himself in a sleazy brothel at the behest of a pimp who has lured him with the tempting bait of a Muslim prostitute. Seizing upon Hari Das's revelation that he is a refugee, the pimp skillfully exploits the latter's displaced subject position to stoke his fantasies of retaliation: "And if you are a refugee, you come with me and I will show you a Muslim girl we have got here. After all that you suffered in Pakistan, here is your chance to enjoy a Pakistani *hoor (houri)*" (19). The *houri,* in fact, is an Indian Muslim girl transformed into a "Pakistani" in an early foreshadowing of the Muslim-as-outsider rhetoric that has been the legacy of Partition in postindependence India.

Hari Das is so concerned with the equalizing logic of his retaliatory mission that the girl's age, her upper-middle class background, the fact that she is the daughter of an erstwhile "prominent citizen," all fit perfectly into his schema of even-handed justice. Like his daughter, the Muslim girl is beautiful, "innocent," and educated. She comes from a "respectable" family, which makes her an "ideal choice to pay the price for Janki's dishonour and humiliation" (21). Although Hari Das is able to perceive that she lacks the animation and vivacity of his daughter—she comes across as a corpse who performs the rituals of the brothel quite mechanically—he is unwavering in his resolve to avenge his daughter's violation on her. The climactic ending of the story, however, effects a complete conversion of the would-be perpetrator. For a price of two hundred rupees, Hari Das is allowed a private soiree with the girl. When he demands that she disrobe completely in front of him, the girl strips but refuses to remove her bra. In his self-appointed patriarchal role as male protector and avenger of his daughter's "dishonor," and by extension, that of his community, Das is closed to all appeals for mercy from the unnamed Muslim girl. With dagger in hand, he snatches the offending apparel, only to recoil at the shocking sight of two horrible scars where her breasts should have been. In a classic melodramatic climax, the potential perpetrator reverts back to the traumatized father, as the single word, "Daughter" slips out of his shocked lips.

Abbas's narrative is driven by the logic of a revelation: to disclose the truth of "what lies behind the woman's veil." Typically, the image of the woman's veil has been put into use as an erotic and tantalizing device of many popular narrative forms—particularly mainstream Hindi cinema—to lure the voyeuristic gaze of the audience; Abbas overturns this popular patriarchal mechanism to confront the voyeur with the mutilating consequence of a specifically male violence.[46] The male avenger is confronted with the disquieting knowledge that someone, some other male, most likely from his own community, has already beat him to his gruesome task, while his anointed target continues to be a victim in this endless cycle of patriarchal brutality. Unlike Manto's narratives of rape, Abbas's story ends with the active transformation of the would-be perpetrator in its climax, a moment that needs to be carefully examined for its extremely effective use of melodrama in order to bring about the cessation of patriarchal violence.

Williams's argument about melodrama is useful here. Informed by Peter Brooks's argument that melodrama seeks to assert "moral truth" in a "post-sacred" modern world where there are no clear moral or religious truths, Williams contends that pathos and action are the two most important means toward the achievement of "moral legibility" (25).[47] Melodrama—the term that best encapsulates both pathos and action—

powerfully channels "paroxysms of pathos" into different forms of action such as the rescue, the chase, the revenge, or the fight. The figures for pathos and action, of course, are more often than not gendered, with the female protagonist consigned to the role of the virtuous sufferer and the male hero assigned the tasks of rescue and revenge. Abbas's "Revenge" is similarly driven by the twin melodramatic imperatives of pathos and action in its effort to establish moral clarity in the context of a post-Partition world gone horribly awry. If Manto's "Open It" and "Cold Meat" end with a crisis of masculinity for the male witness or perpetrator, "Revenge" uses the encounter with the mutilated female other and the ensuing destabilization of Hari Das's maleness to effect a radical alteration in its protagonist. Abbas relies on some classic, subcontinental, patriarchal cultural codes in order to bring about a last-minute "rescue" of the female victim.[48]

What is peculiarly fascinating about this narrative's climax is that in the very moment of transformation, Hari Das moves from the self-assigned identity of perpetrator, once again, to that of a traumatized *father*. As we have seen, the particular scenario of a father having to witness evidence of his daughter's violation appears to be a recurrent one in Partition fiction.[49] It would be interesting to speculate about why this fictional scenario should have so much currency in the subcontinent, especially when it treads so dangerously close to an incestuous situation in terms of the ways in which it implicates both victim and watcher. In deploying this story line, literary fictions underscore the "publicness" of sexual violence during religious or ethnic riots. While everyday rapes tend to be enacted in private and secret spaces, rape in a scene of religious violence is deliberately performed in public and visible spaces in order to transmit the message of victory from one community to another. Moreover, although watching any rape is painful, in a context in which women's chastity and male honor are almost sacrosanct values, the idea of a father's being forced to witness his daughter's sexual assault is at once poignant and repugnant. This melodramatic picture of pathos works not only to heighten the shock value of the rape scene but also to affirm the patriarchal belief that nothing could be more emasculating for a man than to watch his daughter's violation. This kind of patriarchal figuring of women's sexualities as key to the identity of men is often used to justify the language of feud and retribution between groups in times of disruptive violence. In constructing this scenario, both Manto and Abbas are drawing upon available cultural codes of female sexuality and masculine honor, but where Manto's version of the father–daughter story in "Open It" concludes in a bleak and terrifying ironic vision, Abbas's fiction successfully deploys the same trope to bring about a change in the to-be perpetrator.

The subtext underlying this narrative's version of redemption across the father–daughter relationship is the peculiarly Indian, protectivist, patriarchal code: "all women are our daughters or sisters or mothers." Clearly, this is a paternalistic archetype, but it succeeds very potently in cultural terms in its ability to evoke shame and guilt in the would-be assaulter. The religiocultural edict that a "good" Indian man should look at all women other than his wife as daughters, sisters, and mothers dissolves all women—Muslim or Hindu—into such patriarchal archetypes and is meant to ensure protection and safety for women. The verbal rejoinder used by women—"Don't you have a mother or sisters in your home?"—when they are harassed in public spaces utilizes the same code of male honor and shame in a predominantly patriarchal society. In Abbas's story, Hari Das's shocked invocation, "Daughter!" on being viscerally confronted with the impact of brutal male violence on the female body draws on a culture's collective paradigms of shame and honor in order to bring about a drastic change of heart on the part of the male violator. We are led to recognize, then, as Rajeswari Sunder Rajan notes, that "patriarchy is not a monolithic, chinkless ideology—that there is religious, legal, political and humanistic recourse available for women; but also that the holders and dispensers of these institutional remedies are men."[50] By deploying melodrama's combination of pathos and action in its paternalistic climax, Khwaja Ahmad Abbas offers a "moral legibility" that serves to compensate for the perceived loss of moral and religious certitudes in the cataclysmic wake of Partition.

All of the fictions examined thus far, then, contribute to the crucial task of naming, recalling, and bringing to light (making public) a terrible, brutal, painful, and unnameable sexual violence in a context in which an enormous number of women were erased physically or historically. The crises of masculinity staged in these powerful short stories open up difficult ethical questions about male responsibility and complicity in extreme forms of patriarchal violence during communal riots *even for those men who may not have participated directly*. I read the staging of this crisis as an incipient feminist gesture that is important for thinking about the coexistence of disparate religious groups whose very selfhood—ipseity—is based on the virile mastery of a privatized female sexuality. However, these writers are not as concerned with mapping the effects of violence on the female survivor's body and consciousness. These fictions of rape scripted by the male writer are essentially male stories of male trauma around female silencing or of masculine agential transformation. In all the literary works I have discussed so far, the raped woman dies or is near death at the close of the narrative. In Manto's fictions, the raped woman appears only as a dead body—a heap of cold flesh ("Cold Meat") or a barely living corpse ("Open It"). Similarly, in Abbas's "Revenge," the Hindu girl, Janki, is not allowed to survive her rape, and if life is possible after sexual violence for the unnamed Muslim girl, it is only envisioned within the exploitative space of a brothel. Thus, even as these fictions in their use and figuration of death offer powerful ideological critiques of gendered violence, they also open up some obvious concerns around the reification of female victimization that are familiar to critics of "victim-feminism." Although, in their unremitting depiction of female victimization, such literary narratives are able to transmit the ways in which women's bodies are degraded or denied dignity in a profoundly patriarchal world, they also end up incarcerating the female subject of rape in the confining position of merely victim. As a result, the raped woman is denied any agency or capacity for effecting change in her life; indeed, often she is denied the right to life itself.

Feminist critics have questioned this patriarchal equation of rape with death, where female sexual existence and the female self are rendered so inextricable that any injury to the former results in the complete annihilation of the latter. Rajeswari Sunder Rajan points out that it is a commonplace of the conventional rape narrative scripted by the male writer to reify female victimhood: all that is really left for the raped woman to do after the event is either to fade away or to die.[51] Feminist texts of rape, in contrast, counter narrative determinism in a variety of ways: "by representing a raped woman as one who becomes a subject through rape rather than merely one subjected to its violation; by structuring a post-rape narrative that traces her strategies of survival instead of a rape-centred narrative that privileges chastity and leads inexorably to 'trials' to establish it . . . and, finally, by counting the cost of rape for its victims in terms more complex than the extinction of female selfhood in death or silence."[52] In her important work on the psychic life of power, Judith Butler similarly suggests that "subjection signifies the process of becoming subordinated by power as well as the process of becoming a subject."[53] In the discussion that follows, I turn to four feminist fictions that attempt to constitute the subjectivity of the raped/abducted woman by mapping her life after the experience of violation.

Surviving Violence

Recent feminist historical scholarship on Partition has brought to light many new and significant dimensions about the afterlives of the women who did not quite die after being abducted and/or sexually violated during Partition. Relying primarily on a selection of oral survivor narratives, on the testimonials of social workers who were involved in recovering and rehabilitating women as part of a later state-launched operation, and on Constituent Assembly legislative debates in the Indian Parliament, these radical historical projects have sought to "break the silence" surrounding women's experience of 1947 and thus to write women into the history of Partition. In particular, they ask some crucial questions about women and their asymmetrical relationship to the structures of nationality, citizenship, and the liberal democratic secular state. Feminist scholars have uncovered that if the violation of the female body became a widespread means of communicating the message of conquest between Hindus, Muslims, and Sikhs, women also went on to be exploited by a well-meaning yet ill-guided state-sponsored recovery operation that sought to restore them to the body politic of the nation despite their wishes in the matter.[54]

In the immediate aftermath of division, the two new governments were besieged with complaints about "missing" women. Subsequently, in November 1947, these governments entered into an Inter-Dominion Agreement, which laid out steps for the recovery of abducted persons from each country and for their eventual restoration to their families and natal communities. Ordinances were issued in both India and Pakistan, and in December 1949, the Indian Parliament legislated the Abducted Persons (Recovery and Restoration) Act, which was renewed in India every year until 1956, when it was allowed to lapse. Through these legal interventions, each country provided the other with the requisite facilities for search and recovery operations. State policy toward abducted women was generated to some extent by the expectations and clamor of devastated refugees who turned to the fledgling states as the proper recipient of their laments. However, this cannot explain the "uncommon zeal" that the Indian state, in particular, attached to the mission of recovering women in the early years after independence (Menon and Bhasin, 110). Pakistani scholars report that recovery work in Pakistan was not imbued with as much urgency; it is likely that pressure from India impelled most of the recoveries.[55] This difference in effort is especially evident in the contrasting statistics of women recovered in each country. The number of Muslim women recovered from India was almost double that of Hindu and Sikh women "rescued" from Pakistan.[56] How do we view this marked discrepancy in figures between India and Pakistan? For India, a country that was still painfully reconciling itself to the loss of its territory "sacrificed" to a separate Islamic homeland, the task of retrieving its lost women became a project invested with deep emotive charges. National anxiety about the abduction of Hindu women went hand in hand with disquiet about their conversion to Islam, since most abducted women were made to convert to the religion of their abductors. These border-crossing subjects became the visible embodiments of a transgressive and disruptive female sexuality (was she forced or did she choose to go?), the regulation of which is often intrinsic to the policing of borders between nations and communities. The restitution of women to their original families and communities therefore became a national mission charged with urgency and emotion, crucial for asserting the sanctity and inviolability of the male national fraternity. Thus, if the Indian state was driven to carry the story of abduction forward to the climax of recovery, it did so not only out of consideration for female victims of fratricidal violence but also because recovering missing women from Pakistan—the abductor country—became intrinsic to India's self-image as a responsible and civilized state.

By all accounts, however, a number of abducted women did not wish to return to their natal families and communities. As Menon and Bhasin note, part of the problem lay in the very definition of "abducted" persons as introduced in the 1949 Recovery and Restoration Bill, which identified and categorized *all* women found living with men outside of their own religious community as "abducted" and all such intercommunity unions as "illegitimate," although many women may have seized advantage of those disruptive times to marry men of their choice outside of their own communities.[57] Moreover, the state and its agents chose to overlook that several years often had passed by the time recovery was implemented. During this period, many women had forged the beginnings of a new (albeit fragmented) existence with their abductors. A number of women had borne children by their abductors or were pregnant by the time they were recovered. To those of us today who seek to envision the lives and subjectivities of these women, it may seem peculiar that women who had been sexually violated would rather build new lives with the very men who had raped them or who had murdered their families than return to their communities and families. It would be only too easy to attribute their preferred modes of action to false consciousness, but a more careful examination of the multifarious situations of these women discloses that the choices that faced them were tenuous and difficult, at best. In a culture that attaches so much value to the purity and chastity of the female body, the option to return to their natal families was fraught with the dangers of rejection.[58] Indeed, Nehru and Gandhi had to publicly appeal to the consciousness of the populace to accept "recovered" women. Given this context, a considerable number of women who survived the experience of abduction or rape believed that the only recourse available to them was to live on with their abductors, since they would never be able to return to "respectable" lives with their original families. Thus, women often actively resisted recovery. Consequently, the state had to take adequate legal measures to ensure the restoration of these deviant subjects to the patriarchal body of the nation in order to appropriately discipline and contain their sexuality. The omniscient, ostensibly secular democratic state divested these adult women of every right of citizenship, including the writ of habeas corpus. Often recovered under duress from their new homes by the local police (who were invested with almost unlimited powers for carrying out their work), then confined in transitory refugee camps before eventually being deported, "abducted" women were given absolutely no choice in deciding about their own futures or the lives they wanted to lead. In a terrible irony, women once again became the victims of history, only this time, through the execution of a state-sponsored recovery operation that divested them of any agency whatsoever.[59] Forcible abduction was thus followed by forcible recovery.

Although a multitude of family narratives memorialize "martyred" women who voluntarily gave up their lives and others killed by their kinsmen in order to preserve the honor of the community, a shroud of silence surrounds both the experiences of women restored to their families and those who remained with their abductors. Thus, while violence visited on the community remains alive in collective memory—indeed, it is often amplified in present-day accounts of the trauma—the stories of female survivors within the group are rendered completely silent, their pain unacknowledged. It seems as if the silence around women's experiences of violence is key to the social contract—the "forgetting"—that allows the living together of pragmatism and necessity, but only until the next instance of violence. Unless we acknowledge sexual violence as a constitutive element of mass conflict, we cannot hope to inaugurate a more peaceful and just world. Recent feminist work contributes to the important task of publicly recognizing women's stories of violence. Nevertheless, feminists must come to terms with the collective and persistent silence women themselves have chosen to keep about their experiences of violation, even half a century after the event. While recent historical work has provided a rich fund of information about women's traumatic experiences during Partition, it is striking that there is not a single testimonial account of a woman speaking explicitly of sexual violence visited on the self in the new oral histories.[60] Violence can only be relegated to the outside; it is always someone else's story. Veena Das notes that when she asked women to narrate their experiences of violation, she found a "zone of silence" around the event, a silence achieved either by the use of general and metaphoric language or by a complete evasion of the experience of abduction and rape ("Language and Body," 84). How, then, do we read women's silences today, especially in light of much trauma scholarship that advocates bearing witness to one's story or "speaking out" as essential for survival? While, on the one hand, testimony is often unproblematically considered as "evidence" in the juridical tradition, on the other, it is also viewed as the first and necessary step toward any kind of social or personal "healing" in much trauma discourse. One of the most striking changes in the last two decades of trauma thought has been the transformation in the role of the survivor of mass violence from victim to witness—to one who will tell the "tale of survival as a form of self-therapy and inspiration for others."[61] Is this a culturally contingent recommendation?

The mass sexual violence that attended Partition opens up some crucial questions for contemporary trauma discourse—especially Holocaust scholarship—that asserts the imperative of speech as the only path toward survival. Holocaust scholar Dori Laub, for instance, asserts that "the survivors did not only need to survive so that they could tell their stories; they also needed to tell their story in order to survive. There is, in each survivor, an imperative need to tell and thus to come to know one's story, unimpeded by ghosts from the past against which one has to protect oneself. One has to know one's buried truth in order to be able to live one's life."[62] Apparently, the only way out of the timelessness and ubiquity of trauma for trauma survivors is to "re-externalize" the event, transmit the story, literally transfer it to another outside oneself and then take it back again, inside (69). Testimony is viewed as a sort of rite of passage that one has to "pass through in order *to continue and complete the process of survival after liberation*" (85, my emphasis). However, transmitting one's story is not always an option for the gendered survivor of mass violence. The stories of women's lives during and after Partition amply testify to such an inability. Theirs is an experience that is rendered unspeakable not only because it is linguistically impossible to go back to the traumatic event but also because, in a culture where there is no room for the "polluted" (raped) woman, transgressing as she does all known and acceptable categories of womanhood, the sheer exigencies of social survival make silence a necessity.[63] As we seek to understand these women's life stories today, we must not simplistically construct their silence as a symptom of passivity, abjection, or complicity with patriarchy. If abducted women wanted to survive within the structures of patriarchal patronage, silence became imperative; it became the precondition for reabsorption into the traditional structures of family or community. So long as their violation was not made public, women had some chance at survival; often, it could well be their only recourse for living beyond the limit event.

Writing of contemporary historiography's imperative to retrieve suppressed or tabooed histories, Veena Das sensitively notes,

> I have myself found this a very complicated task, for when we use such imagery as breaking the silence, we may end by using our capacity to "unearth" hidden facts as a weapon. Even the idea that we should recover the narratives of violence becomes problematic when we realize that such narratives cannot be told unless we see the relation between pain and language that a culture has evolved. ("Language and Body," 88)

The imperative to *speak* violence—be it in the psychoanalytical encounter or as formal testimony—must be understood, then, as the historically situated dictate of a particularly "modern" consciousness that produced discourses like psychoanalysis in the first place. But this cultural and gendered limit to speaking out need not be the end of the story. If transmitting one's tale is not an option for the female survivor of the Partition, we can still ask what other modes of survival might help women come to grips with a world made strange and desolate by an experience of devastating violence.

Feminist fictions envisage a beyond that is not death or disappearance for the traumatized subject of rape or abduction. In attempting to constitute the fragmented subjectivities of the female subject of mass violence, fictionalized survivor accounts enable us to imaginatively inhabit the traumatic inner worlds of these women as they are confronted with the disquieting *failure* of male hospitality in the aftermath of Partition. Providing powerful indictments of everyday structures of patriarchal oppression that underpin more spectacular instances of mass violence of the kind witnessed during Partition, these narratives take us to the haunting repercussions of sexual violence for the female survivor. Moving away from the stagnating dichotomies of speech and silence, they direct us to a range of possibilities for domesticating and reoccupying life-worlds shattered by violence. Although their protagonists are unable to bear witness to their grief, they are able to narrativize their traumatic pasts and reintegrate these painful events into a historically different present (unlike Manto's Sakina, who can only compulsively reenact her trauma in solitude).[64] As Mieke Bal notes, "To enter memory, the traumatic events of the past need to be made 'narratable'"—that is, they need to be organized into a string of events that can be expanded or reduced, summarized or highlighted, in order to make sense in a particular cultural context (xi). While the process of coming to terms with trauma often takes the form of restorative speech acts that express narrative memory, it is the issue of narrative reintegration that remains the more crucial mechanism for survival.[65] Survival in these fictions is figured as no more and no less than a form of coping—learning to inhabit anew a world made strange and uninhabitable by such horrific violence rather than exorcising painful, traumatic memories through their verbal externalization.

The first of these fictions, Rajinder Singh Bedi's Urdu short story "Lajwanti" dramatizes the impossibility of restorative speech acts for the female survivor of Partition because of the lack of a receptive listener or addressee. The story is set in a riot-devastated town in post-Partition west Punjab, which is struggling to come to grips with the aftereffects of division and violence. It recounts a local community's involvement with the state-initiated recovery operation for abducted women. The narrative focuses on a young married couple, Sunder Lal and Lajwanti, and the ways in which Partition marks their relationship, irrevocably and permanently. The opening lines of the text establish the author's concern with a violence that may not be discernible but that manages to inscribe itself inside the bodies and memories of those who survived: "The country was partitioned. A myriad of wounded human beings staggered out of the shambles and wiped away the blood that still stained their bodies. Then they turned their dazed eyes towards those whose bodies were yet whole and unscathed but whose hearts were torn, bleeding."[66] Bedi describes how the community threw itself into the work of rehabilitating refugees, struggling to provide them with jobs, homes, and lands to offer some measure of compensation for the irreparable losses they had suffered. Yet, he tells, when it came to the women who had been recovered from Pakistan, most families were extremely reluctant to allow readmission into the protective fold of the family.

Against this backdrop, a few concerned individuals of the city set up a committee for the express purpose of rehabilitating recovered women. Sunder Lal is elected unanimously to the position of secretary; the townspeople believe that he will be the most committed and sincere candidate for the position, since his own wife, Lajwanti, had been abducted during the riots. The grieving Sunder Lal immerses himself in the difficult task of converting his community. As is typical of any reformer, Sunder Lal encounters many obstacles in the path of his mission. Thus, while some families, influenced by Sunder Lal's sloganeering, take fitful steps toward the "task of bringing new life to ruined homes," many others persist in refusing to recognize their daughters/sisters/wives who have been brought back by virtue of the recovery operation: "On the contrary they cursed them: Why did they not die? Why did they not take poison to preserve their chastity? Why didn't they jump into the well to save their honour? They were cowards who basely and desperately clung to life" (181). In this passage, Bedi provides a litany of the commonplace patriarchal courses of action expected of women in the midst of communal violence—all options that work to uphold her chastity before her life—in order to establish the ways in which women's sexualities become intrinsic to maintaining the boundaries of the community. His rejoinder to the usual patriarchal lament—"better dead than violated"—is that it takes a terrible kind of bravery to have "lived through the horror and the shame" of it all—to have, in essence, survived (181). In marked contrast to the families that summarily reject these women because they have been "spoilt by the Muslims," Bedi's Sunder Lal has sworn to "enshrine" Lajwanti in his heart if the state ever manages to locate and recover her (187). Eventually, when the state does bring back Lajwanti, Sunder Lal, in keeping with his professed public views, offers refuge to his "recovered" wife.

In many ways, "Lajwanti" is a before and after story; Partition is the watershed that marks the couple's life irrevocably. Like Manto's "Open It," this literary fiction also presents a crucial change in focalization toward the middle of the narrative. Although the first half is narrated from Sunder Lal's point of view, with Lajwanti's return, the story shifts focus to her trauma. The author goes to great lengths to map the changing trajectory of their relationship: we are told that before the abduction, Sunder Lal would often physically abuse Lajwanti, but after her return, he deifies her, now addressing her as "devi," goddess. Recalling Sunder Lal's abusive treatment in the past, Lajwanti is initially overjoyed at not only being allowed sanctuary in her own home (given the fate of others in her situation) but also at her husband's unexpected tenderness and solicitude. Her greatest desire is that she should "pour out all that had happened to her and while narrating her tale of torture she would let her 'sins' be washed away in tears" (188). Clearly, this literary narrative is invested in the therapeutic potential of speech/testimony, but it also underlines the need for a "second person to act as a confirming witness" in order for the traumatized subject to come to terms with her experience.[67] Lajwanti wishes to share her trauma not merely with anyone willing to listen but specifically with her husband, Sunder Lal. As Bal points out, such a second person "confirms a notion of memory that is not confined to the individual psyche (unlike the solitude of traumatic memory, for example), but is constituted in the culture in which the traumatized subject lives."[68]

However, Sunder Lal fails in his capacity as witness. He cannot be the listener she requires; indeed, he shrinks from hearing her story. Only once does he ask her about the identity of her abductor and if the latter had abused her in any way. When Lajwanti hesitantly attempts to share her story with him, telling him that far from abusing her, her abductor actually had treated her well, and yet she feared him (the abductor), Sunder Lal can only say, "Let the past be past, since you are not to blame for what has happened" (189). However, as many sufferers of trauma have testified, a traumatic past can never really be past; it lives on vividly, intruding into the present in many indecipherable ways. As a consequence, there is no possible exorcism or redemption for this traumatized female subject of violence, since "all that was within Lajwanti's heart remained gagged, stifled" (188). Silence falls between the couple like a chasm, cleaving their relationship forever. "Lajwanti" thus stages the impossibility of bearing witness to one's trauma in a cultural context in which there is such a strong interdiction against speech for the female survivor of collective violence. Lajwanti's silence becomes the precondition for their cohabitation. In fact, as long as she remains silent, Sunder Lal can also elide his complicity in the kind of everyday, normalized, patriarchal violence that underpinned the sexual brutality of Partition.

Sunder Lal continues with his public work of reforming the consciousness of society, while Lajwanti is transformed into a devi—a fragile goddess—who will shatter at the merest touch like glass or the lajwanti plant. Bedi deploys, and yokes together, the tropes of devi and the touch-me-not plant (lajwanti) in very effective ways to debunk the patriarchal constitution of the abducted woman's identity as either victim or goddess. Sunder Lal, the reformed beater-become-male-nationalist figure, constructs his abducted wife and all other women in her situation as fragile victims who require the care and the nurturing of the community. Each morning at dawn, he leads processions through the streets, singing the lajwanti folk song in his mission to urge the local community to reinstate abducted women into the structures of family and community: "[T]hese are the tender touch-me-not leaves, my friend; they will shrivel and curl up even if you so much as touch them" (179). As a rhetorical device, the trope of the fragile lajwanti is quite effective in generating sympathy for the pathos of recovered women, as is evident in Sunder Lal's partial success in persuading at least some members of the community to think beyond the prescribed formulas of rejection and banishment. Yet, Bedi also skillfully uses the metaphor of the lajwanti to undercut the patriarchal and conservative imaginaries underlying nationalist reform projects. As feminist historians have amply demonstrated, reform movements, in spite of their well-meaning intentions, often serve to constrain the agency of the female subject of reform.[69] Thus, when the agents of the state eventually do manage to locate Lajwanti, Sunder Lal is somewhat disconcerted to find that she looks healthy, quite unlike the emaciated, suffering, victimized figure that he had constructed in his imagination. Subsequently, in spite of his laudable intentions, the male reformist figure is unable to come to terms with his wife's cohabitation with another man. Thus, Bedi writes, "Now the question of a quarrel between them did not arise for she was a devi and he her worshipper" (189). Only by effacing the corporeality of Lajwanti's now-tainted body and reifying her into the figure of a pristine, untouchable goddess can Sunder Lal bring himself to reintegrate her into the protective fold of his home.[70] In the terms of Das's scenario of gendered hospitality, the male figure thus fails in his ethical obligation to welcome and provide refuge to the female other.

At the close of the narrative, Lajwanti, now in her new incarnation as goddess, feels increasingly incarcerated in a body "which had become the body of a devi and not her own." Her body has been stripped away from her, first by her abductor and then by her husband. Although not stated explicitly, the narrative certainly implies that the sterility of their relationship extends to their intimate life too. The text ends with Lajwanti's indefinable yearning to go back to the physicality of their earlier relationship before the abduction and her insistent awareness that there is no going back: "And Lajo would look at herself in the large mirror and think that she could not be the same Lajo ever again. She had got back everything and yet she had lost everything—she was rehabilitated and she was ruined" (189). The story thus testifies to the uncertain and tenuous mode of Lajwanti's reinstatement into the patriarchal household and dwelling—where the man is the master—and community. By tracing the breakdown of a heterosexual relationship and by constituting the trapped subjectivity of its eponymous protagonist, "Lajwanti" powerfully attests to the enduring trauma of life after Partition for the female survivor.

Several fictions on abducted women, including "Lajwanti," draw upon the story of Sita from the ancient Indian epic, the *Ramayana*.[71] The obvious parallels between Sita's situation—her abduction by Ravana; her incarceration in a strange land, Lanka; and her subsequent "trial by fire" by her own husband—and the plight of the present-day abducted subjects of Partition gave new immediacy and poignancy to this familiar mythical narrative.[72] In a culture where the *Ramayana* and its counterpart, the other ancient Sanskrit epic, the *Mahabharata,* are kept alive every day through performances, religious expositions, and myriad oral narrative forms, the story of Sita in the *Ramayana* understandably provided an older narrative line, a preexisting cultural paradigm, to hold together and represent the chaos and confusion at the time of Partition. In that sense, the abduction of women was not a new story: it had precedents, indeed, epic precedents, in the Indian context. Interestingly, the Sita story was appropriated by two ends of an ideological axis. On the one hand, conservative nationalist interests used the story of Sita to legitimize the Indian state's "rescue and recovery" efforts; on the other, fictional narratives also drew upon Sita's tale to constitute the abducted woman's subjectivity, especially given the rejection and ostracism she was often subjected to once she was recovered.

The widespread currency of the Sita story in the political discourse of the time of Partition is evident even in a perfunctory exploration of the rhetoric deployed during the Constituent Assembly debates over the passing of the Abducted Persons (Recovery and Restoration) Bill, which was moved in Parliament in December 1949 for the consideration of the House. For instance, one Member of Parliament, Pandit Thakur Das Bhargava, declaimed:

> You will remember, Sir, how when Ellis was kidnapped by some
> Pathans the whole of Britain shook with anger and indignation
> and until she was returned Englishmen did not return to their
> senses. And we all know our own history, of what happened at
> the time of Shri Ram when Sita was abducted. Here, where thou-
> sands of girls are concerned, we cannot forget this. We can forget
> all the properties, we can forget every other thing but this cannot
> be forgotten.[73]

Bhargava went on to suggest that India should hold abducted Muslim women in its own territory as "hostages" for some time, as a matter of policy and strategy, in order to put pressure on the intractable Pakistani government, which was not keeping to its part of the bargain by returning an equivalent number of Indian women. In a similar vein, another Member of Parliament, Shibban Lal Saksena declared:

> Sir, our country has a tradition. Even now the *Ramayana* and the *Mahabharata* are revered. For the sake of one woman who was taken away by Ravana the whole nation took up arms and went to war. And here there are thousands, and the way in which they have been treated was told by the Honourable Minister himself . . . what-not was done to them.[74]

Clearly, both these speeches are invoking the narrative tradition of the *Ramayana* in order to incite traditional patriarchal values of male honor and chivalry toward "our" women. Conservative nationalist imaginaries thus drew upon Sita's story to construct an abject female victim who required the legitimate intervention of the modern state to restore her to her "rightful" place within the nation. Thereby, the state, in its own self-fashioning, becomes equated with Rama himself.

Like the political discourse of the time, fictional narratives also draw upon the episode of Sita's abduction and her subsequent trials and tribulations, but unlike the parliamentary debates, literary fictions are concerned to take us to the particular trauma and pain of abducted women. While there has been a long tradition of questioning Ramayanas "within the boundaries of the *Ramayana*," as Paula Richman has pointed out, I argue that the contingencies of Partition gave rise to some particularly powerful feminist revisions of the Sita story that range from interrogation to radical reframings.[75] For example, in "Lajwanti," Bedi invokes the incident of Sita's banishment in order to offer a modern corrective reading of the ancient story.[76] One day, before Lajwanti's return, as Sunder Lal and his followers go about their reformist mission, they come across the conservative stronghold of the local holy man, Narain Baba, while he is preaching to his congregation outside the temple. He is relating the particular section from the *Ramayana* where Rama decides to banish the pregnant Sita on allegedly overhearing the words of a "washerman," who declares to his wife, "I am not like Raja Ramchandra who has accepted Sita even after she has lived for years with Ravana" (Bedi 182). Narain Baba goes on to pontificate that this is the best instance of the prevalence of justice and morality in Rama's kingdom, where even the opinion of an ordinary washerman was upheld. When Sunder Lal tries to intercede, the listening congregation attempts to quiet him, but he appropriates the same episode to argue, successfully, that while in Rama's kingdom even a washerman's opinion was given credence, the present-day espousers of Rama's rule are not even willing to grant him an audience.

Subsequently, once given the forum and the opportunity to speak, Sunder Lal offers a remedial reading of the *Ramayana*, wherein he chastises Rama for turning out the pure Sita. The reformist voice admonishes the people, explaining that, like Sita, Lajwanti and others like her are paying the price for the sins of others. Although Sunder Lal is able to find space for contestation within the *Ramayana* itself, the closure of the text demonstrates how he himself is unable to house her pain once her body has been irretrievably marked by another man. Thus, Sunder Lal and Lajwanti's narrative can only reiterate the trajectory of the Ram-Sita story. Lajwanti is condemned to eternal suffering like her epic counterpart. In this story, Sita is thus "claimed across historical distance, but then surrendered to history."[77]

The story to which I now turn, Jamila Hashmi's "Banished," also alludes to the Sita story as an older narrative paradigm for the present. Like "Lajwanti," this literary fiction attests to the liminal subjectivity of the abducted woman, only it envisages the somewhat different scenario of life with the abductor for the female subject of rape. Narrated on Dasehra day—the Hindu festival that celebrates Rama's destruction of the evil demon Ravana and his brothers by burning their effigies—this fictional narrative is an extended meditation on the thematics of exile, separation, and division that were also constitutive of the experience of Partition. A sense of existential anguish, weariness, and fatigue runs throughout the text. The narrative, largely an interior monologue, is recounted by Bibi, a Muslim woman, who is abducted during the Partition massacres. But Hashmi's protagonist does not return to her natal family and community; instead, she chooses to remain with her Sikh abductor, Gurpal. The narrative delineates the conflictual nature of this decision and the irrevocable sense of loss that attends it. In this short fiction, then, it is not so much the denouement of the plot that assumes significance; rather, the evocation of a mood, a feeling, an aura of inexpressible sadness, is the overarching concern.

The allusion to the *Ramayana*, specifically to Sita's tragic story, is introduced from the first paragraph; indeed, the festival of Dasehra occasions the retrospective narration of the story: "The fire's embers will burn and jump for a long while, giving nearby faces a grotesque look, as if every last face, a veritable image of Ravan, has come to watch with glee Sita's ordeal of separation, her grueling banishment all over again."[78] While the watching people partake in this public celebration of Rama's triumph over evil through the ritual destruction of Ravana and his brothers, the spectacle of the burning Dasehra effigies can only remind the narrator of Sita's forgotten story and its peculiar resonance vis-à-vis her own life.[79] She recalls those devastating days of division when her protected existence was ripped apart at the seams: the country was partitioned, and violence became the rule of the land, but like countless others who were convinced that the violence would abate after a while, her parents refused to migrate. Putting their faith in centuries of peaceful coexistence—"the old life and its values"—they believed that they could continue to live in their home town. However, "Independence and Partition . . . gave the lie to the age-old words of brothers and compatriots—words trampled in the dust under the feet of marauding bands of thugs" (99). The narrator is haunted by the traumatic memories of her father's bloodied body lying near a ditch, her mother impaled by a spear, and her sister's agonizing screams. As for herself, she is brought to Gurpal's home in Sangraon, West Punjab, where she is proffered to her abductor's grandmother as an unofficial *bahu*—daughter-in-law—whose labor can be exploited for useful domestic purposes.

Even today, the narrator avers, when she hears the word *bahu*, she feels it is a travesty, a mockery of everything that marriage stood for, everything that her "marriage" was not. Unlike other brides, she is not brought to her marital home with the usual fanfare and celebration. "No one oiled my dust-coated hair," she recalls, "No *na'in* was sent for to make me up. I became a bride without a single piece of jewelry, without any *sindur* for the parting of my hair" (89). Instead, her abductor lays out a "carpet of corpses" for her. Ever since the fateful day that irretrievably changed her life, she "felt like Sita, enduring her exile, incarcerated in Sangraon" (89). Having been abducted by a modern-day Ravana, she too is destined to a life of perpetual banishment, permanently separated from those she loves. Throughout the text, the narrator explicitly identifies herself with Sita and her abductor with Ravana. For instance, as Gurpal relates the *Ramayana* story to their two boys on their way back from the Dasehra fair, she thinks to herself, "[B]ut how would he ever know that Sita is trailing behind him, that he is Ravan himself" (93).

In the *Ramayana,* Sita is eventually rescued by Rama from the clutches of Ravana, but Hashmi's modern-day abducted subject waits in vain for her brothers to liberate her from a life of banishment and exile. The narrator articulates a profound despair at the complete breakdown of patriarchal and paternalistic structures of protection during that time of anomie and chaos. Significantly, she not only blames Gurpal for her present predicament, she also holds her brothers equally culpable for their failure to rescue her. Many years later, when the paternalistic state does send its agents to Sangraon as part of its recovery operation, she hides herself from the soldiers. The reasons she gives for hiding herself are complex and manifold. They include her awareness of her new responsibilities as a mother to her daughter, Munni; the uncertainty of what lies ahead if she does return to that other country; and, crucially, her feelings of betrayal by her brothers who did not come themselves to secure her release:

> I thought: apart from being a sister to Bhai and Bhaiya, *I was also a mother to Munni.* I wondered: who were these soldiers? And what would that country be like? For the first time I felt unsure of myself. My dreamland turned into dust and vanished. I realized that my roots had sunk deep in Sangraon. . . .
>
> When the army did come to secure my release I hid myself, just like the princess in the fairy tale. I wasn't about to leave with strangers. Why didn't Bhai and Bhaiya come to take me away? I felt hurt by both of them. And I've remained angry with them ever since. (102–3)

What is made evident in this passage is that Bibi views her rescuers as strangers, while her abductor is now perceived as the familiar and known. Consequently, this Sita resigns herself to leading a life with her Ravana— "Munni and I are bound for Sangraon. Rather than embrace a second exile, Sitaji has accepted a life with Ravan" (104). The reference to Sita's *second exile* after her rescue is crucial here, pointing to the narrator's awareness of an uncertain and tenuous future if she were to return to her natal family once the norms of female purity and chastity had been transgressed so irreversibly.[80] Rather than opening herself to the dangers of an uncertain return, she submits to the certainty of life with her abductor. Reflecting that she has traveled with Gurpal far too long to have any strength left to strike out in another direction, she muses, "I know how a boat without oars capsizes and sinks" (92). While feminist historical scholarship has corroborated the veracity of this narrative outline—the fact that many women did resist recovery—it falls upon the literary writer to imagine and re-create the interiority and subjectivity of a woman who makes the difficult decision to stay on with her rapist (often and also the murderer of her family) given the contingencies of her life circumstance.

Caught between past and present, then and now, India and Pakistan, Sikh and Muslim, the abducted subject is represented as a liminal figure condemned to carry her pain and loneliness forever. Above all, then, this is a story about an indefinable sense of loss, grief, and suffering. It is not so much her bodily violation that the narrator mourns but the complete rupture from family and community, one that effectively effaces her sense of being and selfhood: "Faces for which we are willing to sacrifice everything, on the faint hope that we might see them just once, vanish irretrievably. Paths like the watery webs etched on the waves by miniscule crawling marine life, dissolve behind us. We can never backtrack on the paths we have already taken. *Nothing ever returns*" (90; italics added). The narrator's anguish stems from the certain awareness that her past, her home, and her beloved family are permanently lost to her because she has crossed that impalpable yet rigid line of separation that demarcates communities and nations. There is no possibility of return to the other side once that line has been created and crossed. It is the painful, always-present awareness of this loss that runs throughout the text. She thinks of her life as splintered glass that wounds everyone who comes within its vicinity, hence no one ever does. While other women in the village sing nostalgic songs of their parental homes, she is condemned forever to silence because, unlike them, she can never dream of return or reunion: "But there are times when the heart overflows with stories, and yet one remains tongue-tied" (103). Bibi seeks to articulate the pain that is lodged in her body through the use of metaphors and figurative language. Veena Das has drawn attention to abducted women's reliance on metaphoric language to convey their grief: "A woman would say that she is like a discarded exercise book in which the account of past relationships were kept—the body a parchment of losses. At any rate, none of the metaphors used to describe the self that had become the repository of poisonous knowledge emphasized the need to give expression to this hidden knowledge" ("Language and Body," 84). Much like the survivors interviewed by Das, Bibi can only fall upon metaphors of loneliness, solitude, and banishment to articulate her pain and to constitute her subjectivity, likening herself variously to a solitary star, a lonely tree, and a flickering flame.

This fictional text attests to the fact that sometimes there can be no healing after violence; the narrator is destined to bear a burden of grief that never becomes any lighter: "Pain becomes easier to bear if there is hope—just a glimmer of hope—of better days ahead. I was never able to work through it all. What should I erase from my memory? And what should I retain?" (101). At one point in the narrative, Gurpal asks her, "Can't you bring yourself to forget that incident? That was a different time" (99). If, in "Lajwanti," male hospitality is conditional upon the protagonist's silence, in this story, it is contingent upon Bibi's "forgetting." It is evident that Bibi has to give up a crucial part of herself—her past—and indeed to reinvent herself in order to survive in her new persona as Gurpal's wife and Bari Ma's daughter-in-law. Pain is represented as something that she will have to domesticate and cope with on a daily basis rather than something that can be transcended or cured once and for all.

Yet, Jamila Hashmi's "Exile" is also a powerful testimony of survival. Bibi is like her "real-life" counterparts, those women who chose to stay on and build something with their abductors rather than go back to a life of rejection or destitution in an arena of very limited options and restricted agency. By choosing to live with Gurpal and her new family, she silently rewrites the scenario of rape, converting her loss of subjectivity into her agency—in short, refusing the obliterating narrative of rape. This literary fiction thus presents a conscious subversion and "revision" of the ancient Sita story. Hashmi's modern-day Sita accepts her exile with her Ravana rather than return to a life of uncertainty and ostracism, in short, to face a second *vanvas* (exile). Although the narrative works well within patriarchal paradigms in its inability to imagine alternatives outside of paternalistic structures of protection and survival, it is important to underscore that Bibi chooses survival over death or rejection—however difficult or painful such a choice is revealed to be.

The last two fictions I turn to, Jyotirmoyee Devi's Bengali novella, *The River Churning*, and Lalithambika Antherjanam's Malayalam short fiction, "A Leaf in the Whirlwind," also seek to envision the particular dilemmas of life after violence for their female protagonists. However, their narrative trajectories trace a path quite different from the stories examined thus far. Like "Lajwanti" and "Exile," these fictions reveal the violence internal to the home and the family, but unlike the first two, they map the life of a single woman forced to step out of the paternalistic confines of the home into the larger world. First published in a journal in 1967 as *Itihasey Streeparva (The Woman's Chapter in History)*, the original Bengali title of *The River Churning* alludes to a chapter from the *Mahabharata* titled "Stree Parva" (The Woman's Chapter). The title was changed to *The River Churning (Epar Ganga Opar Ganga)* at the behest of the publisher when it was published in book form a year later. In the preface to the novel, however, the author makes clear the link with the "Stree Parva" of the *Mahabharata*. This chapter describes the aftermath of war in a land bereft of men. Women were openly abducted in the presence of the great warrior Arjun, who was rendered helpless. But the poet Vyasa, Jyotirmoyee writes, does not really chronicle what is implied by the title of the chapter; he is not able to give us a complete account:

> *But what happened afterwards.* . . . Which male poet would dare to write about that, and with what ink? No, such a pen, such ink and paper, have not yet been produced in the world. The writer of the epic was a male, after all. He could not possibly describe the savage acts of barbarism, the exploitation of the female body by a group of cowards. . . . History is not written by cowards, and there are no women epic poets.[81]

Born in the last decade of the nineteenth century, married at ten and widowed at twenty-six with six children, this "angry Indian [feminist] voice from the twenties of this century" seeks to remedy the marginalization of women by writing a women's history of Partition.[82] The concern with women's dispossession is made amply clear in the dedication as well: "to the tortured and exploited women of all ages and lands."

The River Churning is essentially a story about survival in the aftermath of Partition for an upper-caste Bengali Hindu girl, Sutara Dutta, whose uneventful existence is altered irredeemably by the 1946 pre-Partition riots in Noakhali district of East Bengal. Like Bedi and Hashmi, Jyotirmoyee is not concerned so much with representing the violence of the event itself as she is with the material and social exigencies of survival for her female protagonist in a fragmented country struggling to come to grips with the trauma of division. The novel opens with Sutara, a history teacher in a Delhi college, ruminating self-reflexively on the inclusions and exclusions of historiography, which takes her to her own suppressed personal history of violence and trauma. She recalls that fateful night in 1946 that changed her life irrevocably. It is a familiar story: a sudden upsurge of religious violence destroys the peace of a small village in East Bengal where Hindus and Muslims have coexisted fairly amicably for many years. In the space of a brief, sparing, and minimalist account, the author recounts how Sutara's Hindu household is destroyed: the father is killed on his way to get help; the mother jumps into a pond to save her honor and is never heard of again; her older married sister also disappears without a trace; while the young, adolescent Sutara loses consciousness under her assault.

The narrative of the event is characterized by blankness, fragmentation, and confusion: "What happened to Didi [her sister]? Sutara couldn't tell. She wanted to reach mother and began to run, but stumbled and fell. *Then everything went blank* (8). On recovering consciousness, she finds herself in the house of her Muslim neighbors, who had come to her rescue. However, in the blurred days that follow, Sutara can only encounter traumatic forgetfulness whenever she tries to remember what happened to her that eventful night:

> She had not recovered from the tremendous shock she had received. It had shaken her to the core. The exact nature of the blow which had stunned her physically and mentally was unknown to her—she was only aware of something terrible having crushed her existence out of shape.
>
> She could not clearly remember what had happened, but the dreadful memories of that night kept returning like a nightmare. Did she fall to the ground or was she pushed down? What happened after that? Who rescued her and when? For how long had she been running a fever? . . . She did not know what had been done to her (16).

The narrative draws attention to the difficulties entailed in incorporating trauma into narrative memory. Bal points out that repression and disso-ciation are two typical and yet different responses to trauma. She notes, "In narratological terms, repression results in ellipsis—the omission of important elements in the narrative—whereas dissociation doubles the strand of the narrative series of events by splitting off a sidelines. . . . In other words, repression interrupts the flow of narratives that shapes memory; dissociation splits off material that cannot then be reincorpo-rated into the main narrative" (ix). If in Manto's "Open It" we witness the dissociation of the female victim in the form of her compulsive reenact-ment of rape, in *The River Churning,* we encounter Sutara's ellipsis of the traumatic event. The novella thus stages the fragmented and partial na-ture of traumatic recall and refuses to provide any conclusive "evidence" about Sutara's rape even years later when, as an adult, she tries to come to terms with the larger national story of abduction and rape.

Her neighbors, Tamijuddin and his family, offer refuge to Sutara in their home for several months and nurse her back to health until she is fi-nally able to join her brothers in Calcutta. It is not due to any effort on her brothers' part, however, that Sutara is able to make her way to Calcutta. In spite of constant letters from Tamijuddin, her brother, Sanat—who is now effectively her guardian—does not express any particular concern for her well-being. Eventually, it is her Tamijkaka who escorts her to the riot-torn Calcutta of 1946–47 at considerable risk to himself and his family. In Calcutta, Sutara finds herself an unwanted visitor in Sanat's father-in-law's home, where the family has temporarily taken shelter because of the rioting in their locality. From the outset, Sutara is treated like a social outcast, especially by the older women of the family, who believe that her very touch and presence will pollute those who come in her vicinity. Her exclusion from caste and community is most emphatically enforced when it comes to the matter of food and the ritually pure domain of the kitchen. When, for example, Sanat's mother-in-law finds Sutara helping out with the chapattis, she almost collapses at the thought of her food being tainted by Sutara's touch: "Have you taken leave of your sense?" she rants to her daughter. "She has spent so many days in a Muslim household, six long months. What is left of her caste, you tell me! It was good of you to bring her over, that is alright. But keep her away from household work as you would a low caste hadi or Bagdi" (36). Notions of ritual purity are of course central to the preservation of the caste order, and upper-caste women are invested with the particular burden of maintaining caste purity in their (sexual) persons.

Even if it is never entirely clear whether Sutara was sexually assaulted or not during the riot, other characters are only too willing to construct her as an "abducted" woman—much like the state cast all women found living with "other" men as abducted.[83] As one aunt rationalizes, "We Hindus have some code of daily rituals. It does not allow *such girls* to be accepted back into the family. They have to be kept apart. She has eaten with Muslims, lived with them—how can she be accepted in the community?" (42). Having transgressed the codes and taboos of orthodox Brahminism by living with a Muslim (read untouchable) family, Sutara cannot be allowed to reenter the fold even though Tamijuddin's family had only offered sanctuary to her. The passage also makes clear how patriarchy and caste mutually reinforce each other—upper-caste norms of pollution are constantly invoked in the text to legitimize Sutara's ostracism from her family and community. In depicting the timeless duration of Sutara's suffering and loneliness, *The River Churning* offers an unsparing indictment of the terrifying hold of rituals of purity that mark out the exclusionary boundaries between communities, most frequently through the regulation and control of women's sexualities.

Ultimately, Sutara is sent off to a missionary boarding school, where she completes her bachelor's and then her master's degrees in history. Menon and Bhasin observe that while Partition made women the target of a never-before-seen epic violence, its disruption also had an ironic liberatory potential, at least for some women, by opening unknown thresholds and vistas of freedom. Forced by the contingencies of economic survival, thousands of women who had never before stepped out of their homes entered public spaces for the first time. Enabled by the "breakdown of traditional constraints on their mobility," they educated themselves and joined the workforce in huge numbers (Menon and Bhasin, 205). One of the women Menon and Bhasin interviewed, Bibi Inder Kaur, who had only studied up to class VIII before the division of the country, but went on to become a teacher in a Delhi college after displacement, claimed: "Partition provided me with the opportunity to get out of the four walls of the house. I had the will power, the intelligence, Partition gave me the chance. In Karachi I would have remained a housewife. Personally I feel Partition forced many people into taking the initiative and finding their own feet. . . . *I had spread my wings*" (Menon and Bhasin, 215). Other scholars have found that a similar phenomenon took place in West Bengal even though the pattern of migration there was quite different. Thus, Rachel Weber notes that a number of women joined the labor force in the 1950s as teachers, office workers, tutors, tailors, and so on, so that "the working woman with the broken sandals became a presence on the crowded streets of central Calcutta."[84]

Similarly, in *The River Churning*, Sutara is forced by the collapse of traditional patriarchal structures to educate herself and subsequently to move to Delhi as a teacher of history. In a significant passage, the author writes:

> Although Sutara found a place to stay, it was neither a home nor a household and least of all a nest created by a woman's love and care. But it was a room, *a room of her own*, and hers through her hard earned money. Did that make it a home? She knew only too well, the bitter truth that she would never have a home. But at least her brothers would no longer have to finance her. She would be a burden no more. (my emphasis, 69)

The echoes from Virginia Woolf are no coincidence: in a 1969 article, Jyotirmoyee, a self-educated Bengali woman writer, divulges the impact that Woolf's *A Room of One's Own* had on her. In it, she found an awareness of the "circumscribed life that women lead, their limited spheres of thought, the plethora of social strictures and the indifference of patriarchy."[85] The spatial movement of this novella, consequently, is very different from either "Lajwanti" or "Exile" as it moves beyond a confining and incarcerating domestic space to public spaces like the college where Sutara teaches and the women's hostel where she lives and encounters other women like herself. Yet, unlike the sentiment expressed by Bibi Inder Kaur in her narrative—"I had spread my wings"—Jyotirmoyee's protagonist does not always experience this passage from inside to outside as merely liberating. She values her newfound economic independence, but like other survivors of gendered violence, she envisions her future to be forever shadowed by loneliness, melancholy, and ostracism.

It is not surprising, then, that this Partition novella also finds in Sita's story a cultural precedent for the trials and dilemmas of its displaced protagonist. Although the benevolent Bengali patriarch, Amulya Babu, feels sorry for Sutara and views her as a "symbol" of the "exiled Sita, Amba or any other neglected girl," he also rationalizes his abdication of his responsibilities toward her by recalling the example of Sita's father, Janak, who remained passive in the face of his daughter's unjust banishment (50). Clearly, Jyotirmoyee holds well-meaning characters like Amulya Babu responsible for their complicity in patriarchal violence against women by virtue of their apathy. By contrast, Amulya Babu's son, Promode, like Sunder Lal in "Lajwanti," evokes Sita's tragic narrative in an effort to inspire some sort of reformist impulse in his male friends. He reminds them, "Sita followed Ram in his forest exile but Ram did not do the same for Sita" (118). But he also highlights the differences between these modern-day Sitas and the female protagonist of the *Ramayana*, for they "cannot die like Sita." "Those who manage to survive lead a most precarious existence on the margins of society" (118). Sita's story thus serves as a subtext that is constantly evoked in *The River Churning;* however, the novella also offers an interesting recasting of Sita's narrative. Whereas the mythical Sita must go through a "trial by fire" to establish her legendary chastity, this text refuses to provide any kind of definite proof of Sutara's "purity." The narrative refuses to fill in this gap in Sutara's memory; it remains until the very end. In this way, the writer repudiates the particular patriarchal logic that only "good" girls are worthy of rescue and redemption.

Interestingly, Sita is not the sole mythological figure to be invoked in this text; the narrative also makes repeated reference to Draupadi, the heroine of the *Mahabharata*. Specifically, the episode of Draupadi's public disrobing and sexual humiliation allows the author to place Sutara's particular predicament in a larger cultural context of women's degradation and oppression.[86] Draupadi, unlike the exemplarily devoted and obedient Sita, is not held up as a role model for Hindu womanhood. On the contrary, the *Mahabharata* represents her as an outraged figure, one who resists sexual humiliation through a variety of maneuvers ranging from physical resistance to legal recourse, pleas for male protection, curses and threats of revenge, and eventually "dignified submission coded as moral triumph."[87] As a consequence, Draupadi has often been appropriated as a proto-feminist cultural heroine in contemporary readings or performances of the *Mahabharata*. In keeping with this narrative tradition,

Sutara too retrieves Draupadi as a "brave and bold" woman, concluding that she would much rather have her students be courageous and outspoken Draupadis than passive and abject Sitas (68–69).

Thus, *The River Churning* constitutes the female subject of violence as a *survivor,* not merely in the sense of one who manages to escape death during the course of a limit event but one who endures and lives on in the face of immense adversity. The metaphor of the journey becomes crucial to Sutara's figuration of the disrupted course of her life. She reflects, "One without a home becomes a traveller—the way has been shown by the one who wrote the Mahabharata. She would *live on, would keep going.* Only the incapable stop half-way—they should stay back" (107; italics added). During the course of her pilgrimage to the Himalayas, Sutara also learns to pay attention to those aspects of life that have been eclipsed by violence: "Every moment there was new magic to behold and her sorrows faded in the face of the serene beauty and the grandeur of her surroundings. She heard a voice within her—all is not yet over, there are other things in life. The world contains a lot more than your tiny little self" (113).

In its closure, the novella seeks to envision the possibilities of a tentative new beginning for its protagonist. Promode proposes marriage in spite of his mother's fierce opposition to the prospect, and for the first time after that fateful night in 1946, Sutara begins to hope and dream of a better future with someone by her side. Yet, the proposal itself can only be proffered in predominantly paternalistic and patronizing terms. It is not offered in the terms of love or equality, but in sympathy and pity. "We talk of you often, Subha and myself," he says to Sutara. "We like you so much. I don't know about love, but we felt so sorry for you. Can you try to like us?" (129). Like the fictions of masculinity I read in the first section, *The River Churning* seeks to imagine men in roles other than perpetrator or passive onlooker. But it can do so only by envisioning a male nationalist figure who seeks to make amends for the nation's (and his family's) crimes against its women. Promode's decision to marry Sutara stems from his reformist desire to reinstate the gendered outcast of the nation—he tells his mother, "I want to marry an ordinary girl, Ma, a refugee" (123). While Sutara silently questions Promode's desire to marry her—"are you doing this out of pity? Charity? Was this love? Was this kindness?"—she is unable to bring herself to articulate these thoughts and eventually submits in abject gratitude.

Strikingly, the text also flirts briefly with the idea of intercommunity marriage but only to reject it as an unviable option at that historical juncture. Tamijuddin's wife becomes a very important figure in this minor though important strand of the narrative. She opens her home and her family to the wounded Sutara in the aftermath of her attack. Furthermore, when she learns of Sutara's rejection by her family, she offers to have her older son marry Sutara and "to make her our very own" (93). Even as her children wonder at her naïveté, the omniscient narrator observes, "All she felt was an overwhelming love for the poor homeless girl. Even now in moments of anger she laments her future . . . Why can't she accept her only option?" (99). Of course, hospitality can only be offered in patriarchal and assimilatory terms with the assumption that the Hindu other would merge into her new family and community. Not surprisingly, Sutara rejects the offer; her enduring trauma will not allow her to forget the events of that night—she can "hardly get her memories out of her system" (90). But it is significant that the novella considers the possibility of a Hindu–Muslim marriage at all; thus, this strand of the narrative ends with Tamijuddin's younger son's hope that (intercommunity) "love would put an end to such barbarities" (102).

Within the terms of Sutara's story, however, marriage can take place only inside the boundaries of caste and religion even if marriage is figured in the paternalistic terms of Promode's proposal. In her essay on the novel, Jill Didur further points out that since Promode's proposal to Sutara comes just as he is planning to leave for England, it can be read as the "ultimate patriotic sacrifice": "As a son of the nation planning to live in exile, he marries Sutara and removes her from the nation rather than directly challenging her treatment by the state and community."[88] Although this Bengali novella is a tremendously moving and poignant feminist account of the traumatic impact of Partition, its narrative ending, like other novelistic closures, limits and constrains the possibilities envisaged in the text itself. But in taking its protagonist past the upper-caste, patriarchal boundaries of her home and community to a secular space— Yajnaseni College, Delhi—inhabited by other women like her, *The River Churning* constructs a radical scenario of gendered survival.

The last fiction I turn to, Lalithambika Antherjanam's Malayalam short fiction, "A Leaf in the Whirlwind" (1948), offers a strikingly different account of survival, one that does not invest any agency for change in male hospitality. In fact, unlike the other stories I have discussed thus far, the story is remarkable for the complete absence of any male figure in the female survivor's attempt to narrativize her trauma and reintegrate it into the present. Instead, the protagonist learns to dwell once again in a world rendered unfamiliar by a catastrophic experience of violence. "A Leaf in the Whirlwind" tells the story of Jyoti, a Punjabi girl, who finds herself alone and pregnant in an Indian refugee camp after being brutally raped during the riots that attended Partition. Like *The River Churning*, this narrative envisions life beyond the paternalistic confines of the home for the raped subject but maps a different public space, that of a refugee camp. Here the state takes over as patriarch instead of the husband or the abductor of the previous fictions. From the start, Lalithambika constitutes her female protagonist as a resistant figure who repeatedly calls into question the authority of the state and the nation.

The story begins with the exchange of abducted women at the border between India and Pakistan: "An agreement had been made to hand over fifty women who had been held captive this side of the border, in return for an equal number from the other side."[89] The opening paragraphs of Lalithambika's fiction set the tone of the narrative with the use of words like "refusing," "reluctant," "held back," and "resisted." The author establishes Jyoti from the beginning as an insubordinate and defiant subject who calls into question the patriarchal authority of the state both through speech and action. For example, when she is handed over to the agents of the Indian state at the border, she refuses to divulge her name or her caste; moreover, when they attempt to take her to the refugee camp, she resists physically, asking: "[A]re you taking us from one prison to another, then?" (79). At the refugee camp, she refuses to speak to anyone and declines the social workers' offer of food, cursing them in anger: "Throw away your rotten pieces of bread. Give me a gun or a dagger—or even some poison. That's all I want from you" (80). Although Jyoti's verbal defiance establishes her as an outraged figure, her speech provides an instance of what Rajeswari Sunder Rajan has termed "linguistic excess" rather than any active agency. Sunder Rajan notes that women's exclusion from public spaces such as pulpits, courts of law, parliaments, and educational institutions often limits their speech to the space of the home. When women are allowed entry into public spaces, the very exceptionality of that entry may produce various kinds of "linguistic excess" such as

confession, curse, polemic, diatribe, or prophecy.[90] But patriarchy effectively deflects the significance and force of women's speech not by explicit
injunction alone but by the operation of more covert strategies, including preempting it as hysteria, gossip, ignorance, or lies. Indeed, speakers
often elicit a fierce backlash in the form of containment or repression.
Jyoti's physical and verbal defiance is futile and inappropriate, since it is
not able to achieve anything of consequence in changing her situation. If
I read Lalithambika's protagonist as a resistant figure, it is not because of
the linguistic excess in the story but because the trajectory of her narrative actively challenges the patriarchal order of both state and religious
community.[91]

Veena Das views the traumatized raped women of Partition as "occupying a zone between two deaths," one from violation and the other from
rejection. Lalithambika similarly constructs the subject status of these female victims of violence as ghosts returning from the dead: "[B]undled
shapelessly in black, the women glided from one side to the other like
ghosts released from a tomb" (79). The omniscient narrator recounts the
individual, traumatic life stories of the inmates of the refugee camp, yet
even as she wonders how these violated women were still alive given the
horror and the trauma they had endured, she is also careful to affirm their
enduring existence. She tells the story of one old woman, with nine children and fifty grandchildren, who had been like a mother to the entire
village. When the violence broke out, she had given refuge to Hindus
and Muslims alike but had refused to move from the place of her birth.
Eventually, her beloved home was burnt to ashes, while all her children
lost their lives. Yet, "she was still alive," the narrator insists. She cried
constantly, but "continued to talk, greedy for a part in life" (80). In another instance, the narrator recounts the story of a woman in the camp
who had been raped while her husband and children were murdered in
front of her eyes: "She had been barely alive when she was picked up
from a railway track—*yet she had not died*" (80, my emphasis).

In this fiction, the refugee camp becomes an enormous and in-
hospitable state-controlled public space, which brings together these victims of the disaster from different parts of the country. As the numbers
of devastated refugees grow, the turmoil and the confusion also increase.
In the midst of this vast sea of traumatized humanity, Jyoti finds herself
friendless and pregnant. When she refuses to eat even after several days

in the camp, a doctor is summoned to examine her. The doctor, as the official voice of nationalism in the narrative, attempts to interpellate Jyoti as a subject of the new nation, asking her to drink some milk if not for her own sake, at least for the sake of their "beloved country," which values every life it has (81). But as the victim of a fratricidal nationalistic violence, Jyoti refuses to be seduced by the lures of nationalism, angrily accusing the nation of having destroyed many lives in its mission to achieve independence at any cost, including Partition. Instead, she asks the doctor to help her abort the child she is carrying in her womb, a child who she describes as "the fruit of animal force and ignorance" (81). We are told that Jyoti doesn't even know who the father of her child is, having been brutally and violently gang-raped. However, the Gandhian doctor refuses to comply, and Jyoti is forced to carry her pregnancy to full term.[92]

As an unmarried, expectant mother, Jyoti makes all possible efforts to conceal her "shameful" secret from the other inmates of the camp by confining herself to deserted areas of the camp all day and sleeping in lonely corners at night. Providing a very embodied account of Jyoti's pregnancy, Lalithambika describes how Jyoti experiences her pregnancy as a suffocating burden that "invaded every atom of her being" (83). In fact, when she hears of a dead baby found abandoned in the camp lavatory, she resolves to kill her child and "come out into a new world full of hope" (83). Jyoti views the baby's murder as an act of agency, an example of the mother's remarkable courage. However, the narrative traces the subsequent transformation in Jyoti from her secret resolution to murder her child and thus to bury her "shame" to her decision to accept this painful relationship with a child conceived in violence and hate yet so undeniably a part of her life.

As she goes through the excruciating throes of labor in a lone corner of the camp, she feels an empathetic connection with her mother, who must have gone through the same pain to give birth to her. Yet, in marked contrast to her mother, who was surrounded by relatives, friends, doctors, and nurses as she delivered her child, Jyoti delivers her baby alone and forsaken in the relative anonymity of a refugee camp. In her pain, she recalls that brutal night of violation when innumerable men had raped her, "maddened with communal fever," and wonders which one of them her child would look like. Finally, lying exhausted on the ground, Jyoti decides that she must not merely kill her newborn child but also bury it, since "this was her cross, she had borne it, and she had to lay it down herself." But when she moves to pick up the "mass of moving flesh" and touches its hot body, she is halted in her resolve (86). While Manto's "Cold Meat" presents a visceral account of the encounter with the dead as other in the form of the cold corpse, "Leaf Caught in a Whirlwind" provides a thick, evocative, and tactile description of the young mother's first encounter with her living, breathing baby. She wonders, "Had it taken this heat from her own body?" (86). Overwhelmed by a mesh of contradictory emotions, Jyoti considers the possibility of abandoning the baby but eventually resolves to accept this "bond that was so inextricably interwoven with her life, even if it brought her great sorrow" (87). The child becomes a visible embodiment of the pain that survivors like Jyoti would have to learn to bear within their bodies. Grief is not depicted as something that will be transcended; instead it is experienced as something the female survivor will have to carry forever within her body. By learning to accept her relationship with pain, Jyoti is able to reinhabit a world made strange and bleak by the experience of a shattering violence.

The narrative closes on a hesitant and fragile "redemptive" note with the new mother holding her child close and walking back toward the camp. But Lalithambika feels the need to end her narrative on a sentimental note and enact some sort of closure. The last sentence of the story reads: "The stars smiled down on her as if they had found the answer to a difficult question" (87). However, the greater body of the narrative makes clear that there is often no closure after violence; living in the shadows of violence requires continuous coping and working through rather than a once-and-for-all cure or recovery.

In mapping the story of a single mother who makes the active choice to accept her illegitimate child—the visible symbol of her rape—Lalithambika's powerful feminist narrative offers a radical reframing of abducted women's stories by refusing available paternalistic solutions like living with the abductor or returning to her family. Jyoti refuses patriarchal efforts to constitute her either as a polluted being who can never completely be accepted by her community or as an abject victim who requires the benevolent intervention of the state.

In this chapter, I argue that fictional narratives of inhuman violence have an important role in inaugurating a more just and peaceful world. Using

Partition fictions as an example, I demonstrate how literature took upon itself the difficult and complicated task of pulling together the tatters of culture in the wake of the catastrophic violence of 1947. In contrast to recent historiographical turns to literature, my study strives to develop a method for the use of literature in the study of mass violence that does not seek to complete the historical record (as if that is ever really possible) or provide "evidence," but rather uses these fictions of inhuman violence for envisioning a way of living together in peace and accord with the other.

In their delineation of a radical crisis of masculinity brought about by the encounter with the wounded female body, the fictions I examine in the first section are examples of incipient efforts to imagine men in transformative and unconventional roles. I argue that such a reframing of the meaning of masculinity is crucial to the peaceful cohabitation of religious and ethnic groups whose very identities rest upon patriarchal norms of gender and sexuality in conditions of proximity to the other. (This was also evident in more recent instances of communal violence such as in Gujarat, where women's bodies were subjected to brutal and gruesome regimes of torture.) However, I also argue that Manto and Abbas are unable to take on the difficult task of exploring radical possibilities of subject constitution for the female survivor of mass violence because of the cultural equation of rape with death. This inability is also indicative of a larger cultural paralysis in the face of a limit event like Partition. Literature often turns to older narrative lines to comprehend what is happening in the present (as evidenced in the turns to the Sita story in a number of fictions), but limit events by definition surpass available paradigms of representation—that is, they pass beyond what lives in myth or in the cultural memory of a people. The predicament of the testimonial writer is how to describe such events. The enormity of the catastrophe prevents the writer-as-witness from taking the story further: the imagination balks and literature itself breaks down under the duress. In my reading, I have tried to show how we might use the gaps, fissures, and moments of rupture in these narratives as a means of understanding the gendered vocabulary of pain, survival, and coping that a culture has developed.

While the fictions of masculinity I read in the first section are preoccupied with revisioning maleness in a way that might allow men and women to live together after women's bodies have been subjected to brutal violation, the feminist literary narratives I address in the second section are unable to envision men in anything but complicit roles. Thus, almost all of the fictions of survival trace the failure or the impossibility of male hospitality toward the violated female other. Of the narratives I have examined, *The River Churning* is the only example of a woman's narrative that gestures toward a "new man" in the person of Promode. But this novella too can only represent male hospitality—men taking women's pain in their own bodies and making a home for them—toward the female survivor in primarily paternalistic terms. Men are understood to be so deeply implicated in the horrifying violence against women that it is nearly impossible to imagine the possibility of loving or nurturing heterosexual relationships. Rather, these feminist narratives are more concerned with the complicated issue of exploring possibilities of living, managing, sustaining—in short, surviving in the aftermath of violence. They enable us to question if violence really ever ends and whether survivors can ever *transcend* memories of violence. Veena Das and Arthur Kleinman suggest that the task of ethnographies of violence is to grapple with long-term and "little" consequences of violence as opposed to participating in "judicial or media-oriented confessional modes of truth-telling."[93] The moment of destruction is but one moment; hence, they remind us to attend to the "manner in which processes of resistance, contestation and accommodation begin to happen," but without looking for miraculous exceptions and hopeful endings. By enabling us imaginatively to inhabit the fractured world of the female survivor of mass violence, these fictions, like new ethnographies of violence, take us to the long-term ramifications of violence. They depict how surviving violence is an ongoing process of coping—domesticating worlds shattered by violence—that the survivor must struggle with every day of her life after violence.

In taking us to realms of pain and suffering that are a direct consequence of religio-nationalist conflict, these fictions of inhuman violence make a strong suit for a lasting peace rather than a temporary armistice or an armed peace. By attending to mass sexual violence against women, they point to the dangers of identity politics—especially when the identities of groups are predicated on the "despotic sovereignty" of female sexuality (to use Derrida's term)—and underscore the crucial importance of a feminist critical theory (as a persistent form of critique) to any program of multireligious and multiethnic coexistence.

5

∨

It's My Home, Too:
Minoritarian Claims on the Nation

What happened to those Muslims who remained in India in spite of the creation of a separate Islamic homeland across the border? A central argument of this book is that any effort at thinking about multireligious coexistence in India necessarily entails a rethinking of the anomalous place of Muslims in the modern Indian nation, not just in the more virulent discourses of the Hindu Right but also in the discourses of secularism, nationalism, and citizenship. One of the first steps toward such a task, as I have indicated, is rethinking the demand for Partition itself. While the accepted nationalist wisdom in India views the creation of Pakistan as the inevitable end point of the Muslim separatist impulse, I argue instead that Partition be read as the culmination of the (Indian) nationalist effort to contain Muslims in the role of national minority. Nationalism needs and produces its minorities—defined as such—in order to reinforce and validate its own center: the presence of oppressed minoritarian groups is therefore crucial to the self-definition of the majority group. One significant consequence of this successful minoritization of Muslims in post-Partition India has been that Indian Muslims have come to bear the difficult burden of blame for India's national vivisection. If Indian nationalism is haunted by its "other"—Pakistan—then, the figure of the Indian Muslim comes to occupy a strange, liminal place in this drama between self and "other." Placed in the uncomfortable position of national scapegoats, India's remaining Muslims continue to be defined as refugees, living on borrowed time, always bound for Pakistan—affectively and emotively, if not literally—no matter how valid their citizenship. Muslim minoritarian existence in India is thus defined by specific forms of estrangement

and othering vis-à-vis both state and society. In this final chapter of my
book, I address the particular legacies of a divided nation for the minoritarian Muslim community of post-Partition India. I examine some notable
Hindi films that give expression to the sense of a beleaguered Muslim
identity that has emerged in response to the blatantly anti-Muslim agenda
of the Hindu Right.

As a crucial realm of representation and refraction around the issues of
nationalism, religion, and minoritarian identities, Hindi cinema provides
a fascinating site of analysis. Mainstream Hindi cinema's mass appeal
and expansive reach in a context of widespread illiteracy is undeniable.
Cinema's form of viewership is social and collective, which makes viewing films a rather different activity than the typically private one of reading literary fiction. The very act of collective viewing entails a certain
kind of democratization and blurring of boundaries—if only for the time
we are in the social space of the auditorium—since it allows everyone
watching simultaneous access to the fictional realm despite the actually
existing hierarchies among different members of the audience (reflected
in the very organization of space in Indian movie theaters).[1] In its visual
and auditory address, as well, cinema as a medium works in a different
register than literature, since it introduces the relationship of spectator-
ship to narrative. As Ravi Vasudevan points out, cinema as an audiovisual
medium "places new demands on the human sensorium" as we enter into
a compact to become part of its imaginary domain.[2] Cinema's enormous
potential as an affective and accessible medium therefore cannot be overemphasized. I turn to Hindi cinema in this last chapter of a book that primarily addresses literary narratives because of the wider reach and impact
of the medium and also because the particular films I examine open up a
space for thinking about the dilemmas of Muslim minoritarian existence
in contemporary Hindutva-inflected India.

The films I examine, Mahesh Bhatt's *Zakhm* (1998), Khalid Mohamed's
Fiza (2000), and Shyam Benegal's *Mammo* (1994), are part of what I call
an emergent genre in Hindi cinema, the Muslim minoritarian film. I consider M. S. Sathyu's *Garam Hawa* (1973) the prototypical text of this
genre; I also include films like Saeed Akhtar Mirza's *Saleem Langde Pe
Mat Ro* (1989) and *Naseem* (1995) within this category. Like the fictions
of Salman Rushdie, Amitav Ghosh, and Mukul Kesavan, these films are
concerned with the ambivalent and anomalous place of Muslims in dis-

courses of Indian nationhood and citizenship, but in a significantly different register. They ask us to consider what happens when one *inhabits* a marginalized and dispossessed subject-position. What kind of ethical and political claims can be articulated from such positions? To understand the significance I claim for these films, it is important to first situate them within the grammar of popular Hindi cinema.

Bombay cinema has long been affirmed as one of the most enduring secularist cultural sites of contemporary India with its diverse personnel coming from various religious and regional backgrounds. Yet the anxieties surrounding the figure of the Indian Muslim in discourses of Indian nationalism are also generated in the Bombay cinema, which, after all, is a primary site for constructions of the Indian nation.[3] Popular Hindi cinema tends to rely on a characteristic suppression of minority ethnic and religious groups either through hyper-visibility (the stereotype) or through invisibility (absence). As Ravi Vasudevan points out, "While the working premise of social representation in mainstream cinema is the stereotype, we must understand that Bombay cinema has always tended to reserve a notion of normalcy for the Hindu hero, the apex figure in the composite nationalism of its fictions. Exaggeration in cultural behaviour is attributed to other social groups, especially Muslims, Christians and Parsis."[4]

Just as nationalism constructs (upper-caste) Hindu beliefs and practices as universal and secular—with minority groups construed as saturated by their religious and cultural identities—popular Hindi cinema also figures the North Indian Hindu male as the representative secular-nationalist self. By means of its visual culture and characteristic narrative forms, this cinema invites the spectator to assume a majoritarian Hindu, North Indian male identity. This unmarked Hindu male identity is thus positioned as the normative spectator of popular Hindi cinema.[5] If and when Muslims find figuration in this cinema, their representation has largely been in keeping with popular Hindu perceptions about Muslims as a backward, deeply religious, and conservative community. Popular Hindi cinema reproduces with unfailing regularity what Mukul Kesavan has called "a repertoire of ghetto stereotypes" of Muslims, which includes such stock characters as the simple, perpetually Quran-reading Muslim, the burqa-clad Muslim *khatoon* (woman), the refined *tawaif* (courtesan), and so on. Clearly defined external markers of speech, dress, appearance, and religious practice are used to identify and segregate Muslims in most Hindi films.[6] Muslims are rarely placed at the center of popular Hindi cinema's narratives.

To be sure, there are some notable mainstream films, such as *Coolie* (Manmohan Desai, 1983), *Amar Akbar Anthony* (Manmohan Desai, 1977), and *Allah Rakha* (Ketan Desai, 1986), in which Muslims figure as protagonists. However, the star personae of actors like Amitabh Bachchan and Rishi Kapoor often overwhelm the characters they are playing in these films—hence, Muslims cannot be represented as Muslims in these films. And while particular genres, such as the Muslim Social or the Historical, have depicted Muslim sensibilities in mainstream Bombay cinema, they have also contributed to the consolidation of the Muslim as the self-consolidating other of the normative secular Hindu self. As Sumita Chakravarty notes, the Bombay cinema has "not so much addressed the Hindu–Muslim relationship as sublimated it by displacing it on to the canvas of history."[7] Nationalist anxieties around the figure of the Indian Muslim are thus managed in the cinematic imaginary through a series of proscriptions—including official censorship—and repressions. Until recently, these prohibitions ensured that "'communal passions' or Muslim religio-political identities except of an oppressively benevolent variety remained unnamed and unexaminable."[8] Muslims in mainstream Hindi cinema therefore tend to be represented as an undifferentiated homogeneous entity—the site of the traditional, the antiquated, and the premodern. Differences of class and region among Muslims are often completely elided or dismissed. Once Muslims are constructed as a particular kind of "other"—that which consolidates the subject status of the ethnocentric (upper-caste) Hindu subject—it becomes fairly routine and easy to contain them within the dominant narratives of the Bombay cinema. What is largely occluded in such monolithic constructions is a figuration of the modern Muslim subject.

Despite these typological representations, however, mainstream Hindi cinema also offers some interesting ways of thinking about Hindu–Muslim coexistence. In a complex and wide-ranging essay that extends Christian Metz's work on the cinematic apparatus, Vasudevan argues that popular Hindi cinema—by way of its narratives and as a medium that serves to dematerialize both the object and the viewer—is able to constitute a "transcendent subject," one that is not bound by an identity.[9] Thus, for example, an early film such as D. G. Phalke's *Shree Krishna Janma* (1918) depicts characters from different castes—who were initially shown successively and divided from each other by means of intertitles preceding separate shots—eventually occupying the same frame in a single shot that has them crowding together. Vasudevan reads this film as an "important ur-text for images of intercommunity mingling and self-transcendence" (246). He also identifies the city—and especially the street—in the cinema of the postindependence period as an important space that provides a release from hierarchy and bounded identities. In this context, he offers the interesting example of Manmohan Desai's *Chhalia* (*The Cheat*, 1960), which cleverly mobilizes Raj Kapoor's famous screen persona of the tramp as the means for "intercommunity tolerance and renewal" (255). Although the use of the term "transcendence" to subsume the range of possibilities of Hindu–Muslim cohabitation found in these films is, to my mind, problematic, Vasudevan provides some fascinating examples of multireligious coexistence in earlier popular Hindi cinema. While participating in and consolidating popular stereotypes of Muslims as innately backward, deeply religious, and conservative, cinema also channels its energies to come up with imaginative scenarios of cohabitation and living with the other.

The films of the late 1980s and 1990s, however, signaled an important departure in mainstream cinema's depictions of Muslims and of Hindu–Muslim relations. This conjuncture is defined by the rise of the Hindu Right in India; it also saw the intensification of separatist movements in Kashmir and the North-East. Concurrently, Hindi cinema of this period, in contrast to the films of the previous decades, saw the emergence of the "evil" Muslim. Films like *Tezaab* (N. Chandra, 1988), *Gardish* (Priyadarshan, 1993), and *Angaar* (Shashilaal Nayar, 1992) identify their villains as Muslim, though "Muslims in these narratives come from Bombay's criminal groups."[10] The 1990s, however, gave rise to a spate of popular filmic narratives that explicitly constitute Muslims as a belligerent community. For example, Mani Ratnam's *Bombay* (1995) despite its well-meaning effort to reveal the futility of communal violence, may well be the first film to "figure [Muslim] aggression as residing *within* the community rather than characterizing its communal offshoots" (Vasudevan, "Bombay," 194). Thus, *Bombay* inaugurates an alliance between mainstream cinema's representation of Muslims and nationalist anxieties about the Muslim as a stranger in our midst. Such constructions are further exacerbated and legitimized in popular cinema as Muslim militancy becomes the subject of several films in the 1990s, including Ratnam's *Roja* (1992) and *Mission Kashmir* (Vidhu Vinod Chopra, 2000). The aftermath of the Kargil war with Pakistan also saw the emergence of a spate of patriotic films such as *Hindustan ki Kasam* (Veeru Devgun, 1999), *Pukar* (Boney Kapoor, 2000), and *L. O. C. Kargil* (J. P. Dutta, 2003), which clearly identify Pakistan as the enemy nation. In still other films, such as *Sarfarosh* (John Mathew Mathan, 1999) and *Refugee* (J. P. Dutta, 2000), the disquiet around the figure of the Indian Muslim takes the form of a split between the "good" Indian Muslim who is made ritually to swear allegiance to the nation and the "evil" Pakistani other who is clearly established as the enemy who dares to challenge Indian sovereignty. Films often invoke this split quite explicitly by figuring the "good" and "bad" Muslims as brothers—for example, in films like *Refugee* and, more recently, *Insan* (K. Subhash, 2005)—a revision of an old formula found in earlier films such as *Mother India* (Mehboob Khan, 1957) and *Deewar* (Yash Chopra, 1975).

In such a polarized context, the Muslim minoritarian film comes to occupy a very important emergent space for new ways of thinking about Hindu–Muslim relations. These films are important to examine because they stand as significant exceptions to the regular fare of much Hindi cinema in the ways in which they allow a rare spectatorial identification with the figure of a besieged Muslim subject. Identification is effected both by means of narratives that draw attention to the plight of Muslims in contemporary Hindutva-dominated India and by the visual address of these films. In inviting the normative spectator of popular Hindi cinema to identify with the figure of the beleaguered Muslim, these films enable the majoritarian (and male) Hindu self to come as close as possible to imagining the (Muslim) other as a self, a task that is central to ethics.[11] However, while these films invite empathy from the normative spectator of mainstream Hindi cinema—who is typically aligned with a majoritarian and male subjectivity—they do not allow for the assimilation of the Muslim other into the representative (upper-caste) Hindu self. (This refusal to allow the appropriation of the other distinguishes the Muslim minoritarian film from Hindu–Muslim/Indian–Pakistani romances ranging from *Bombay* [1995] to *Veer Zaara* [Yash Chopra, 2004], which stage the fantasy of incorporating the exotic Muslim/Pakistani woman into the secular Indian self that can only be imagined as male and Hindu.)[12] They make it possible for us to consider how Muslims might be figured as Muslims without rendering their different religious beliefs and practices as exhaustive of all subjectivity and identity. Most importantly, they assert a specific claim on the Indian nation from an embodied minoritarian location, a claim moreover that is not a simple plea but an assertion: *It's my home, too!*

In staking a claim to the nation, the protagonists of these films compel us to consider the possibility of a radical hospitality without invitation. Derrida differentiates between the hospitality of invitation and that of visitation by proposing that there is a "hidden contradiction" between hospitality and invitation. He argues that "the awaited *hôte* (thus invited, anticipated, there where everything is ready to receive him) is not a *hôte, not an other as hôte*" (my emphasis).[13] It is precisely the invitation that marks conditional hospitality: "If I welcome only what I welcome, what I am ready to welcome, and that I recognize in advance because I expect the coming of the hôte as invited, there is no hospitality" (362). In contrast, an unconditional hospitality would be open to the visitation, where one "waits without waiting, awaiting absolute surprise, the unexpected visitor, awaited without horizon of expectation" (362). The "visitor" is someone who could come at any time and who does not have to be an "invited guest." The films I examine here exemplify Derrida's notion of "visitation" as the "arriving of the other who could come at any moment *without asking my opinion.*"[14] The protagonists of these films insist on their claims on the Indian nation and their right *to be* in India. In fact, there *is* no host within the narratives of these films, one who is given the power to block the threshold or even to say, "I welcome you"—and hence to claim ownership of the nation. Like the novels of Rushdie and Ghosh, these films radically reject the authority of (caste) Hindus as the hosts—those who have prior claims—and hence as the original inhabitants of India. But, since they function within the realm of a cinema that has traditionally invited its spectators to assume an upper-caste Hindu (male) identity, I argue that these films position the normative spectator of Hindi cinema as the self who is now being asked to give up all claims to mastery and sovereignty. The spectator is faced with the ethical choice of either unconditionally welcoming the Muslim other—that which has been deemed "strange" and "foreign" to the nation—into his home, his dwelling, and his self, or of barring the threshold yet again.

Interestingly, in different ways, all three of the films I focus on occupy an important intermediate space between Hindi commercial cinema and art cinema. Having emerged at a historical moment when such categories have increasingly become diffused, especially as attested to by the recent appropriation of popular cinematic modes by parallel cinema auteurs such as Shyam Benegal and Govind Nihalani, these films inhabit an interesting middle ground between popular and parallel modes of filmmaking. If Mahesh Bhatt emerges mainly from the mainstream cinema tradition, then Benegal is closely identified with art cinema, while Khalid Mohamed attempts to construct a creative middle space with his very first film as a director, *Fiza*. With *Zakhm* and *Mammo,* both Bhatt and Benegal also move closer to an in-between space between commercial and parallel cinema.[15] Bhatt dilutes the element of the popular in *Zakhm* and returns once again to the mode of his earlier critically acclaimed yet less mainstream films such as *Arth* (1982), *Saaransh* (1984), and *Janam* (1985). And, although Benegal's *Mammo* emerges from a realism-driven art cinema, it too seems to mark a turning point in his authorship in its episodic narrative, its deployment of humor, and its use of songs on the soundtrack. Of the three, *Fiza* is most clearly allied with popular cinematic conventions in its use of song and dance sequences and popular stars, while both *Zakhm* and *Mammo* rely on long takes and focus on particular spaces to simulate reality.

All three films are family melodramas, which use the private family setting to work over the ambivalent public position of Muslims in Indian society and structures of citizenship. While each of these films employs certain melodramatic conventions of popular cinema, they also subvert them in very interesting ways. *Zakhm* most evidently relies on the excess of melodrama and the centrality of pathos to convey its affect, while Benegal veers closer to realism by means of more subdued acting and less histrionics. But what marks *all* these films off from mainstream Hindi cinema is not just their imaginative attempt to elicit identification with the Muslim other but also their refusal to rely on spectacle in the same way as commercial cinema. There are hardly any chase scenes, fights, rescues, or action sequences in these films, and even sectarian violence is rarely depicted on screen.

Given cinema's enormous potential for epic representations of "big events" like communal violence, what are we to make of this avoidance? As an affective and audiovisual medium, cinema can elicit a visceral response from the spectator through its depictions of inhuman violence. Why, then, do these films eschew what has by now become an iconographic representation of crowds in cinematic representations of mass violence? This reticence about depicting violence or massed crowds on screen distinguishes these films from what I call the "riot film," among which I include such works as *Bombay, Hey Ram* (Kamal Haasan, 2000), *Gadar: Ek Prem Katha* (Anil Sharma, 2001), and *Dev* (Govind Nihalani, 2004). (Nihalani's televisual drama on Partition, *Tamas*, is undoubtedly the ur-narrative of this genre.) A central semantic element of these latter films is the crowd sequence, which establishes iconic images of collective violence by means of shots of Hindu and Muslim mobs armed with swords or *lathis* (sticks), shouting terrifying slogans, and charging at each other. Typically, these sequences involve shots of people dousing petrol on their victims, of rioters carrying flaming torches, of burning cars, of looting and plunder. But while they establish an iconography of the riot in the spectator's memory, they also risk creating a monotonous or banal effect by dint of sheer repetition. At times, violence can also take on a sensationalizing and gratuitous aspect, inviting a voyeuristic view (for example, in some of the riot sequences of Kamal Haasan's *Hey Ram*). I do not mean to suggest that all representations of violence are necessarily prone to sensationalism or banality, especially given my argument about the power of inhuman images and stories of violence to mobilize against violence in the last chapter. But certainly the pitfalls of representing violence, especially because of the disjunction between intention and reception, are more likely with cinematic spectacles of violence.

In contrast, the Muslim minoritarian film rarely depicts scenes of mass violence or frenzied Hindu–Muslim crowds charging at each other. I argue that the refusal to represent violence on screen is not determined by budgetary constraints alone, but rather it is a deliberate choice of the directors. One of the formal aspects that brings these films closer to the tradition of art cinema is their hesitancy or unwillingness to exploit violence by reducing it to spectacle. Moreover, representing antagonistic crowds pitted against each other can only serve to stage contemporary religious violence as a war among equals—a conflict between two equally guilty parties—whereas Bhatt, Mohamed, and Benegal are more concerned with establishing the plight of Muslims in a post–Babri masjid India by means of their affective narratives. They seek to convey the collective sense of vulnerability, insecurity, and alienation among Muslims, a feeling not limited to specific sections of the community but engulfing the community as a whole. (This is amply testified to in the recent Sachhar Commission Report). Like the feminist fictions I examined in chapter 4, these films focus on the long-term impact of everyday forms of violence and discrimination rather than on the climactic riot scene itself. Before examining these more recent films, I turn briefly to what I consider the prototypical narrative of the Muslim minoritarian film, M. S. Sathyu's debut feature, *Garam Hawa* (*Hot Winds*, 1973).

Garam Hawa

Released two years after India's 1971 war with Pakistan, *Garam Hawa* is a brave and idealistic reaffirmation of Indian Muslims' claim on the Indian nation. Set in Agra after the first major exodus of Muslims to the new Islamic nation of Pakistan, the film traces the story of a particular Indian Muslim family in the immediate years after Partition. Like many North Indian Muslim families of the time, this family is divided on the issue of emigrating to Pakistan or staying on in their ancestral home in Agra. The film delineates an increasingly hostile and antagonistic anti-Muslim environment in the recently truncated India. At the center of this beleaguered minoritarian narrative stands Salim Mirza, an elderly Muslim who refuses to migrate to Pakistan at the time of Partition. Mirza is established as a hero precisely because of his rejection of the idea of Pakistan—unlike his brother Halim, he never gives in to separatist sentiments. Gradually, however, Mirza is forced to reconsider his conviction that the ties of region and commerce transcend those of religion in the face of the many trials and tribulations he has to face as a Muslim in post-Partition India. The film maps the breakdown of Mirza's fortitude from his initial resolve to continue to live in his hometown—emerging from the idealistic conviction that after Gandhi's death ("martyrdom") there will be no more bloodshed in India—to his eventual painful decision to migrate to Pakistan toward the end. The concluding sequence of the film takes us to the shrunken family in a horse carriage—Mirza, his wife, and their younger son, Sikander—on their way to the train station. However, the film's idealistic closure does not allow the seeming inevitability of this depressing conclusion. As their carriage moves toward the station, they are interrupted by a peaceful communist rally with people waving red flags proclaiming the unity of all the dispossessed. Mirza's son Sikander jumps into the fray, believing that they must stay and fight with the "common man," and soon Mirza too joins him. In its conclusion, the film affirms a tentative and fragile hope in the possibility of a better future, one that will allow for the emergence of new political coalitions and alignments across religious communities. Clearly, the film is an early (albeit belated) secular-nationalist account of Partition, but one that emerges from the specific experiences of a besieged Indian Muslim subjectivity in the immediate aftermath of Partition.

At the same time, the film also inaugurates the binaries of "good" Indian and "evil" Pakistani in the figures of the secular-nationalist Salim Mirza, who refuses to migrate to Pakistan, and the separatist Halim Mirza, who is set on the road to Pakistan. While the film draws attention to the specific concerns and traumas of the minoritarian Muslim community in India in the early years after division, it is unable to call into question the construction of Pakistan as the "other" of Indian nationalism. But undeniably, Sathyu's film remains the only film to directly address the issue of a minoritarian Muslim identity in the first three decades after Partition. It has taken the destruction of the Babri masjid and the spiraling communal violence of the subsequent years to inspire a new set of films that attempt to articulate similar concerns about the construction of Muslims as strangers within the nation. These films emerge as a specific response to the predicaments and dilemmas of Muslims in a Hindu Right–inflected India and attest to the ways in which historical "moments of crisis" provide the impetus for radical literary and cultural production.

Assimilation and Burial in *Zakhm*

Set in Bombay in the days following the destruction of the Babri masjid, *Zakhm* is a powerful narrative about concealed identities, assimilation, and the eventual assertion of a distinct Muslim selfhood. It is the story of a Muslim woman (Pooja Bhatt) and her lover, an upper-caste Hindu man, Ramesh (Nagarjuna), who have been unable to marry because of strong resistance from the man's mother. Told largely as a flashback from the adult son Ajay's perspective, the film moves between representing the everyday indignities of the past for the single mother and her child and the dangers of a Hindu Right–dominated present. The film opens with a melancholy Ajay (Ajay Devgan) listening to news about the riots that have been sparked off in Bombay as a consequence of the destruction of the Babri masjid. The television anchor announces that there is a curfew in various localities such as Dharavi and Behrampara—thus establishing a sense of danger in the city. Ajay's wife Sonia has decided to leave for England because she does not want to give birth to their child in this atmosphere of communal discord and violence "where daggers are drawn in the name of religion." Ajay tries to dissuade her by saying that running away is not the answer, since this is their home. However, their argument is interrupted when his brother calls to say that their mother has been missing since morning. When he goes to the church where she usually prays to try to find her, he learns from some policemen that she has been burned by a Muslim mob, which had mistakenly taken her to be a Hindu. In the hospital, a chance question about her identity by a Muslim reporter who has heard her cry out "Allah" leads Ajay to reflect on his past and his parents' deeply complicated relationship. In an extended flashback, the film takes us to the boy Ajay (Kunal Khemu) who witnesses his mother's daily humiliation and anxiety given her illegitimate status in a society in which marriage and motherhood are crucial to middle-class norms of femininity. Although he claims to love her, Ajay's father is not able to assert himself to his mother, who resorts to all kinds of stratagems to prevent him from marrying his Muslim "concubine." Eventually, he succumbs to his mother's emotional blackmail and agrees to marry another woman of his own caste and religion. Despite her pain and anguish, Ajay's mother agrees to continue with their illegitimate relationship.

Much of the plot is driven by Ajay's eventual discovery of his mother's Muslim identity—which she has kept hidden from him—in a climactic moment of heightened drama. When his father dies in a car accident, Ajay and his mother go to the father's house to pay their last respects. The crazed grandmother cannot bear the thought of their polluted Muslim presence in her sanctified home and calls them "dirty Muslims," which is when Ajay finally learns the truth about his mother. Significantly, even after this discovery, his mother instructs him to hide his Muslim lineage, since it brings so much humiliation and indignity. This knowledge must remain a secret that they will not share with anyone, not even Ajay's little brother. However, after the brutal attack on his mother by the Muslim mob, the adult Ajay decides to reveal everything to his wife and his brother.

The impetus for sharing this information has to do with his mother's wish that she be buried—rather than cremated—in accordance with Muslim rites when she dies. Ajay wants to honor her decree, but his brother, Anand, cannot grasp the thought that their mother, who had passed herself off as a Hindu, is actually a Muslim. Anand is a member of a right-wing Hindu organization (a proxy for the Shiv Sena); the chief of this organization, Subodh Bhai, has taken Anand under his wing and has been instrumental in indoctrinating him into the group's blatantly anti-Muslim agenda, which seeks to cleanse and purify the nation of all Muslims. Thus, when Anand finds out about the attack on his mother, he immediately wants to avenge himself on the imprisoned Muslim man who assaulted her. However, Ajay comes to the man's rescue by divulging to Anand that their mother was a Muslim—and hence they too are half Muslim. But despite Ajay's avowal of the truth, Anand refuses to believe him and insists, with Subodh's support, that she be cremated according to normative Hindu rituals and practices. Subodh wants to use the event to incite retaliatory violence against all Muslims in Bombay; however, Ajay refuses to allow him to use their mother's body as a pawn in his political gamesmanship. Despite much opposition from Subodh and a character-istic corrupt police inspector, the quiet but determined Ajay insists on carrying out his mother's wishes. In the end, the film depicts how Anand also comes around, since maternal love overwhelms all other affiliations, and the two brothers, together, lay their mother to rest in keeping with Muslim rites for the dead.

Bhatt's own history as the product of an illicit relationship between a Guajarati Brahmin man and a Muslim woman brings an extradiegetic text to the film and heightens its emotional impact. *Zakhm* explicitly ac-knowledges its autobiographical referent in the epigraph—"For Nanabhai Bhatt and Shirin . . . who gave me life." Bhatt is well known for proclaim-ing autobiographical sources for his films, most famously for *Arth*, which explored his extramarital relationship with Praveen Babi.[16] Indeed, he has often been criticized for exploiting and sensationalizing his own life in order to make his films. In this film, while Bhatt once again draws on his own childhood and his parents' relationship, he also makes an important intervention in the broader discourse of Hindu–Muslim relationships. Although he has explored the meaning of illegitimacy and what it means to grow up with a single mother in earlier films like *Janam,* only with *Zakhm* does he bring the Hindu–Muslim aspect of the relationship to the fore. Writing of *Zakhm,* he states:

> After having found dizzying success and after making senseless and meaningless movies, the time had now come to make *the defining film of my career.* I am glad that before I hung up my gloves as a director, I dared to revisit the wounds of my childhood. I told a tale *that moved out into the larger domain, the public domain*—the post–Babri Masjid demolition period and the subsequent bloodshed. This was *Zakhm.* I dared to make this film with my own funds, without State help, in a very repressive atmosphere. . . . *Zakhm* had bought me a lot of dignity. It washed me clean, it purged me of the aftertaste of having made some senseless films.[17] (my emphasis)

Bhatt also underscores how the making of this film was cathartic for him: "One can hardly claim exorcism, but the act of story-telling helps you to cope with the anguish of life."[18] Evidently, *Zakhm* occupies an important place in his oeuvre (in his own estimation) in its effort to take on broader sociopolitical issues about the subordinate place of Muslims in the Indian polity.

Unlike his more recent "potboilers" (his term), *Zakhm* deploys many conventions that derive from the art cinema: slow pace, entire scenes shot in long takes to simulate reality, the use of mostly medium to medium-long shots punctuated by very few extreme long shots, rudimentary establishing shots, and a preoccupation with space. Most of the drama takes place in limited spaces—the hospital (in the present) and the house (in the past)—with a few interspersed sequences in the father's studio and the house that he shares with his wife. At the same time, the film also draws on some of the conventions of popular cinema, particularly in its use of songs, which allow it to reach out to a broader audience. Nevertheless, the songs in *Zakhm* do not evoke a realm of fantasy as they often do in mainstream cinema. In contrast to the picturized song and dance sequences of commercial cinema, in this film, songs are played over the soundtrack and are used to convey a first-person point of view. For example, the mother's worshipping adoration of her lover is established by means of songs that express her desire and longing as she waits for him to visit them. However, it is in its use of melodrama that the film most evidently aligns itself with the modes of popular Hindi cinema.

Zakhm employs some of the dominant features of melodrama to achieve moral legibility in an unjust world. Once again, Linda Williams can instruct us about the appeal of melodrama as a pervasive mode of the popular imagination. She usefully identifies some key features of melodrama, including its need to establish a (lost) "space of innocence" usually typified in the realm of the home, its focus on victim-heroes whose suffering constitutes their virtue, and its deployment of a Manichaean universe. Pathos is central to the melodramatic mode—"the suffering body caught up in paroxysms of mental or physical pain" is the means to the recognition of the victim's virtue.[19] *Zakhm* draws on such melodramatic conventions to establish both the pain of the long-suffering mother and the cruelty of the casteist grandmother. Both are set up as Manichean opposites throughout the film. While Ajay's and his mother's multiple indignities are used to elicit viewer sympathy, the grandmother's hysterical responses serve to alienate the spectator. The grandmother's incessant invective against Ajay and his mother disallows any kind of sympathy on the part of the spectator. On one occasion, when Ajay calls and asks to speak to his father, she warns him that if after today he were to address her son as "Daddy," she would snip off his tongue with a pair of scissors, and if he were to dial their number again, she would chop off his fingers. As she puts the phone down, she mutters, "Dirty blood"—at this point we don't know that Ajay's mother is Muslim—while her oblivious son framed at a distance with his back to the camera continues to pray in front of a Ganapati idol.

The grandmother's excessive behavior is heightened in the scene when Ajay's father tells her that he plans to marry his lover. The sequence begins with Ramesh's point-of-view shot as he looks at a photograph of his lover and his child concealed behind the clothes in his closet. The hidden photograph serves as an apt metaphor for their relationship, which is literally "in the closet." Ramesh is interrupted in his wistful reverie by his mother, who asks him to join their guests. As he continues to look at the picture, she walks into the room. The camera follows her as she peers into the closet and discovers the photograph. Covering her eyes and muttering chants to purify herself, she castigates him for showing her the (impure) faces of Ajay and his mother. When he tells her that he plans to bring them both to his home, she breaks into a rant: "What else will you do for that sorceress? You have already bought her a house, given her a child, and committed your monthly salary to her." When he avers that he plans to marry her, she walks out of the room, and the soundtrack turns loud and ominous. A sound bridge comprised of clanging vessels leads us into the next scene of heightened melodrama. As Ramesh follows the sound of the banging, he discovers his mother in the kitchen. Composed in a medium-long shot with her back to the camera, she is dousing fuel all over herself. As the frightened man calls out, "Ma," she turns around to face us and tells him that after she dies, he is welcome to bring "prostitutes" to the house, but she will not let him commit this "sin" in her lifetime. As he holds her, she cries, "Those two will not be allowed to come to this house while I am alive." The excess of this scene establishes the grandmother as a frenzied and hysterical character and solicits our alienation from her while simultaneously evoking our sympathy for the "illegitimate" mother–son duo that is the target of her invective. Melodramatic pathos in the person of Ajay's long-suffering mother then invites the normative spectator of mainstream Hindi cinema to feel the pain of his intimate other, the Indian Muslim, at precisely the moment when the Muslim protagonist is excluded from upper-caste Hindu society on the basis of notions of ritual purity and impurity. Pathos is further heightened by the extradiegetic knowledge that Bhatt's real-life daughter, Pooja, is playing the role of his mother's persona in the film.

I want to dwell on a particularly evocative scene that foreshadows the eventual proclamation of the mother's submerged Muslim identity. This scene occurs right after the grandmother's threat to immolate herself. The mise-en-scène shifts radically from the trappings of an upper-caste Hindu household, with its idols, its miniature temple, its swastikas, and its oms, to an explicitly Muslim milieu announced by the sound of the *azan*—the Islamic call to prayer—and a long shot of a minaret at dawn. The seemingly extradiegetic sound of the *azan* accompanies the camera to Ajay's room in the form of a sound bridge. The camera pans slowly to the right from the objects on the table to Ajay as he sleeps on the bed. A dazed Ajay wakes up to the sound of the muezzin's call, but now a chanting voice is also heard over the soundtrack with the *azan* in the background. The intoning voice is not clearly audible or incomprehensible, but it sounds as though someone is praying. The tracking camera follows a visibly bewildered Ajay as he walks in the direction of the voice, but the soundtrack ceases suddenly just before he reaches the door. As he opens the door leading out to the balcony, his mother calls him from the inside. He turns around, and along with him, we see her composed in profile praying in front of a statue of Ganesh. Her brisk and routine demeanor reestablishes the façade of a "normal" Hindu household and allows us to forget the "strange," inexplicable sounds we have heard along with Ajay.

However, the scene acquires importance retrospectively when Ajay finally registers the meaning of the sounds he had heard. This recognition takes place during the crucial sequence when Ajay and his mother go to his father's house after they learn of the latter's death. Ajay's mother wants her newborn child to receive his dead father's blessings. Predictably, the grandmother commands them to get out of her house, but her virtuous (legitimate) daughter-in-law comes to their rescue. Taking the child from his mother, she holds him close to the photograph of the dead man. At this, the grandmother completely loses control and tells her that she has touched her son with a Mussalman's child, and now he can never receive salvation. The absurdity of casteist notions of pollution and impurity is conveyed by means of the grandmother's melodramatic reaction; the irony, of course, is that the sexual taboo has already been transgressed. As she seethes wildly in front of her son's photograph, the two women along with the children all cower together at the edge of the frame—thereby signifying a solidarity of the oppressed. Her son's loyal servant Baadal is also in the same frame, but he stands a little to the side, indicating his different class position. What is most potent about this scene of intensified melodrama is that it is the moment of revelation for Ajay. The shot of the raging grandmother proclaiming their Muslimness cuts to a medium close-up of Ajay's shocked face while his mother looks anxiously at him. As they walk out and sit on the stairs, his mother starts praying audibly in Arabic, and the camera moves in to a medium close-up of her rocking back and forth with the baby in her arms as a bemused Ajay watches her. Gradually, the camera tracks in on a dazed Ajay in a close shot, eliminating his mother from our view, as he tries to come to terms with her—and his own—Muslim identity. The sound of his mother's chanting reminds him of that fateful day when he had heard her barely audible voice interspersed with the sound of the *azan* over the soundtrack. A retrospective subjective shot takes us once again to the past with Ajay as he follows the sound of his mother's voice—only now the sound is clearly audible on the soundtrack and merges with her incantations in the present.

The film's assertion of Muslim religiocultural practices is highlighted in the very next sequence when Ajay's mother is explicitly represented as Muslim for the first time in the film. As mother and son discuss why Hindus and Muslims are not allowed to intermarry, she instructs him to make sure that she should get a burial befitting a Muslim when she dies. She believes that as a Muslim, she will only achieve salvation if she is buried according to Muslim norms and practices. Although the osten- sible reason for this is to reunite with his father in paradise, it does not take away from her *refusal to be assimilated in death as she has been in life*. Simultaneously, she tells him never to divulge their secret to his brother, who must become a Hindu like his father so that he (the brother) never has to undergo the humiliation and indignity that they had to suffer on that day. As mother and son are composed in profile for us, she en- folds him in her arms and says, "My identity *(pehchaan)* is like a wound *(zakhm)* in both your lives. Hide this wound in your chest, my son." A melancholy song starts playing on the soundtrack, expressing her desire that her son grow up fast and answer his own difficult questions, while the young Ajay holds his mother close and rocks her—slowly taking on the mantle of the parent. The song ends with a powerful point-of-view shot of Ajay's gazing at his mother as she performs the *namaz*. Composed in profile and in a long shot, she is dressed in black with her head covered in the prescribed Islamic way. As the camera gradually tracks in to a close shot of her face, her son continues to watch and take in his mother's new persona. Although the image of the pious Muslim is part of the semantics of much commercial Hindi cinema, this iconic image takes on a subver- sive and powerful charge in this film, since the mother has for so long concealed her Muslim identity. For most of the film, we have seen her in the garb of a traditional, middle-class Hindu woman who wears *bindis*, *mangalsutras*, and *gajras*. The sequence thus *forcefully* figures her as a

Muslim. Unfortunately, this figuration is also somewhat diluted, since it is followed by a shot of her holding a cross to her eyes and another one of her bowing in front of the Ganapati idol. This blurring of identities initially serves the plot well, since we are taken by surprise when the mother's identity is eventually revealed, but Bhatt's need to affirm a somewhat simplistic *Amar, Akbar, Anthony* version of syncretism at this crucial moment tends to undermine the film's assertion of the right to be at once Muslim and Indian. Perhaps this is to be expected from Bhatt, given his own hybrid lineage, but it weakens the compelling statement that the film is able to make through its story of a closeted Muslim identity.[20]

To be sure, the overall impetus of the film remains establishing Muslim claims on the nation, as is made especially evident in the emotionally charged sequence in which Ajay's brother Anand finds out that their mother is a Muslim. After hearing the news of his mother's death, he rushes toward her killer in a frenzy and swears that he will drive all Muslims out of the country. Anand's tirade iterates the common sense of Hindu—and Indian—nationalism, which constructs Muslims as invaders and Hindus as the original inhabitants of the nation. Restraining him physically, Ajay asks: "Is this your father's country? Who are you to drive anyone out of the country?" He tells Anand that if he wants to cleanse the nation of Muslims, he will first have to remove his own "polluted blood," which is also half Muslim.[21] Besides, he will also have to get rid of his mother's body, since she is Muslim. In this obviously allegorical story of cultural admixture and intermingling, the film reconstitutes the nation as a complex intersection of diverse and multiple cultural claims rather than as the sole domain of any one group. In its depiction of the two brothers, it also offers an interesting subversion of the binaries of "good" and "bad" Muslim that have come to be a staple of recent Hindi films such as *Sarfarosh, Refugee,* and *Insan.* While the good Muslim of these films swears undying allegiance to the nation, the evil militant Muslim/Pakistani is admonished for bringing a bad name to the community. *Zakhm* also enacts a split between the "secular" brother and his "fundamentalist" sibling—only here the antagonist is the brother who has come under the sway of the Hindu Right.

Ultimately, the film draws on the sanctity of the mother–son relationship, a characteristic element of much mainstream Hindi cinema, to ensure that the mother is buried and to bring Anand, the wayward brother,

Ajay's mother figured as a Muslim woman for the first time in *Zakhm* (Mahesh Bhatt, 1998).

back into the familial fold.[22] An enraged Subodh Bhai threatens an implacable Ajay with violence if he persists with the idea of burying his mother. An understated yet firm Ajay comes right up to Subodh and says that no religion in the world can stop a son from fulfilling his mother's last wishes. This dialogue about a son's filial duties to his mother is very recognizable within the semantics of mainstream Hindi cinema and works well to pro-

Ajay and his brother finally lay their mother to rest according to Muslim rites for the dead.

vide a rationale for the burial. As Ajay walks out with his dead mother in his arms and his wife and two faithful neighbors at his side, Subodh Bhai's goons attempt to restrain them. At one point, Subodh pushes Ajay and he almost falls, but the dutiful son in Anand reemerges and comes to his mother's rescue in the nick of time. Finally, he turns on Subodh for disrespecting his mother.

The penultimate sequence takes us to the two brothers who, helped by the Muslim journalist and their two faithful neighbors—a stereotypical Sikh and a Muslim—lay their mother to rest in her grave. The cumulative shots of the bier, the grave, and the rituals establish a specific Muslim milieu, while the soundtrack replays the song, "Today is the day of my hope / Today is the day of my Eid." This is followed by a subjective shot of Ajay as he looks up and imagines his parents united in a bizarre depiction of heavenly space. At this point, the subgenre of the intercommunity romance takes over and to some extent dilutes the film's effort to assert Muslim religiocultural practices. In its closure, then, the film reverts to the melodramatic mode and returns to the "space of innocence" so central to melodrama. As Williams notes, "[E]ven if this space is not literally represented, and the narrative cannot begin there, *even if it has never been possessed,* the most enduring forms of the mode are often suffused with nostalgia for a virtuous place that *we like to think we once possessed,* whether in childhood or the distant past of the nation" (my emphasis).[23] Ajay's longing to see his parents united after death is complicated by our knowledge that this togetherness is imaginary and did not really exist in the first place. The return to this imagined space of plenitude establishes a compensatory "feeling for justice"—a characteristic of the melodramatic form—rather than the reality of justice as such. It is the burial that leaves us with some sense that justice has been achieved. Melodramatic "action" is refigured in this film in the form of Ajay's act of ensuring his mother's burial rather than the spectacle of rescue typical of most melodrama.[24]

Through its narrative of a Muslim woman forced to closet her identity, *Zakhm* enacts powerful resistance to the assimilatory logic of both secular nationalism and Hindu nationalism, which demand—to different degrees—that the figure of the Muslim subsume itself into the majoritarian nationalist self. The film also makes a simultaneous intervention in the discourse of concealed Muslim identities in the world of Hindi cinema, which has been a part of its history since its inception. For a long time, Muslim actors took on Hindu names when they entered the world of Hindi cinema. Examples of such figures include famous actors Dilip Kumar, Madhubala, Meena Kumari, and Ajit, among others. Although Dilip Kumar has said that he was never asked to change his name—and in fact even considered Jehangir at one point—it is apparent that many Muslim actors of the 1940s and 1950s felt the need to pass themselves off as Hindu. Although their "Muslimness" was well known in popular off-screen discourses, clearly "an abnegation of identity was undertaken in the development of the star personality."[25] Thus, Muslim actors often had to ritually exorcise the excess that was connoted by their very names in order to become eligible for star status.

Zakhm also recalls for us the controversy over well-known film star Nargis's burial in the 1980s.[26] As a figure who became the embodiment of the nation, Nargis was viewed as someone who had transcended her Muslimness both by way of her iconic role in the film *Mother India* and by her eventual marriage to the Hindu actor Sunil Dutt. She married him in an Arya Samaj ceremony, and their children were given Hindu names. But when she died, Sunil Dutt decided to give her a Muslim burial rather than a cremation, which led to public speculation about her "return to Islam." Parama Roy has discussed the anxieties surrounding the figure of Nargis as the embodiment of the "good" (assimilated) Muslim: "Even after death, she remains as good Muslimness remains in the Indian polity and in Indian Hindu public culture, as a phantasm, a ghost that lives and moves uncannily in our midst, not quite tangible and never fully exorcisable."[27] In depicting the painful consequences of minority invisibility both in the world of Hindi cinema and in Indian nationalism, *Zakhm* provides powerful resistance to the majoritarian demand that Muslims fold into the internal law of the normative Hindu self. The film's emphasis on lived bodily practices, such as rites for the dead, demonstrates the imbrication of religion and culture and affirms the crucial importance of such practices to one's subjectivity.

Burial in this film also becomes a hugely symbolic act, *a way of laying claim by death,* by the insertion of the Muslim body into the space of the nation. As Derrida reminds us, typically, the birthplace underpins the definition of the stranger as nonautochthonous: "The stranger is first of all he who is born elsewhere. The stranger is defined from birth rather than death" (Hostipitality, *Angelaki,* 14). Consequently, he asks us to consider the possibility of hospitality from death no less than from birth. One might extend this line of inquiry to ask what it could mean to assert a claim—there where one has been designated as a "stranger"—by means of death. The emphasis on burial in *Zakhm* becomes a way of "taking root" in a "foreign" land—or rather in a land where the protagonist has been deemed "foreign"—by way of death rather than from birth. The physical burial allows Ajay's mother to insert her self into the space of the nation and at last to be "at home" in the nation—in death if not in life.

"Terrorism" and the State of the Law in *Fiza*

The next film I address, Khalid Mohamed's *Fiza* (2000), offers a fascinating site for thinking about issues of communal conflict, minoritarian identities, law, and the state in postindependence India. Although in this chapter I read *Fiza* as a Muslim minoritarian film, it is also important to situate the film in terms of its affinities with other contemporary films. *Fiza* is representative of a new hybrid or hyphenated subgenre in mainstream Hindi cinema that I call the vigilante-terrorist film, which includes films like Gulzar's *Maachis* (1996), Vidhu Vinod Chopra's *Mission Kashmir* (2000), and Mani Ratnam's *Dil Se* (1998). I use *vigilante*-terrorist to suggest the difference of this subgenre from "terrorist" films like *Sarfarosh* (John Mathew Mathan, 1999), *Pukar* (Boney Kapoor, 2002), and *Roja* (Mani Ratnam, 1992) that figure the militant or separatist group as the "other" of Indian nationalism that must be destroyed. In contrast, through a narrative of state violence and persecution, these vigilante-terrorist films represent the point of view of the disaffected group and create a great deal of sympathy for the much-maligned figure of the "terrorist."[28] Like earlier vigilante films, most famously those of Amitabh Bachchan, these films are also organized around a cause-and-effect structure of oppression and revenge. However, what sets apart films like *Fiza, Maachis,* and *Dil Se* from previous revenge films that rely on similar patterns is that the persecuted protagonist is figured as a representative of a minority group rather than as an isolated individual—a victim of unjust state policies— and hence as one who claims to act on behalf of his/her entire group. I examine *Fiza* in light of its efforts to unleash extralegal fantasies of justice through vigilante actions that go beyond the law of the state. While *Fiza* offers a clear indictment of the state and its fundamental culpability in persecuting the minority Muslim community, my reading suggests that the film simultaneously subverts and recasts the codes of the vigilante film by rejecting the violent resolution of justice, closing with an appeal to the secular state to redress the wounds of 1992 and 1993 *within the framework of its laws*. I examine the implications of this return to the (secular) state in this vigilante-terrorist film.

Like *Zakhm* and Mani Ratnam's *Bombay, Fiza* has features that distinguish it from the commercial cinema: its recalling into public memory "real" political-historical events in the life of the nation, the use of dates and place names to situate and historicize its time frame, the employment of newspaper stills of the riots to establish its claims to truth and authenticity, and so on.[29] These devices contribute to making the film an explicit intervention in the context of controversial political issues that continue to be hotly debated, especially the issue of attributing accountability to those individuals and groups who perpetrated the violence of 1992–93 in Bombay. Speaking of the genesis of this film, Khalid Mohamed, the director and screenwriter, explains:

> The idea for the film, particularly the terrorist angle, was catalyzed by what I had seen around the Mohammed Ali neighborhood and among lower economic class Muslims in general. The

riots (1992–93) had made them lose their sense of worth and proportion—many of them wanted to go militant and did. The basic premise of the film was that many young men have gone missing (official figure is over 800 for Bombay) and their families are still waiting for their return. I'd met several families with lost sons and brothers which became the basis for the film. I spoke to a lot of *mohallawallas* and their families. I wanted to know what happened to these missing boys. Many people were willing to talk. Many of them have gone into terrorist outfits which I researched. They would write letters to Osama in blood saying, "We want to join you." There was a dialogue in the film just before they kill the politician that they'd have to take permission from Osama. Thank god, we didn't retain it because it would really have become charged by now. These boys want 5 to 15 minutes of fame . . . one big binge in life and then kill themselves.[30]

Significantly, the movie's call to justice follows closely upon the submission of the Justice Srikrishna Report. The report is based on the findings of a Judicial Commission of Inquiry that was appointed on January 25, 1993, under a judge of the Bombay High Court, Justice B. N. Srikrishna, by the government of the state of Maharashtra, at the insistence of Prime Minister Narasimha Rao, to investigate the "circumstances, events and immediate causes" of the communal riots that took place in Bombay between December 1992 and January 1993.[31] The Commission was given the express charge of determining the culpability of specific individuals, groups, or organizations that contributed to the violence. Moreover, it was also asked to determine the role of the Bombay police in terms of the measures they took to prevent the riots as well as the police shooting, which, according to the Report, resulted in the deaths of 356 people out of total casualty figures estimated at 900. In addition, the Commission was asked to recommend "the measures, long and short term, which are required to be taken by the administration to avoid recurrence of such incidents, to secure communal harmony and also to suggest improvements in law and order machinery." The Terms of Reference of the Report were later expanded to include an investigation of the serial bomb blasts of March 12, which also took place in Bombay in the same year. The report was submitted to the state government on February 16, 1998.

While the Report has been widely praised by the liberal and left intelligentsia for restoring faith in commissions of inquiry, it was held in contempt by the Maharashtra state government, led at the time by the Hindu nationalist BJP–Shiv Sena alliance. In its Action Taken Report, the state government simply dismissed the painstaking work that went into the Report. Significantly, the Report clearly indicts the Shiv Sena and its leader, Bal Thackeray, for their role in orchestrating the violence: "From January 8, 1993, at least, there is no doubt that the Shiv Sena and Shiv Sainiks took the lead in organizing attacks on Muslims and their properties under the guidance of several leaders of the Shiv Sena from the level of Shakha Pramukh to the Shiv Sena Pramukh (chief), Bal Thackeray, who, like a veteran general, commanded his loyal Shiv Sainiks to retaliate by organized attacks against Muslims." When the Shiv Sena chief was eventually arrested in July 2000 at the behest of a new government in the state, he was discharged on the same day in a travesty of justice. The magistrate in charge ruled that the case was "time-barred" as per the law, since seven years had passed between registration of the offense and filing of the charge sheet. *Fiza*'s call to return to the violence of 1992–93 and to bring justice to the perpetrators, then, has to be situated within this highly charged political scenario. Indeed, Khalid Mohamed maintained that his film was "time-bound," which is why he had to ensure that the film was released within 2000.

Yet, *Fiza* is also very much a mainstream Hindi film that makes use of a number of generic conventions and modes of commercial cinema: an emphasis on music and spectacle, including the characteristic song and dance sequences intrinsic to popular Hindi cinema; major stars such as Karisma Kapoor, Hrithik Roshan, and Jaya Bachchan; a guest appearance by Sushmita Sen in a sensually filmed dance sequence; the obligatory comic sequence provided by Johnny Lever; and catchy songs by popular music director Anu Malik. In fact, *Fiza* was an eagerly anticipated film for a number of reasons, the most significant being the Hrithik Roshan factor—at the time of the film's release, Roshan was well on his way to becoming the latest superstar in the Hindi cinema circuit. *Fiza* had the fortuitous distinction of being his first film after his debut feature *Kaho Na Pyar Hai* (Rakesh Roshan, 2000), one of the biggest successes of Hindi cinema in recent years. Karisma Kapoor, who plays the role of the eponymous female lead, was also a very successful, popular actress in her own right, although her character in *Fiza* was a significant departure from her usual roles until that time. (She went on to play a somewhat similar role in Shyam Benegal's *Zubeidaa*). The star text that actors like Roshan and Kapoor bring with them to their roles is crucial to the spectatorial identification elicited by the film. A significant portion of the audience is aware that these are Hindu actors playing Muslim roles, which can often solicit empathy for the characters. These popular elements form the basis of the film's spectatorial address and enable the spectator to "listen to the other as if it were a self."[32]

Fiza tells the story of a Muslim family—Fiza (Karisma Kapoor), her brother Amaan (Hrithik Roshan), and their widowed mother Nishatbi (Jaya Bachchan)—whose happiness is shattered by a single traumatic night of violence during the Bombay riots of December 1992 and January 1993. The film begins with a classic melodramatic trope—home as a "space of innocence." An extended credit sequence establishes the break-up of the family by virtue of Amaan's persecution and disappearance that fateful night. Clearly announcing its historical moment with the onscreen title "Bombay, 1993," the film opens with a montage sequence of Amaan as Fiza's offscreen voiceover nostalgically speaks of her brother and how happy they all used to be. The next sequence takes us to an intimate and happy family scene with Fiza, Amaan, and their mother facing the viewer in the same frame as they watch Raj Kapoor's classic teen romance *Bobby* and apply oil to one another's hair. However, the tranquil harmony of the small family is rent asunder the same night. The scene is presented from Fiza and Nishatbi's point of view as they helplessly watch a clearly overwhelmed Amaan trying to defend himself and his Muslim friend against their Hindu attackers. A slightly low angle shot of the traumatized and helpless mother–daughter duo framed at the window is followed by a high-angle shot of Amaan and his persecutors on the street outside, prompting us to view the scene from their perspective. The frame within a frame and the accompanying dialogue, "Run, Amaan, Run" work to consolidate the sense of Fiza's and Nishatbi's gendered and minoritarian vulnerability—the sheer sense of helplessness that constitutes their subjectivity as Muslim women in Bombay at the time. The sequence ends with a close-up of a besieged Amaan looking up at his traumatized mother and sister before running away and finally fading out of the scene, mirroring his disappearance and invisibility to them ever since. The remaining credits appear on the screen interspersed with black and white photographic stills of a riot-torn Bombay. The opening sequence thus demonstrates an interesting blurring of fiction and documentary modes, establishing the film's location in a specific historical moment and simultaneously recalling into public memory a horrific violence from a not-too-distant past.

Subsequently, the movie opens six years later in the present of the audience, once again marked by a title, "Mumbai, 1999." The use of "Mumbai" rather than "Bombay" to indicate the Bombay of 1999 is not an insignificant or incidental change. It is of course a politically correct act in keeping with the official name-change of the city from the anglicized Bombay to the nativist, indigenous, Mumbai; however, it is also a telling comment on the ways in which a cosmopolitan Bombay has been transformed into the present-day stronghold of the Shiv Sena. This second opening sequence of the film takes us to Nishatbi sitting outside a police station as she waits to talk to the woman police officer sitting inside. The purpose of Nishatbi's visit is soon made clear: she is there to find out if the police have any new information about her son, who has been missing all these years. Dighibai is apparently used to these visits, since Nishatbi has been coming regularly for the past six years to inquire about Amaan, but the police have no new information for her. She is told that "one hundred sixty people are still reported missing (presumed dead), Hindus as well as Muslims, you are not alone, there are many who are crying." The sequence opens and closes with a crucial close-up of the police officer's hand pressed against a hand-bell as she calls out "Next" to summon the subsequent person in line. Although Dighibai is constructed as somewhat sympathetic in her dealings with Nishatbi, the repeated shot of the disembodied hand and voice reinforce an image of indifferent bureaucratic state authority.[33]

Amaan is among the many victims of the Bombay riots—missing, presumed dead. His mother, however, refuses to believe that Amaan is dead and holds fast to her hope that he will return one of these days. "Let my enemies cry," she tells the police officer in an assertion of faith, "I am convinced that he is alive and he will certainly come back." Her daughter Fiza, on the other hand, is tired of her mother's blind conviction and charges her with turning their life into a "waiting room." She decides to take matters into her own hands to find out once and for all if Amaan is dead or alive. To this end, Fiza sets up a meeting with the police officer who had testified in court about his encounter with Amaan on that fateful night; writes a provocative article for a newspaper about her missing brother, which gets her a lot of media and political attention; and eventually takes a trip to an unnamed border area in response to her Hindu boyfriend Aniruddh's tip that he has come across a picture on the Internet of a wanted terrorist who looks surprisingly like Amaan. Fiza's worst fears are confirmed when she does meet her brother in a village (which is obviously in the Kutch-Rajasthan desert region that borders Pakistan) in the person of an Islamic terrorist. Amaan fills in the incomplete story of what drove him first to murder and then to armed militant action. Invoking filial love, Fiza manages with some difficulty to bring him back to the fold of the family, and they set off for Bombay.

However, the ill-fated family's happiness is once again doomed to be short-lived, since a frustrated Amaan, imbued by the notion of revolution and change, is unable to adjust to the monotony and purposelessness of everyday life and rejoins the terrorist group. Significantly, the sequence that portrays the disruption of the (briefly) reconstituted familial unit is shot as a repetition of the happy family scene of 1993. The state appears as the "villain" that intrudes upon this idyllic space in the guise of two policemen. The mise-en-scène depicts the tiny family dancing together along with their neighbor, Ulfatbi, as they watch a song sequence from the same film *(Bobby)* as before, when the police come in to arrest Amaan for his role in the 1993 violence at the behest of two local hoodlums who have been beaten up by Amaan in a previous sequence. (In *Fiza*, then, *Bobby* serves as a melodramatic signifier of past innocence and happiness, which is eventually destroyed). When his mother accidentally finds out about his new incarnation as an Islamic terrorist, she is driven to take her own life. Subsequently, Amaan is chosen by his group to assassinate two politicians: one Hindu, the other Muslim, who have formed a new electoral alliance for purposes of political expediency (an obvious comment on the new era of coalition politics in India). Amaan succeeds in his mission but then finds out that his group members had planned to kill him all along after the execution of the plan. The last sequence, once again, finds him helpless, besieged, and terrorized, only this time surrounded by the police on a railway track. His agonized sister, the voice of sanity and tolerance in the film, begs him to throw away his weapons, but he manages to convince her to shoot him and put an end to his weary existence.

My reading of the film proposes that there is a specific pattern of ambivalence in the narrative construction of this film wherein Fiza's and Amaan's narratives seem to work against each other such that the radical possibilities opened up by Fiza's story are somewhat constrained by Amaan's paradoxical narrative. At the most obvious level, the opposition between Amaan and Fiza is fairly self-evident: he is the jihad-waging Islamic terrorist, while Fiza represents the voice of reason in the film. Ironically, however, Fiza articulates and raises specific concerns about a Muslim minoritarian identity in contemporary India, while Amaan is effectively transformed into a *secular* militant fighting against a corrupt political system, even though he is part of an armed Islamic organization. Why does the film feel this need to mask Amaan's militant Islamism once he becomes a terrorist and consequently risk a reading as yet another male vigilante film of the individual against the establishment in the line of Bachchan films of the 1970s? A careful examination of Fiza's and Amaan's narratives that situates their characters within the larger context of Muslim representation in Hindi cinema reveals some interesting answers to this question.

I have already suggested some of the ways in which Muslims have been stereotyped in popular Hindi cinema in which normalcy is the sole privilege of the Hindu hero. If Muslims by and large are characterized as a backward, orthodox, and deeply religious group marked out by their peculiar dress, appearance, and speech, Muslim women in particular are constituted as inherently passive, submissive, and retrogressive, evidenced most obviously in the figuration of the perpetually burqa-clad Muslim woman.[34] Even specific mainstream genres like the Muslim Social, which encompass a predominantly Muslim world, tend to fetishize Muslim women as the exotic "other" of the representative secular nationalist self—thus, women in such films as *Pakeezah* (Kamal Amrohi, 1972) and *Umrao Jaan* (Muzzafar Ali, 1981) often appear in the role of the mysterious courtesan. Most of the scenes that center on the women are set inside the domestic space of the home. Space is expressed mainly through huge sets and long shots; the emphasis is on spectacle and grandeur. When viewed within this context, *Fiza* appears as a radical refiguration of the Muslim woman's subjectivity in mainstream Hindi cinema.

From the outset, the female protagonist of *Fiza* is represented as a bold, outspoken, and resistant subject who refuses the mantle of victimization and is thus set up in explicit opposition to the figuring of Muslim women in Hindi cinema generally. An apex of "normality" is established throughout for Fiza. At the most apparent level, this is effected by the film's refusal to code Fiza overtly and crudely as Muslim according to the usual cinematic device of deploying such explicit external markers of identity as the burqa (or the white filigreed cap for men). Emerging from a lower middle-class Muslim family that subsists primarily on the dead father's pension, Fiza is shown to be an educated, English-speaking woman who traverses secular public spaces in her search for employment; in short, she is not that different from the "normal" Hindi film heroine. For example, in one sequence, her mother speaks of how the financial responsibility for taking care of the family now falls squarely on Fiza's shoulders, thus rupturing many abiding stereotypes about the victimized, submissive, confined Muslim woman, so beloved of Hindu right-wing rhetoric. At the same time, the film meticulously sets up the family's middle-class Muslim milieu, not in the clichéd manner of the mainstream Hindi film but through the use of Muslim-specific kinship terms, shots of Nishatbi and Fiza saying the namaaz as a normal part of their everyday routine (unlike the iconic figuration in *Zakhm*), a beautifully constructed mise-en-scène in the Haji Ali shrine in Bombay, and the sensitively shot sequence of Nishatbi's funeral rites interspersed with Ulfatbi's song of mourning for her friend. All of these become effective representational ways of allowing spectatorial identification with Muslim subjects without either effacing their alterity or making them hyper-visible, as much popular Hindi cinema tends to do.

Fiza is represented as an independent and self-respecting woman who is set up in opposition not just to the caricatured Muslim women of commercial Hindi cinema but also to the general sexualized representation of women who don't have much to do other than sport designer outfits, dance and sing, and provide the romantic angle in popular film. She is portrayed as someone who is self-reliant to the point of obduracy and capable of determining her own course of action. Thus, when her boy-friend Aniruddh (who is significantly Hindu) offers to accompany her to the border-area to look for Amaan, since "it is not right for a girl to go there alone," she informs him that this is not a question of being a man or a woman—this is one task that she must complete by herself. In another sequence, as Fiza stands surrounded by press photographers in response to her newspaper article on Amaan and other victims of the Bombay riots, Aniruddh asks her if she needs any help. Her response, delivered in English ("I'll handle it"), sums up the image of a self-sufficient gendered Muslim subject that Mohamed seeks to foreground in his film.

The two song sequences that focus on Fiza, the title song and the

"Nachon bin Payal" ("I'll dance without *payals*," loosely translated as ornaments) song, also serve as an important part of the film's diegesis (unlike "inserted" songs), working to consolidate the film's figuration of its female protagonist as a self-reliant woman who demands respect on her own terms. The title song "Fiza" is shot as a fantasy sequence from Aniruddh's point of view as he imagines singing a song of yearning and invitation to his unattainable beloved to come to his *ashiaana* (dwelling, refuge, shelter). The entire sequence is edited by alternating long and medium-long shots of a lovelorn Aniruddh standing against the backdrop of the ocean with close-ups of Fiza dressed in a glamorous blue outfit (more in keeping with Karisma's usual screen persona) as the camera moves in and out from her face, emphasizing her unattainability for Aniruddh. The word "Fiza" itself translates to weather or atmosphere, and the lyrics of the song underscore Fiza's inaccessibility, or more accurately, her transience. Even in Aniruddh's fantasy, Fiza affirms through the song that she is like the wind that cannot be held down, that she is not of this earth/world *(zameen)*, and that she has no dwelling, thus overturning the cozy gendered fantasy of domesticity, which is the staple of much Hindi cinema.

The second important song sequence crucial to Fiza's figuration is set in a discotheque and shows Fiza dancing and singing a song in a very uncharacteristic moment. Dressed in black leather pants (apparently at the behest of her friend Gitanjali), Fiza is there in response to Aniruddh's invitation ("You really need to unwind sometimes"). The song sequence is set up as a rejoinder to Aniruddh when he asks her (upon her refusal to dance) why she can't be like other girls and have fun sometimes. A wounded Fiza retorts in English: "You want me to be like them" (meaning the vacuous women in the club), "then watch the spectacle." The sequence is shot with Fiza in the center of the dance floor and a spotlight follows her as she dances in a series of stylized acrobatic and aerobic moves with the lyrics reiterating her representation as an independent woman who has faith only in herself. The dance shots are alternated with shots of Fiza walking right up to Aniruddh and wagging a finger at him to emphasize her point. If that were not enough, the sequence closes with Fiza walking out, while Gitanjali tells a chastened Aniruddh to leave Fiza alone for some time and he apologizes for wanting to change Fiza. Many critics disparaged the sequence, but the director views it as central to his representation of Fiza. He says: "I think the disco element was essential . . . to show that a Muslim girl can be, well . . . in tune with the so-called hip things of life. Unfortunately, the disco set piece was seen as a commercial compromise. Believe me, it wasn't" (Interview).

Critics have often tended to dismiss Hindi film songs as nondiegetic spectacles bearing only a tangential link to the narrative. Lalitha Gopalan, however, has suggested that "song and dance sequences deserve another look, differentiating their relationship to the diegesis," since they serve to delay plot development, distract us from other scenes of the narrative through spatial and temporal disjunctions, and bear an integral link to the plot.[35] In keeping with the spirit of Gopalan's argument, I have tried to emphasize the significance of these two song and dance sequences to Fiza's figuration in the film. However, song and dance sequences also work to provide the crucial element of pleasure for viewers, and it is at the level of pleasure that the song in the discotheque seems to fail, especially as compared to the other song sequences in the film. Rather than dismissing it as a "commercial compromise," I suggest that this sequence appears as a case of overkill in its attempts to refigure the conventional representation of Muslim women in popular Hindi cinema, especially in the quality of its choreography with its many overtly macho moves. But undoubtedly, through his figuration of Fiza, Mohamed does manage to encapsulate the image of the modern, self-sufficient, gendered Muslim subject. In light of this alone, Fiza could well be a landmark portrayal in the history of popular Hindi cinema.

From this grounded minoritarian location, *Fiza* stakes an explicit claim to the nation, especially by indicting the postcolonial state for fashioning nationalism in its own intolerant image. The film's indictment of the state comes through most clearly in its representation of corrupt politicians, a communalized police force, and an inept legal system. The sequences in which Fiza encounters the two politicians—V. K. Singh, clearly the representative of the Hindu Right in the movie, and Syed Sahab, his Muslim counterpart—are remarkably similarly constructed in the way in which the "minority" subject chastises the self-serving politicians for their communal agenda, the first for being explicitly anti-Muslim, the second, for his expedient and contingent Muslim identitarian politics. Both Singh and Syed seek out Fiza once she is propelled to the forefront of public attention as a result of her newspaper piece on her missing brother. The episode with Singh is striking for the ways in which Fiza, the minoritarian Muslim subject, reappropriates the nation from the representative Hindu nationalist self. Singh initially engages Fiza in some small talk about her family, but his skewed motives are clear. He will offer Fiza some help as she searches for Amaan in return for her enrollment in the youth wing of his party, which will help to establish the "secular" (the word is used in English) credentials of his right-wing political organization. Fiza's sharp retort to Singh—"so that you can place me on the flag and display me to the world in order to obtain some Muslim votes"—clearly exposes the assimilatory tactics of the Hindu Right. The sequence exemplifies the ways in which secularism has become such a contested terrain in contemporary India that even the Hindu Right has come to selectively appropriate the concept in order to validate its claim to be representative of all communities. At the same time, Singh does not make any attempt to disguise his blatant anti-Muslim sentiments. Accordingly, in an echo of some of the most strident positions of the Hindutva parties today, he tells Fiza: "Now see, the Mughals attacked and captured us, we didn't say anything; *you people* made a separate country for yourselves there, we still didn't have a problem." This significant speech, though delivered in the clamorous voice of a caricatured politician, in fact enunciates many mainstream nationalist (mis)perceptions. The sweeping statement conflates centuries and configures the Hindu community as a beleaguered, silently suffering majority that has been passively enduring Islamic rule and domination for too long, and it also equates all subcontinental Muslims with the Mughal rulers of the past. The specter of Pakistan as the unnamed "other country," not quite here but always there in the shadows, is also typically invoked in Singh's anti-Muslim tirade. But Fiza once again provides an effective rebuttal to Singh: "Don't say you people, Singh Sahab," she declares. "Those who wanted to create Pakistan have already gone there and those who didn't go are largely dead. There is no one remaining in this country who wants to make a Pakistan. *We are as much Indian ("Hindustani") as you are.*"

Similarly, Fiza also firmly counters the Muslim communal sensibility, represented in the figure of Syed in the film. The meeting with Syed takes place in a local Muslim gathering. Fiza has gone along with her mother to attend the wedding of Shahnaz, Amaan's former love interest. Syed, who is also in attendance at the wedding, recognizes Fiza from her pictures on television and summons her for a private meeting. Syed Sahab, unlike his Hindu counterpart, appears as a very sophisticated and old-world representative of Muslim culture; he speaks, for example, in an upper-class accent. However, like Singh, he too has an opportunistic interest in Fiza. He wants Fiza to give up her search for Amaan—the ostensible reason he gives her is that raking up this "old issue" once again could well prove to be very dangerous for the entire Muslim community. Yet, later we find out that he has no qualms in aligning with the Hindu Right in order to be appointed as Home Minister. Fiza, at this point, disassociates herself from the so-called larger interests of the Muslim community and asserts her right as a sister to look for her brother. This is also the crucial moment in the film when Fiza brings up the Srikrishna Report on the Bombay riots in a thinly veiled reference (in deference to the censors) as the Justice "Hare Krishna Report" when she asks Syed what has been done to bring justice since the judicial commission published its report.[36] In response to his spurious claim that he only wants to establish peace, she says, "There will be peace [equilibrium] only when each person learns to live within his or her limits. The truth is, green and saffron [the representative colors of Muslims and Hindus respectively] are parts of the Indian flag; they should not attempt to be the whole flag." This provocative statement, though delivered to Syed, once more seems to be implicitly directed against the assimilatory tendencies of the Hindu Right. Both encounters close with very similar shots of Fiza walking out, as the camera follows her, while the soundtrack plays the very recognizable tune of the popular patriotic song "Sare Jahan se Acha Hindustan Hamara" (translated roughly as "My India is better than the entire world"). *Fiza* therefore makes some of its most charged political interventions through dialogue. Together, the two sequences underscore Muslim claims on the Indian nation and reject Hindu assertions of ownership and mastery over the nation. In a refiguration of the hegemonic rules of popular Hindi cinema, *Fiza* explicitly figures the Muslim woman as the repository of a radical minoritarian nationalist consciousness, one that also makes very specific claims and demands on the legal collectivity of the nation. The nation is not just an abstract entity to which all citizens by default owe allegiance, but it can be claimed by the very people who constitute its political geography.

If Fiza is the representative of a minoritarian Muslim subjectivity in the film, Amaan is constituted as the victim-turned-Islamic-terrorist who seeks to wage war against a moribund and decayed political system. Amaan's militant narrative is largely framed against the events of that fateful night of January 1993. The film offers a piecemeal and fragmented version of his story. His harrowing experience is related to us in three broken segments: the first, as I have discussed, is presented to us right at the beginning of the film from Fiza's and Nishatbi's point of view; the second, appearing in a flashback sequence, is narrated by the corrupt police inspector, Prakash Ingle, to Fiza; the third, recounted by Amaan himself, is also depicted through the cinematic device of the flashback. For six years, all Fiza and her mother know about the events of that night is what they had witnessed with their own eyes. When Fiza decides to do something more constructive than passively waiting for Amaan, she calls on the police inspector who had submitted an affidavit in court about his encounter with Amaan on the same night. At first, the Inspector attempts to convince Fiza to forget everything, but on being bribed by her, he reveals a rather different story from the one he had testified to in court.

The sequence shows a desperate Amaan running toward the uniformed inspector, pleading for help: "Sahab [Sir] help me, they'll kill me, they killed my friend too." The Inspector's unabashedly anti-Muslim answer—"You want to save yourself, then go, go to Pakistan," undoubtedly may seem exaggerated, but it offers an explicit indictment of the conduct of the Bombay police in the 1992–93 riots, particularly in terms of their entrenched anti-Muslim attitudes. (This mind-set has been clearly exposed in the Srikrishna Report.)[37] When Fiza finally asks the indifferent Ingle if Amaan is dead or alive, he is unable to give her a definite answer. The cumulative images of a perpetually fleeing, scared, helpless, victimized Amaan in these first two segments set up a catalogue of horrors that constitute Amaan as a victim of both an anti-Muslim violence and an indifferent state, which fails in its duty to protect him as a citizen—indeed, refuses to acknowledge him as citizen. Thus, the film successfully invokes the sense of a terrorized Muslim identity in the figure of a persecuted Amaan.

From terrorized to terrorist—finally, when Fiza does find Amaan in the desert, he appears in a different persona than when she last saw him: that of a masked terrorist making an attack on a shop. Significantly, this scene also marks the halfway point of the film, the "interval" so characteristic of popular Hindi cinema, which also announces a shift in the focus of

Amaan, the "terrorist": Fiza and Amaan meet in the desert in *Fiza* (Khalid Mohamed, 2000).

the film from its female protagonist to Amaan (here, Hritik's newly begotten star status is also important).[38] In response to Fiza's persistent prodding, he finally completes the story of that traumatic night. A flashback sequence takes us once again to a bloodstained, devastated Amaan who witnesses a man being attacked while the man's terrified wife watches impotently. The moment is presented as a turning point, since the besieged Amaan decides to resort to violence in order to help the unknown man. A series of close-ups portray a shocked Amaan looking down at the man he has murdered, followed by a graphic sequence of Amaan brutally killing again, this time armed with a butcher's knife, though evidently in self-defense, as he wanders wildly through the devastated, carnage-riven city. Eventually, in what is perhaps the weakest link in the plot—because totally coincidental—the flashback depicts his accidental encounter with Murad Khan, the leader of an Islamic terrorist group.

Murad Khan incites Amaan with a militant Islamic rhetoric that expresses the many ways in which Muslims are denied dignity in contemporary India. His recruiting speech is a typical instance of incendiary rhetoric articulating the sense of an oppressed and victimized group identity: "If you can tolerate injustice," he says, "if you can tolerate our people being humiliated, if you can see our mothers and sisters being raped, then, this place is not for you. If you can watch our homes and our dignity being taken away then go, but remember where you are going, let alone a dignified life, even a dignified death is not possible." Murad Khan is the representative of a separatist Muslim sensibility in the film, taking on an explicitly organized and militant form, to which the overall film is evidently opposed, especially as embodied in the person of Fiza. The film thus clearly establishes the one night as formative in the making of Amaan, the Islamic terrorist, allowing Amaan's constant refrain that he didn't choose to pick up arms but was forced to adopt such militant methods. In that sense, the film is not making a very different statement than other contemporary films that examine (though in varying ways) the rise of separatist movements in different contexts, including *Maachis, Dil Se,* and *Mission Kashmir,* which claim that terrorists are not born terrorists but are made or created by the inefficient policies of a culpable state. This sympathetic understanding itself marks a significant moment within popular consciousness.

However, even though Amaan becomes part of a militant *Islamic* outfit, he is simultaneously at pains to distance himself from specific religious causes and often reiterates that he has nothing to do with religion or community. Even Murad Khan, at one point, explicitly employs a nonsectarian rhetoric to incite Amaan: "We have all seen our dignity and self-respect being taken away from us in meaningless riots," he says. "From now on we won't let that happen to anyone else, *whether they are Hindu or Muslim.*" Similarly, while Amaan explicitly draws on the vocabulary of Islam to constitute himself as a jihad-waging warrior, he also sees himself as fighting a nonsectarian, *secular* war against "injustice, oppression and hatred" on behalf of *all* "ordinary" citizens who are victims of conniving politicians. This is an extraordinary and paradoxical claim, emanating as it does from an organization whose very rationale for existence is the sense of an injured Muslim community. Such a claim, I argue, transforms Amaan's narrative from a powerful indictment of state policies of persecution and discrimination against a minority group into a conventional vigilante story about the individual outlaw versus the establishment (in which class consciousness is the absent-presence), a much-reiterated theme in popular Hindi cinema. Amaan is neutralized into just one more "ordinary" victim of state policy and manipulative politicians rather than a victim of his specific minoritarian location. This ambivalence in the film's representation of Amaan diminishes the impact of the successful invocation of a besieged, minoritarian *Muslim* identity through the cumulative images of a defenseless and victimized Amaan in the first half of the film.

Why does the film neutralize Amaan's Muslim identity at precisely the moment when he aligns himself with a militant organization, after it has gone to such lengths in the first half to foreground the sense of a beleaguered Muslim identity in his person? The answer seems fairly obvious: Amaan, as the male protagonist of the film, especially as played by Hrithik Roshan, cannot be so alienated from conventional modes of representation in the Bombay film as to disallow any possibility of spectatorial identification with him. Islamic/Pakistani terrorists are the newfound villains of Hindi cinema, especially following the recent border war fought with Pakistan at Kargil. If Amaan is allowed to mouth militant Islamic rhetoric (even though it would be very much in keeping with his new persona), he will become the absolute "other" of recent Hindi film, and that could certainly take away from his newly acquired star status and the commercial viability of the film. Indeed, Khalid Mohamed explains that both official and unofficial censorship played a role in diluting this powerful strand of the film:

> There were all kinds of pressures and political compulsions because of which I had to soften the politics of the film—whether it was from my producers or because Hrithik had become so popular. It would have been too volatile at a time when the hero had become the heartthrob of the nation. . . . Hrithik's father was also quite anxious about what it would do to his son's image. So we had to make the terrorist group into a sort of a *lala*-land—a vigilante group which I hoped people wouldn't pay much attention to. I think I said what I wanted to say. Yes, many people were missing; many of the community's boys were being misled into terrorism and other things. They have their own reasons, but were basically humans. The state should take notice instead of felling them down with bullets and forcing them to retaliate. Who knows where these people have gone? What were they doing? One imagines the worst. It was a kind of cautionary story: treat us like dogs and dogs bite back. At that point, it was very extreme. I've seen things which I couldn't have imagined. (Interview)

Hence the paradox in Amaan's representation: he is an *Islamic* terrorist waging a *secular* war against the state on behalf of a self-defined militant Islamic outfit. As a consequence of Amaan's inconsistent representation, the film tends to lose some of its narrative coherence.

In the concluding sequence in which Amaan stands in a forsaken railway compartment and is eventually shot by his distressed sister, the director attempts once again to foreground the sense of a beleaguered Muslim identity in the figure of the overwhelmed Amaan. In an incisive reading of the female vigilante genre in Hindi cinema, Lalitha Gopalan suggests that there is a significant difference in the closure of the male and female revenge dramas. While the state is repeatedly undermined in male vigilante films, the unfettered power of the avenging woman is finally undercut "by reeling in the authority of the state" and revealing the woman's own investment in restoring the social imaginary.[39] *Fiza* can be read as a radical refiguring of both the male and female revenge stories. The film's bleak conclusion in which Fiza is forced to shoot her brother *at his own behest*, refuses to fall into the mode of either type of closure. The ending emphasizes once again that the state cannot be trusted to uphold its guarantees of "protection" to the minority Muslim community. Amaan tells Fiza, "I would rather that you kill me than deliver me to them," since he knows that his options are either death at the hands of the police in an "accidental encounter" or a death sentence by way of the law. Clearly, the law is established as a site of violence in *Fiza*. The film offers a clear indictment of the postcolonial state and its culpability in alienating its minority Muslim population. Thus, even though *Fiza* foregrounds melodrama by beginning in a space of innocence (their home) and by ending with Fiza's and Amaan's evocation of nostalgia for that lost space, the closure of the film also departs from melodrama's "achievement of a felt good."[40] The sequence depicting Amaan's death ends with an uncomfortably long take of Fiza looking right at the camera and therefore at the viewer before she fades from our view. Several critics, including Ashish Rajadhyaksha and Ravi Vasudevan, have commented on the widespread use of frontality and direct address in mainstream Hindi cinema.[41] However, while in most films frontal positioning is used to solicit and lure the look of the spectator, in *Fiza*, the direct address of that unnerving shot disallows the viewer the comfort of passivity or a place outside the film's frame of reference. Above all, it works to foreground the increasing sense of vulnerability

Frontal shot of Fiza looking directly at the camera as Amaan dies in her arms.

and alienation among Muslims and underscore spectatorial complicity in being passive bystanders, or worse, perpetrators.

The film's use of space is especially relevant in this context. As a *mainstream* film deploying a number of popular conventions, *Fiza* stands out for its unusual use of space. For the most part, Mohamed relies on medium shots and medium-long shots not only while framing the protagonists but also in those sequences in which we might typically expect long shots or extreme long shots to cover the vista, such as Fiza's and Amaan's meeting in the desert and Fiza's visit to the Hindu politician's house. This technique creates an overwhelming sense of closed spaces that emphasize the central characters' sense of entrapment and vulnerability. It seems as if the city or public spaces can only be safe in their fantasies, expressed in the song sequences, which typically depict vast expanses of space. Almost all other spaces are shot with a sense of containment.

Notably, the only space that evokes the extreme long shot (outside of the song sequences) are the scenes around the Haji Ali shrine in Bombay. The first time we see Haji Ali in all its splendor is during the moving "Piya Haji Ali" qawwali sequence composed by A. R. Rahman. The cinematographer, Santosh Sivan, lovingly covers Haji Ali from the inside and the outside in a series of shots that are juxtaposed with subjective shots of Nishatbi and Shanaaz as they remember Amaan. The next time we see

Haji Ali in the film, once again in an extreme long shot, is when Fiza tells her mother about what she has learned from Inspector Ingle. They are both sitting amidst the rocks behind the shrine. While Haji Ali has typically been evoked as an icon of a diverse, tolerant, and "secular" Bombay, most famously in the films of Manmohan Desai and Prakash Mehra, Mohamed's use of Haji Ali is not a mere reiteration of this semantic convention (even though Rahman's song asserts that this is a syncretic place of worship where Hindu, Muslims, Sikhs, and Christians *all* find comfort). I argue that Haji Ali appears as the only space of relief and solace for its Muslim protagonists in this film. This is especially accentuated in the final extreme long shot of the Sufi shrine just after Fiza shoots Amman. As she looks directly at us and eventually fades out from our view, there is a cut to an extreme long shot of Haji Ali, followed by a shot of Amaan cradled in his mother's arms in front of the shrine. Subsequently, the camera tracks in to a lone Fiza gazing out of the window in a retrospective subjective shot. As she turns away from the window, we realize that Fiza is trying to find some consolation in the image of her mother and brother together and in her faith—represented here by Haji Ali. This shot is followed by a medium shot of Fiza composed in profile as she prays and her voiceover says, "Allah, give me strength." In marked contrast to a film like *Mother India* in which Nargis literally becomes the mother of the entire village and metonymically that of the nation (as signaled by the title) after she shoots her wayward son Birju in public space, Fiza's loneliness and solitude are underscored in this film once she kills Amaan. Typically, the male love interest would be represented as her support structure at this point, but Aniruddh doesn't figure anywhere in the end even though he accompanied Fiza when she goes to find Amaan at the political gathering. The space of faith—represented through Haji Ali—becomes the only site of solace for Fiza. The intensely personal use of Haji Ali in this film gives us some sense of what the destruction of the Babri masjid meant to many Indian Muslims. We are left with the overriding feeling that justice has *not* been served rather than the compensatory recognition of virtue or the "feeling for justice" so crucial to the melodramatic mode.

Yet, significantly, this male vigilante film doesn't abandon the state—and its laws—altogether. In fact, it returns full circle to the state in the final close-up of the police officer's disembodied hand pressing against the bell and calling out, "Next." Only this time, the camera rotates as the bell

Extreme long shot of the Haji Ali shrine right after Amaan's death.

goes out of focus slowly. The importance of this repeated shot in the film cannot be overemphasized. While it works to reiterate the indifference of bureaucratic authority, it also serves as a call to the secular state to redress the injuries of 1992 and 1993 *within* the laws of the state—a significant departure from the conventions of the male vigilante film. To be sure, as Derrida reminds us, law is not justice, and justice by definition exceeds the law, but justice also requires laws to be effective.[42] The movie's injunction to the state's (juridical) regime of justice appears more urgent than ever in light of the atrocities against Muslims in Gujarat and the collusion of the state in perpetuating such violence and injustice. However, to envision a justice that is not limited by the laws of the (Indian and Pakistani) state, we will have to turn to another one of Mohamed's screenplays, the film *Mammo*.

Claiming "Home" in *Mammo*

The last film I address, indeed the last fictional narrative I examine in this book, is noted film director Shyam Benegal's *Mammo* (1994). Unlike Bhatt and Mohamed, Benegal is closely identified with art cinema. He is considered one of the pioneers of the "New Indian Cinema," a set of state-sponsored films that emerged in the late 1960s and early 1970s. The

New Cinema was the name given to a body of films that dealt with socio-political issues and took realism as their aesthetic imperative. With this movement, art cinema attained a new visibility and impetus and was no longer limited to the works of (Bengali) auteurs such as Satyajit Ray and Ritwick Ghatak. It came to be associated with a number of filmmakers like Mrinal Sen, Mani Kaul, M. S. Sathyu, Kumar Sahani, Girish Karnad, and Benegal. Typically, these filmmakers employed formal techniques such as deep focus and long takes to simulate reality. Often shot in limited spaces because of budgetary constraints, the films expressed a deep preoccupation with space and meticulously delineated particular locales. *Mammo* emerges from this realism-driven tradition but also marks a subtle shift in Benegal's oeuvre in its comparatively quicker pace, its relative verbosity, and its episodic narrative. The film was co-produced by the state-run television channel Doordarshan and the National Film Development Corporation of India in order to be premiered on television—thereby ensuring a larger middle-class audience for it. Like *Zakhm* and *Fiza*, *Mammo* is also a family melodrama that relies on pathos to evoke sympathy for its Muslim protagonist, but unlike Bhatt's reliance on the excess of melodrama, Benegal tends to control the melodrama, especially at heightened moments. Melodrama is diluted primarily by means of the warmth and humor of the film's central character and by her figuration as a resistant subject rather than as the object of our pity.

While all the cinematic narratives I have considered thus far in this chapter attempt to stake a claim to the nation from an excluded minoritarian location *within* the nation, *Mammo* lays claim to the nation from the liminal space of the Partition refugee who, to borrow Vazira Fazila-Yacoobali's resonant phrase, is both "Pakistani-Indian" and yet "not-Pakistani-not-Indian."[43] Fazila-Yacoobali, in a fascinating essay, proposes that we consider Partition a "rite of passage" into what Liisa Malkki has called the dominant "national order of things." This order conceives of the world as a school atlas that depicts discretely partitioned territorial nations. In such a divided world, refugees, the unwanted migrants, pose a disturbing "problem." Inhabiting as they do a liminal subject position, they are considered to be inherently threatening, polluting, and dangerous to the naturalized order of nation-states.

While most contemporary refugees are understood to occupy a liminal space because of a legal and institutional apparatus that clearly contains them in that space, Fazila-Yacoobali notes that millions of Partition refugees were assumed to have been incorporated into the new national orders of India and Pakistan and thus to have negotiated the rite of passage quite successfully. As a result, Partition displacements have been rendered largely invisible in the emerging fields of "refugee" and "migration" studies. However, while there are many Partition narratives that testify to the successful incorporation of both Indian and Pakistani subjects into the new nations, there are other marginalized stories that fall clearly within the realm of liminality, such as those of abducted women and divided families whose absorption into this national order may not have been as complete or finished as dominant nationalist narratives in all three postcolonial states would have us believe.[44] *Mammo* is the story of one such liminal subject who radically calls into question the national order instituted by the Partition by affirming a vision of justice that exceeds the laws of both the Indian and Pakistani states. I choose to conclude my own narrative with this film because it enacts a situated and manifest act of resistance to the geographical and political divisions created and naturalized by the Partition fifty years after the event.

Scripted by Khalid Mohamed, the director and screenplay writer of *Fiza, Mammo* is part of a loose trilogy along with two other films, *Sardari Begum* (1997) and *Zuebidaa* (2000). All three narratives are loosely based on women from Mohamed's family. (While the characters of Mammo and Sardari Begum are based on his grandmother's sisters, Zubeidaa is a fictional reconstruction of his mother's life.) *Mammo* is the moving story of a Muslim woman, Mehmooda Begum Ahmed Ali, known as Mammo, who migrated to Pakistan with her husband at the time of Partition; after he dies, she wishes to return to India to be with her surviving family: her sister, Fayyazi, and Fayyazi's grandson, Riyaz. The film opens with a montage sequence of the eponymous protagonist (sensitively played by Farida Jalal): the images are linked by fade-outs and quick-cutting, providing a sense of immediacy and fear. As the credits appear on screen, the camera frames an adult Riyaz (Rajit Kapur) in a close shot, sleeping on his bed, and as he wakes up startled, we realize that he has been dreaming of Mammo. From the outset, then, the film is set up largely from Riyaz's perspective. The next sequence has him asking his grandmother (Surekha Sikri Rege) about Mammo's whereabouts, and they wonder if she is even alive, since they haven't heard any news of her for a long

time. The doorbell rings, and as Riyaz walks toward the door, his grandmother looks up expectantly. A cut suddenly transports us to the past
with Mammo standing at the doorway composed frontally in a medium
shot, facing a younger Riyaz (Amit Phalke).

Riyaz is confronted with an old woman who talks interminably. The
storyline traces the fourteen-year-old's initial resistance to his grand-
aunt and her busy-bodying ways to his eventual anguish at being forcibly
parted from her. In fact, in the beginning, he is ashamed of this burqa-clad
old lady from Pakistan who seems to take over and invade his home from
the minute she arrives. His discomfort at acknowledging her as family is
made explicit in the sequence when, after she drops him off at his school,
he denies any relationship with her and tells his friends that she is a
stranger who happened to give him a ride. Yet the same Mammo, he discovers, is also a sport who does not snitch to his grandmother even when
she discovers him smoking on the sly or when it comes to light that he has
been deploying her burqas to gain entry to an "adult" Hitchcock film. On
the contrary, she even surprises him by sharing his cigarettes, reminiscing
about the times when she used to steal some from her husband's pack.

Riyaz lives with his grandmother, having been abandoned by his father
after his mother's death. In spite of his grandmother's financial difficulties,
he goes to an elite school, listens to Beethoven and Vivaldi, and reads the
Lebanese poet Khalil Gibran. His ambition is to become a writer, an as-
piration that is met with much amusement and scorn in a society that can
only imagine medicine or engineering as viable professions for a young
man of his class. His grandmother gets angry at the very thought, but his
Mammo Nani, as he calls her, actually takes his desire to write seriously.
To Mammo's query about what he wants to write, he replies: "I want to
write about what I *see*. I want to take in a lot of experiences in life so that
I can write about them." Invoking Saadat Hasan Manto's testimonial fiction, Mammo asks him: "So you want to write like Manto? He too wrote
about what he saw." And yet, she cautions him, there are some things in
life that are better not experienced, like "hell."

A flashback takes us briefly to 1947 through images of flames and
people running in confusion accompanied by the tormented sounds of
screaming on the soundtrack as Mammo recalls those "apocalyptic" days
when millions of people found themselves divested of their homes and
attempted to cross the newly drawn borders of India. She narrates the

calamitous story of a woman with two children, one of whom died during the journey; traumatized by the incident, the tortured woman threw her living offspring into a nearby river and kept holding tight to the dead one. Mammo continues to be haunted by her "torn eyes" and horror-stricken scream of realization. Significantly, the story that Mammo narrates is a distilled version of Gulzar's Urdu short story, "Ravi Paar" (acknowledged in the credits). What I find most telling about this sequence is that the visual medium of cinema turns to literary narrative in order to represent the carnage of Partition. Violence is hardly depicted on screen except for two very brief shots that are used to convey a sense of confusion more than anything else. The sequence represents an important instance of Benegal's deliberate refusal to provide epic portrayals of mass violence on screen. In passing on this story to Riyaz, the child of a new generation, Mammo bears witness to that woman's personal tragedy, a tragedy that made it impossible to remain uninvolved for all who lived through those catastrophic times. Drawn by her contiguity to another's experience of pain and grief, Mammo, the witness, is unable to stand outside the event. In turn, Riyaz is summoned by the exigencies of Mammo's traumatic history to be her witness and to record her story: the narrative of the film becomes the adult Riyaz's testimonial (and by extension that of Khalid Mohamed). It is a story that he had begun writing many years ago from the perspective of the child who had encountered Mammo, a story that attests to the simple fact that "everyone returns to their roots."

This thematic of home, belonging, and roots is central to the film's structure of feeling. In a particularly evocative intertextual moment, the film pays homage to Sathyu's *Garam Hawa*. (Sathyu's wife, Shama Zaidi, is a long-time collaborator of Benegal and wrote the additional screenplay and dialogues for Mammo.) The sequence takes us to Mammo, Fayyazi, and Riyaz sitting in a movie theater and watching the episode from *Garam Hawa* in which the old, displaced grandmother finally dies in her ancestral home. Instinctively identifying with the grandmother's tragedy, Mammo cries out: "It looks as though they've filmed my story." The very next sequence has Mammo recalling the treatment meted out to her by her brothers-in-law after her husband died. She remembers how they called her a "barren witch," since she had not borne any children, and cursed her for "devouring their brother." As a widow with no children, Mammo has no rights in her husband's family; there is no room for Mammo's nonreproductive sexuality within the patriarchal structure of the heterosexual family—which is why she decides to return to India. Mammo's story therefore is a gendered narrative that attests to women's experiences of displacement and exile.

Mammo wants to live in India to be with her surviving family, but as a Pakistani national, she is not allowed to visit independent India for more than three months at a time. The duration of her stay in the country of her birth, then, as she says, is dependent upon the will of Allah and the visa. The two sequences in the film in which Mammo meets with the police official who registers her visit reveal interesting facets about subaltern speech and its encounter with authority. She is very discreet and respectful—the "normal" attitude toward bureaucracy—but by taking an interest in his personal and familial life, she resists the usual anonymity of such encounters, thereby attempting to reduce the distance between her own subaltern subject position and his "authoritative" location. Yet, in spite of all her efforts to extend her visa, including bribing the same Inspector Apte, Mammo is deported from the country and put on the train to Pakistan. She is forcibly removed from her home and not even given enough time to collect her personal effects. Much like the scene in *Fiza* depicting Amaan's arrest and the break-up of the briefly united family, the sequence that portrays Mammo's eviction draws upon melodrama's figuration of home as a space of innocence, which is then disrupted by the intrusion of the villain—once again, the Indian state. The sequence begins languidly as the camera pans slowly around the house, ultimately coming to rest on Mammo and Fayyazi as they sit in their room peeling pistachios in preparation for Eid while the soundtrack plays an old film song. The doorbell rings, disturbing the tranquil scene: the police have come to deport all "illegal" Pakistani migrants. The woman police officer drags Mammo out while her distraught sister runs after her to try to give her her belongings. A high-angle shot from the maid Shanta Bai's point of view depicts Mammo being yanked into the police jeep while Fayyazi's offscreen voice screams, "Where are you taking my sister? She hasn't done anything." As the jeep drives away, the camera pans and comes to rest on Fayyazi, eliminating Mammo from our view. The sequence ends with a medium shot of a distraught Fayyazi, framed in profile, crying for her sister, thereby inviting the spectator to empathize with her trauma.

Mammo is dragged away by the agents of the Indian state in *Mammo* (Shyam Benegal, 1994).

When Riyaz returns, dressed in the *sherwani* that Mammo bought for him, and learns of Mammo's eviction, he rushes to the visa office and finds out that all Pakistani "illegals" are being deported from the country. The next sequence shifts to Bombay central station where a distressed Mammo pleads with her captors to let her go, since this is her home. The same impersonal voice of authority, this time the agent of the state who deports her, wonders abstractly: "Why do *these people* want to remain in India? What do they hope to get?" Mammo's poignant cry—"This is my home, my earth, if you give me a little piece of this land what would you lose?"—falls on deaf ears. By the time Riyaz reaches the station, Mammo is already sitting inside the train. A visibly upset Riyaz rushes to her window crying out—"Mammo Nani, where are you leaving us and going?"—while the train slowly pulls out of the station. The haunting title song, "Yeh Faasle Teri Galiyon Ke / Hamse Te Na Ho Sake" (I could not traverse the distances of your streets), starts playing on the soundtrack as Riyaz runs along the side of the train and waves goodbye to Mammo. The sequence ends with a fade-out as Mammo disappears from our vision and from Riyaz's life. In the new ordering of the world instituted by Partition, Mammo can only be distinctly "Pakistani" or "Indian"; she cannot be

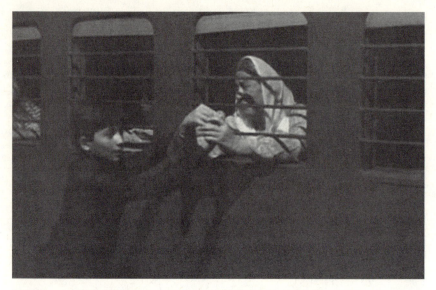

Mammo and Riyaz at the station as she is deported to Pakistan.

A visibly older Mammo returns to India in a repetition of the first arrival scene.

allowed to transgress the border between India and Pakistan, at least not within the rationale of nations and states.

In what appears to be the final sequence of the film, we view the adult Riyaz, typing in the concluding words of his account: "This true story is twenty years old." We realize that this has been Riyaz's testimony, but this is a narrative that Riyaz can only end inconclusively for he and his grandmother never discover what became of Mammo after she was deported to Pakistan, in spite of all their inquiries. Yet "life" takes over where "art" leaves off, as Mammo forcefully inserts herself into her own story. Just as Riyaz wonders if she is alive or . . . he is not allowed to pronounce the word "dead," the doorbell rings, and the film comes full circle, as a visibly older yet still indefatigable Mammo confronts her nephew once again at the doorway in a repetition of the first arrival scene. Mammo affirms her living presence: "You thought I was dead," she says, completing his sentence, "I won't die so easily!"

This resilience and ability to survive is celebrated in the film. "I am still alive" is what Mammo had asserted twenty years ago, even as she recounted her distressing story of (domestic) displacement and eviction to her sister. What makes this scene even more potent to me is the retrospective offscreen knowledge that the "real" Mammo returned to India after many years during the making of the film. Accordingly, Mohamed and Benegal changed the ending of the film in order to incorporate her return (the original script was supposed to end with her deportation). Thus, this time, the fictional Mammo makes certain that no "son of his mother" *(mai ka lal)* will be able to handcuff and dislocate her yet again. The movie closes with a radical disruption of state authority—and of the laws of the Indian and Pakistani states—through a manifest act of subaltern agency. In a triumphant refusal of the borderlines imposed by the two states, Mammo forges her own death certificate and submits it to the Pakistani and Indian authorities. Her witness, Riyaz, becomes her collaborator, aiding her in getting a false death certificate. Mammo's story then becomes a very corporeal act of resistance to the cartographies of Partition. If, in *Zakhm*, burial provides the means finally to lay claim to the nation as a Muslim, in *Mammo*, the protagonist asserts her right *to be* in India by inserting her very body, her tactile being, into the space she calls "home." In doing so, she disallows the state the authority to interpellate her as a citizen-subject and to define her identity solely along the binaries of "Indian" or "Pakistani." The film ends with a shot of the reconstituted familial unit positioned frontally in the same frame as a triumphant Mammo holds her sister and Riyaz.

Mammo stakes her claim on the Indian nation—"The hell with this visa-shisa"—by taking recourse to a notion of justice that is beyond the laws of both states. As Derrida writes, "The justice of law, justice as law is not justice. Laws are not just in as much as they are laws. One does not obey them because they are just but because they have authority. . . . The authority of laws rests only on the credit that is granted to them. *One believes in it; that is their only foundation.*"[45] Mammo, the ostensibly nonautochthonous stranger, is able to lay claim to the Indian nation by refusing the (unjust) authority of the law and the state-decreed frontiers that separate her from her family. However, the film does not leave us with an uncomplicated endorsement of subaltern agency. On the contrary, it allows us to see how manifestations of subaltern agency are tenuous and complicated and how we cannot merely endorse or celebrate agency without thinking through its implications and consequences. For even as we may validate Mammo's successful defiance of the state's juridical regime, we also realize that she must "die" to the state in order to do so. It is important, then, to ask and imagine what it might mean for a living subject to cope with the experience of not being recognized as one. Why should Mammo have to resort to such a drastic rejection of her legal status as a living subject? Thus, even though Mammo asserts her claim to the Indian nation from her liminal—not quite Indian, not quite Pakistani—subject position, she must efface her very "life" in order to be able to do so. It seems as if the Muslim must either literally die *(Zakhm)* or symbolically die by sacrificing all entitlement to the structures of citizenship and the law *(Mammo)* in order to be able to lay claim to the Indian nation.

Throughout this book, I have argued that a fundamental reconsideration of what "Indian Muslim" has meant for secular nationalism in India is necessary for thinking coexistence in the subcontinent today. In inviting the normative spectator of Hindi cinema to identify with besieged Muslim subjectivity at particular "moments of crisis" in the history of the Indian nation, the Muslim minoritarian films I engage in this chapter enable the representative secular-nationalist self to figure the other as "imaginative actant" and to come as close as possible to "listen[ing] to the other as if it were a self"—but without negating the alterity of the other.[46] By asserting their entitlement on the Indian nation, the Muslim protagonists of these films assert the significance of minoritarian claims on national culture. Going an important step further, Benegal's *Mammo,* in staking a place in the post-Partition Indian nation for the quintessential outsider—the

Pakistani—also contests the invented national identities of "Indian" and "Pakistani" that came to be naturalized with the creation of a separate Muslim nation in the subcontinent. I have argued that such an interrogation of normative nationalist subjects is crucial to the peaceful coexistence of religious groups and nations in the subcontinent.

Postscript

> Pakistan need not cross the borders and attack India. Two hundred fifty million Muslims in India will stage an armed insurrection. They form one of Pakistan's seven atomic bombs.
>
> ⟩ Shiv Sena Chief, Bal Thackeray, *Saamna* 1992

> In Indonesia, Malaysia, wherever Muslims are living they don't want to live in harmony. They don't mix with others in society *[ghul milkar nahin rehte]*. They are not interested in living in peace.
>
> ⟩ Former Indian Prime Minister Atal Bihari Vajpaye, April 2002

> The war we fight today is more than a military conflict. It is the decisive ideological struggle of the twenty-first century.
>
> ⟩ U.S. President George W. Bush, speech at
> American Legion convention, September 1, 2006

On July 11, 2006, eight bombs exploded aboard seven commuter trains in Bombay in less than fifteen minutes, killing about 180 people. The incident has been referred to as 7/11 in the English-language media of India, an obvious allusion to the events of September 11, 2001. What makes this a self-conscious effort at validation by correlation is the use of 7/11 rather than the typical 11/7. Clearly, the idea is to establish the magnitude of the attack by means of association with what has now been constituted as a limit event—a kind of yardstick by which all future "terrorist" attacks must be measured. The effort to set up an identity between the two instances of violence demonstrates how the figuration of the Indian Muslim as a "stranger" within the nation cannot be divorced from the global politics of "terror."

In fact, the coordination and scale of these newest blasts have led many investigators to believe that the event involved both a "home-grown cell" (similar to attacks in the United Kingdom and elsewhere) and the likely participation of militants based in Pakistan. While India's allegations of state-sponsored terrorism against Pakistan are not new or atypical, a recent *New York Times* article reports that a growing number of educated Indian Muslims are being drawn toward militancy.[1] Apparently, an active recruitment drive is underway to mobilize Indian Muslims to turn militant. Although the report is careful to outline that "no more than 50 Indians attended military and religious training camps in Pakistan and the Pakistani-controlled part of Kashmir on average each year"—based on interviews with senior officials of the *Lashkar-e-Taiba*—it also suggests that the call of Islamic radicalism among Indian Muslims is gradually becoming a cause of some disquiet and concern. India's national security adviser, M. K. Narayanan, recently claimed on television that often the motivation among many Muslims is: "You know what happened in Gujarat." Whether this emerging militancy has to do with the rise of the Hindu Right in India or with the sense of a perceived solidarity with Muslims elsewhere, it is apparent that we are witnessing the phenomenon of an increasingly beleaguered "Islamic" identity, one which cannot be disassociated from Bush's "war on terror" or the recurrent crises in the Middle East. Thus, one of the men interviewed in the *New York Times* report states that the lesson he learned after Gujarat was that "as minority Muslims we are unprotected. . . . According to the current situation, *Muslims in the whole world are not protected.*"

Simultaneously, and unsurprisingly, we are also viewing the emergence of new alliances between disparate Islamist groups on a global stage as a response to the perceived larger threats of Israel and the United States. Thus, for example, the Shiite Hezbollah has been able to garner some support from Sunni groups such as Hamas and the Muslim brotherhood in Egypt and Jordan, especially since Hezbollah's self-proclaimed victory in the recent conflict against Israel. Similarly, the Saudi cleric Salman al-Awda proclaims on his Web site, "[T]his is not the time to express our differences with the Shiites because we are all confronted by our greater enemy, the criminal Jews and Zionists"[2] Even Al-Qaeda, which has traditionally distrusted and disparaged Shiite groups like Hezbollah, has publicly expressed something akin to a statement of solidarity: "We cannot just stand idly by while we see all these shells fall on our brothers in Gaza and Lebanon."[3] The crystallization of a transnational "Muslim" identity—one which has emerged in opposition to the U.S.–Israeli axis—is abundantly demonstrated in these instances even as accelerated instances of violence among Shias and Sunnis continue with frightening regularity in countries such as Iraq.

Clearly, the "local"—in this instance, the Indian nation—must be understood with reference to the "global"—as attested to by the striking similarity in the sentiments expressed in my epigraph. Certainly, the monolithic figure of a transnational "Islamic terrorist" gives credence to the myth of the aggressive Indian Muslim/Pakistani. The image of a worldwide *jihadi* only serves to reinforce and consolidate the construction of the Indian Muslim as "the intimate enemy." However, as Yoginder Sikand points out, "[I]t is striking how general discourse on terrorism in India, as elsewhere as well, is now so heavily lopsided, focusing as it does, largely on militant acts committed by some Muslims. Terrorism in India is now talked about almost wholly in the context of fringe Islamic or Muslim militant groups, whereas similar acts of terrorism by other actors, including the state or by *Hindutva* outfits, are rarely described as such in the 'mainstream' media or by politicians."[4] We cannot afford to ignore or dismiss the trauma and suffering of thousands of Muslims who have died or survived the many instances of anti-Muslim violence since independence. As Sikand notes, "Islamophobia has today become a fashion in large circles and demands for justice to Muslims are quickly branded as 'communal' and 'anti-national' by those who mistakenly see 'Islamist terrorism' in a political vacuum."[5] Moreover, a mere politico-legal approach to the problem of "terrorism" will not suffice—in fact, if anything, it can result in tragic consequences, as amply borne out by recent events on a global stage. Militancy, in a wide variety of contexts, is often a symptom of a deep-rooted sense of oppression and injustice (real or perceived), and unless we address these concerns, we cannot hope to bring about justice and peace.[6] What this would mean in the contemporary Indian landscape is not just ensuring justice to the victims of anti-Muslim pogroms by means of the legal system but also addressing the growing feelings of insecurity, fear, and vulnerability among many Indian Muslims. The recent Sachhar Committee report has clearly recorded the immense sense of alienation and helplessness among Muslims across a spectrum of classes. From all accounts, it is evident that this sense of insecurity is resulting in deep-seated changes in the lifestyle of the community—thus Muslims are moving into ghettos; parents are not sending their daughters to schools, especially if the girls need to use public transport systems; Muslim names are missing from voters' lists in several states because of the ways in which these lists have been used in the past to target Muslim homes during incidents of communal violence; women, in particular, are afraid to move out of the "safe" space of their neighborhoods. Ironically, as Seema Mustapha points out, the report has not made any far-reaching recommendations on the issue of an increasingly beleaguered Muslim identity—despite going to some length to foreground the community's growing feeling of being under siege—perhaps because that would mean acknowledging the state's own complicity in contributing to Muslim insecurity.[7] Clearly, unless the state makes concerted efforts to address Muslims fears and the broader marginalization of the community in the Indian polity, we will not be able to move toward a lasting peace. Writing of another context, Derrida asserts, "Palestinians and Israelis will live truly together only on the day when peace (not only armistice, cease-fire, or the peace-process) comes into bodies and souls, when what is necessary will have been done by those who have the power for it or who, quite simply, have the most power, State power, economic, military, national or international power, to take the initiative of peace *in a manner that is first of all wisely unilateral.*"[8] State-led efforts to prevent violence and to rectify inequities among differently located religious groups therefore continue to be crucial for the living together of these groups.

As someone who grew up in a not-quite-Hindu-not-quite-Sikh family in post-Partition India, I, like many others of my generation, inherited an implicit othering of Muslims and Pakistanis. As an "upper-caste" Hindu-Sikh, my "ensemble" is based on the positioning of the Muslim as a stranger. Like many Punjabi families, my family was among those millions who migrated from places that are now in Pakistan to a newly carved out India. I remember hearing stories as a child about how my maternal grandfather offered water to wounded and suffering Muslims during the long trek from Pakistan. In family history, this act comes to take on a larger-than-life heroic significance, not so much because he stopped to offer water to a hurt and afflicted human being in that time of immense chaos and suffering but because he offered water to a *Muslim*. Although today I have come to understand that gesture as a singular act of kindness toward the other in a time of conflicted and intensified identities, I also recognize the ways in which "the Muslim" is being cast as the self-consolidating other of the normative (tolerant) Hindu self in these familial narratives.

A poll conducted by *Outlook* magazine during the fiftieth year of India's independence reveals the startling ignorance of those who came after Partition about the "facts" of that catastrophic divide, which leads many to conclude that Partition has been forgotten and consigned to the past (where it belongs) by the children of "midnight's children." The thrust of this book has argued against such a view to suggest, instead, that the traumatic memories of Partition and the very specter of Pakistan—as that other nation—have shaped the subjectivities of subsequent generations in formative, and often undesirable, ways. For example, I recall another incident from when I was in the fifth grade: a friend in school—one of the few Muslims in my hometown of Chandigarh, the capital of the new, truncated Punjab—is told by another classmate that she belongs in Pakistan, since she is a Muslim. Clearly, the figuration of the Muslim as the stranger or as the "enemy within" persists as one of the primary legacies of Partition for subsequent generations of Hindus and Sikhs. In a recent hard-hitting and powerfully written piece, journalist Farzana Versey asks:

> Why do 800 million Indians find us [Muslims] a threat? *The Muslim is an abstraction now.* S/he would be forced to ask: Who am I? And the response would be . . . I am the AK-47 rifle, I am the detonated bomb, I am the dynamite that has blown up cars, trains, bodies, I am the beard, the burqa, I am the voice that shouts out loud in the streets to support dictators who look like thieves, I am the bent over figure taking up public space for my prayers, I am the loudspeaker that beckons believers and is a nuisance to the ears, I am the butcher with a knife over a poor goat's neck, I am the one that the metal detector detects faster than anyone else. *I am not like you anymore.* (my emphasis)[9]

While Versey views this othering of Muslims as the legacy of the destruction of the Babri masjid (the immediate occasion for the writing of this essay), I have underscored how Indian nationalist understandings of Partition and the creation of Pakistan have played a crucial role in consolidating the figure of the Muslim as an "abstraction." The ethical task before the normative nationalist self, then, is to imagine different ways of relating to the other that must interrupt the totality of the ensemble given to it by blood, birth, belonging, or convention, and to imagine the other as another human being. This book has been an effort to heed the call of the other by moving past "identity as reference"—to "try opposite."[10]

Limiting Secularism has argued that secularism as a concept is not capacious enough to take on the program of multireligious coexistence that it has been asked to fulfill in postindependence India. Its scope must be minimized if it is to ensure the reasonable coexistence of different religious groups in society. I argue that literary and cinematic fictions enable us to imagine possibilities of living together that are not restricted to the enforced tolerance of the secular state and the juridical contract. The cosmopolitan fictions of Salman Rushdie and Amitav Ghosh allow us to envision a hospitable world that is welcoming to all others, especially those rendered strange or foreign to one's ensemble, without asserting the prior claim of any one group. The fictions of memory I address in chapter 3 posit an uncanny mode of remembrance that is crucial for rendering the representative nationalist self strange and unfamiliar. This mode of approaching the traumatic past of Partition, I argue, is imperative for calling into question the nationalist binaries of "Indian" and "Pakistani" and hence for envisioning coexistence in the present. The powerful and moving stories of inhuman and gendered violence I address in chapter 4 enable me to underscore the crucial role of a feminist perspective to any agenda of coexistence. I read these literary fictions not only as traumatic testimonials but as compelling imaginative accounts that point to ways of remaking worlds and selves shattered by violence. The crises of masculinity staged within the melodramatic fictions of Manto and Abbas open up difficult questions about male responsibility and complicity in communal riots and emphasize the importance of reconfiguring masculinity for the living together of diverse religious groups. The fictions of survival I read in the second part of this chapter take us to the long-term consequences of violence. In revealing the tremendous impact of mass sexual violence on survivors, these literary fictions articulate a powerful poetics of resistance to the conflict between communities and make an eloquent plea for a world without terror and violence. Finally, the Muslim minoritarian films by Mahesh Bhatt, Khalid Mohamed, and Shyam Benegal I examine in chapter 5 make a powerful case for Muslim claims on the Indian nation. Not only are they stirring, imaginative accounts of a beleaguered Muslim subjectivity in a world that increasingly equates "Muslim" with "terrorist," they also call into question the Indian nationalist construction of the Muslim as the stranger who exceeds all statutory conventions, but one who must be tolerated.

Literature is a place where ethical work takes place; our imaginative making and remaking of the affective materials of life is one of the things that can enable us to respond to the call of the other. In different ways, each of these narratives directs us to the possibility of an ethical relationship with those who have been rendered outside the conditional circles of family, religious group, or nation. Although my literary examples have focused on India, I argue that the ethical implications of these fictions are broader and relevant as well for thinking about possibilities of peaceful coexistence in the subcontinent as a whole. Together, these fictions of coexistence aim to reorient the ethical sensibilities of their readers by radically calling into question the law of identity—the "being-oneself in one's own home"—and allow us to envision ways of living well "at home" with the "stranger."

Notes

Introduction

1. See, for example, Tapan Basu et al., eds., *Khaki Shorts and Saffron Flags: A Critique of the Hindu Right* (New Delhi: Orient Longman, 1993); Tanika Sarkar and Urvashi Butalia, eds., *Women and the Hindu Right: A Collection of Essays* (New Delhi: Kali, 1995); Gyanendra Pandey, ed., *Hindus and Others: The Question of Identity in India Today* (New Delhi: Viking, Penguin, 1993).

2. Banu Subramaniam, "Archaic Modernities: Science, Secularism, and Religion in Modern India," *Social Text* 18.3 (2000): 74.

3. Basu et al., *Khaki Shorts*, 2.

4. The rationale behind this brutal act of cultural desecration was that the Mughal emperor Babur had constructed a mosque on this ostensibly most sacred site of the Hindus, the birthplace of the Hindu god Ram. Present-day Hindus now desired to reclaim the site and build a temple to honor Ram. In the months following the destruction of the mosque, large-scale communal riots between Hindus and Muslims erupted across the country in which thousands were killed or wounded.

5. Jacques Derrida, "Hostipitality," trans. Barry Stocker and Forbes Morlock, *Angelaki* 5.3 (December 2000): 14.

6. For example, in his 1923 treatise *Hindutva: Who Is a Hindu?*, the Hindu nationalist leader Vinayak Damodar Savarkar wrote: "Their [Muslims'] holyland is far off in Arabia or Palestine. Their mythology and godmen, ideas and heroes are not the children of this soil. Consequently their names and their outlook smack of foreign origin." See Vinayak Damodar Savarkar, *Hindutva: Who Is a Hindu?* (first published 1923; Poona: Bharat Mudranalaya, 1949), 94.

7. Mushirul Hasan, "Introduction," in *India's Partition: Process, Strategy and Mobilization*, ed. Mushirul Hasan (Delhi: Oxford University Press, 1993), 1.

8. Thus, my study is closely aligned with Prasenjit Duara's more historiographical project, which interrogates the nation as the subject of linear teleological Enlightenment histories. Arguing that "national history secures for the contested and

contingent nation the false unity of the self same, national subject evolving over time," Duara proposes a notion of bifurcated histories that would pay attention to the ways in which historical narratives appropriate dispersed histories according to the needs of the present (4–5). See *Rescuing History from the Nation: Questioning Narratives of Modern China* (Chicago: University of Chicago Press, 1995). I am indebted to Amit Baishya for directing me to Duara's work.

9. See Jacques Derrida, "Différance," in *Margins of Philosophy*, trans. Alan Bass (Chicago: University of Chicago Press, 1985).

10. Gayatri Spivak, "The Setting to Work of Deconstruction," in *A Critique of Postcolonial Reason* (Cambridge, Mass.: Harvard University Press, 1999), 425.

11. See, for example, Ayesha Jalal, *The Sole Spokesman: Jinnah, the Muslim League and the Demand for Pakistan* (Cambridge, U.K.: Cambridge University Press, 1985), and Asim Roy, "The High Politics of India's Partition," in Hasan, ed., *India's Partition.*

12. Aamir Mufti, "Auerbach in Istanbul: Edward Said, Secular Criticism, and the Question of Minority Culture," *Critical Inquiry* 25 (1998): 95–125, 117–18.

13. Aamir Mufti, "Secularism and Minority," *Social Text* 14.4 (1995): 75–96, 86–87.

14. See Wendy Brown, "Reflections on Tolerance in the Age of Identity," in *Democracy and Vision: Sheldon Wolin and the Vicissitudes of the Political*, eds. Aryeh Botwinick and William E. Connolly (Princeton: Princeton University Press, 2001), and *Regulating Aversion: Tolerance in the Age of Identity and Empire* (Princeton: Princeton University Press, 2006). I am deeply grateful to Professor Brown for sharing sections of her manuscript with me.

15. See "Tolerance as/in Civilizational Discourse" in *Regulating Aversion.*

16. Jacques Derrida, "Avowing—The Impossible: 'Returns,' Repentance and Reconciliation," keynote address of the conference "Irreconcilable Differences? Jacques Derrida and the Question of Religion," trans. Gil Anidjar, University of California, Santa Barbara, October 2003 (hereafter cited in text with page numbers). I am very grateful to Elisabeth Weber for sharing this text with me. I would also like to thank Gil Anidjar for his help with clarifying some of my questions about this essay.

17. I elaborate on Derrida's concept of hospitality in chapter 2.

18. Similarly, Gayatri Spivak envisions the "ethics of alterity" as a "social practice of responsibility *based on an imperative grounded on alterity*" (72, my emphasis). Accordingly, she asks us to envision ourselves as "planetary subjects," subjects who are radically oriented toward the other: "If we imagine ourselves as planetary subjects rather than global agents, planetary creatures rather than global entities, alterity remains underived from us, it is not our dialectial negation, it contains us as much as it flings us away" (46). Significantly, her account of ethics underscores that both the dominant and the subordinate must rethink themselves

as intended by planetary alterity. The onus is not just limited to Europe as "the giver of hospitality" (84). See Gayatri Chakravorty Spivak, *Imperatives to Re-Imagine the Planet / Imperative zur Neuerfindung des Planten,* ed. Willi Goetschel (Vienna: Passagen, 1999). I am very grateful to Professor Spivak for providing me with a copy of this essay and to Sangeeta Ray for recommending this essay.

19. Jacques Derrida, "Faith and Knowledge: The Two Sources of 'Religion' at the Limits of Reason Alone," in *Acts of Religion,* ed. Gil Anidjar (New York: Routledge, 2002), 60.

20. For an elaboration, see Gayatri Chakravorty Spivak, "A Moral Dilemma," in *What Happens to History: The Renewal of Ethics in Contemporary Thought,* ed. Howard Marchitello (New York: Routledge, 2001), 215–36.

21. Spivak, "The Setting to Work of Deconstruction," 423–31, esp. pp. 427 and 425.

22. As Spivak explains: "To be born human is to be born angled toward an other and others. To account for this, the human being presupposes the quite-other. This is the bottom-line of being-human as being-in-the-ethical relation. By definition, we cannot—no self can—reach the quite-other. Thus the ethical situation can only be figured in the experience of the impossible." See "A Moral Dilemma," 215. See also "The Setting to Work of Deconstruction" for a lucid elaboration of these insights, esp. pp. 424–27.

23. For a succinct elaboration of the *partage*—the division and the sharing—between ethics and politics, see Sara Guyer's review of *On Cosmopolitanism and Forgiveness, MLN* 116.5 (December 2001): 1115–18.

24. Gayatri Spivak, "Terror: A Speech after 9-11," *boundary 2* 31.2 (2004): 83. Hereafter cited in text with page numbers.

25. See Spivak, "A Moral Dilemma," 230. On the uncanny, see *Death of a Discipline,* especially the last chapter, "Planetarity." I elaborate on Spivak's use of Freud's theory of the uncanny in chapter 3.

26. Spivak, *Death of a Discipline,* (New York: Columbia University Press, 2003), 23. Spivak writes, "the image of the other as self, produced by imagination supplementing knowledge or its absence, is a figure that marks the impossibility of *fully realizing* the ethical." I take her to mean not that ethics are impossible but that the effort to heed the call of the other by means of the imagination can only ever be incompletely realized. See "A Moral Dilemma," 221.

27. Leela Gandhi et al., Editorial, *Postcolonial Studies* 5.1 (2002): 7.

1. Rethinking Secularism

I am very grateful to Rajeswari Sunder Rajan, Laura Rigal, Barbara Eckstein, Judith Pascoe, and Amit Baishya for their comments on earlier versions of this chapter.

1. Following sociologists Roy Wallis and Steve Bruce, I differentiate between secularism as normative doctrine and secularization as social phenomena that emerged in the wake of modernization. Although secularism in its hegemonic version desires the *decline* of religion, secularization is often understood in a more restricted way as a *process* that led to the "diminishing social significance of religion." See Roy Wallis and Steve Bruce, "Secularization: The Orthodox Model," in *Religion and Modernization: Sociologists and Historians Debate the Secularization Thesis* (Oxford: Clarendon, 1992), 11.

2. See Talal Asad, *Formations of the Secular: Christianity, Islam, Modernity* (Stanford, Calif.: Stanford University Press, 2003); Jose Casanova, "Private and Public Religions," *Social Research* 59.1 (1992): 17–57; Gauri Viswanathan, *Outside the Fold: Conversion, Modernity, and Belief* (Princeton: Princeton University Press: 1998); William E. Connolly, *Why I Am Not a Secularist* (Minneapolis: University of Minnesota Press, 1999); Homi Bhabha, "Unpacking My Library . . . Again," in *The Post-Colonial Question: Common Skies, Divided Horizons*, ed. Iain Chambers and Lidia Curti (London: Routledge, 1996) 199–211; "On Subaltern Secularism," *Women Against Fundamentalisms* 6 (1995): 6; Janet Jakobsen and Ann Pellegrini, "World Secularisms at the Millenium: Introduction," *Social Text* 18.3 (2000): 1–27.

3. For more on the ways in which secularization can be traced back to the Reformation, see Lori Branch's *Rituals of Spontaneity: Sentiment and Secularism from Free Prayer to Wordsworth* (Waco, Tex.: Baylor University Press, 2006). Branch notes that secularization is an "ongoing yet perpetually incomplete process" that takes place first of all within religious discourse itself, "a result of religious thinkers embracing forms of rationalization which are themselves simultaneously transcendentalizing and secularizing." Emergent economic and empirical discourses made it difficult to speak of the value of faith and belief in terms other than those of certainty and possession. This is evident, for example, in a religious thinker like Calvin, who was particularly invested in maintaining a separation between this (material) world and the next (spiritual). I am grateful to Lori Branch for some very interesting conversations on the imbrication of secularism and religion.

4. Immanuel Kant, "An Answer to the Question: What Is Enlightenment?" http://www.english.upenn.edu/~mgamer/Etexts/kant.html (accessed on July 4, 2007).

5. Indeed, it is only retrospectively that the term "secularism" has come to be associated with Enlightenment thinking about religion. Freethinkers who sought to dissociate themselves from atheists introduced it into English in the mid-nineteenth century. Asad tells us that the word secularism was coined by George Jacob Holyoake in 1851 and was meant to differentiate his position from Brad-

laugh's antithesitic one. See Talal Asad's *Formations of the Secular* for a more elaborate account of the origins of the term, especially chapter I.

6. Jacques Derrida, "Faith and Knowledge: The Two Sources of 'Religion' at the Limits of Reason Alone," *Acts of Religion*, ed. Gil Anidjar (New York: Routledge, 2002), 65.

7. Derrida, "Faith and Knowledge," 65.

8. Dorinda Outram's *The Enlightenment* (Cambridge, U.K.: Cambridge University Press, 1995) provides a useful account of diverse perspectives on religion among Enlightenment thinkers.

9. Asad, *Formations of the Secular*, 192. Hereafter cited in text with page numbers. Asad proposes that the "secular" as a variety of behaviors, practices, and sensibilities is an *aspect* of secularism as a political and governmental doctrine that has its origins in the nineteenth century but is conceptually prior to it (16). Following Asad, this study sets out to unravel the fraught meanings of the term "secularism" by exploring its connections with the "secular."

10. John Locke, *The Second Treatise of Government and a Letter Concerning Toleration* (1956; Mineola, N.Y.: Dover, 2002). Hereafter cited in text with page numbers.

11. Jose Casanova, "Private and Public Religions."

12. See Casanova's "Private and Public Religions" for an exposition of how these binaries are constructed.

13. This is not to suggest that he views liberalism and secularism as unrelated—for Connolly, the secularization of public life is crucial to the primacy of the state. See Connolly, *Why I Am Not a Secularist*, 10.

14. Gayatri Spivak, *In Other Worlds* (New York: Methuen, 1987), 103.

15. On deconstructing the private/public binary, see also Nivedita Menon, *Recovering Subversion: Feminist Politics Beyond the Law* (New Delhi: Permanent Black, 2004), esp. pp. 9–17.

16. For an incisive account of how (western) Christianity invented the distinction between the religious and the secular, and hence "made religion," see Gil Anidjar, "Secularism," *Critical Inquiry* 33 (August 2006): 52–77, esp. p. 62. See also Talal Asad, *Genealogies of Religion: Discipline and Reasons of Power in Christianity and Islam* (Baltimore: Johns Hopkins University Press, 1993).

17. In a similar insight, Robert Baird, in his analysis of David Hume's *The Natural History of Religion*, notes that the idea of "world religions" that has undergirded the study of religion condenses different social phenomena as "religion," even as it simultaneously naturalizes the object of its study, based largely on a post-Reformation Protestant model. See Robert J. Baird, "Late Secularism," *Social Text* 18.3 (2000): 123–36.

18. As Hent De Vries, one of Derrida's most careful readers, avers, citations

from religious traditions are fundamental to the structure of language and experience and indeed constitute the unseen, the unsaid, and the unthought of a philosophical logos. See *Philosophy and the Turn to Religion* (Baltimore: Johns Hopkins University Press, 1999), 5.

19. "Faith and Knowledge," 64–65. Hereafter cited in text with page numbers.

20. Jacques Derrida, "Force of Law: The 'Mystical Foundation of Authority,'" *Acts of Religion*, 228–98, 241.

21. Judaism and Islam are thus the last two monotheisms that are revolting against everything "that in the Christianizing of our world, signifies the death of God . . . two non-pagan monotheisms still alien enough at the heart of Graeco-Christian, *Pagano-Christian* Europe alienating themselves from a Europe that signifies the death of God" by affirming that monotheism is no less than belief in a single God. Derrida, "Faith and Knowledge," 51.

22. Gayatri Spivak provides a succinct gloss on the story of western secularism: "In the seventeenth and eighteenth centuries Christianity is recoded, laundered and sublated into philosophy and ethics," which subsequently is "not called Christian but simply secular," and transported to the rest of the world through the process of imperial expansion. This process is routinely presented as a "law of motion"—the benevolent extension of the European project of modernity by which "other" cultures are brought into the ambit of civilization. Gayatri Spivak, "Reading the Satanic Verses," in *Outside in the Teaching Machine* (New York: Routledge, 1993), 240–41.

23. Gayatri Spivak's "Terror: A Speech after 9-11," *boundary 2* 31.2 (2004): 81–111, 88. Hereafter cited in text with page numbers.

24. Spivak picks up on Kant's use of the word "effect" in his statement that we have to make room for "the effects of grace" and reads it as his effort at de-transcendentalizing "grace." Grace is figured as near metalepsis—"unverifiable effect of an effect" (109). Since pure reason is unable to know the cause, all that it has is inscribed as an effect (108).

25. I elaborate on this conception of religion in the pages that follow.

26. Arjun Appadurai suggests as much when he speaks of "ideoscapes" as aspects of Enlightenment worldview, which comprise a "concatenation of ideas, terms and images, including 'freedom,' 'welfare,' 'rights,' 'sovereignty,' 'representation' and the master-term 'democracy'" that are flowing across borders with an unprecedented velocity. Significantly, however, he maintains that their scattering across the world, especially since the nineteenth century, has "loosened the internal coherence that held these terms and images together in a Euro-American master-narrative" (though one might question if such an internal coherence ever existed). The differential diaspora of these keywords entail problems of both a semantic and a pragmatic nature: "semantic to the extent that words (and their

lexical equivalents) require *careful translation* from context to context in their global movements; and pragmatic to the extent that the use of these words by political actors and their audiences may be subject to very *different set of contextual conventions* that mediate their translation into public context."

See his "Disjuncture and Difference in the Global Cultural Economy," *Public Culture* 2.2 (1990): 10.

27. Brenda Cossman and Ratna Kapur, *Secularism's Last Sigh?: Hindutva and the Misrule of Law* (Delhi: Oxford University Press, 1999), xi.

28. Anuradha Needham and Rajeswari Sunder Rajan, Introduction, *The Crisis of Secularism in India,* eds. Anuradha Needham and Rajeswari Sunder Rajan (Durham, N.C.: Duke University Press, 2007), 3. I am deeply indebted to them for sharing this and other essays from the anthology with me.

29. It is important to recall, though, that while Muhammad Ali Jinnah led the movement for a separate nation for India's Muslims, in his inaugural speech, as the first President of Pakistan, he proclaimed that Pakistan would be a secular state, where Muslims and non-Muslims could be citizens with equal rights, and that religion would not impinge upon state administration. Six months after his death, however, Pakistan was declared an Islamic state. India, on the contrary, has continued to define itself constitutionally as a "sovereign, socialist, secular, democratic republic," words that resound with the Nehruvian vision of an India catching up with the modernity of the post-Enlightenment west.

30. Amartya Sen, "The Threats to Secular India," *The New York Times Review of Books* XL-7 26 (April 8, 1993): 60–67.

31. Gyanendra Pandey, *The Construction of Communalism in Colonial North India* (Delhi: Oxford University Press, 1990), 6–7.

32. Thus, for example, Rajeev Bhargava, the editor of a recent collection of essays on secularism, writes: "It was earlier thought that the ideology of secularism enabled people with different faiths as well as believers and nonbelievers not merely to coexist but to live together as well." See Rajeev Bhargava, "What Is Secularism For?" in *Secularism and Its Critics,* in Bhargava, (Delhi: Oxford University Press, 1998), 487.

33. Partha Chatterjee, "Secularism and Tolerance," in Bhargava, *Secularism and Its Critics,* 349.

34. Donald E. Smith, "India as a Secular State," in Bhargava, *Secularism and Its Critics,* 177–233; hereafter cited in text with page numbers.

35. Shefali Jha, "Secularism in the Constituent Assembly Debates, 1946–1950," *Economic and Political Weekly,* July 27, 2002.

36. What is particularly telling about advocates of the second and third positions is their understanding of all western state secularism as necessarily antagonistic to religion rather than as a doctrine of privatization, a perception that

shadows contemporary Hindu nationalist (Rashtriya Swayamsevak Sangh, RSS) critiques of secularism as an alien western ideology. The U.S. "wall of separation" (in a largely religious landscape), the French tradition of *laïcité,* and the English secular state with the anomalous existence of a state church are only some of the most obvious examples that can be cited to argue for the heterogeneity of western secularism.

37. Cited in Neera Chandhoke, *Beyond Secularism: The Rights of Religious Minorities* (New Delhi: Oxford University Press, 1999), 53.

38. Derrida cites the prominent linguist Benveniste to recall that the Indo-European language had no term for what we call "religion," since they did not conceive of "religion" as a "separate institution" (72).

39. Smith, "India as a Secular State," 213. Hereafter cited in text with page numbers.

40. Timothy Scanlon reminds us that nonestablishment has entailed a different strategy—indeed a different political compromise—in different western countries at different historical conjunctures, so we cannot afford to talk unproblematically about some sort of homogeneous "western" secularism. See "The Difficulty of Tolerance" in Bhargava, *Secularism and Its Critics,* 54–72.

41. Moreover, under Nehru, the Indian secular state undertook a massive reform of Hindu religious institutions and practices in the early years after independence, clearly violating the principle of separation of state and religion.

42. Ashis Nandy, "The Politics of Secularism and the Recovery of Religious Tolerance," in Bhargava, *Secularism and Its Critics,* 321–44; T. N. Madan, "Secularism in Its Place," in Bhargava, *Secularism and Its Critics,* 297–320.

43. M. K. Gandhi, *An Autobiography or the Story of My Experiments with Truth* (Boston: Beacon Press, 1993), 383.

44. Cited in Ajay Skaria, "Gandhi's Politics: Liberalism and the Question of the Ashram," *South Atlantic Quarterly* 101.4 (Fall 2002): 955–86, 962.

45. Skaria suggests that state-centered politics is denoted in Gandhi by the Gujarati words *rajkaran* and *rajkiya,* which he rejects in favor of notions like *satyagraha* (peaceful noncooperation) and *ahimsa* (rendered as "neighborliness" by Skaria rather than Gandhi's preferred translation, "love."). Gandhi saw practices like *sarva dharma sambhava* and *satyagraha* (peaceful noncooperation) as providing checks to the modern state's practices of governmentality. The absence of the state in Gandhian religious politics is not to be understood as an antistatist communitarianism, even if Gandhi did believe that after independence the Congress should disband itself and make no claim to state power; rather it should devote itself to the *seva* (service) of India's villages. But this "politics" did see itself as disciplining modern discipline in the form of modern power and the modern state. I am very grateful to Ajay Skaria for his help with this section of my chapter.

46. Jawaharlal Nehru, *The Discovery of India* (1946; New Delhi: Oxford University Press, 2002), 519–20.

47. Jawaharlal Nehru, *Toward Freedom: The Autobiography of Jawaharlal Nehru* (New York: John Day Company, 1941), 240.

48. Jawaharlal Nehru, *Jawaharlal Nehru: An Anthology*, ed. S. Gopal (New Delhi: Oxford University Press, 1980), 327.

49. Jawaharlal Nehru, *Jawaharlal Nehru: An Anthology*, 330.

50. Ashis Nandy, "The Politics of Secularism and the Recovery of Religious Tolerance," and Partha Chatterjee, "Secularism and Tolerance," in *Secularism and Its Critics*. Chatterjee, for example, takes as his point of departure the parallels that have been drawn between the rise of fascism in Europe and the consolidation of Hindu majoritarianism in India in the past few years. Nazi Germany and Fascist Italy, he points out, are only two examples of a central conundrum in the analysis of the development of the modern state in many countries of the world: namely, that state policies of religious or other kinds of intolerance do not necessarily call for the collapse of state and religion, nor do they require the existence of theocratic institutions. Similarly, he suggests, the Hindu Right in India, in its most mature and formidable statement of the new political conception of Hindutva, seeks to mobilize the legal powers of the secular state to "persecute and terrorize a specific religious minority within its population," namely, the Muslims of India, and "to supply in the name of national culture, a homogenizing content to the notion of citizenship" (347). Given this peculiar conundrum, Chatterjee asks, "[I]s the defence of secularism an adequate or even appropriate ground on which to meet the political challenge of Hindu majoritarianism? Or should it be fought where the attack is being made, i.e. should the response be a defense of the duty of the democratic state to *ensure policies of religious tolerance*?" (348). Thus, he calls for a radical rejection of the existing structures of the liberal secular state itself in favor of a communitarian framework that will allow minorities their own autonomous representative institutions based on internal democratic norms and procedures.

51. Jacques Derrida, "Taking a Stand for Algeria," *Acts of Religion*, 306.

52. The BJP proposes *panthnirpekshata*, but *panth* is as misleading as *dharma* for a translation of the Latin noun *religion*.

53. I am very grateful to Simona Sawney for her help with clarifying these terms.

54. Bhargava suggests that the Indian state has followed a "contextual secularism" of the "principled distance" kind by excluding religion for some purposes and including it for others, but always on the basis of nonsectarian considerations. Rather than making the case for the complete separation of religious and nonreligious practices, he argues for the separation of some religious and nonreligious

institutions. See his "What Is Secularism For?" in *Secularism and Its Critics*, 486–542.

55. I draw upon Étienne Balibar's distinction between individual nationalities that exist in the world and the "nation-form," or the form of nationality as such. Balibar defines the nation-form as a "type of 'social formation,' that is a mode of combination of economic and ideological structures," which provides a model for legitimizing the administrative and symbolic functions of the state. See his *We, the People of Europe?: Reflections on Transnational Citizenship* (Princeton: Princeton University Press, 2004), esp. pp. 16–17; hereafter cited in text as *We the People* with page numbers.

56. Benedict Anderson, *Imagined Communities: Reflections on the Origins and Spread of Nationalism* (1983; London: Verso, 1991).

57. Wendy Brown, "Subjects of Tolerance: Why We are Civilized and They are the Barbarians," in *Regulating Aversion: Tolerance in the Age of Identity and Empire,* manuscript, p. 22. (Princeton: Princeton University Press, 2006).

58. See Étienne Balibar, "Ambiguous Universality," *Differences: A Journal of Feminist Cultural Studies* 7.1 (1995): 52. For a similar argument about the subordinate place of Sri Lankan Tamils, see Qadri Ismail's incisive essay, "Speaking to Sri Lanka," *Interventions* 3.2 (2001): 296–308.

59. As Ernest Gellner notes, the nation-form, in most circumstances, cannot survive without its normative political "shell"—the state. See *Nations and Nationalism* (Ithaca, N.Y.: Cornell University Press, 1983).

60. Kymlicka writes, "The religion model, with its strict separation of church and state, is altogether misleading as an account of the relationship between the liberal-democratic state and ethnocultural groups" (17). In this account, religion is therefore construed as a matter of private faith, which has nothing to do with ethnocultural groups. Moreover, even though he questions the idea of what he calls "ethnocultural neutrality" in the liberal state, these insights are not carried over into an interrogation of the presumed neutrality of the secular state since religion is only understood to be about individual choice.

See the Introduction to *Can Liberal Pluralism Be Exported? Western Political Theory and Ethnic Relations in Eastern Europe*, eds. Will Kymlicka and Magda Opalski (Oxford: Oxford University Press, 2001).

61. Clifford Geertz, *The Interpretation of Cultures* (New York: Basic, 1973). However, recent work in cultural anthropology and cultural studies has challenged this traditional account of cultures as distinct, bounded entities that can be clearly demarcated from each other. James Ferguson and Akhil Gupta's "Beyond 'Culture': Space, Identity and the Politics of Difference" in *Cultural Anthropology* 7.1 (1992): 6–23 is a good example of this kind of work. For an interesting exploration of the relationship between religion and culture, see Tomoko Masuzawa's

"Culture" in *Critical Terms for Religious Studies,* ed. Mark C. Taylor (Chicago: Chicago University Press, 1998) 70–93.

62. Informed by Jyoti Puri's work, I take ethnicity to mean a form of collective identity based on cultural commonalities such as those of language, custom, or descent. This is not to suggest that some sort of primordial or biological ties constitute ethnicities as compared to nations; indeed ethnic groups, like nations, can often be premised on fictive constructions of commonality while sharing some cultural affinities. Both nationalism and ethnicity center on affects like belonging, identity, a shared past, links to a historic homeland, as well as, crucially, boundaries of inclusion and exclusion between self and other. What differentiates the two concepts most critically is the relationship to the state and territorial boundaries; nationalism, unlike ethnicities, seeks *sovereignty* over a bounded territory. When an ethnic group comes to fashion itself with notions of sovereignty and statehood, it comes to be viewed as a nationalist or subnationalist group. For a very clear and succinct account of the overlaps and the differences between nationalisms and ethnicities, see Puri's *Encountering Nationalism* (Malden, Mass.: Blackwell, 2004). However, unlike Puri, I do not view religion as an aspect of ethnicity—as I go on to elaborate.

63. Gayatri Spivak, "Terror: A Speech after 9-11," 104. Hereafter cited in text with page numbers.

64. See Derrida's "Faith and Knowledge" for an account of religion as the experience of the sacred or holy, as well as an experience of faith.

65. Although Žižek is writing of the relationship between nationalisms and ethnic communities, his account of the excess that constitutes minority groups within the nation is very relevant to religious groups as well. See Slavoj Žižek's "Eastern Europe's Republics of Gilead," *New Left Review* 183 (1990): 50–62, 54. I am very grateful to Kathy Lavezzo for recommending this essay.

66. Aamir Mufti "Secularism and Minority," *Social Text* 14.4 (1995): 75–96. Hereafter cited in text with page numbers.

67. This is an important claim because it asks us to consider the minoritarian positioning of Indian Muslims even before the momentous event of Partition.

68. On the Round Table discussions, see Shabnun Tejani's essay, "Reflecting on the Category of Secularism in India" in *The Crisis of Secularism in India,* ed. Needham and Sunder Rajan (Durham, N.C.: Duke University Press, 2007); on the Constituent Assembly debates, see Rochana Bajpai's "Constituent Assembly Debates and Minority Rights," *Economic and Political Weekly,* May 27, 2000.

69. Kymlicka and Opalski, *Can Liberal Pluralism Be Exported?*

70. Cited in Cossman and Kapur, *Secularism's Last Sigh,* 65.

71. Cited in Cossman and Kapur, *Secularism's Last Sigh,* 65.

72. Speech to Parliament, November 11, 1990, cited in Ratna Kapur and Brenda

Cossman, "Communalizing Gender, Engendering Community: Women, Legal Discourse and the Saffron Agenda," *Women and the Hindu Right: A Collection of Essays,* eds. Tanika Sarkar and Urvashi Butalia (New Delhi: Kali, 1995), 89–90.

73. For a succinct outlining of the various positions involved in the personal law/uniform civil code controversy, see Rajeswari Sunder Rajan's "Women Between Community and State: Some Implications of the Uniform Civil Code Debates" in *The Scandal of the State: Women, Law and Citizenship in Postcolonial India* (Durham, N.C.: Duke University Press, 2003), 147–76.

74. Chandhoke, *Beyond Secularism,* 92 and 87. Hereafter cited in text with page numbers.

75. This statement does seem to contradict the previous one, but by and large the tenor of her argument is that secularism as a concept cannot cope with demands for minority rights. A little later, she writes, "For majority groups can legitimately insist—if the argument has been carried out within the realm of the secular principle per se—that by making these demands the minority groups violate the secular principle, that the state shall treat all groups equally" (87–88).

76. See especially the last chapter, "Negotiating Collective and Individual Rights," for an account of minority cultural rights, esp. pp. 288–89.

77. Neera Chandhoke, "Re-presenting the Secular Agenda for India," *Will Secular India Survive?* ed. Mushirul Hasan (Gurgaon: ImprintOne, 2004), 65. Hereafter cited in text with page numbers.

78. When she does suggest going "beyond secularism" in this new essay, it is to grapple with the thorny question of *intragroup* relations such as gender justice within the group. In her view, this is where the principle of democratic equality is particularly useful, since secularism as a concept is designed to regulate intergroup rather than intragroup relationships.

79. Thus, for example, Rustom Bharucha writes: "[A]t the risk of essentialisation, one is compelled to name a concept around which a struggle has emerged, and without which it cannot be sustained." Rustom Bharucha, "The Shifting Sites of Secularism: Cultural Politics and Activism in India," *Economic and Political Weekly* 24 January (1998), 168.

80. I concur with Anuradha Needham and Rajeswari Sunder Rajan's observation that "it is the exacerbated expectations of secularism as political ideology and civic practice that have led to the inflation of its significance in the Indian context." See their Introduction to *The Crisis of Secularism,* 20.

81. See Gyan Prakash, "Secular Nationalism, Hindutva and the Minority," 177–90, and Gyanendra Pandey's "The Secular State and the Limits of Dialogue," 157–76, in Sunder Rajan and Needham's *The Crisis of Secularism in India.* In this, they echo William Connolly's desire for a "multidimensional pluralism," wherein "public culture inside and outside the state is now constituted by multiple mi-

norities divided along more numerous lines of religion, linguistic habit, economic interest, irreligion, ethnicity, sensuality, gender performances. . . ." with no place for an unquestioned majority. See *Why I Am Not a Secularist,* 92. For a somewhat similar position about Muslims in Europe, see Talal Asad's "Muslims as a 'Religious Minority' in Europe" in *Formations of the Secular,* 159–180.

82. Aamir Mufti, "Auerbach in Istanbul: Edward Said, Secular Criticism, and the Question of Minority Culture," *Critical Inquiry* 25 (1998): 95–125, particularly p. 107.

83. Pandey, "The Secular State," 170, 172, and 176.

84. Étienne Balibar, *We the People of Europe,* viii.

85. The immense difficulties of this process are evident even in Europe, as manifested, for example, in the recent French and Dutch votes against the new European constitution.

86. See, for example, Partha Chatterjee's early essay on this issue, "Secularism and Toleration." His more recent work presents an interesting turn away from this initial formulation. See "The Contradictions of Secularism" in *The Politics of the Governed: Reflections on Popular Politics in Most of the World* (New York: Columbia University Press, 2004), 113–30.

87. For a very incisive argument about the limits of both privatization and protectionism as a solution to cultural claims, see Courtney Jung, "From Contingency to Proceduralism," *Yale Conference on Contingency in Honor of Robert Dahl,* December 3–4, 2004, Yale University, http://www.yale.edu/polisci/info/ conferences/contingency%20conference/jung.pdf (accessed on March 7, 2005).

88. Jung, "From Contingency to Proceduralism," 26.

89. See Wendy Brown's *Regulating Aversion* for a similar move toward questions of emancipation and equality rather than "tolerance" as a tool for addressing politicized cultural claims.

90. Zoya Hasan, "Social Inequalities, Secularism and Minorities in India's Democracy" in ed. Mushirul Hasan, *Will Secular India Survive?* 240–41.

91. Yamini Aiyer and Meeto Malik, "Minority Rights, Secularism and Civil Society," *Economic and Political Weekly* October 23, 2004.

92. Seema Mustapha, "Sachhar Committee Report on the Backwardness of Indian Muslims," *Asian Age,* December 1, 2006.

93. While acknowledging the risks involved in any kind of appeal to collective identity, Bruce Robbins and Elsa Stamatopoulou suggest that cultural rights' discourses (for example, in U.N. human rights treaty bodies and international instruments) can in fact provide an alternative to the concept of discrete and bounded cultures that often underlie movements for *full* political sovereignty and the right to self-determination of peoples. Cultural rights are of immense political importance because they are a means of attaining material objectives that cannot be

attained more directly. They conclude that the opportunities match and indeed outweigh the difficulties. See "Reflections on Culture and Cultural Rights," in "And Justice for All? The Claims of Human Rights," eds. Ian Balfour and Eduardo Cadava, special issue, *South Atlantic Quarterly* 103.2/3 (2004): 419–34.

94. One way out of this predicament of fixed authenticity, as Robbins and Stamatopoulou suggest, is to place temporal limitations on human rights laws or affirmative action policies to ensure that these measures do not fix the very identities they set out to protect. See "Reflections on Culture," 431.

95. Rustom Bharucha, "The Shifting Sites of Secularism," 167.

96. Nandy believes that secularism is an alien and statist ideology, which is part of a broader package of modernization, bureaucratization, national security, and scientific development that has been imposed by India's middle-class cosmopolitan elite on the nonmodern majority of believers. In his view, secularism has become a faith intolerant of other faiths, and thus it must be rejected altogether (333). In opposition to Nandy's wholesale denunciation of secularism, my argument underscores the importance both of a reformulated liberal secular state and a reason-based secularism toward the project of multireligious coexistence. Needless to add, my vision of ethical coexistence is also quite different from his account of "tolerance"—which he locates in the diverse religious communities of India. See "The Politics of Secularism."

97. Needham and Sunder Rajan, Introduction, *The Crisis of Secularism*, 22.

2. For God's Sake, Open the Universe a Little More

1. Martha Nussbuam, "Patriotism and Cosmopolitanism," *For Love of Country: Debating the Limits of Patriotism*, ed. Joshua Cohen (Boston: Beacon Press); Anthony Appiah, "Cosmopolitan Patriots," in *For Love of Country*, ed. Nussbaum, 21–29; Paul Rabinow, "Representations are Social Facts," in *Writing Culture: The Poetics and Politics of Ethnography*, eds. James Clifford and George E. Marcus (Berkeley: University of California Press, 1986); Pheng Cheah and Bruce Robbins, eds., *Cosmopolitics: Thinking and Feeling Beyond the Nation* (Minneapolis: University of Minnesota Press, 1998); David Hollinger, "Not Universalists, Not Pluralists: The New Cosmopolitans Find Their Own Way," *Constellations* 8.2 (2001): 236–48; Homi Bhabha, "Minority Culture and Creative Anxiety," http://www.britishcouncil.org/studies/reinventing_britain/bhabha_1.htm (accessed on July 4, 2007).

2. Jacques Derrida, "Hostipitality," in *Acts of Religion*, trans. and ed. Gil Anidjar (New York: Routledge, 2002), 361.

3. Bruce Robbins, "Comparative Cosmopolitanism," *Social Text* 31/32 (1992): 171.

4. Timothy Brennan, "Cosmopolitans and Celebrities," *Race and Class* 31 (1989): 1–19. Hereafter cited in text with page numbers.

5. Timothy Brennan, *At Home in the World: Cosmopolitanism Now* (Cambridge, Mass.: Harvard University Press, 1997), 37.

6. Salman Rushdie, *Midnight's Children* (London: Jonathan Cape, 1981).

7. See Josna Rege, "Victim into Protagonist? *Midnight's Children* and the Post-Rushdie National Narrative of the Eighties" in *Studies in the Novel* 29.3 (1997): 342–75 for an insightful analysis of the considerable influence of this novel.

8. Bishnupriya Ghosh, *When Borne Across: Literary Cosmopolitics in the Contemporary Indian Novel* (New Brunswick, N.J.: Rutgers University Press, 2004), 8.

9. Martha Nussbuam, "Patriotism and Cosmopolitanism," 7. Hereafter cited in text with page numbers.

10. Subsequently, several humanities and social sciences journals in the 1990s came up with special issues on cosmopolitanism. See, for example, *Constellations* 7.1 (March 2000); *The Partisan Review* (Spring 1996); *Dissent* (1999); *Public Culture* 12.3, later published as a book, *Cosmopolitanism* (Durham, N.C.: Duke University Press, 2002). See also Pheng Cheah and Bruce Robbins, eds., *Cosmopolitics: Thinking and Feeling Beyond the Nation;* David Hollinger, "Not Universalists, Not Pluralists: The New Cosmopolitans Find Their Own Way"; David Harvey, "Cosmopolitanism and the Banality of Geographical Evils," *Public Culture* 12.2 (2000): 529–64.

11. Timothy Brennan, "Cosmo-Theory," *South Atlantic Quarterly* 100.3 (2001): 662.

12. Homi Bhabha, "Minority Culture and Creative Anxiety." Hereafter cited in text with page numbers.

13. See Hollinger, "Not Universalists, Not Pluralists: The New Cosmopolitans Find Their Own Way." Hereafter cited in text with page numbers.

14. Robbins and Cheah, *Cosmopolitics.*

15. Martha Nussbaum, *Upheavals of Thought: The Intelligence of Emotions* (Cambridge, U.K.: Cambridge University Press, 2001), 359.

16. Ross Posnock, *Color and Culture: Black Writers and the Making of the Modern Intellectual* (Cambridge, Mass.: Harvard University Press, 1998); David Hollinger, *Postethnic America: Beyond Multiculturalism* (New York: Basic Books, 2000). Interestingly, Hollinger affirms both the national and the transnational versions of cosmopolitanism in his more recent essay, "Not Universalists, Not Pluralists."

17. See Brennan, "Cosmo-Theory." Brennan aims to demonstrate how a "national-political myth of multicultural inclusion (U.S. pluralism) dovetails under specific conditions, with a purportedly supranational ethos of global cooperation (cosmopolitanism)" ("Cosmo-Theory," 669). In his view, the desire for a

"structure of underlying unity" and a "supranational ethos of global cooperation" to be found in cosmo-theory unwittingly serves to support the image of America as a universal nation, "the globally sought after, the desire of all" (669). Even though this new discourse is critical of the American government's expansionism, he contends that it also masks a veiled Americanism in its affirmation of the desirability of American cultural life. While Brennan's concerns about how cosmopolitanism can lapse into an alibi for American imperialism (much like the risks of contemporary human rights' discourses) are well founded, he doesn't differentiate between versions of cosmopolitanism. Bruce Robbins and Homi Bhabha, for example, share many of his concerns. The important point of disagreement between them, of course, is Brennan's notion of the nation-state as a "manageable community" that allows subalterns to petition the state as opposed to Robbins's efforts to constitute a transnational ethos of solidarity (along with his affirmation of the welfare state).

18. Bruce Robbins, "What's Left of Cosmopolitanism?" *Radical Philosophy* November/December (2002): 33.

19. Gayatri Chakravorty Spivak, *Death of a Discipline* (New York: Columbia University Press, 2003), 84.

20. See Jacques Derrida, *Of Hospitality: Anne Dufourmantelle Invites Jacques Derrida to Respond*, trans. Rachel Bowlby (Stanford, Calif.: Stanford University Press, 2000); "On Cosmopolitanism," *Cosmopolitanism and Forgiveness*, trans. Mark Dooley and Michael Hughes (London: Routledge, 2001); "Hostipitality," trans. Barry Stocker and Forbes Morlock, *Angelaki* 5.3 (December 2000): 3–18; and "Hostipitality" in *Acts of Religion*.

21. Jacques Derrida, "Avowing—The Impossible: 'Returns,' Repentance and Reconciliation," keynote address of the conference "Irreconcilable Differences? Jacques Derrida and the Question of Religion," University of California, Santa Barbara, October 2003, trans. Gil Anidjar, 18.

22. Likewise, Gaytari Spivak suggests that we imagine ourselves as "planetary subjects" rather than as continental, global, or worldly, since "the planet is in the species of alterity, belonging to another system; and yet we inhabit it on loan" (*Death of a Discipline*, 72). Spivak's invocation of planetarity allows us to embrace an "inexhaustible taxonomy" of others rather than limit ourselves to other human beings.

23. In fact, as Derrida points out, there is also a semantic and etymological link between hostis (as host) and hostis (as enemy) and hence between hospitality and hostility. See "Hostipitality," *Angelaki*, 15. Hereafter cited in text with page numbers.

24. Derrida, *Of Hospitality*, 25. Hereafter cited in text with page numbers.

25. See "Hostipitality" in *Acts of Religion* for an elaboration of the themes of holding oneself hostage and as the substitute of the other in the work of Levinas and Massignon.

26. Derrida, *On Cosmopolitanism*, 16–17. Hereafter cited in text with page numbers.

27. Derrida differentiates between the absolute Law of hospitality and the conditional laws of hospitality (in the plural), which come to limit this infinite notion in its inscription as a law. Yet, absolute hospitality also requires these laws in order to become concrete and effective, or else it would risk becoming utopian (even as the inscription in law of hospitality always threatens it from within). If the first notion of hospitality implies the unconditional—and hence the impossible—and dispenses with law, duty, and politics, the second takes in the conditional and the juridico-political. Ethics straddles these two regimes of hospitality, since the second, more limited kind of hospitality can also entail a conditional ethics. *Of Hospitality*, 135–37.

28. Saul Bellow, *The Dean's December*, quoted by Salman Rushdie in "Imaginary Homelands" in *Imaginary Homelands: Essays and Criticism 1981–1991* (London: Granta, 1991), 21.

29. Rushdie, "Imaginary Homelands," 20.

30. Homi Bhabha, "Minority Culture and Creative Anxiety," 3.

31. Vinayak Damodar Savarkar, *Hindutva: Who Is a Hindu?* 1923; Poona: Bharat Mudranalaya, 1949, 104.

32. Salman Rushdie, *The Moor's Last Sigh* (London: Jonathan Cape, 1995), 260. Hereafter cited in text with page numbers.

33. Prasenjit Duara, *Rescuing History from the Nation: Questioning Narratives of Modern China* (Chicago: University of Chicago Press, 1995), 9.

34. Dohra Ahmad, "'This Fundo Stuff Is Really Something New': Fundamentalism and Hybridity in *The Moor's Last Sigh*," *The Yale Journal of Criticism* 18.1 (2005): 1–20. Hereafter cited in text with page numbers.

35. For example, see some of his recent essays, particularly, "Not About Islam?" and "The Attacks on America" in *Step Across This Line: Collected Nonfiction 1992–2002* (New York: Random House, 2002).

36. Interview, *India Today* 30 September (1995): 101.

37. The novel's perspective on Bombay as the repository of cosmopolitanism echoes a fairly popular view of the city.

38. Derrida, "Avowing the Impossible," 21.

39. As Bruce Robbins notes, the sense of privilege that is intrinsic to most understandings of the term cosmopolitanism is underscored by the first entry under "cosmopolitan" in *The Oxford English Dictionary*, from J. S. Mill's *Political Economy*, which indicates the imbrication of capital with cosmopolitanism: "Capital," wrote Mill in 1848 "is becoming more and more cosmopolitan." See Bruce Robbins, "Comparative Cosmopolitanism," *Social Text* 31/32 (1992): 171.

40. Of course, Conrad, unlike Rushdie, figures Africans as "savages" throughout his novella.

41. Mary Lou Emery, *Modernism, the Visual, and Caribbean Culture* (Cambridge, U.K.: Cambridge University Press, 2007), 239–40. I am very indebted to Mary Lou Emery and Eddie Mallot for their insights on ekphrasis.

42. The historical accuracy of Rushdie's construction of Moorish Spain as an exemplarily coexistent world is, of course, open to contestation and interpretation.

43. Jawaharlal Nehru, cited in Sunil Khilnani, *The Idea of India* (1997; New Delhi: Penguin, 2004), xv.

44. See Aamir Mufti, "Secularism and Minority: Elements of a Critique," *Social Text* 45 (1995): 75–96, on the ways in which Nehru's *The Discovery of India* constructs Muslims as invaders (and Islam as an interruption) who were eventually absorbed into the subcontinent.

45. In Derrida's account of "love" as abandonment, it is the self—one that is aware of itself—which elects to offer itself to the other; it does not require a reciprocal abandonment from the other.

46. Derrida, "Avowing the Impossible," 32, 21.

47. My reading of the significance of the above passage in the novel differs quite significantly from Jill Didur's interpretation. She believes that the novel interrogates this "fantasy of deracination" or "transcendence of the body" (555), since Moor views the recounting of his story as a painful reworking of the dream: "A painful dream, that I do not deny; for in the waking world a man's not as easy to flay as a banana, no matter how ripe he may be" (Rushdie, 136). I suggest, however, that he sees this "flaying" or "peeling off" as a necessary, albeit painful, process so that the "truth about myself" can struggle out at last, and (in an echo of Joyce) "our souls, so long suppressed, can find utterance" (Rushdie, 136). We find resonances of this desire for a transcendent and unified naked self reiterated toward the end of the novel, as well, in the passage I cite next. See Jill Didur, "Secularism Beyond the East/West Divide: Literary Reading, Ethics, and *The Moor's Last Sigh*," *Textual Practice* 18.4 (2004): 541–62.

48. Hannah Arendt, most famously, first pointed out the paradox that human rights do not underlie political rights, but national citizenship determines human rights. See "The Decline of the Nation-State and the End of the Rights of Man" in *The Origins of Totalitarianism* (1951, New York: Schocken Books, 2004), 341–86.

49. Ian Balfour and Eduardo Cadava, eds., "The Claims of Human Rights: An Introduction," in "And Justice for All? The Claims of Human Rights," special issue, *South Atlantic Quarterly* 103.2/3 (2004): 282.

50. For a thoughtful analysis of *The Satanic Verses,* see Sara Suleri, "Contraband Histories: Salman Rushdie and the Embodiment of Blasphemy." *Yale Review* 78.4 (1989): 604–24.

51. One of the characters in the novel, Aires, names his dog Jawaharlal after Nehru, and in the last section of the novel, we see the dead dog stuffed and carried

on wheels. This, of course, caused yet another predictable controversy in India, but as Bharucha points out, the dog is more an object of pathos than of derision. See Rustom Bharucha, *In the Name of the Secular: Contemporary Cultural Activism in India* (Delhi: Oxford, 1998), 4–5.

52. Alan Villiers, *The Indian Ocean* (London: Museum Press Limited, 1952). See also Auguste Touissaint, *History of the Indian Ocean Trade,* trans. Jane Guicharnaud (Chicago: University of Chicago Press, 1966); Janet L. Abu-Lughod, *Before European Hegemony: The World System A.D. 1250–1350* (Oxford: Oxford University Press, 1989); Kenneth McPherson, *The Indian Ocean: A History of People and the Sea* (Oxford: Oxford University Press, 1993); Michael Pearson, *The Indian Ocean* (London: Routledge, 2003). I am grateful to Ned Bertz for directing me to these historical sources. See his forthcoming work on Indian Ocean world travelers.

53. Leela Gandhi, "'A Choice of Histories': Ghosh vs. Hegel in an Antique Land," *New Literatures Review* 40 (2003): 30.

54. Clifford Geertz, "Review of Amitav Ghosh's *In an Antique Land,*" *The Australian* 25 (August 1993): 30.

55. Amitav Ghosh, *In an Antique Land* (New Delhi: Ravi Dayal, 1992), 80–81. Hereafter cited in text with page numbers.

56. James Clifford, "The Transit Lounge of Culture," *Times Literary Supplement,* 4596, May 3, 1991, 8. In this article, Clifford is responding to Ghosh's short piece, "The Iman and the Indian," that was published in *Granta* 20 before the book came out in 1992.

57. Clifford, "The Transit Lounge," 8.

58. Recent historical research has revealed the immense diversity of Indian Ocean travelers. See note 52 for citations of historical work.

59. Part of this text was published in *Subaltern Studies,* VII (1992) as the essay "The Slave of MS.H.6."

60. Amitav Ghosh, *The Shadow Lines* (Delhi: Ravi Dayal, 1988) 24. I discuss this text in greater detail in chapter 3.

61. Ghosh, *The Shadow Lines,* 31.

62. The phrase is Meenakshi Mukherjee's in "The Anxiety of Indianness: Our Novels in English," *Economic and Political Weekly* (November 27, 1993): 2613.

63. Gayatri Chakravorty Spivak, "A Moral Dilemma," in *What Happens to History: The Renewal of Ethics in Contemporary Thought* (New York: Routledge, 2001), 229.

64. Gauri Viswanathan, "Beyond Orientalism: Syncretism and the Politics of Knowledge" *Stanford Humanities Review* 5.1 (1996): 7. Hereafter cited in text with page numbers. See also *Outside the Fold: Conversion, Modernity,*

Belief (Princeton: Princeton University Press: 1998) for an elaboration of these questions.

65. As an example, Aamir Mufti points out that the forces of Hindutva are quite capable of drawing to their religio-political rallies individuals who quite unconsciously may visit Sufi (Islamic) shrines at Ajmer Chishti or Nizamuddin, Delhi. See Aamir Mufti, "Auerbach in Istanbul: Edward Said, Secular Criticism, and the Question of Minority Culture." *Critical Inquiry* 25 (1998): 115.

66. Viswanthan, "Beyond Orientalism," 1.

67. Neelam Srivastava, "Amitav Ghosh's Ethnographic Fictions: Intertextual Links Between *In an Antique Land* and His Doctoral Thesis," *Journal of Commonwealth Literature* 36.2 (2001): 55.

68. Nivedita Menon, "Surviving Gujarat 2002," *Economic and Political Weekly* (July 6, 2002), 7–8.

69. This is not to suggest that there is a monolithic Hindu identity or to obscure the many differences of caste, region, or sect that are grouped under the moniker "Hindu," but to point to the ways in which "Hindu" and "Muslim" have been constructed in a relational context.

70. Anita Desai, *Baumgartner's Bombay,* cited in Aamir Mufti, "Auerbach in Istanbul: Edward Said, Secular Criticism, and the Question of Minority Culture," *Critical Inquiry* 25 (Autumn 1998): 112.

3. Acts of Return

1. Rukmini Bhaya Nair suggests as much when she invites attention to Wittgenstein's statement that "momentary grief" works like a linguistic oxymoron because it is a psychological impossibility. She writes, "'Grief' describes a pattern which recurs, with different variations in the weave of our lives. If a man's bodily expression of sorrow and of joy alternated, say with the ticking of a clock, here we should not have the characteristic formation of the pattern of sorrow or of the pattern of joy. 'For a second he felt violent pain'—[but] why does it sound queer to say: 'For a second he felt deep grief'?" See Rukmini Bhaya Nair, "Acts of Agency and Acts of God: Discourse of Disaster in a Postcolonial Society," *Economic and Political Weekly* 32.11 (1997): 541.

2. See Ana Douglass and Thomas A. Vogler, *Witness and Memory: The Discourse of Trauma* (New York: Routledge 2003); Mieke Bal, Jonathan Crewe, and Leo Spitzer, eds., *Acts of Memory: Cultural Recall in the Present* (Hanover, N.H.: University Press of New England); Marianne Hirsch and Valerie Smith, "Feminism and Cultural Memory," *Signs* 28.1 (2002): 1–19; Dagmar Herzog, "'Pleasure, Sex and Politics Belong Together': Post-Holocaust Memory and the Sexual Revolution in West Germany," *Critical Inquiry* 24.2 (1998): 393–444; Dominick LaCapra, "Trauma, Absence, Loss," *Critical Inquiry* 25 (1999): 696–727.

3. If Partition serves as national trauma for the Indian national conscious-ness, it is, after all, the moment of the creation of a new Muslim homeland for Pakistan, while in Bangladesh it persists largely as an absence, since the 1971 war of liberation from Pakistan has displaced it from national memory. On the absence of Partition in Bangladeshi public discourse and memory, as well as the absence of Bangladesh in recent discussions on Partition, see Shelley Feldman, "Feminist Interruptions: The Silence of East Bengal in the Story of Partition," *Interventions* 1.2 (1999): 167–82.

4. Jacques Derrida, "Avowing—The Impossible: 'Returns,' Repentance and Reconciliation," keynote address of the conference, "Irreconcilable Differences? Jacques Derrida and the Question of Religion," University of California, Santa Barbara, October 2003, trans. Gil Anidjar, 3–4. Hereafter cited in text with page numbers.

5. Derrida differentiates between two kinds of forgiveness: one that is de-pendent on and demands *teshuva*/repentance and the other a pure forgiveness without expectation of confession or reconciliation.

6. Dominick LaCapra "Trauma, Absence, Loss," *Critical Inquiry* 25 (1999): 724.

7. LaCapra, "Trauma, Absence, Loss," 724.

8. LaCapra, "Trauma, Absence, Loss," 717.

9. Priya Kumar, "Testimonies of Memory: Partition and the Haunting of a Nation," *Interventions* 1.2 (1999): 201–16.

10. Elie Wiesel, "Foreword," *Indelible Shadows: Film and the Holocaust,* by Annette Insdorf , 2nd ed. (Cambridge, U.K.: Cambridge University Press, 1989), xi.

11. Peter Novick, *The Holocaust in American Life* (Boston: Houghton Mif-flin, 1999), 15.

12. For more on the implications of comparative genocide studies, see Doug-lass and Vogler's *Witness and Memory.*

13. Gyanendra Pandey, "The Prose of Otherness," *Subaltern Studies VIII: Es-says in Honour of Ranajit Guha,* eds. David Arnold and David Hardiman (New Delhi: Oxford University Press, 1994), 194. See also his *Remembering Partition: Violence, Nationalism and History in India* (Cambridge, U.K.: Cambridge Uni-versity Press, 2001), especially chapter 2, "Historians' History," for an incisive elab-oration of these insights. Hereafter cited in text with page numbers.

14. For example, see Alok Bhalla, ed. *Stories about the Partition of India,* 3 vols. (New Delhi: Indus, Harper Collins, 1994), and Mushirul Hasan, ed., *India Partitioned: The Other Face of Freedom* (Delhi: Roli, 1995).

15. Notable among these works for its attention to the related yet different ex-perience of Bengal is Jasodhara Bagchi and Subhoranjan Dasgupta's *The Trauma and the Triumph: Gender and Partition in Eastern India* (Kolkatta: Stree, 2003).

16. Ritu Menon and Kamla Bhasin, *Borders and Boundaries: Women in India's Partition* (New Delhi: Kali for Women, 1998), xi.

17. Similarly, in 1997, Partition came to the forefront again, this time very consciously (and sometimes superficially) as India celebrated its fiftieth year of independence. As is typical of such moments of stocktaking, the nation meditated self-reflexively upon the successes and failures of modernity and nation-statehood, concluding that it is impossible to disentangle the memories of anticolonial struggle from the more distressing and fragmented recollections of Partition.

18. For an insightful elaboration of these questions, see Gyanendra Pandey's *Remembering Partition*, especially "Historians' History."

19. On the contemporary phenomenon of global movements of reconciliation, healing, and apology, see Rajeswari Sunder Rajan, "Righting Wrongs, Rewriting History," *Interventions* 2.2 (2000): 159–70.

20. Marianne Hirsch and Valerie Smith define cultural memory as "an act in the present by which individuals and groups constitute their identities by recalling a shared past on the basis of common and therefore often contested norms, conventions and practices." These may be conscious or deliberate or involuntary and repetitive. While I agree with Hirsch and Smith's definition of cultural memory as an act in the present, I do not believe that all acts of cultural memory necessarily serve to consolidate group identities. In fact, an uncanny practice of remembrance, as I will outline, can be used to move past identity politics. See Hirsch and Smith, "Feminism and Cultural Memory," 5. See also Mieke Bal's "Introduction" to *Acts of Memory: Cultural Recall in the Present*, eds. Bal, Crewe, and Spitzer, vii–xvii.

21. Gyanendra Pandey, *Remembering Partition*, 62.

22. Javed Alam and Suresh Sharma, "Remembering Partition," *Seminar* 461 (1998): 100. Hereafter cited in text with page numbers.

23. See, for example, Menon and Bhasin, *Borders and Boundaries;* Urvashi Butalia, "Blood," *Granta* 57 (1997): 14–22, esp. p. 15; and Uma Chakravarti and Nandita Haskar, *The Delhi Riots: Three Days in the Life of a Nation* (Delhi: Lancer International, 1987).

24. Deepak Mehta and Roma Chatterji, "Boundaries, Names, Alterities: A Case Study of a 'Communal Riot' in Dharavi, Bombay," in *Remaking a World: Violence, Social Suffering and Recovery*, eds. Veena Das, Arthur Kleinman, Margaret Lock, Mamphela Ramphele, and Pamela Reynolds (Berkeley: University of California Press, 2001), 201–49. Hereafter cited in text with page numbers. See Rakesh Sharma's documentary *Final Solutions* for a similar re-territorialization of space that draws upon the vocabulary of the India-Pakistan "border" in the aftermath of the anti-Muslim riots in Gujarat.

25. Toni Morrison, *Beloved* (1987; New York: Vintage, 2004).

26. In the next chapter, I take up the question of "testimony" as healing for the individual survivor of violence—a commonplace of much Holocaust scholarship.

27. Ana Douglass and Thomas A. Vogler, *Witness and Memory,* 33 and 35.

28. Veena Das and Arthur Kleinman, "Introduction," *Remaking a World,* eds. Das et al., 19.

29. LaCapra, like many others, takes his point of departure from Freud's work on mourning and melancholia. He uses these terms to distinguish between what he calls "acting out" and "working through" as two different modes of remembrance. See "Trauma, Absence, Loss," 696–727.

30. Marianne Hirsch, "Marked by Memory: Feminist Reflections on Trauma and Transmission," in *Extremities: Trauma, Testimony, and Community* (Urbana: University of Illinois Press, 2002), 71–91. See also *Family Frames: Photography, Narrative and Postmemory* (Cambridge, Mass.: Harvard University Press, 1997).

31. Hirsch differentiates between Morrison's notion of "rememory" as "a memory that communicated through bodily symptoms becomes a form of repetition and reenactment" and "postmemory" as "one that works through indirection and multiple mediation." See "Marked by Memory," 74.

32. Gayatri Chakravorty Spivak, *Imperatives to Re-Imagine the Planet / Imperative zur Neuerfindung des Planten,* ed. Willi Goetschel (Vienna: Passagen, 1999), 72.

33. See Gayatri Chakravorty Spivak, *Death of a Discipline* (New York: Columbia University Press, 2003). Hereafter cited in text with page numbers.

34. Amitav Ghosh, "The Ghosts of Mrs. Gandhi," *The New Yorker* 17 July 1995: 40.

35. Amitav Ghosh, *The Shadow Lines* (Delhi: Ravi Dayal, 1988), 39. Hereafter cited in text with page numbers.

36. Liisa Malkki, "National Geographic: Rooting of People and the Territorialization of National Identity among Scholars and Refugees," *Cultural Anthropology* 7.1: 26.

37. For an account of this shared culture, we must turn to Qurratulain Hyder's novels: *River of Fire, Sita Betrayed,* and *Fireflies in the Mist.*

38. Gayatri Chakravorty Spivak, "A Moral Dilemma," in *What Happens to History: The Renewal of Ethics in Contemporary Thought,* ed. Howard Marchitello (New York: Routledge, 2001), 221.

39. Gayatri Chakravorty Spivak, *Imperatives to Re-Imagine the Planet,* 52. Hereafter cited in text with page numbers.

40. Gayatri Chakravorty Spivak, "A Moral Dilemma," 221.

41. Strikingly, the novel simultaneously falls into the trap of reinforcing the very boundaries of nationality it seeks to repudiate when it comes to constructing and consolidating gendered identities. The intersection of gender and nationality is most visible in the narrator's ambivalent attitude toward his love interest, Ila. Ila is desirable to him precisely because she is "exotic" and different from the "Indian" women he has known, but he also constructs her as promiscuous because of

her liminal diasporic identity. Indeed, women in this narrative often come to bear the unfair burden of what Suvir Kaul terms "narratorial scapegoats." Thus, both Tha'mma's exclusionary nationalism and Ila's rootlessness and ostensibly deviant sexuality must be contested in order for the Bildungsroman elements of this narrative to be realized, allowing the male narrator to come into his own as an adult. See Suvir Kaul, "Separation Anxiety: Growing up Inter/National in Amitav Ghosh's *The Shadow Lines*," *Oxford Literary Review* 16 (1993): 125–46.

42. Mukul Kesavan, *Looking through Glass* (New Delhi: Ravi Dayal, 1995), 8 and 15. Hereafter cited in text with page numbers.

43. For an elaboration of the ways in which the figure of the Muslim becomes the site of excess in the discourse of Indian nationalism, see the section "Nationalism, Religion/Culture and Minorities" in chapter 1.

44. Spivak, *Death of a Discipline*, 58.

45. See chapter 1 for an elaboration of these perspectives.

46. On evolutionary models of religion that differentiate between post-Reformation Christianity and other religions like Islam and Hinduism, see Talal Asad, "Interview: Modern Power and the Reconfiguration of Religious Traditions," *Stanford Humanities Review* 5.1 (1996): 1–12.

47. Padma Challakere, "Witnessing 'History' Otherwise: Mukul Kesavan's Looking Through Glass," *Studies in the Novel* 30.4 (1998), 584–85.

48. Although Baldwin draws attention to the minoritization of Sikhs in several stories in this collection, in this story, "Hindu" and "Sikh" converge in the notion of the normative male nationalist subject, since the Muslim/Pakistani is deemed as the self-consolidating other of both Hindus and Sikhs.

49. Shauna Singh Baldwin, "Family Ties," in *English Lessons and Other Stories* (New Brunswick, N.J.: Goose Lane, 1999), 22. Hereafter cited in text with page numbers.

50. Urvashi Butalia recounts the story of the Sikh women of Thoa Khalsa, a village in present-day Pakistan, who threw themselves into a well in order to preserve the sanctity and purity of their religion and to avoid invasion of their religious/bodily space by men of the other community, Islam in this instance. Today, these women are remembered as heroines and martyrs who upheld the honor of their community in annual remembrance services held by survivors in a Delhi *gurudwara*. In a similar episode, a survivor relates how his father personally beheaded 26 women of his own family in order to protect the inviolability of their community: "First of all my father, Sant Raja Singh, when he brought his daughter, he brought her into the courtyard to kill her, first of all he prayed (he did *ardaas*) saying *sacche badshah*, we have not allowed your Sikhi to get stained, and in order to save it we are going to sacrifice our daughters, make them martyrs, please forgive us." See "Community, State and Gender: Some Reflections on the Partition

of India," *Oxford Literary Review* 16 (1994): 36–37. I elaborate some of the contexts of this violence in chapter 4.

51. Toni Morrison, *Beloved,* 323–24.

52. Kamila Shamsie's *Kartography* is an excellent example of what I call an uncanny practice of remembrance in its effort to defamiliarize the legacies of 1971 for the Pakistani nationalist narrative. See *Kartography* (Orlando, Fla.: Harvest, 2002).

4. Fictions of Violence

1. For an incisive analysis of the trope of "mobilizing shame" in human rights discourses and the ways in which it is being subverted not just through the indifference or the voyeurism of the audience but also through the brazen and shameless enjoyment of perpetrators appearing on camera, see Thomas Keenan's essay "Mobilizing Shame" in "And Justice for All? The Claims of Human Rights," eds. Ian Balfour and Eduardo Cadava, special issue, *South Atlantic Quarterly* 103.2/3 (2004): 435–50.

2. Judge Roling, cited in Keenan, 438.

3. Urvashi Butalia writes that estimates of the dead vary from 200,000 (the contemporary British figure) to 2 million (a later Indian figure), but that somewhere around a million people died is now widely accepted. More recently, Gyanendra Pandey has questioned the accuracy of these "widely accepted" figures. He contends that the existing records make it difficult to come to any kind of conclusive inference in terms of statistics, but these figures have come to be legitimized as "true" through recycling and repetition. The "tertiary discourse" on Partition therefore continues to function as a "gigantic rumor," now presented as "testimony" or "history." At the same time, as Pandey notes, there is no denying that there was incredible destruction and loss of life. See Butalia's *The Other Side of Silence: Voices from the Partition of India* (Delhi: Viking-Penguin, 1998), 3; Pandey's *Remembering Partition: Violence, Nationalism and History in India* (Cambridge, U.K.: Cambridge University Press, 2001), esp. pp. 88–91.

4. Jason Francisco, "In the Heat of Fratricide: The Literature of India's Partition Burning Freshly." *The Annual of Urdu Studies* 2 (1996): 227.

5. The account that follows is largely based on Ritu Menon and Kamla Bhasin's *Borders and Boundaries: Women in India's Partition* (New Delhi: Kali, 1998); Veena Das's *Critical Events: An Anthropological Perspective on Contemporary India* (Delhi: Oxford University Press, 1995), and Urvashi Butalia's *The Other Side of Silence.*

6. G. D. Khosla, a civil servant, had access to the Government of India's Fact

Finding Organization on the communal violence during Partition. Cited in Das, *Critical Events*, 59.

7. Menon and Bhasin, *Borders and Boundaries*, 7.

8. The recent work of Veena Das represents an important exception. For example, bemoaning the inadequacy of the social sciences in articulating trauma and suffering, she writes: "In repeatedly trying to write the meaning(s) of violence against women in Indian society, I find that the languages of pain through which social sciences could gaze at, touch, or become textual bodies on which this pain is written often elude me." (67) Consequently, she turns to what she calls the "register of the imaginary . . . not in the manner of a thief who has stolen another voice but in the manner of one who pawns herself to the words of this other" to write a more affective—and thus effective—history (69). See "Language and Body: Transactions in the Constructions of Pain," *Social Suffering*, eds. Arthur Kleinman, Veena Das, and Margaret Lock (Delhi: Oxford University Press, 1997), 67–91.

9. For surveys of Partition literature, see Alok Rai, "The Trauma of Independence: Some Aspects of Progressive Hindi Literature 1945–47," in *Myth and Reality: The Struggle for Freedom in India 1945–47*, ed. Amit Kumar Gupta (Delhi: Manohar, 1987); S. S. Hans, "The Partition Novels of Nanak Singh" in Gupta ed., *Myth and Reality;* Aijaz Ahmad, "In the Mirror of Urdu: Recompositions of Nation and Community, 1947–65" in *Lineages of the Present* (Delhi: Tulika, 1996), 191–220.

10. Aijaz Ahmad, "In the Mirror of Urdu." Hereafter cited in text with page numbers.

11. Therefore, to write in Urdu in India today, as noted Urdu critic C. M. Naim points out, is in itself a political act. C. M. Naim, "The Situation of the Urdu Writer: A Letter from Bara Banki, December 1993/February 1994," *World Literature Today* (Spring 1994): 246.

12. Ahmad argues that the separations and divisions instituted by Partition did not succeed in rupturing the Urdu literary community until the early 1960s when the 1965 India-Pakistan war inaugurated a "different kind of literary map" in ways that have subsequently appeared to be irrevocable. See "In the Mirror of Urdu," 191.

13. For example, Urdu writers like Qurratulain Hyder often moved between India and Pakistan, exemplifying the dilemmas of "home" and "belonging" in their personal lives that they so movingly evoke in their fictions. On Qurratulain Hyder's poignant novella of exile and displacement, *Sita Betrayed (Sita Haran)*, see my "Testimonies of Loss and Memory," *Interventions* 1.2 (1999): 201–15.

14. Shoshana Felman and Dori Laub, *Testimony: Crises of Witnessing in Literature, Psychoanalysis, and History* (New York: Routledge, 1992), xx. Hereafter cited in text with page numbers.

15. Jacques Derrida, *Demeure: Fiction and Testimony*, trans. Elizabeth Rottenberg (Stanford, Calif.: Stanford University Press, 2000). Hereafter cited in text with page numbers.

16. Avital Ronell, "The Testamentary Whimper," Balfour and Cadava, 489–500.

17. Abbas's writings cover the gamut from literary fiction to journalism, essays, plays, and films screenplays. He often translated his own work from Urdu into English or Hindi, and from film to fiction and vice versa. Although Abbas wrote "Revenge" both in Urdu and English, I treat Abbas primarily as an Urdu writer, since his literary writings draw upon the tropes and conventions of Urdu literature and Hindi cinema. (I have tried to provide original dates of publication wherever possible.)

18. Other examples include Amrita Pritam's Punjabi novella, *Pinjar*, and Yashpal's Hindi novel, *Jhoota Sach*. For a more recent moving film on abducted women, see Sabiha Sumar's *Khamosh Pani (Silent Waters)*.

19. As Roberta Culbertson evocatively writes, "Healing is competence / not cure. / No memory dies or clarifies / Just rises and falls like / the contours of a hill / some line of iron inside / always, still." See "Healing," *Sacred Bearings* (Fall 1999): 15. I am grateful to Roberta Culbertson for sharing many insights on issues of violence and survival with me.

20. On the importance of securing everyday life, see Veena Das and Arthur Kleinman's groundbreaking work on remaking worlds disrupted by violence. They argue, "While everyday life may be seen as the site of the ordinary, this ordinariness is itself recovered in the face of the most recalcitrant of tragedies: it is the site of many buried memories and experiences" (4). See "Introduction," *Remaking a World: Violence, Social Suffering, and Recovery*, eds. Veena Das et al. (Berkeley: University of California Press, 2001), 1–30.

21. Das, "Language and Body," 82. Hereafter cited in text with page numbers.

22. Drawing upon Wittgenstein's work, Das argues that pain does not have to be something radically "other" or essentially incommunicable (as argued, for instance, in the work of Elaine Scarry), but it can be conceptualized as a "claim asking for acknowledgment, which may be given or denied." The statement "I am in pain" is not an indicative statement, though it may appear to be one, but it is a cry asking for a response from the other, and it is up to the other to deny or acknowledge this pain. In effect, it becomes the ethical responsibility of the listener, the addressee, or the witness to recognize the other's pain and to house it not just in language but also in the body. See "Language and Body," 70.

23. Das provides an insightful account of the division of labor between men and women in the work of mourning in Punjabi families. While men exercise control over speech in the course of everyday life, they are rendered strikingly mute in the mourning process. In contrast, women are invested with the responsibility of

bearing witness to the grief and loss that death has brought in its wake. But, it is men who must ritually create the conditions for finding a home in the cosmos for the dead. Thus, men carry the corpse on their shoulders to the cremation grounds and give the sacred fire to the dead person. On the fourth day, they gather the bones and ritually immerse these into a sacred river. For a period ranging from ten to thirteen days, the dead person is believed to be hovering between the living and the dead; male mourners make possible the conditions for the ghost finally to become an ancestor through these rituals of mourning ("Language and Body," 81).

24. Ahmad, "In the Mirror of Urdu," 194.

25. Many of these writers have been anthologized in the three-volume anthology of translated Partition fictions, *Stories about the Partition of India*, ed. Alok Bhalla (New Delhi: Indus, Harper Collins, 1994).

26. Ritu Menon, "Trimmed in Black," *Indian Review of Books* (August–September 1998).

27. Thus, for example, in one famous fragmentary sketch, titled "Mishtake," Manto writes: "Ripping the belly cleanly, the knife moved in a straight line down the midriff, in the process slashing the cord which held the man's pyjamas in place.

"The man with the knife took one look and exclaimed regretfully, 'Oh no! . . . Mishtake.'"

See Saadat Hasan Manto, *Partition Sketches and Stories,* trans. Khalid Hasan (Delhi: Viking, Penguin, 1991).

28. Ahmad, "In the Mirror of Urdu," 193.

29. Menon, "Trimmed in Black," 5.

30. Keki N. Daruwalla, "The Craft of Manto, Warts and All," *The Annual of Urdu Studies* 11 (1996): 118.

31. Cited in Daruwalla, 119. For a lucid and very useful account of the emergence and concerns of the Progressive Writers' Association (PWA), see Priyamvada Gopal's *Literary Radicalism in India: Gender, Nation and the Transition to Independence* (London: Routledge, 2005).

32. Cited in Khalid Hasan, "Introduction," 1987, *Mottled Dawn: Fifty Sketches and Stories of Partition,* by Saadat Hasan Manto, trans. Khalid Hasan (New Delhi: Penguin, 1997), xix.

33. As Derrida points out, "[P]ower (despotic sovereignty and the virile mastery of the master of the house [one could add religious community or nation]) is nothing other than ipseity itself, the same of the selfsame, to say nothing of the subject which is a stabilizing and despotic escalation of ipseity, the being oneself or the Selbst." See Jacques Derrida, "Hostipitality," trans. Barry Stocker and Forbes Morlock, *Angelaki* 5.3 (December 2000): 15.

34. Saadat Hasan Manto, "Khol Do" (my translation). Although Khalid

Hasan's prolific translations have provided me with a very useful point of entry into Manto's works, like others, I have found his translations of "Khol Do" and "Thanda Ghosht" somewhat limited. Thus, I have provided my own translations, working from Devinder Issar's Devanagri transliterations, although admittedly that method also comes with its own set of constraints. See Devinder Issar, ed., *Mantonaama [The Works of Manto]* (Delhi: Indraprastha Prakashan, 1991).

35. The image of the speeding trains carrying their dead cargo seems to have captured the literary imagination and becomes an oft-invoked trope in the literature and film on the Partition. See, for instance, Khuswant Singh's *Train to Pakistan* and Bapsi Sidhwa's *Ice-Candy-Man (Cracking India)*. For cinematic representations, see Deepa Mehta's *Earth* and *Gaddar: Ek Prem Katha*.

36. Priyamvada Gopal makes the important point that the story should be read as a critique of the state-launched recovery operation (about which I will have more to say), since Sakina is raped by a group of Pakistani volunteers. Gopal's reading underlines that "a very thin line separates patriarchal violence from patriarchal protectionism," a point underscored by "Family Ties," as well. See "Dangerous Bodies: Masculinity, Morality and Social Transformation in Manto," *Literary Radicalism in India*, 109.

37. Dominick LaCapra, "Trauma, Absence, Loss," *Critical Inquiry* 25 (Summer 1999): 699.

38. Saadat Hasan Manto, "Thanda Ghosht" ("Cold Meat") (my translation), in *Mantonaama*, ed. Devinder Issar.

39. Cited in Khalid Hasan, "Introduction," 1987 *Mottled Dawn: Fifty Sketches and Stories of Partition*, by Saadat Hasan Manto, trans. Khalid Hasan (New Delhi: Penguin, 1997) xix.

40. Priyamvada Gopal, *Literary Radicalism in India*, 105. Hereafter cited in text with page numbers.

41. Linda Williams, *Playing the Race Card: Melodramas of Black and White From Uncle Tom to O.J. Simpson* (Princeton: Princeton University Press, 2001), 12–13. (Hereafter cited in text with page numbers.) Williams makes an argument about the centrality of melodrama to American popular cultural forms, but her claims are very relevant for the Indian context.

42. I borrow the resonant term "noncathartic" from Julia Kristeva, who uses it to describe the postwar literature of Marguerite Duras. Kristeva writes: "Duras's texts tame the malady of death to become one with it, part of it every step of the way, no distance, no escape. There is no purification at the end of these novels, laden with disease, no heightened sense of well-being, no promise of a beyond, not even the enchanting beauty of style or irony that would provide a bonus of pleasure beyond the ill revealed." However, unlike Kristeva's reading of Duras, I have tried to underscore how Manto compels his reader to respond to the call

of the other. See Julia Kristeva, "The Pain of Sorrow in the Modern World: The Works of Marguerite Duras," *Publications of the Modern Language Association* 102.2 (1987): 141.

43. Khwaja Ahmad Abbas, "Revenge," in *Orphans of the Storm: Stories about the Partition of India,* eds. Saros Cowasjee and K. S. Duggal (New Delhi: UBS Publishers, 1995), 14. All subsequent references will appear in the text itself.

44. While the paternalistic images deployed by Abbas to convey the violence enacted on the female body work to make visible the suffering of the hapless female victim, arguably, they also contribute to antifeminist and reactionary understandings of rape as violations of chastity, modesty, or honor.

45. Sudhir Kakar points out that the manifestation of mutilated breasts and castrated penises during a riot situation incorporates the more or less conscious desire to wipe the hated enemy off the face of the earth by eliminating its means of its reproduction and the nurturing of its infants. See *The Colors of Violence: Cultural Identities, Religion, and Conflict* (Chicago: University of Chicago Press, 1996), 33.

46. The most famous example of this cinematic device is the titillating hit song from the film *Khalnayak* (*The Terrorist,* 1993) that pictures then Hindi screen icon Madhuri Dixit asking, *"Choli ke peeche kya hai?"* (What lies behind my blouse?). For a recent, powerful literary interrogation of this voyeuristic image, see Mahasweta Devi's story, "Choli Ke Peeche." Interestingly, Mahasweta's story figures a similar scenario in which the middle-class male is thrown into crisis by his encounter with the subaltern woman whose breasts have been mutilated. See "Choli Ke Peeche," *Breast Stories,* trans. Gayatri Spivak (Calcutta: Seagull Books, 1997).

47. The notion of a "post-sacred" world, of course, has been complicated in my first chapter.

48. Like many other Urdu writers, Abbas was very closely involved with Hindi cinema—in the capacity of both screenplay writer and director—which frequently employs melodramatic conventions and tropes. However, the relationship between Urdu and the Hindi film is not just one of personnel, as evidenced in the predominance of the Urdu lyric writer in the world of Hindi cinema, for example. As Mukul Kesavan points out, the very architecture of Hindi film "has been fashioned out of the rhetorical and demotic resources of Urdu." Like any metropolitan pan-Indian cultural form, Hindi film has had to create and refine an idiom for itself over time, and Urdu helped constitute both this idiom and the narratives characteristic of Hindi cinema. Urdu's ability to find "sonorous words for inflated emotions" was very appropriate to the purpose of stylized melodrama; thus, Kesavan argues that "the operatic abandon of the Parsi theatre and the Hindi cinema is a function of the metaphoric extravagance of Urdu." The worlds of Urdu and

Hindi cinema, then, have always been mutually constitutive of each other. Consequently, melodrama remains a fundamental mode of both Urdu literature and popular Hindi cinema. See Mukul Kesavan, "Urdu, Awadh and the Tawaif: The Islamicate Roots of Hindi Cinema," in *Forging Identities: Gender, Communities and the State,* ed. Zoya Hasan (New Delhi: Kali, 1994), 246.

49. Manto's "Bitter Harvest" is another example of this particular version of the rape story. In yet another brief but powerful sketch, "Out of Consideration," Manto tells of a father pleading with his attackers to not rape his daughter in front of him, and they, "out of consideration," lead him to the other room as they proceed with their task. See "Black Margins" in *Mottled Dawn.*

50. Rajeswari Sunder Rajan, "The Story of Draupadi's Disrobing: Meanings for Our Times," in *Signposts: Gender Issues in Post-Independence India,* ed. Sunder Rajan (New Delhi: Kali, 1999), 339.

51. Rajeswari Sunder Rajan, "Life after Rape," in *Real and Imagined Women: Gender, Culture and Postcolonialism* (London: Routledge, 1993).

52. Sunder Rajan, 77.

53. Judith Butler, *The Psychic Life of Power: Theories in Subjection* (Stanford, Calif.: Stanford University Press, 1997), 2.

54. Ritu Menon and Kamla Bhasin, *Borders and Boundaries;* Urvashi Butalia, *The Other Side of Silence;* Veena Das, *Critical Events* and "Language and Body." My discussion in this section derives primarily from Menon and Bhasin's analysis in the chapter titled "Borders and Bodies" and Das's "National Honour and Practical Kinship: Of Unwanted Women and Children" in *Critical Events.*

55. These reports are based on preliminary discussions conducted by Menon and Bhasin with scholars working on similar issues in Pakistan. These scholars report that it is very likely that the community stepped in to help rehabilitate women in Pakistan, given that the level of destitution of women was appreciably lower. The Muslim League and the All Pakistan Women's Association also made active efforts to arrange marriages for women. See especially *Borders and Boundaries,* 122–23.

56. The official estimates for the number of women abducted, according to the figures given in the context of Constituent Assembly legislative debates, were 50,000 Muslim women in India and 33,000 Hindu and Sikh women in Pakistan. Until December 1949, 12,552 recoveries had been made in India and 6,272 in Pakistan. Taken together, about 30,000 women were recovered by both countries over an eight-year period as a result of this joint state-launched operation; significantly, however, the number of Muslim women recovered in India was 20,728, much higher than the total number of Hindu and Sikh women recovered in Pakistan, 9,032 (Menon and Bhasin, 70).

57. According to this definition: "an 'abducted person' means a male child

under the age of sixteen years or a female of whatever age who is, or immediately before the 1st day of March, 1947, was a Muslim and who, on or after that day and before the 1st day of January, 1949, had become separated from his or her family and is found to be living with or under the control of any other individual or family, and in the latter case includes a child born to any such female after the said date. If any police officer, not below the rank of an Assistant Sub-Inspector . . . has reason to believe that an abducted person resides or is to be found in any place, he may after recording the reasons for his belief, without warrant, enter and search the place and take into custody any person found therein who, in his opinion, is an abducted person, and deliver or cause such person to be delivered to the custody of the officer in charge of the nearest camp with the least possible delay" (cited in Menon and Bhasin, 116)

58. Veena Das introduces the cautionary note that such rejections may not have occurred as widely as is alleged in accounts of the Partition—it is not as if all families arbitrarily rejected and dismissed their daughters/sisters/wives. Indeed, she contends that so long as women's violation was not made public, many families bent kinship norms in various directions in order to reabsorb recovered women into the networks of family and community. Thus, girls could be married off to older men who had lost their wives in the turmoil or to members of the community who would have normally fallen under the category of prohibited kin so long as the unspoken censorship on speech was maintained by all concerned. Still, undeniably, the power of cultural archetypes like female purity and chastity prevailed, thus, "to be masculine when death was all around was to be able to hand death to your violated daughter without flinching—to obliterate any desire for the concreteness and uniqueness of this human being who once played in your family yard." See Das, "Language and Body," 77, and *Critical Events.*

59. Feminist scholars have been careful to point out that it is not their intention to suggest that every woman resisted recovery or that the state should not have carried out its recovery operation; what they hope to have revealed through their research are the many discordant notes and ruptures that were struck during the work of recovery in spite of the welfarist and humanitarian objectives of the Indian state.

60. For example, Menon and Bhasin have collected a number of valuable personal narratives that recall the witnessing of sexual violation of women by other women, but it is important to note that none of these personal testimonials speak of violence visited on the self, with the singular exception of one voice in *Borders and Boundaries*, who can only say: *"Dafa karo, hun ki yaad karna hai. Main sab bhula ditta hai."* (Let it go, what is the point in remembering all this now? I have forgotten everything) (95).

61. Ana Douglass and Thomas A. Vogler, *Witness and Memory: The Discourse of Trauma* (New York: Routledge, 2003), 41.

62. Felman and Laub, *Testimony*, 78. Hereafter cited in text with page numbers. Deepika Bahri's "socially constituted rejoinder" to Laub from the perspective of the "fallen women" of the Partition is eloquent and succinct: "[O]ne has to bury one's known truth in order to be able to live one's life." "Telling Tales: Women and the Trauma of Partition in Sidhwa's Cracking India," *Interventions* 1.2 (1999): 220.

63. The inadequacies of human language to express or articulate extreme trauma have often been acknowledged in contemporary scholarship on trauma. For example, Dori Laub writes: "This imperative to tell and to be heard can become itself an all-consuming life task. Yet no amount of telling ever seems to do justice to this inner compulsion. There are never enough words or the right words, there is never enough time or the right time, and never enough listening or the right listening to articulate the story that cannot be fully captured in thought, memory and speech." See *Testimony*, 78.

64. In her important work on trauma and memory, Mieke Bal notes that it is in the very nature of traumatic memories that they cannot become narratives, since they are often vividly present and tend to be mechanically reenacted as drama as opposed to the "mastery" of narrative. The term "traumatic memory" is therefore a misnomer, since such memories refuse integration. See Mieke Bal, "Introduction," *Acts of Memory: Cultural Recall in the Present,* eds. Mieke Bal, Jonathan Crewe, and Leo Spitzer (Hanover, N.H.: University Press of New England), vii–xvii; (x).

65. As Bal writes, the point is not that ordinary narrative memories, in contrast to "traumatic (non)memory," are necessarily conveyed to others, but that they "could be." Narrative memory can make sense of the past in the present to others "who can understand it, sympathize with it, or respond with astonishment, surprise, even horror." Bal, "Introduction," x. On restorative speech acts, see Susan Brisson, "Trauma Narratives and the Remaking of the Self," in Bal et al., *Acts of Memory.*

66. Rajinder Singh Bedi, "Lajwanti," *India Partitioned: The Other Face of Freedom*, ed. Mushirul Hasan (Delhi: Roli, 1995) 178–79. All further references will be in the text.

67. Bal, "Introduction," x.

68. Bal, x.

69. See, for example, the volume edited by Sudhesh Vaid and Kumkum Sangari, *Recasting Women: Essays in Colonial History* (New Delhi: Kali, 1989) on national reform movements.

70. In a more recent translation of the story, Muhammad Umar Memon makes Bedi's interrogation of the metaphor of the lajwanti even more evident: "Sunder

Lal had convinced her that she was in fact a lajwanti, a glass object too fragile to withstand the barest touch" (29). Much like the figure of the untouchable
goddess, the touch-me-not plant cannot withstand the physical and the intimate
connection that the eponymous protagonist, in fact, yearns for so intensely. See
"Lajwanti," in *An Epic Unwritten: The Penguin Book of Partition Stories* (Delhi:
Penguin, 1998).

71. First narrated in Sanskrit by the poet-sage Valmiki some two thousand
years ago, innumerable versions of the *Ramayana* have subsequently been retold
in ensuing centuries by poets in various regional Indian languages—most notably
for Northern India, the influential sixteenth-century Hindi retelling by Tulsidas,
the *Ramcaritmanas*. For more than two millennia, this tradition has flourished
throughout the subcontinent, extending to Thailand, Cambodia, Laos, Vietnam,
and Indonesia. Though the core story of Rama and Sita has remained more or less
the same in different versions, each storyteller has embellished and re-created the
story according to regional traditions and his/her own preoccupations, leading to
a multiplicity of Ramayanas. See Philip Lutgendorf, "Interpreting Ramraj: Reflections on the Ramayana, Bhakti and Hindu Nationalism" in *Bhakti Religion in
North India: Community Identity and Political Action,* ed. David N. Lorenzen
(1995; New Delhi: Manohar, 1996), 253–87 for an account of the resonance of the
Ramayana in contemporary contexts. For a sense of the diverse tellings of the Ramayana, see Paula Richman, ed., *Many Ramayanas: The Diversity of a Narrative
Tradition in South Asia* (Berkeley: University of California Press, 1991).

72. A brief recapitulation of the bare outlines of the *Ramayana* story is useful
here. Prince Rama, the rightful heir to the kingdom of Ayodhya, is deprived of his
kingdom because his scheming stepmother, Kaikeyi, demands that her husband,
King Dasratha, banish Rama to the forest for fourteen years and appoint her son,
Bharata, as king in his stead. Consequently, Rama, Sita, and his faithful brother
Laksmana depart for the forest. While they are in the forest, Ravana, a ten-headed
demon king, abducts the beautiful Sita and incarcerates her in his island kingdom,
Lanka. Subsequently, Rama and Laksmana launch a massive rescue mission to
recover Sita. Along with Hanuman, the monkey god, they lay siege to Lanka, and
after a protracted battle, Rama kills Ravana. But unable to accept his beloved
Sita without reservation, once she is restored to him, Rama requires her to prove
her chastity in a trial by fire. In deference to her husband, Sita steps into the fire
and comes out unscathed, thus affirming her eternal purity. Interestingly, various versions of the story have dealt with this section somewhat differently: while
Valmiki's ancient Sanskrit text allows Sita an extended and eloquent response
to Rama's unexpected and cruel remarks, Tulsi's comparatively more recent and
influential version glosses over the unpalatable reunion in one line, merely rendering Sita speechless. (Indeed, in Tulsi's text, the abducted Sita is rendered into

a "shadow" of the real Sita, thus completely dismissing her trauma). Eventually, Rama, Sita, and Laksmana return victorious to the kingdom of Ayodhya amid much celebration among the residents of the city, and Rama goes on to rule the land for many golden years. The epic itself is an extended meditation on Rama, the divine or spiritualized king, and his exemplary behavior and acts. Sita, as the pure and obedient wife of Rama, is correspondingly held up as a paragon of virtue. Her legendary chastity establishes her as a model for Hindu womanhood. (I am indebted to Philip Lutgendorf for his help with clarifying some of the differences between the Valmiki and Tulsi versions).

73. Constituent Assembly of India (Legislative) Debates, December 15, 1949, cited in Das, *Critical Events*, 70.

74. Constituent Assembly Debates, cited in Menon and Bhasin, 114.

75. See Paula Richman, *Questioning Ramayanas: A South Asian Tradition* (Berkeley: University of California Press, 2000).

76. Qurratulain Hyder's novella *Sita Haran (The Abduction of Sita)* also makes powerful use of the Sita story in depicting the impossibility of loving or nurturing heterosexual relationships in a post-Partition context, although the eponymous protagonist of her story is not literally abducted.

77. Rajeswari Sunder Rajan makes a similar point about modern feminist retellings of Drauapdi's story from the *Mahabharata*. See "The Story of Draupadi's Disrobing," *Signposts*, 338.

78. Jamila Hashmi, "Banished," *An Epic Unwritten: The Penguin Book of Partition Stories from Urdu*, trans. Muhammad Umar Memon (New Delhi: Penguin, 1998) 87. All subsequent references will be cited in parentheses in the text.

79. It is not insignificant that Hashmi's Muslim protagonist draws on one of the major myths of Hindu religiocultural tradition to come to terms with her own traumatic situation—thus providing an interesting and concrete instance of cultural syncretism in the text.

80. Valmiki's Ramayana does not end with Rama's enthronement and his subsequent utopian rule. In the controversial concluding section, *Uttarakanda*, Rama banishes the pregnant Sita to the forest yet again because it comes to his attention that his subjects have been questioning her chastity in spite of the trial by fire. Many contemporary retellings of the story in performance or in exposition omit this section or undermine it with various ingenious explanations. In Valmiki, however, Sita has to go through a second exile or banishment (a *vanvas*, literally forest dwelling), once again in deference to her husband's dictates because he puts his *dharma*, his duty as a king, over and above everything, including his loyalty to his wife. In the forest, the pregnant Sita is offered refuge by the poet-sage Valmiki, the attributed writer of the ancient Sanskrit epic, to whom she tells her tragic story. In Valmiki's *ashram*, she gives birth to Rama's twin sons Luv and Kush. Many years

later, when Rama is reunited with his sons, Sita, as a final demonstration of her chastity, summons forth the Earth, her mother, which cracks open to let her in.

81. Jyotirmoyee Devi, *The River Churning: A Partition Novel*, trans. Enakshi Chatterjee (New Delhi: Kali, 1995), xxxv. All further citations will follow parenthetically in the text.

82. Jasodra Bagchi, "Introduction," *The River Churning*, xxvi.

83. At one point, even Tamijuddin considers handing Sutara over to the state's relief workers, since people are alleging that he had forcibly kept Sutara in his home.

84. Cited in Menon and Bhasin, *Borders and Boundaries*, 207. Ritwick Ghatak's famous film, *Meghe Dhaka Tara* (*The Cloud Capped Star*, 1960) provides a moving account of Bengali women refugees forced to step out of the confines of their homes.

85. Jyotirmoyee Devi, "Beginnings," *The River Churning*, xviii.

86. See Sunder Rajan, "The Story of Draupadi's Disrobing," *Signposts*, for an incisive account of Draupadi's appropriation by both feminist and patriarchal currents in contemporary cultural narratives.

87. Sunder Rajan, "Draupadi," 337.

88. Jill Didur, "At a Loss for Words: Reading the Silence in South Asian Women's Partition" *Topia* 4: 53–71, 69.

89. Lalithambika Antherjanam, "A Leaf in the Whirlwind," in *Cast Me Out If You Will: Stories and Memoir*, trans. and ed. Geeta Krishnakutty (New York: Feminist Press, City University of New York, 1998), 78. Hereafter cited in text with page numbers.

90. Sunder Rajan, *Real and Imagined Women*, 88.

91. Following Sunder Rajan, I conceptualize individual resistance not in the traditional sense of its performative intentionality but in terms of its social function. See *Real and Imagined Women*, 12.

92. This perhaps is an instance of fictional misrepresentation. Menon and Bhasin have uncovered that a number of women were sent to state-run abortion camps (even though these were illegal at the time) once recovered so that they could be assimilated into the community.

93. Das and Kleinman, "Introduction," *Remaking a World*, 26.

5. It's My Home, Too

I am grateful to Corey Creekmur and Swarnavel Pillai for illuminating discussions on these films.

1. For an interesting argument on cinema and citizenship, see Ashish Rajadhyaksha, "Viewership and Democracy in the Cinema," in *Making Meaning*

in Indian Cinema, ed. Ravi Vasudevan (Delhi: Oxford University Press, 2000), 267–296.

2. Ravi Vasudevan, "Neither State Nor Faith: The Transcendental Significance of the Cinema," in *The Crisis of Secularism in India,* eds. Anuradha Needham and Rajeswari Sunder Rajan (Durham, N.C.: Duke University Press, 2007), 240 and 242. I am extremely grateful to Ravi Vasudevan not only for sharing this essay with me but also for an insightful discussion of this piece during his trip to the University of Iowa in the Spring of 2005.

3. On constructions of the nation in popular Hindi cinema, see Sumita Chakravarty, *National Identity in Indian Popular Cinema, 1947–1987* (Austin: University of Texas Press, 1993) and Jyotika Virdi, *The Cinematic ImagiNation: Indian Popular Films as Social History* (Delhi: Permanent Black, 2004).

4. Ravi Vasudevan, "Bombay and Its Public," in *Pleasure and the Nation: The History, Politics and Consumption of Public Culture in India,* eds. Rachel Dwyer and Christopher Pinney (Delhi: Oxford University Press, 2001), 193–94.

5. See Ravi Vasudevan, "Addressing the Spectator of a 'Third World' National Cinema," *Screen* 36.4 (1995): 305–24 on the positioning of the spectator in Hindi cinema.

6. Mukul Kesavan, "Urdu, Awadh and the Tawaif: The Islamicate Roots of Hindi Cinema," in *Forging Identities: Gender, Communities and the State,* ed. Zoya Hasan (New Delhi: Kali, 1994), 245.

7. Thus, the historical film becomes a fascinating site for the displaced working out of Hindu–Muslim relations in the present. See Chakravarty, *National Identity in Indian Popular Cinema,* 165.

8. Parama Roy, "Figuring Mother India: The Case of Nargis," in *Indian Traffic: Identities in Question in Colonial and Postcolonial India* (Berkeley: University of California Press, 1998), 165.

9. Ravi Vasudevan, "Neither State nor Faith." Hereafter cited in text.

10. Vasudevan, "Bombay," 194. Hereafter cited in text with page numbers.

11. I do not mean to suggest that these works are viewed only by the normative spectator of Hindi cinema—and not by Indian Muslims, for example—but I argue that by means of their narratives and their visual culture, Muslim minoritarian films invite this idealized spectator to assume a position different from that of an unmarked Hindu male identity.

12. This is by no means to take away from what these films are able to achieve through their narratives of love across borders, especially since the taboo against miscegenation is central to the maintenance of religious and national boundaries. In particular, *Veer Zaara* opens up an interesting space to think about Indian–Pakistani relationships by introducing an almost Gandhian vocabulary of neighborliness.

13. Jacques Derrida, "Hostipitality," trans. Gil Anidjar, *Acts of Religion*, ed. Gil Anidjar (New York: Routledge, 2002), 361. Hereafter cited in text with page numbers.

14. "Hostipitality," trans. Barry Stocker and Forbes Morlock, *Angelaki* 5.3 (December 2000): 17.

15. This kind of intermediate cinema had antecedents in the cinema of the 1960s and 1970s, but it lost ground with the advent of television. It is identified with filmmakers such as Hrishikesh Mukherji, Basu Chatterji, Basu Bhattacharjee, and Gulzar, who affiliated themselves with Bimal Roy's style of filmmaking.

16. More recently, he has produced *Woh Lamhe*, which once again explores his relationship with Babi, significantly, after she died in tragic circumstances.

17. Mahesh Bhatt, "Cinema and Secularism," *Communalism Combat* 105 (February 2005).

18. Interview with Ashish Virmani, *Afternoon Dispatch and Courier*, Internet edition, 1. http://www.cybernoon.com/features/celebs.html (accessed on September 2, 2002).

19. Linda Williams, *Playing the Race Card: Melodramas of Black and White From Uncle Tom to O.J. Simpson* (Princeton: Princeton University Press, 2001), 29.

20. Bhatt has described the syncretism practiced by his mother: "My mother, who was the driving force behind my life, the lifeblood of my existence, died in April this year. And I found a Quransharif under her head and a Cross that she had made with her own hands on her chest. My father came chanting shlokas and offering Gangajal. Secularism was a habit, we did not have to labour to embrace it or rise up to acquire it—it was an actuality in our day-to-day life. . . . But my mother was almost pathological about prayers, she numbed her anguish with prayer. She would go to the Satsang as well as to the Imambara for Muharram. I remember her in sari with a flaming red tikka on her head at Diwali, as well as blank-faced, and dressed in a black chaddar for the majlis. I also remember her standing transfixed in front of Jesus on the Cross and touching the blood, then lifting us up and touching our foreheads to the blood too." (*Communalism Combat*, July 1998, as told to Deepa Gahlot)

21. For a similar earlier moment in Hindi cinema, see Yash Chopra's *Dharmaputra* (1961), in which the Hindu nationalist protagonist discovers that he is a Muslim.

22. One of the most famous examples of such a relationship is to be found in the roles played by Nargis and Sunil Dutt in Mehboob's magnum opus, *Mother India*, an onscreen relationship that was complicated by the duo's marriage after the film.

23. Williams, *Playing the Race Card*, 28.

24. As I indicated in chapter 5, Williams argues that melodrama's recognition of virtue entails a simultaneous dialectic or tension between pathos and action, which typically takes the form of rescues, chases, or fight sequences. These spectacles of pathos and action are often interpreted as the "excess" of melodrama but also constitute its allure.

25. Vasudevan, "Addressing the Spectator," 322.

26. Nargis's mother, Jaddanbai, was a courtesan, and her father, Mohanbabu, was a Hindu who converted to Islam to marry her mother.

27. Roy, "Figuring Mother India," 173.

28. To be sure, however, the extent to which they contain the figure of the "terrorist" in their narrative resolutions differs substantially in each instance. *Mission Kashmir*, for example, ends by incorporating the figure of the Muslim militant into its nationalist imaginary.

29. See Vasudevan's "Bombay and Its Public" for an incisive elaboration of such devices in *Bombay*.

30. See Priya Kumar, "Interview with Khalid Mohamed," *Framework* 47.2 (2006): 106. Conducted in July 2004.

31. The Justice Srikrishna Report, http://www.sabrang.com/srikrish/sri%2omain.htm (accessed on January 10, 2007).

32. Gayatri Chakravorty Spivak, "Terror: A Speech after 9-11," *boundary 2* 31.2 (2004): 83.

33. Indeed, the Missing Persons Bureau is now more or less nonexistent. Mohamed told me that he had tried to go to the Bureau, but by the time he went there, it had been disbanded: "There was just this one clerk. But for drama, I created a policewoman there." See Interview with Mohamed.

34. See Fareed Kazmi, "Muslim Socials and the Female Protagonist" in *Forging Identities: Gender, Communities and the State*, ed. Zoya Hasan (New Delhi: Kali, 1996): 226–43.

35. Lalitha Gopalan, *Cinema of Interruptions: Action Genres in Contemporary Hindi Cinema* (London: British Film Institute, 2002), 19.

36. Mohamed explains the minor change: "The producer insisted that if we wanted the Justice Srikrishna report reference to remain intact, we should change the name and we would get through (the censors). He was right. We made it "Harekrishna" (Interview).

37. The Justice Srikrishna Report clearly indicts the Mumbai police for what it calls a "built-in bias of the police force against Muslims": "The response of the police to appeals from desperate victims, particularly Muslims, was cynical and utterly indifferent. On occasions, the response was that they were unable to leave the appointed post; on others, the attitude was that one Muslim killed was one Muslim less."

38. On the significance of the interval in Hindi cinema, see Gopalan's *Cinema of Interruptions.*

39. Gopalan, *Cinema of Interruptions,* 49.

40. Williams, *Playing the Race Card,* 21.

41. Ashish Rajadhyaksha, "The Phalke Era: Conflict of Traditional Form and Modern Technology," *Journal of Arts and Ideas* 14–15 (1987): 47–78; Ravi Vasudevan, "Addressing the Spectator."

42. In his seminal essay "Force of Law: The 'Mystical Foundation of Authority,'" Derrida differentiates between law and justice: "Law is not justice. Law is the element of calculation, and it is just that there be law, but justice is incalculable." It is an experience of the impossible. Thus, he insists on the possibility of a justice that "not only exceeds or contradicts law but also, perhaps, has no relation to law, or maintains such a strange relation to it that it may just as well demand law as exclude it." See "Force of Law" in *Acts of Religion,* ed. Gil Anidjar (New York: Routledge, 2002), 244, 233.

43. Vazira Fazila-Yacoobali, "A Rite of Passage: The Partition of History and the Dawn of Pakistan," *Interventions* 1.2 (1999): 183–200.

44. The most famous literary example of such liminality is, of course, the eponymous protagonist of Manto's famous short story "Toba Tek Singh." See Saadat Hasan Manto, "Toba Tek Singh," in *Kingdom's End and Other Stories,* trans. Khalid Hasan (London: Vero, 1987), 11–19.

45. Derrida, "Force of Law," 240.

46. Spivak, "Terror: A Speech after 9-11," 94 and 83.

Postscript

1. Somini Sengupta, "India Fears Terrorism May Attract Its Muslims," *New York Times* August 9, 1994.

2. Cited in Bernard Haykel, "The Enemy of My Enemy Is Still My Enemy," *New York Times* July 26, 2006.

3. Cited in *Council on Foreign Relations,* August 14, 2006, http:www.cfr.org/publication/11275 (accessed on September 1, 2006).

4. Yoginder Sikand, "The Discourse on Terrorism and the Missing Muslim Voice," *Countercurrents.org,* September 29, 2006, http://www.countercurrents.org/comm-sikand250906.htm (accessed on December 23, 2006).

5. Sikand, 2.

6. For a similar argument about the significance of social humiliation in understanding "terrorist" violence, see Dipankar Gupta, "The Cry of the Terrorist: The Absentee Discourse of Social Humiliation," in *Will Secular India Survive,* ed. Mushirul Hasan (Gurgaon: imprintOne, 2004), 356–74.

7. See "The Sachhar Committee Report on the Backwardness of Muslims in India," *Asian Age,* December 1, 2006.

8. Jacques Derrida, "Avowing—The Impossible: 'Returns,' Repentance and Reconciliation," keynote address of the conference "Irreconcilable Differences? Jacques Derrida and the Question of Religion," University of California, Santa Barbara, October 2003, trans. Gil Anidjar.

9. Farzana Versey, "The Legacy of Babri Masjid," *Countercurrents.org,* December 6, 2006, http://www.countercurrents.org/comm-versey061206.htm (accessed on December 23, 2006).

10. Gayatri Chakravorty Spivak, "Terror: A Speech after 9-11," *boundary 2* 31:2 (2004): 110–11.

Index

Abbas, Khwaja Ahmad, xv, xxv, 44–45, 131, 140, 175; "Revenge," 140–44; as an Urdu writer, 265n17, 268n4809

Abducted Persons Recovery and Restoration Act, 146–47, 156

abducted women, 146–48, 269n56, 269–70n57; Sita story, 155–162; subjectivity of, 158–62. *See also* "recovered" women

abduction, child, 269–70n57

abortion, 173

Advani, L. K., 34

Ahmad, Aijaz, 132, 264n12

Ahmad, Dohra, 61, 69

Aiyar, Yamini: and Meeto Malik, 39–41

Ajay (character in *Zakhm*), 188–89, 193–95; burying his mother, 196–98; discovery of his mother's Muslim identity, 193–94, 196

Ajay's grandmother (character in *Zakhm*), 191–92

Ajay's mother (character in *Zakhm*): concealment of her Muslim identity, 187–89, 192–93, 198; desire for Muslim burial rites, 189, 194; Muslim burial of, 196–98; revelation of Muslim identity, 193–94, 196

Alam, Javeed, "Remembering Partition," 92–93, 95

Alan Trewasen (character in *The Shadow Lines*), 107

al-Awda, Salman, 232

"A Leaf in the Whirlwind" (Antherjanam), 131

Algerian crisis (France), 24

Alhambra fort, 64–65

All-India Backward Muslims Morcha, 39

All-India Progressive Writers' Association (AIPWA), 134

All Pakistan Women's Association, 269n55

Al-Qaeda, 232–33

Amaan (character in *Fiza*), 203–5; death of, 216–218; found by Fiza, 212–13, 217; as a secular militant, 206, 214–16; as victim-turned-terrorist, 205–6, 211–14

Ambedkar, B. R., 18–19

American Indians, 66

Ammi (character in *Looking through Glass*), 114–15

amnesia, 85, 91, 96, 135, 164; traumatic forgetting and, 91–92, 96

Amulya Babu (character in *The River Churning*), 168–69

colonial plan for Partition, xvii, 124–25, 228–29

communalism, 15

"communities of fate," 37

"conflictual democracy," 42. *See also* Balibar, Étienne

Congress-League, 113–14

Connolly, William, 250–51n81

Conrad, Joseph, 56; *Heart of Darkness*, 63, 98

Constituent Assembly, 16, 18, 156. *See also* Indian Constitution

Constitutional discourse, 3, 16–20, 32–33, 38, 89, 179; and the Hindu Right, 33–34. *See also* Indian Constitution

construction: fictional, 79, 103, 205, 236n42, 249n62; of history, 95; of Muslim identity, 31, 182, 187, 233, 257; of nationalism, 59, 275n3; transcendental (*see* transcendental constructions)

cosmopolitan ideal, xxiii–xxiv, 48–49; borderless place as, 104; set in a mercantile past, 72–73. *See also In an Antique Land*

cosmopolitanism, 45, 48; Derrida on, 45, 49–52, 58; as hospitality, 52–55, 65. *See also* minority cosmopolitanism; pluralism

"cosmo-theory" (Brennan), 51, 243–44n17

Cossman, Brenda, and Ratna Kapur: *Secularism's Last Sigh*, 13

Culbertson, Roberta, 265n19

cultural rights, 251–52n93

cultural syncretism, 76–77, 273n79, 276n20

culture: religion secularized as, 26, 28–32. *See also* collective memory; religiocultural identity

Das, Hari and Janki (characters in "Revenge"), 140–43

Das, Veena, 91, 95, 96, 265n22; "Language and Body," 149–50; on women's experience of violence, 131, 161–62, 172, 264n8, 270n58

Dasehra festival, 158–59

death, 267n35; of a Muslim terrorist (film), 216–18; rape equated with, 137, 145–46, 175, 270n58; remembrance of a character's, 75, 100, 102–4. *See also* burial

deconstructive approach, xvii, 241n22. *See also* construction; narrative

democracy, 33, 42; rights of minorities, 2–3, 12, 32–33, 41

Derrida, Jacques, xxv, 4, 9–10, 18, 24–25; on cosmopolitanism, 45, 49, 51–52, 58; on despotic sovereignty, 266n33; on "the ensemble," 51–52; "Faith and Knowledge," 10; on forgiveness, 259n5; on "founding violence," xvii, 86, 117; "Hospitality," 52–55, 65, 70, 132, 255n27; on justice vs. law, 219, 228, 278n42; on Kant, 10–11; on "living together," xix–xx; on love as abandonment, 256n45; "Reflections," xix; on the "stranger," xvi, 51, 199; on testimony, 129

Desai, Manmohan: *Chhalia (The Cheat)*, 181

devdasi practice, 17

Devgun, Veeru: *Hindustan ki Kasam*, 182

LaCapra, Dominick: on "founding trauma," 87, 136, 261n29
"Lajwanti" (Bedi), 131, 151–55, 157–58, 271–72n70
Lajwanti (character in "Lajwanti"), 152–55, 157–58
Laub, Dori, 150, 270n63
"Leaf in the Whirlwind, A" (Antherjanam), 131, 170–74; self-agency in victimization, 174
Lever, Johnny, 202
liberal secularism, 5–6, 14, 25, 36; "ethnocultural neutrality" and, 248n60; limits of, 110, 112–13, 250n80, 251n87; in *The Moor's Last Sigh*, 68–70; pluralist approach, 33, 36–37; reason-based, 2, 3–4, 11. *See also* secularism
liberal secular state, 2–3, 15; clarifying the role of, 7–8; transformation of, 42–43
liberal societies, 27–28
linguistic competence, 81
"linguistic excess," 171–72
literary narrative, 96–97; fictional construction, 79, 103, 205, 236n42, 249n62. *See also* Partition literature
literature: crossing borders, 128, 147; ethics and, xxiii–xxiv, 237. *See also* post-Partition literature
Llosa, Mario Vargas, 46
Locke, John, 39; "Letter concerning Toleration," 6
Looking through Glass (Kesavan): Hindu narrator encounters Muslim other in, xxiv–xxv, 108–12, 115–16, 121; post-Partition memory in, 87; the uncanny *(unheimlich)* in, 98
Lumières, French, 4

Madam Bose (character in *Looking through Glass*), 109–10
Madan, T. N., 21
madrasas (Muslim religious schools), 40
Mahabharata, 156, 168
majoritarian nationalism, xxii, 36–37, 59, 96
Malayalam fiction, 131, 170
male feminist politics, 132. *See also* feminism; masculinity
male vigilante genre, 219. *See also* vigilante-terrorist film
Malik, Anu, 202
Malkki, Liisa, 103–4
Mammo (Benegal), xxvi–xxvii, 219–222; filmic space in, 224–25; flashback sequences, 222–23; gendered experience of the Partition in, 223–25; "outsider" lays claim on the nation in, 227–29; song sequence in, 225
Mammo (character in *Mammo*), 219, 221, 222–224; as a refugee, 224–27; return of, 224–26; as strong, 227–28
Manicheanism, 139–40
Manto, Saadat Hasan, xv, xxv, 133–35, 175, 222, 266n27; "Bitter Harvest," 269n49; *Black Margins (Siyah Hashiye)*, 133, 136, 138; "Cold Meat" *(Thanda Gosht)*, 134, 137–40, 174; "Open It" *(Khol do)*, 134–37, 151, 153, 165
masculinity: crisis of, 138, 140, 143–44, 175; male feminist politics, 132; patriarchal norms of (*see also* patriarchy), 116–20, 134, 144, 152–54; reframing of, 131, 134, 175, 176, 236–37; and the trauma of witness-

PRIYA KUMAR is associate professor of English at the University of Iowa. She teaches and writes in the areas of postcolonial studies and South Asian literature and culture. Her recent publications include an interview with Hindi filmmaker and screenplay writer Khalid Mohamed in the film studies journal *Framework*.